The Definitive
LUTON TOWN F.C.

A statistical history to 1997

Steve Bailey, Brian Ellis
and Alan Shury

Volume 10 in a series of club histories.
A *Soccer Data* Publication from Tony Brown,
on behalf of the Association of Football Statisticians

Published in Great Britain by Tony Brown,
4 Adrian Close, Beeston, Nottingham NG9 6FL.
Telephone 0115 973 6086. E-mail soccer@innotts.co.uk

Other volumes in this series are:

Rochdale
Northampton Town
Chesterfield
Portsmouth
Barnsley
Queen's Park Rangers
Scunthorpe United
Aldershot
Torquay United

Please write to the publisher for news of future volumes.

ISBN 1 899468 10 2

FOREWORD BY THE CHAIRMAN

Luton Town Football Club ("The Town" or "The Hatters") was formed in 1885 as a fusion of local sides Wanderers and Excelsior. Early games were played on a friendly basis apart from the annual excursions into the F.A. Cup. Gradually better players were attracted to the Town because of the growth of industry in the area.

In 1891, Luton became the first professional club in the South, paying the whole team plus an additional allowance for working time lost travelling to away games. Luton Town moved to Kenilworth Road in 1905 with the current main stand being acquired second hand from Kempton Race Course in 1920.

It is amazing when one travels the country and discusses our nation's favourite sport, how Luton Town is held with great affection by most football supporters. This book is by definition historical fact and indeed a great reference and benchmark upon which this football club needs to go forward.

We at Luton Town have a proud history and hopefully an even prouder future.

David Kohler BSc (Hons) ARICS
Chairman/Managing Director

INTRODUCTION BY THE AUTHORS

This is the first complete statistical record of Luton Town in the Football League. Partial but valuable records have been published before, but this book contains the full record of every Football League and major Cup game played by the club. We cannot pretend that there are no errors, although we have checked and checked again. Other statisticians might disagree with a point here and there as, particularly for early games, it is often difficult to be sure who scored a goal due to the extravagant mode of newspaper writing of the day. What we have done though is set a marker, put down in black and white all the records and checked as thoroughly and completely as we can. The authors will always be glad to hear from anyone who can shed more light on the more obscure corners of the club's history.

The division of labour on this book was that Steve Bailey did the computer data entry with Brian Ellis and Alan Shury providing detailed input from their copious and thorough paper records which they have diligently and carefully maintained over a number of years. It was then over to Tony Brown of the Association of Football Statisticians to assemble the records into this book.

The authors would like to thank the AFS for inviting us to contribute to the "Definitive" series. Thanks are also due to Simon Pitts and Jeremy Goodwyn for checking computer print outs and providing help on the seasons from the mid 60s to the 90s in the early days of writing the book; Michael Joyce for providing the database on which the player details are based; Leigh Edwards for checking the player details from his records; Brian Tabner for providing the League attendances from the official records; and finally, Chris Grabham of the Luton Museum and John Pyper for their help with the photographs.

Steve Bailey, Brian Ellis and Alan Shury, November 1997

1905/06: Back: E Gibbs (director), J Bygrave (groundsman), Bert Else, Fred Hawkes, J Blackett, AE Lewis, W McCurdy (vice-captain), H Watkins, A Wales, C Green (secretary), W Lawson (trainer). Middle: P Gallacher, A Warner, JM Dow, J Pickering, A McDonald, W Barnes. Front: F White, Alex Brown, Bob Hawkes (captain).

September 13th, 1958. Back: Bingham, Hawkes, Morton, Shanks, Dunne, TS Mackey (trainer), McNally, Adam, Middleton, Cummings. Next to back: Chambers. Kelly, Smith, Marsh, Owen, Groves, Baynham, McLeod, Folwell, Brown. Seated: Messrs Frank King (head trainer), Duncan, Hodgson, Tooley, AF England (vice chairman), PG Mitchell (chairman), Hewson, Wright, Crarer and Coley (secretary). Front: Parin, Pacey, Legate, Turner, D King, Lesnick.
© The Luton Museum Service/Luton News

27th July 1967. Back: Moore, Slough, Dougan, McDonald. Next to back: Readhead (secretary), Read, French, Allen, Jardine, McDerment, Bruce Rioch, Brown, Hare, Branston, Whittaker, Walker, Evans (trainer), Allan Brown (manager). Seated: LS Hawkins, AF England (vice chairman), T Hodgson (chairman), DG England, RI Burr, JAC Bain. Front: Mooney, Neil Rioch, Bevan, Wainwright.
© The Luton Museum Service/Luton News

19th August 1982, with the Division Two Championship Cup. Back: Johnson, Turner, Goodyear, Small, Bunn, Kellock, Fuccillo, Walsh. Next to back: John Moore (coach), Donaghy, Money, Findlay, Saxby, Judge, Antic, Aizlewood, Trevor Hartley (coach). Seated: David Coates (chief coach), Hill, Stevens, Horton, David Pleat (manager), Moss, Brian Stein, John Sheriden (physio). Front: McConville, Daniel, Mark North, Stacey North, Watts, Breaker, Beasley, Thomas, Parker.
© The Luton Museum Service/Luton News

LUTON TOWN RECORDS PAGE

PLAYERS:

Most Appearances

Bob Morton 572 (495 League, 58 FA Cup, 7 FL Cup, 12 other)
Ricky Hill 507 (436+33+38+0)
Brian Stein 496 (427+31+35+3)
Mal Donaghy 488 (415+36+34+3)

Most Goals

Gordon Turner 276 (243+18+4+11)
Andy Rennie 163 (148+15)
Brian Stein 154 (130+6+15+3)

Most League Goals in a Season   Joe Payne, 55 1936/37

Most International Appearances   Mal Donaghy, Northern Ireland, 58

THE CLUB:

Honours:

Champions of Division Three (South) 1936/37
Champions of Division Four, 1967/68
Champions of Division Two, 1981/82
Football League Cup winners 1987/88

Best League Performance   7th in Division One, 1986/87
Best F.A. Cup Performance   Beaten finalists 1958/59
Most League Points   88, Division Two 1981/82 (3 points for a win)
          66, Division Four 1967/68 (2 points for a win)
Most League Goals   103, 1936/37
Most League wins in a season   27, 1936/37, 1967/68
Best League win   12-0 v. Bristol Rovers 13th April 1936
Best League away win   5-0 v. Exeter City, 21st October 1967
Best F.A. Cup win   15-0 v. Great Yarmouth, 1914/15
Best League Cup win   7-2 v. Mansfield Town, 1989/90
Best League run undefeated   19, from 20th January 1968 and 8th April 1969
Undefeated League games, home   39, from September 26th 1925
Undefeated League games, away   10, from 20th April 1981
Best run of League wins   9, from 22nd January 1977
Best run of home League wins   15, from 12th April 1967
Longest run of League draws   5, in 1928/29 and 1971/72

Most appearances: Bob Morton

Most goals: Gordon Turner

LUTON TOWN: THE EARLY YEARS

The Luton Town club was formed by the merger of two local sides, Excelsior and Wanderers, at a meeting in the Town Hall on the 11th April 1885. The new committee decided that the colours of the club's shirts and caps should be blue and pink halves. Their first ground was that belonging to Excelsior, in Dallow Lane.

Organised football under Association Rules had first appeared in Luton in 1880, with a 15 a side match on the 23rd October 1880 between Excelsior and Luton Rovers at Dallow Lane, won by the former 2-0. On 4th December 1880, a return match at the Richard III field of the Rovers ended in a 0-0 draw. Rovers played eleven games in their first season, all fifteen a side, under both Association and Rugby Union rules. The first Rugby game seems to have been a match between St. John's College and Woodlands of Hitchin on 12th November 1879.

The following season 1881/82 saw the end of Rovers. Their last reported match was on the 28th January 1882. Seven of their players went on to play for Excelsior, including their captain J.G. Hunt. This season also saw the appearance of Wanderers, who first played on the 26th December 1881, losing to Excelsior. By the following season there were four clubs of comparable strength in Luton. Looking at the results, Wanderers were the strongest, followed by Excelsior, St. John's College and St. John's Mission School. In 1883/84, the strength of the clubs was such that only nine defeats were incurred in the combined records of Excelsior, Wanderers and St John's College.

Somewhat confusingly for today's historians, Wanderers changed their name to Luton Town on 13th January 1885 at a meeting at St. Matthews School, Havelock Road, just three months before the merger with Excelsior.

St. John's College faded from the scene as their most prominent players left the club. Several joined the Town club, including Deacon, the celebrated Lomax brothers EH, DAN, and JC along with Wright and Wheeler.

For the 1885/86 season, fixtures were arranged against teams such as St. Albans, Wellingbrough Grammar School, Watford Rovers, United London Scottish, Dulwich, Hanover United and Notts County (whom they defeated 2-0). The F.A. Cup was entered for the first time, although Wanderers had appeared in 1884/85. Wanderers also played in 1885/86! Some of the former members decided to continue playing under the old name.

In 1889, Town changed its colours to cochineal. As a consequence, they were known for several years throughout the South as the "Reds".

In December 1890, Luton took the plunge as regards to professionalism. They decided to pay three of their players, Tom Read and the brothers Frank and Harry Whitby, the sum of five shillings a week for their football services. It is not on record that all three players accepted this offer, but Harry Whitby certainly did. It is probable that he was the first player to sign a professional form in the South of England. On the 9th February 1891, an application from Frank Whitby, who worked outside the town, for payment to cover travelling expenses and lost time was rejected by the committee.

By the following season the committee were faced with the fact that they had either to pay the whole team or see the players drift away to other clubs. When the committee met on August 10th 1891, it was resolved that each player should be allowed half a crown a week, an additional sixpence being allowed for away matches. So Town put into the field the first fully professional eleven in the South of England: Burley; Sanders, Hoy; Taylor (captain), Paul, Wright; Frank Whitby, Harry Whitby, Deacon, Chesher, Oclee. Eight of these players lived in the town, whilst Taylor, Paul and Oclee came from Bedford.

The following season, the players wages were doubled. The committee made their first bid for an outside professional when they secured Julian, an Arsenal player, who was made captain in 1892. They also signed Hugh Galbraith, the forward. Matters were progressing on the field, and in 1893-94 Luton gained fame by defeating Old Westminsters in the F A Cup. The Old Boys were very strong at the time, containing half a dozen men who had played for England in International matches. Progressing to the first round proper, Town had to travel to the North East to meet the then celebrated Middlesbrough Ironopolis club, who defeated them 1-2.

The success of the Football League led to the formation of the Southern League on January 12th 1894. The first games were played on 22nd September 1894. Luton's first game was on 6th October at home to Millwall, resulting in a 3-4 defeat. The first two season ended with Luton as runners-up to Millwall, with Southampton third. Luton players were honoured by being chosen for the Southern League XI against the London F.A. on the 24th February 1896 at the Clapton ground. The game resulted in a 2-2 draw. The Luton players involved were Williams, McEwen, Stewart, Gallacher and Galbraith.

Luton, Millwall and Southampton left the

Southern League in 1896, looking for stronger competition. Luton made an unsuccessful bid to join the second division of the Football League. Blackpool (19 votes) Walsall (16), Gainsborough (15) were elected. Port Vale and Luton (10 votes) were among those unsuccessful. Luton joined the newly formed United League, but with only nine clubs affiliated, the fixtures did not fill the season. At this time a new ground had to be found. The club moved just a few yards, onto the site of what is now Hazelbury Crescent and Avondale Road, often referred to as Bury Park. The opening of the new Dunstable Road ground took place on April 3rd 1897. The Duke of Bedford kicked off, the occasion being the United League match with Loughborough. Luton at this time had a powerful team, the stars being McCartney, Stewart, Coupar (ex Manchester United) Williams (ex Everton), Docherty (ex Derby County) and Ekins, formerly of Burton Swifts. The club again finished second to Millwall!

The decision to convert the club into a Limited Company was taken on June 11th 1897, the name being Luton Town Football and Athletic Company Limited. The club was elected to the Second Division of the Football League in 1897, taking the place of Burton Wanderers. Lincoln gained 21 votes, Burton Swifts 15 and Luton Town 13. They did well in their first season finishing with 30 points. However, the season was not a success financially, with the consequence that the team with which they had started their venture into the Football League could not be retained. Newcomers replaced them with inevitable results. It was in season 1898/99 that they suffered their worst ever defeat, 0-9 against Small Heath (now Birmingham City), eventually finishing fifteenth. In their third season in the Football League they filled the penultimate position in the table, and decided not to apply for re-election. The decision was made to return to the Southern League for which they were accepted for season 1900-01, finishing in the lower reaches.

The following season saw the arrival of the great Robert (Bob) Hawkes, who played for the club until 1920. He was one of half a dozen locals appearing in the side; the others being Fred Hawkes (no relation), Jack Durrant, Fred White, Herbert Moody and Harry Williams. The club had their poorest season to date in the Southern League in 1904-05 when they finished second from bottom. Fortunately, their application for re-election was supported unanimously. They were forced to leave their Dunstable Road ground, making today's ground at Kenilworth Road their new home.

The 1905/06 season opened on September 4th with the "Green" game versus Plymouth Argyle. It was so called because Plymouth played in green, the kick off was performed by JW Green, Charles Green was the Luton Secretary, and the referee was also called Green! The result was 0-0. Next season saw the first Luton player to be honoured at full international level, when Bob Hawkes was capped by England against Ireland for the match at Liverpool.

Season 1911-12 ended with relegation to the second division of the Southern League, marking the lowest point in the clubs history. Luton found themselves for two years in a league made up almost entirely of Welsh clubs! In the first season the only English opposition came from Croydon and Southend. After threatening to climb back into Division One at the first attempt, they eventually finished fifth. However the following season promotion was achieved and the regular visits to Wales ceased.

The town continued in the Southern League and finished fourteenth in 1914/15. Competition was then suspended for the duration of the Great War. Jack Jarvie, Arthur H. Wileman and Ernest J. Dodd died on active service. Those wounded included Arthur Roe and Ernest Simms, and those who suffered in gas attacks included Frank Lindley, Sid Hoar and Westby Heath. During the war the club carried as best it could, playing in the London Combination in 1915/16 and 1916/17, but could no longer compete after 1917 since it was restructured so only metropolitan clubs could play. Luton then played friendly matches until the War was over. There was one more season in the Southern League before they were elected (with the other clubs) to the newly formed Football League Third Division in 1920.

In their first Football League game for twenty years they were beaten 1-9 at Swindon, this being their second worst League defeat ever recorded, but they recovered to finish ninth. One feature of note the following season came on October 22nd 1921, when they became the only Third Division side to have three players in the same International match; Ernie Simms at centre-forward for England, and Alan Mathieson and Louis Bookman as the right wing partnership for Ireland. Luton defeated Portsmouth in a League game on the same day.

For the remainder of the Luton Town story, please turn to the following pages!

LUTON TOWN IN NON FOOTBALL LEAGUE SEASONS

Luton's score first in the left hand columns

Southern League 1894/95

home	away:		p	w	d	l	f	a	pts
3-4	2-2	Millwall Athletic	16	12	4	0	68	19	28
		Luton Town	16	9	4	3	36	22	22
4-1	2-1	Southampton St. Mary's	16	9	2	5	34	25	20
1-1	1-3	Ilford	16	6	3	7	26	40	15
5-2	3-2	Reading	16	6	2	8	33	38	14
2-1	2-2	Chatham	16	4	5	7	22	25	13
3-0	0-2	Royal Ordnance Factories	16	3	6	7	20	30	12
2-0	1-1	Clapton	16	5	1	10	22	38	11
2-0	3-0	Swindon Town	16	4	1	11	24	48	9

Southern League 1895/96

home	away		p	w	d	l	f	a	pts
0-3	0-2	Millwall Athletic	18	16	1	1	75	16	33
		Luton Town	18	13	1	4	68	14	27
3-0	1-2	Southampton St. Mary's	18	12	0	6	44	23	24
7-2	3-0	Reading	18	11	1	6	45	38	23
9-1	1-2	Chatham	18	9	2	7	43	45	20
8-1	1-0	New Brompton	18	7	4	7	30	37	18
7-1	2-0	Swindon Town	18	6	4	8	38	41	16
6-0	6-0	Clapton	18	4	2	12	30	67	10
4-0	0-0	Royal Ordnance Factories	18	3	3	12	23	44	9
5-0	5-0	Ilford	18	0	0	18	10	81	0

United League 1896/97

home	away		p	w	d	l	f	a	pts
2-3	1-3	Millwall Athletic	14	11	1	2	43	22	23
		Luton Town	14	10	1	3	52	16	21
5-2	2-2	Woolwich Arsenal	14	6	3	5	28	34	15
1-0	5-2	Loughborough	14	6	1	7	29	31	13
11-0	3-1	Rushden	14	6	1	7	25	42	13
3-0	0-1	Kettering Town	14	4	4	6	23	24	12
7-0	8-0	Wellingborough	14	3	3	8	17	39	9
2-1	2-1	Tottenham Hotspur	14	1	4	9	25	34	6

Southern League 1900/01

home	away		p	w	d	l	f	a	pts
3-4	0-5	Southampton	28	18	5	5	58	26	41
2-0	0-1	Bristol City	28	17	5	6	54	27	39
2-4	0-2	Portsmouth	28	17	4	7	56	32	38
2-0	1-3	Millwall Athletic	28	17	2	9	55	32	36
2-4	2-3	Tottenham Hotspur	28	16	4	8	55	33	36
2-0	0-2	West Ham United	28	14	5	9	40	28	33
0-1	0-1	Bristol Rovers	28	14	4	10	46	35	32
2-2	3-1	QPR	28	11	4	13	43	48	26
2-0	1-0	Reading	28	8	8	12	24	25	24
		Luton Town	28	11	2	15	43	49	24
2-0	0-2	Kettering Town	28	7	9	12	33	46	23
4-2	1-3	New Brompton	28	7	5	16	34	51	19
5-2	2-2	Gravesend United	28	6	7	15	32	85	19
2-0	0-2	Watford	28	6	4	18	24	52	16
2-1	1-2	Swindon Town	28	3	8	17	19	47	14

Southern League 1901/02

home	away		p	w	d	l	f	a	pts
2-1	0-1	Portsmouth	30	20	7	3	67	24	47
0-0	0-0	Tottenham Hotspur	30	18	6	6	61	22	42
0-2	0-1	Southampton	30	18	6	6	71	28	42
0-3	1-4	West Ham United	30	17	6	7	45	28	40
1-1	1-1	Reading	30	16	7	7	57	24	39
1-0	0-1	Millwall Athletic	30	13	6	11	46	31	32
		Luton Town	30	11	10	9	31	36	32
1-0	2-2	Kettering Town	30	12	5	13	44	39	29
1-1	0-4	Bristol Rovers	30	12	5	13	43	39	29
3-1	0-3	New Brompton	30	10	7	13	39	38	27
0-0	4-2	Northampton Town	30	11	5	14	53	65	27
1-0	2-2	QPR	30	9	6	15	34	55	24
1-0	0-2	Watford	30	9	4	17	36	58	22
1-0	2-2	Wellingborough	30	9	3	18	34	72	21
1-1	1-0	Brentford	30	7	6	17	34	61	20
3-0	2-1	Swindon Town	30	2	3	25	17	92	7

Southern League 1902/03

home	away		p	w	d	l	f	a	pts
1-3	0-2	Southampton	30	20	8	2	83	20	48
0-3	3-5	Reading	30	19	7	4	72	30	45
0-2	0-3	Portsmouth	30	17	7	6	69	32	41
3-0	1-1	Tottenham Hotspur	30	14	7	9	47	31	35
1-1	1-4	Bristol Rovers	30	13	8	9	46	34	34
1-1	1-1	New Brompton	30	11	11	8	37	35	33
0-1	0-1	Millwall Athletic	30	14	3	13	52	37	31
4-0	0-0	Northampton Town	30	12	6	12	39	48	30
4-1	1-3	QPR	30	11	6	13	34	42	28
4-0	1-4	West Ham United	30	9	10	11	35	49	28
		Luton Town	30	10	7	13	43	44	27
0-0	1-2	Swindon Town	30	10	7	13	38	46	27
1-0	1-1	Kettering Town	30	8	11	11	33	40	27
3-1	1-2	Wellingborough	30	11	3	16	36	56	25
4-1	1-0	Watford	30	6	4	20	35	87	16
2-0	3-1	Brentford	30	2	1	27	16	84	5

Southern League 1903/04

home	away:		p	w	d	l	f	a	pts
1-0	1-1	Southampton	34	22	6	6	75	30	50
3-2	1-1	Tottenham Hotspur	34	16	11	7	54	37	43
1-0	1-3	Bristol Rovers	34	17	8	9	64	42	42
1-1	0-3	Portsmouth	34	17	8	9	41	38	42
1-0	1-2	QPR	34	15	11	8	53	37	41
2-1	1-1	Reading	34	14	13	7	48	35	41
1-1	3-2	Millwall	34	16	8	10	64	42	40
		Luton Town	34	14	12	8	38	33	40
1-1	0-0	Plymouth Argyle	34	13	10	11	44	34	36
3-0	0-1	Swindon Town	34	10	11	13	30	42	31
0-0	0-1	Fulham	34	9	12	13	34	36	30
1-0	0-0	West Ham United	34	10	7	17	39	44	27
1-0	1-2	Brentford	34	9	9	16	34	48	27
1-2	0-2	Wellingborough	34	11	5	18	44	63	27
1-0	0-0	Northampton Town	34	10	7	17	36	60	27
1-0	2-2	New Brompton	34	6	13	15	26	43	25
2-0	2-2	Brighton & Hove Alb.	34	6	12	16	46	69	24
2-1	2-1	Kettering Town	34	6	7	21	39	76	19

Southern League 1904/05

home	away		p	w	d	l	f	a	pts
1-2	2-3	Bristol Rovers	34	20	8	6	74	36	48
2-0	0-1	Reading	34	18	7	9	57	38	43
1-2	1-4	Southampton	34	18	7	9	54	40	43
0-2	0-3	Plymouth Argyle	34	18	5	11	57	39	41
1-0	0-1	Tottenham Hotspur	34	15	8	11	63	34	38
6-0	0-0	Fulham	34	14	10	10	46	34	38
1-1	2-1	QPR	34	14	8	12	51	46	36
4-3	0-1	Portsmouth	34	16	4	14	61	56	36
1-0	1-2	New Brompton	34	11	11	12	40	40	33
2-1	0-3	Watford	34	15	3	16	44	45	33
0-2	2-6	West Ham United	34	12	8	14	48	42	32
2-0	1-1	Brighton & Hove Alb.	34	13	6	15	44	45	32
4-2	1-2	Northampton Town	34	12	8	14	43	54	32
1-0	0-3	Brentford	34	10	9	15	33	38	29
1-2	0-2	Millwall	34	11	7	16	38	47	29
4-1	0-1	Swindon Town	34	12	5	17	41	59	29
		Luton Town	34	12	3	19	45	54	27
4-0	0-2	Wellingborough	34	5	3	26	25	107	13

Southern League 1905/06

home	away		p	w	d	l	f	a	pts
0-1	0-3	Fulham	34	19	12	3	44	15	50
5-0	1-2	Southampton	34	19	7	8	68	39	45
3-2	0-2	Portsmouth	34	17	9	8	61	35	43
		Luton Town	34	17	7	10	64	40	41
2-0	0-1	Tottenham Hotspur	34	16	7	11	46	29	39
0-0	0-2	Plymouth Argyle	34	16	7	11	52	33	39
2-1	1-1	Norwich City	34	13	10	11	46	38	36
7-1	2-3	Bristol Rovers	34	15	5	14	56	56	35
0-2	1-2	Brentford	34	14	7	13	43	52	35
3-0	1-1	Reading	34	12	9	13	53	46	33
1-1	2-1	West Ham United	34	14	5	15	42	39	33
6-1	2-1	Millwall	34	11	11	12	38	41	33
3-2	3-2	QPR	34	12	7	15	58	44	31
2-0	1-1	Watford	34	8	10	16	38	57	26
4-0	1-1	Swindon Town	34	8	9	17	31	52	25
4-1	1-2	Brighton & Hove Alb.	34	9	7	18	30	55	25
2-1	1-1	New Brompton	34	7	8	19	20	62	22
1-0	2-1	Northampton Town	34	8	5	21	32	79	21

Southern League 1906/07

home	away		p	w	d	l	f	a	pts
2-0	0-0	Fulham	38	20	13	5	58	32	53
3-1	0-1	Portsmouth	38	22	7	9	64	36	51
3-1	3-1	Brighton & Hove Alb.	38	18	9	11	53	43	45
		Luton Town	38	18	9	11	52	52	45
1-1	1-5	West Ham United	38	15	14	9	60	41	44
0-2	2-1	Tottenham Hotspur	38	17	9	12	63	45	43
1-1	1-5	Millwall	38	18	6	14	71	50	42
1-0	1-3	Norwich City	38	15	12	11	57	48	42
2-0	2-2	Watford	38	13	16	9	46	43	42
2-0	1-0	Brentford	38	17	8	13	57	56	42
2-1	0-1	Southampton	38	13	9	16	49	56	35
1-1	2-7	Reading	38	14	6	18	57	47	34
5-3	0-1	Leyton	38	11	12	15	38	60	34
1-0	1-0	Bristol Rovers	38	12	9	17	55	64	33
3-2	0-0	Plymouth Argyle	38	10	13	15	43	50	33
0-2	0-0	New Brompton	38	12	9	17	47	59	33
6-2	0-4	Swindon Town	38	11	11	16	43	54	33
1-1	0-2	QPR	38	11	10	17	47	55	32
2-1	1-0	Crystal Palace	38	8	9	21	46	66	25
1-0	0-0	Northampton Town	38	5	9	24	29	88	19

Southern League 1907/08

home	away:		p	w	d	l	f	a	pts
0-0	1-3	QPR	38	21	9	8	82	57	51
0-0	1-2	Plymouth Argyle	38	19	11	8	50	31	49
3-1	0-0	Millwall	38	19	8	11	49	32	46
4-0	2-4	Crystal Palace	38	17	10	11	54	51	44
1-0	0-4	Swindon Town	38	16	10	12	55	40	42
0-2	1-0	Bristol Rovers	38	16	10	12	59	56	42
3-1	2-1	Tottenham Hotspur	38	17	7	14	59	48	41
0-1	0-0	Northampton Town	38	15	11	12	50	41	41
2-0	0-1	Portsmouth	38	17	6	15	63	52	40
0-3	0-1	West Ham United	38	15	10	13	47	48	40
0-2	1-2	Southampton	38	16	6	16	51	60	38
3-1	0-3	Reading	38	15	6	17	55	50	36
1-0	0-1	Bradford Park Avenue	38	12	12	14	63	54	36
1-1	1-2	Watford	38	12	10	16	47	59	34
1-0	1-3	Brentford	38	14	5	19	49	52	33
0-0	1-6	Norwich City	38	12	9	17	46	49	33
1-0	0-1	Brighton & Hove Alb.	38	12	8	18	46	59	32
		Luton Town	38	12	6	20	33	66	30
0-3	0-5	Leyton	38	8	11	19	51	73	27
1-2	1-0	New Brompton	38	9	7	22	44	75	25

Southern League 1908/09

home	away:		p	w	d	l	f	a	pts
3-1	0-3	Northampton Town	40	25	5	10	90	45	55
1-0	1-4	Swindon Town	40	22	5	13	96	65	49
1-0	0-6	Southampton	40	19	10	11	67	58	48
5-1	0-1	Portsmouth	40	18	10	12	68	60	46
1-0	0-1	Bristol Rovers	40	17	9	14	60	63	43
0-2	1-2	Exeter City	40	18	6	16	56	65	42
3-0	0-1	New Brompton	40	17	7	16	48	59	41
2-2	2-2	Reading	40	11	18	11	60	57	40
		Luton Town	40	17	6	17	59	60	40
1-3	1-1	Plymouth Argyle	40	15	10	15	46	47	40
0-1	0-0	Millwall	40	16	6	18	59	61	38
3-0	0-2	Southend United	40	14	10	16	52	54	38
2-1	0-2	Leyton	40	15	8	17	52	55	38
1-0	3-0	Watford	40	14	9	17	51	64	37
1-0	0-4	QPR	40	12	12	16	52	50	36
4-1	0-2	Crystal Palace	40	12	12	16	62	62	36
1-0	0-4	West Ham United	40	16	4	20	56	60	36
3-1	0-0	Brighton & Hove Alb.	40	14	7	19	60	61	35
4-0	2-3	Norwich City	40	12	11	17	59	75	35
6-1	2-5	Coventry City	40	15	4	21	64	91	34
3-1	2-2	Brentford	40	13	7	20	59	74	33

Southern League 1909/10

home	away:		p	w	d	l	f	a	pts
1-1	0-3	Brighton & Hove Alb.	42	23	13	6	69	28	59
1-1	0-0	Swindon Town	42	22	10	10	92	46	54
1-1	0-4	QPR	42	19	13	10	56	47	51
0-3	1-6	Northampton Town	42	22	4	16	90	44	48
3-4	2-3	Southampton	42	16	16	10	64	55	48
0-1	2-3	Portsmouth	42	20	7	15	70	63	47
2-4	3-1	Crystal Palace	42	20	6	16	69	50	46
4-1	2-6	Coventry City	42	19	8	15	71	60	46
4-2	2-1	West Ham United	42	15	15	12	69	56	45
1-1	0-3	Leyton	42	16	11	15	60	46	43
3-2	2-4	Plymouth Argyle	42	16	11	15	61	54	43
1-0	0-4	New Brompton	42	19	5	18	76	74	43
2-1	1-2	Bristol Rovers	42	16	10	16	37	48	42
4-2	2-2	Brentford	42	16	9	17	50	58	41
1-1	1-6	Luton Town	42	15	11	16	72	92	41
4-1	2-2	Millwall	42	15	7	20	45	59	37
1-1	0-6	Norwich City	42	13	9	20	59	78	35
3-1	2-1	Exeter City	42	14	6	22	60	69	34
4-2	1-1	Watford	42	10	13	19	51	76	33
3-3	1-4	Southend United	42	12	9	21	51	90	33
1-1	3-2	Croydon Common	42	13	5	24	52	96	31
2-1	1-0	Reading	42	7	10	25	38	73	24

Southern League 1910/11

home	away:		p	w	d	l	f	a	pts
2-1	1-4	Swindon Town	38	24	5	9	80	31	53
1-3	1-3	Northampton Town	38	18	12	8	54	27	48
1-0	3-3	Brighton & Hove Alb.	38	20	8	10	58	36	48
1-1	1-3	Crystal Palace	38	17	13	8	55	48	47
1-1	0-2	West Ham United	38	17	11	10	63	46	45
0-1	3-3	QPR	38	13	14	11	52	41	40
4-1	0-3	Leyton	38	16	8	14	57	52	40
0-0	0-4	Plymouth Argyle	38	15	9	14	54	55	39
		Luton Town	38	15	8	15	67	63	38
3-1	2-3	Norwich City	38	15	8	15	46	48	38
4-2	1-1	Coventry City	38	16	6	16	65	68	38
1-1	0-1	Brentford	38	14	9	15	41	42	37
3-1	2-4	Exeter City	38	14	9	15	51	53	37
3-1	0-1	Watford	38	13	9	16	49	65	35
1-0	3-1	Millwall	38	11	9	18	42	54	31
4-0	2-4	Bristol Rovers	38	10	10	18	42	55	30
3-2	0-0	Southampton	38	11	8	19	42	67	30
3-0	1-2	New Brompton	38	11	8	19	34	65	30
3-1	4-1	Southend United	38	10	9	19	47	64	29
4-1	1-2	Portsmouth	38	8	11	19	34	63	27

Southern League 1911/12

home	away:		p	w	d	l	f	a	pts
1-3	0-2	QPR	38	21	11	6	59	35	53
0-3	0-2	Plymouth Argyle	38	23	6	9	63	31	52
3-3	0-1	Northampton Town	38	22	7	9	82	41	51
0-3	2-4	Swindon Town	38	21	6	11	82	50	48
1-0	0-1	Brighton & Hove Alb.	38	19	9	10	73	35	47
2-4	0-1	Coventry City	38	17	8	13	66	54	42
0-1	1-3	Crystal Palace	38	15	10	13	70	46	40
0-1	1-1	Millwall	38	15	10	13	60	57	40
1-1	1-0	Watford	38	13	10	15	56	68	36
1-1	3-4	Stoke	38	13	10	15	51	63	36
7-1	1-1	Reading	38	11	14	13	43	59	36
0-1	2-2	Norwich City	38	10	14	14	40	60	34
2-1	0-3	West Ham United	38	13	7	18	64	69	33
0-0	1-0	Brentford	38	12	9	17	60	65	33
4-2	0-2	Exeter City	38	11	11	16	48	62	33
1-1	2-3	Southampton	38	10	11	17	46	63	31
3-1	1-2	Bristol Rovers	38	9	13	16	41	62	31
3-0	0-0	New Brompton	38	11	9	18	35	72	31
		Luton Town	38	9	10	19	49	61	28
4-1	1-1	Leyton	38	7	11	20	27	62	25

Southern League Division Two 1912/13

home	away:		p	w	d	l	f	a	pts
2-0	0-3	Cardiff City	24	18	5	1	54	15	41
4-3	1-1	Southend United	24	14	6	4	43	23	34
0-4	0-2	Swansea Town	24	12	7	5	29	23	31
3-1	2-4	Croydon Common	24	13	4	7	51	29	30
		Luton Town	24	13	4	7	52	39	30
2-0	1-1	Llanelly	24	9	6	9	33	39	24
2-2	2-1	Pontypridd	24	6	11	7	30	28	23
3-1	2-2	Mid Rhondda	24	9	4	11	33	31	22
3-1	0-3	Aberdare	24	8	6	10	38	40	22
5-0	1-5	Newport County	24	7	5	12	29	36	19
1-0	3-2	Mardy	24	6	3	15	38	38	15
4-0	3-0	Treharris	24	5	2	17	18	60	12
7-1	1-2	Ton Pentre	24	3	3	18	22	69	9

Southern League Division Two 1913/14

home	away:		p	w	d	l	f	a	pts
2-1	1-1	Croydon Common	30	23	5	2	76	14	51
		Luton Town	30	24	3	3	92	22	51
3-1	0-0	Brentford	30	20	4	6	80	18	44
5-0	1-0	Swansea Town	30	20	4	6	66	23	44
2-1	2-1	Stoke	30	19	2	9	71	34	40
1-0	0-2	Newport County	30	14	8	8	49	38	36
8-1	1-1	Mid Rhondda	30	13	7	10	55	37	33
3-0	2-3	Pontypridd	30	14	5	11	43	38	33
5-1	0-3	Llanelly	30	12	4	14	45	39	28
3-1	3-1	Barry	30	9	8	13	44	70	26
6-0	2-1	Abertillery	30	8	4	18	44	57	20
2-0	4-0	Ton Pentre	30	8	4	18	33	61	20
1-0	2-1	Mardy	30	6	6	18	30	60	18
4-0	9-0	Caerphilly	30	4	7	19	21	103	15
7-0	5-1	Aberdare	30	4	5	21	33	87	13
6-0	2-1	Treharris	30	2	4	24	19	106	8

Southern League 1914/15

home	away:		p	w	d	l	f	a	pts
0-2	4-2	Watford	38	22	8	8	68	46	52
1-2	0-4	Reading	38	21	7	10	68	43	49
2-1	0-3	Cardiff City	38	22	4	12	72	38	48
1-2	0-3	West Ham United	38	18	9	11	58	47	45
1-1	3-0	Northampton Town	38	16	11	11	56	51	43
3-2	3-3	Southampton	38	19	5	14	78	74	43
0-2	1-3	Portsmouth	38	16	10	12	54	42	42
0-2	3-3	Millwall	38	16	10	12	50	51	42
2-2	2-2	Swindon Town	38	15	11	12	77	59	41
0-1	1-0	Brighton & Hove Alb.	38	16	7	15	46	47	39
0-2	2-1	Exeter City	38	15	8	15	50	41	38
2-4	3-0	QPR	38	13	12	13	55	56	38
1-1	1-5	Norwich City	38	11	14	13	53	56	36
		Luton Town	38	13	8	17	61	73	34
1-2	3-2	Crystal Palace	38	13	8	17	47	61	34
3-1	0-1	Bristol Rovers	38	14	3	21	53	75	31
2-1	3-3	Plymouth Argyle	38	8	14	16	51	61	30
3-4	0-1	Southend United	38	10	8	20	44	64	28
2-1	1-1	Croydon Common	38	9	9	20	47	63	27
3-1	4-2	Gillingham	38	6	8	24	43	83	20

Southern League 1919/20

home	away:		p	w	d	l	f	a	pts
2-0	1-1	Portsmouth	42	23	12	7	73	27	58
1-2	1-4	Watford	42	26	6	10	69	42	58
1-4	1-4	Crystal Palace	42	22	12	8	69	43	56
2-2	1-2	Cardiff City	42	18	17	7	70	43	53
1-2	0-1	Plymouth Argyle	42	20	10	12	56	29	50
2-1	0-4	QPR	42	18	10	14	62	50	46
0-2	2-1	Reading	42	16	13	13	51	43	45
0-1	1-2	Southampton	42	18	8	16	72	63	44
1-1	0-3	Swansea Town	42	16	11	15	53	45	43
3-1	2-3	Exeter City	42	17	9	16	57	52	43
1-1	0-3	Southend U	42	13	17	12	46	48	43
1-1	1-1	Norwich City	42	15	11	16	64	57	41
3-1	0-1	Swindon Town	42	17	7	18	65	68	41
2-2	0-2	Millwall	42	14	12	16	52	55	40
0-0	1-3	Brentford	42	15	10	17	53	69	40
2-0	3-4	Brighton & Hove Alb.	42	14	8	20	60	72	36
1-1	0-5	Bristol Rovers	42	11	13	18	62	78	35
4-0	0-0	Newport County	42	13	7	22	45	70	33
0-2	4-1	Northampton Town	42	12	9	21	64	103	23
		Luton Town	42	10	10	22	51	76	30
0-4	3-1	Merthyr Town	42	9	11	22	47	79	29
2-0	0-2	Gillingham	42	10	7	25	34	74	27

INTRODUCTION TO THE STATISTICS PAGES

The season by season grids show the results of games in the Football League, F.A. Cup, Football League Cup, Full Members' Cup, Associate Members' Cup, Texaco Cup, Watney Cup, Anglo-Italian Cup, the Third Division (South) Cup and the Southern Professional Floodlit Cup. The two World Wars caused the abandonment of League seasons 1915/16 to 1918/19 and 1939/40 to 1945/46. However, details of three League games played in 1939/40 and the FA Cup results from 1945/46 will be found in later sections.

Home games are identified by the opponents name in upper case, away games by the use of lower case. Luton's score is always given first. Attendances for League games are taken from the official Football League records since 1925/26; before that, estimated attendances based on newspaper reports have to be used.

Substitutes have the numbers 12, 13 and 14. 12 is used if only one substitute appeared (no matter what number was on the player's shirt). The players who were substituted are underlined.

A full player list is provided for every player who made a League appearance. Date and place of birth are shown, where known, and the year of death. Players with the same name are given a (1) or (2) after their name to avoid confusion. The next two columns, "seasons played", act as an index to the season by season grids. The years shown are the "first year" of the season; for example, 1971 is season 1971/72. The two columns show the season in which the player made his League debut; and the final season that he played. However, if he only played in one season, the second column is blank. An entry of "1996" in the second column does not imply that the player has left the club, but means that he appeared in the "final season" of the book.

Note that some players also made F.A. Cup appearances before 1897/98, between 1900/01 and 1920/21, and in 1945/46. If a player also made a League appearance his F.A. Cup appearances from these seasons are included in the list.

Previous and next clubs show where he was transferred from, and the club he moved to. Non-league club information is included when known.

The appearance columns have separate totals for the League, F.A. Cup, Football League Cup and the miscellaneous cup tournaments listed above. League play-off appearances are included in the "miscellaneous" games. "Goals scored" are also shown under the four headings.

If a player has had more than one spell at the club, a consolidated set of appearance and goals are shown on the first line. Subsequent lines show the seasons involved in his return, and his new pair of previous and next clubs.

A full record of meetings against all other League clubs is included. Some clubs have played in the League under different names, but the totals are consolidated under the present day name in this table. Other pages show the club's record in the F.A. Cup in non League seasons and the list of managers.

1897/98   8th in Division Two

#	Date	Opponent	Res	Scorers	Att	Birch E	Catlin W	Clarke J	Coupar J	Davies S	Docherty J	Donaldson R	Durrant AF	Ekins FG	Gallacher W	Little T	McCartney WJ	McEwen J	McInnes T	Perrins G	Stewart WS	Williams R
1	Sep 4	Leicester Fosse	1-1	Ekins		9			8	4	6			11	7		2	3	10		5	1
2	11	GAINSBOROUGH TRIN.	4-0	Ekins, Little, McInnes, Gallacher					8	4	6			11	7	9	2	3	10		5	1
3	18	Newton Heath	2-1	McInnes, Little	7000				8	4	6			11	7	9	2	3	10		5	1
4	Oct 2	WOOLWICH ARSENAL	0-2		5000			9	8	4	6				7	11	2	3	10		5	1
5	9	Woolwich Arsenal	0-3		10000				8		6			11	7	9	2	3	10	4	5	1
6	16	Loughborough	0-2		1500				8		6			11	7	9	2	3	10	4	5	1
7	Nov 6	BURTON SWIFTS	1-1	Gallacher	3000				8	4	6			11	7	9	2	3	10		5	1
8	13	Burnley	0-4		3000	10				4	6			11	7	9	2	3	8		5	1
9	27	Gainsborough Trinity	3-3	McInnes, Gallacher, Little					8	4	6			11	7	9	2	3	10		5	1
10	29	BLACKPOOL	3-1	Little 2, Coupar					8	4	6			11	7	9	2	3	10		5	1
11	Dec 4	Lincoln City	2-4	Stewart, McEwen					8	4	6			11	7	9	2	3	10		5	1
12	18	LINCOLN CITY	9-3	* See below	3000	9			8	4	6				7	10	2	3	11		5	1
13	25	Burton Swifts	1-2	Donaldson		8					6	9		11	7	10	2	3			5	1
14	27	GRIMSBY TOWN	6-0	McInnes, Ekins, Donaldson 2, Coupar, Davies (p)	5000				8	4	6	9		11	7		2	3	10		5	1
15	Jan 1	MANCHESTER CITY	3-0	Donaldson, Coupar, McInnes	4000				8	4	6	9			7	10	2	3	11		5	1
16	8	Walsall	0-5		4000				8	4	6	9			7	10	2	3	11		5	1
17	15	LOUGHBOROUGH	7-0	Coupar 2, Stewart 2(1p), Donaldson 2, Little	3000				8		6	9			7	10	2	3	11	4	5	1
18	22	Grimsby Town	3-1	Donaldson, McInnes, Coupar	5000				8	4	6	9			7	10	2	3	11		5	1
19	Feb 5	WALSALL	6-0	Stewart 4 (1p), Little 2	2000	6			8		2	9			7	10		3	11	4	5	1
20	12	Small Heath	2-4	Stewart, Donaldson	4000	6			8		2	9			7	10		3	11	4	5	1
21	19	NEWCASTLE UNITED	3-1	Birch, Stewart, Donaldson	3500	11			8	4	6	9			7		2	3	10		5	1
22	26	Darwen	2-0	Gallacher, Birch		11			8	4	6	9			7		2	3	10		5	1
23	Mar 12	Newcastle United	1-4	Birch	15000	11			8	4	6	9			7		2	3	10		5	1
24	19	BURNLEY	2-0	Donaldson, Gallacher		11				2	6	9			7	8		3	10	4	5	1
25	21	NEWTON HEATH	2-2	Durrant, McInnes	2000					4	6	9	11		7	8	2	3	10		5	1
26	26	Manchester City	1-2	Coupar	5000	11			8	4	6	9			7		2	3	10		5	1
27	Apr 2	SMALL HEATH	1-2	Coupar	3000	11			8	4	6	9			7		2	3	10		5	1
28	8	LEICESTER FOSSE	0-1		3000	11			8	4	6	9			7		2	3	10		5	1
29	11	DARWEN	3-0	Gallacher, McInnes, Catlin			9		8	4	6				7	11	2	3	10		5	1
30	30	Blackpool	0-1		200				8	4	6	9			7	11	2	3	10		5	1
		Apps				13	1	1	26	25	30	17	1	12	30	22	27	30	29	6	30	30
		Goals				6	1		9	1		10	1	3	7	9			1		10	

Scorers in game 12: Birch 3, Stewart, Coupar, McInnes 2, Little, Gallacher

F.A. Cup

	Date	Opponent	Res	Scorers	Att	Birch E	Catlin W	Clarke J	Coupar J	Davies S	Docherty J	Donaldson R	Durrant AF	Ekins FG	Gallacher W	Little T	McCartney WJ	McEwen J	McInnes T	Perrins G	Stewart WS	Williams R
Q4	Nov 20	Tottenham Hotspur	4-3	Davies, Stewart, McInnes, Ekins	12000				10	4	6			11	7	9	2	3	8		5	1
Q5	Dec 11	Clapton	2-0	Stewart, Little	2500				10	4	6			11	7	9	2	3	8		5	1
R1	Jan 29	BOLTON WAN.	0-1		4500				8	4	6	9			7	11	2	3	10		5	1

Drawn against Marlow in Q3; Marlow scratched

	Team	P	W	D	L	F	A	W	D	L	F	A	Pts
1	Burnley	30	14	1	0	64	13	6	7	2	16	11	48
2	Newcastle United	30	14	0	1	43	10	7	3	5	21	22	45
3	Manchester City	30	10	4	1	45	15	5	5	5	21	21	39
4	Newton Heath	30	11	2	2	42	10	5	4	6	22	25	38
5	Woolwich Arsenal	30	10	4	1	41	14	6	1	8	28	35	37
6	Small Heath	30	11	1	3	37	18	5	3	7	21	32	36
7	Leicester Fosse	30	8	5	2	26	11	5	2	8	20	24	33
8	LUTON TOWN	30	10	2	3	50	13	3	2	10	18	37	30
9	Gainsborough Trin.	30	10	4	1	30	12	2	2	11	20	42	30
10	Walsall	30	9	3	3	42	15	3	2	10	16	43	29
11	Blackpool	30	8	4	3	32	15	2	1	12	17	46	25
12	Grimsby Town	30	9	1	5	44	24	1	3	11	8	38	24
13	Burton Swifts	30	7	3	5	25	21	1	2	12	13	48	21
14	Lincoln City	30	6	3	6	27	27	0	2	13	16	55	17
15	Darwen	30	4	1	10	21	32	2	1	12	10	44	14
16	Loughborough	30	5	2	8	15	26	1	0	14	9	61	14

1898/99   15th in Division Two

#	Date	Opponent	Score	Scorers / notes	Att	Birch E	Boutwood	Brock JS	Clarke W	Crump WH	Dow JM	Durrant AF	Ekins FG	Farr H	Ford C	Ford WG	Galbraith H	Gentle	Hawkes T	Hewitt G	Kemplay J	McInnes T	Moore JAO	Palmer JF	Perkins WH	Ralley W	Sharpe DA	Smith GH	Williams H
1	Sep 3	WOOLWICH ARSENAL	0-1		5000			11	5	6		7			4	9				8		10	3		1				2
2	10	Barnsley	1-2	McInnes				11	6			7			4	9				8		10	3		1		5		2
3	17	Leicester Fosse	1-1	Hewitt				2				7				6	11			10	9	8			1	4	5		3
4	24	DARWEN	8-1	* see below								7	11		4	10				6	9	8	3		1		5		2
5	Oct 1	Gainsborough Trinity	3-2	McInnes, Kemplay, Brock				10			2	7			4	11				6	9	8	3		1		5		
6	8	MANCHESTER CITY	0-3		3000						2	7	11		4	10				6	9	8	3		1		5		
7	15	Glossop	0-5		2500				4	6	2	7	11			10					9	8	3		1		5		
8	22	WALSALL	3-2	McInnes, Hewitt, Durrant	2000						2	7	11		6	4				10	9	8			1		5		3
9	Nov 5	BURSLEM PORT VALE	0-1		2000							6	10	7	4	5	9			11		8	3		1				2
10	12	Small Heath	0-9		4000					6	2	7	11		4	5	9			10		8	3		1				
11	26	Blackpool	3-2	Ekins, Hewitt 2	1000			7		6	2		11		4					10	8	9	3		1		5		
12	Dec 3	GRIMSBY TOWN	3-1	Durrant 2, Kemplay	2000					6	2	7	11		4					10	9	8			1		5		3
13	17	NEW BRIGHTON TOWER	2-3	Hewitt, Williams	3000			7		6	2		11		4					10	9	8			1		5		3
14	24	Lincoln City	0-2			7				6	2		11		4	10					9	8	3		1		5		
15	26	Burton Swifts	1-1	Brock		10		7		6			11								9	8	3		1	4	5		3
16	31	Woolwich Arsenal	2-6	Kemplay 2	4000			7		6	2		11		4					10	9	8	3		1		5		
17	Jan 7	BARNSLEY	4-1	Kemplay, Birch 3		10		7		6	2		11								9	8	3		1	4	5		
18	14	LEICESTER FOSSE	1-6	W Ford						6		7	11		4	10					9	8	3		1		5		2
19	28	GAINSBOROUGH TRIN.	4-2	Brock, McInnes, Kemplay 2		10		7		6			11		4						9	8	3		1		5		2
20	Feb 4	Manchester City	0-2		8000	10		7		11	3				4	8					9				1	6	5		2
21	11	GLOSSOP	0-2			10		11		6	2	7			4						9	8			1		5		3
22	18	Walsall	0-6		3000	10		7		6	2		11		4						9	8			1		5		3
23	Mar 4	Burslem Port Vale	1-4	Birch	4000	10		7		11	2				6				9			8	3		1	4	5		
24	11	SMALL HEATH	2-3	Dow, W Ford	2000	10		7		6	2				4	11					9	8			1		5		
25	18	Loughborough	1-4	Brock		11		8			2	7			6						9	10	3		1	4	5		
26	25	BLACKPOOL	3-2	W Ford 2, Kemplay		10		7		6	2		11		4	8					9				1		5		3
27	31	LOUGHBOROUGH	2-2	McInnes, Durrant	4000						2	7	11				9	1				8	3			5	4		6
28	Apr 1	Grimsby Town	0-5		5000	6					2	7	11			10		1			9	8				5	4		3
29	3	BURTON SWIFTS	3-0	W Ford, Kemplay, Brock		8		6			2	7	11			10					9					5	4	1	3
30	8	NEWTON HEATH	0-1		2000	4		7		6	2		11			10		1			9	8					5		3
31	11	Darwen	1-4	McInnes				7		6	2	5	11		4	10		1			9	8							3
32	12	Newton Heath	0-5		3000			7		6	2		11		8	10		1			9	5	3						4
33	15	New Brighton Tower	0-4			5	7		4				11			10				2	9	8		1		6			3
34	22	LINCOLN CITY	2-0	W Ford, McInnes		4		7		6	2		11	1		10					9	8					5		3
				Apps		16	1	21	4	25	26	22	21	1	24	23	3	5	1	12	29	31	19	1	26	11	21	1	30
				Goals		4		5		1	6	2				7				6	11	8							1

Scorers in game 4: Hewitt, McInnes, Kemplay 2, Ekins, Durrant 2, W Ford

F.A. Cup

#	Date	Opponent	Score	Scorers	Att	Birch E	Boutwood	Brock JS	Clarke W	Crump WH	Dow JM	Durrant AF	Ekins FG	Farr H	Ford C	Ford WG	Galbraith H	Gentle	Hawkes T	Hewitt G	Kemplay J	McInnes T	Moore JAO	Palmer JF	Perkins WH	Ralley W	Sharpe DA	Smith GH	Williams H
Q3	Oct 29	WATFORD	2-2	Dow, Durrant	2500			11			2	7			6	4	9			10		8			1		5		3
rep	Nov 2	Watford	1-0	Galbraith	2000			11	5		2	7			6	4	9			10		8	2		1				3
Q4	Nov 19	SHEPHERDS BUSH	4-3	Crump, Durrant, Kemplay, Hewitt	2000			11	5		2	7			6					10	9	8	4		1				3
Q5	Dec 10	Tottenham Hotspur	1-1	Hewitt	4000				5		2		11		6	4				10	9	8			1		7		3
rep	Dec 14	TOTTENHAM HOTSPUR	1-1	McInnes	3500				5		2	4	11		6					10	9	8			1		7		3
rep 2	Dec 19	Tottenham Hotspur	0-2		4500				5		2		11		6	4					9	8			1		7		3

Q5 second replay at Tufnell Park   Played at 10 in Q5 second replay: F Draper

		P	W	D	L	F	A	W	D	L	F	A	Pts
1	Manchester City	34	15	1	1	64	10	8	5	4	28	25	52
2	Glossop	34	12	1	4	48	13	8	5	7	23	39	46
3	Leicester Fosse	34	12	5	0	35	12	6	4	7	29	30	45
4	Newton Heath	34	12	4	1	51	14	7	1	9	16	29	43
5	New Brighton Tower	34	13	2	2	48	13	5	5	7	23	39	43
6	Walsall	34	12	5	0	64	11	3	7	7	15	25	42
7	Woolwich Arsenal	34	14	2	1	55	10	4	3	10	17	31	41
8	Small Heath	34	14	1	2	66	17	3	6	8	19	33	41
9	Burslem Port Vale	34	12	2	3	35	12	5	3	9	21	22	39
10	Grimsby Town	34	10	3	4	39	17	5	2	10	32	43	35
11	Barnsley	34	11	4	2	44	18	1	3	13	8	38	31
12	Lincoln City	34	10	5	2	31	16	2	2	13	20	40	31
13	Burton Swifts	34	7	5	5	35	25	3	3	11	16	45	28
14	Gainsborough Trin.	34	8	4	5	40	22	2	1	14	16	50	25
15	LUTON TOWN	34	8	1	8	37	31	2	2	13	14	64	23
16	Blackpool	34	6	3	8	35	30	2	1	14	14	60	20
17	Loughborough	34	5	4	8	31	26	1	2	14	7	66	18
18	Darwen	34	2	4	11	16	32	0	1	16	6	##	9

1899/00 17th in Division Two: Did not apply for re-election

#		Date	Opponent	Score	Scorers	Att	Barnes WT	Brock JS	Brown J	Brown WR	Burbage RW	Daw EC	Dawson	Dimmock R	Dow JM	Draper F	Durrant AF	Eckford J	Fairgrieve RW	Garratt A	Hawkes F	Hawkes T	Holdstock H	Inglis JA	Marshall FR	McCurdy W	McInnes T	Morrison FR	Ralley W	Stewart WS	Williams H
1	Sep	2	Grimsby Town	3-3	Fairgrieve, Brock 2	4000		8				1			2			11	9					7		3	10	4		5	6
2		9	WOOLWICH ARSENAL	1-2	Dow	3000		8				1			2			11	10					7		3	9	4		5	6
3		16	Barnsley	1-2	Williams	2500		8				1			2			11	9					7		3	10	4		5	6
4		23	LEICESTER FOSSE	0-0				8		7		1			2	9		11								3	10	4		5	6
5		30	BURTON SWIFTS	5-2	Fairgrieve, Brock 2, Eckford, W Brown			8		7		1			2			11	9							3	10	4		5	6
6	Oct	7	Burslem Port Vale	0-1		2000		8		7		1			2			11	9							3	10	4		5	6
7		14	WALSALL	4-0	Brock, Fairgrieve, Bunch (og), McInnes	3000		8		7		1			2			11	9							3	10	4	6	5	
8		21	Middlesbrough			7000		8		7		1			2			11	9							3	10	4	6	5	
9	Nov	4	Gainsborough Trinity	2-2	Brock, Fairgrieve			8		7		1			2			11	9							3	10	4	6	5	
10		11	BOLTON WANDERERS	0-2				8		7		1			2			11	9							3	10	4	6	5	
11		25	NEWTON HEATH	0-1		3000		8				1			2		7	11	9		3						10	4	6	5	
12	Dec	2	Sheffield Wednesday	0-6		10000	6	4		7		1				8		11	9				3				10			5	2
13		16	Small Heath	0-3		2000		4		7		1			2			11	8				9			3	10			6	5
14		23	NEW BRIGHTON TOWER	1-4	Marshall			4		7		1			2			11	8				9			3	10			6	5
15		26	CHESTERFIELD TOWN	0-3		2000			5			1			2			11	8				7	9		3	10	4	6		
16		30	GRIMSBY TOWN	0-4		500		9		7		1			2			11	8							3	10	4	6	5	
17	Jan	6	Woolwich Arsenal	1-3	Eckford	3000		4		7		1			2	9	11	10					6			3	8				5
18		13	BARNSLEY	3-0	J Brown, Brock, Draper			4	6	7		1			2	9	11	10								3	8				5
19		20	Leicester Fosse	2-2	Draper 2	6000		4		7		1			2	9	11	10					5			3	8				6
20	Feb	3	Burton Swifts	1-3	W Brown	300		4		7	11	1			2	9		10								3	8				6
21		10	BURSLEM PORT VALE	1-1	Draper	500		4	5	7	11	1			2	9		10								3	8				6
22		17	Walsall	3-7	Dimmock, Eckford, Draper	1000		4	6	7		1		11	2	9		10					5			3	8				
23		24	MIDDLESBROUGH	1-1	W Brown	1000		4	6	7		1		11	2	9		10					5				8				3
24	Mar	3	Lincoln City	0-2		2500	4		6			1		11	2		8	9								3	10				5
25		10	GAINSBOROUGH TRIN.	4-0	Holdstock, Dimmock, Draper, Brock			8	6	7		1		10	2		8	11					5			3	4				
26		17	Bolton Wanderers	0-3		3658			4	7		1		11	2		8	10					5			3	9				
27		24	LOUGHBOROUGH	4-0	Dow, Brock 2, Hawkes			9	6	7		1			2			11		4	8					3	10				
28		26	Chesterfield Town	0-2				8		7		1	4		2		11	10					5			3	9				
29		31	Newton Heath	0-5		3000		4	6	7		1		11	2		8	10								3	9				
30	Apr	7	SHEFFIELD WEDNESDAY	0-1		1000		8	6		9	1			2	7		11					5			3	10				4
31		16	LINCOLN CITY	0-2		1500	4			7	9	1		11				10					5	8		3			6		2
32		17	Loughborough	1-1	Durrant	300		4	6	7		1		5	9		8	11								3	10				2
33		21	SMALL HEATH	1-2	Burbage	1000		8	6	7	9	1			2			11					5			3	10				4
34		28	New Brighton Tower	1-5	McInnes			4	6	7		1		11			8	10								3	9				2
			Apps				6	31	13	26	3	34	2	12	30	9	9	34	15	1	2	1	13	4	3	31	33	13	10	15	24
			Goals					9	1	3	1			2	2	3	1	4	5				1			1	3	1			1

Two own goals

F.A. Cup

#		Date	Opponent	Score	Scorers	Att	Barnes WT	Brock JS	Brown J	Brown WR	Burbage RW	Daw EC	Dawson	Dimmock R	Dow JM	Draper F	Durrant AF	Eckford J	Fairgrieve RW	Garratt A	Hawkes F	Hawkes T	Holdstock H	Inglis JA	Marshall FR	McCurdy W	McInnes T	Morrison FR	Ralley W	Stewart WS	Williams H
Q3	Oct	28	Lowestoft Town	2-0	McInnes, Eckford	1000		8		7		1			2			11	9							3	10	4	6	5	
Q4	Nov	18	WATFORD	3-2	Brown, Brock, Fairgrieve	4500		8		7		1			2			11	9							3	10	4	6	5	
Q5	Dec	9	QUEEN'S PARK RANGERS	1-1	McInnes	3000		8		7		1			2			11	9							3	10	4	6	5	
rep	Dec	13	Queen's Park Rangers	1-4	Fairgrieve	2000				7		1			2		8	11	9							3	10	4	6	5	

		P	W	D	L	F	A	W	D	L	F	A	Pts
1	Sheffield Wed.	34	17	0	0	61	7	8	4	6	23	15	54
2	Bolton Wanderers	34	14	2	1	47	7	8	6	3	32	18	52
3	Small Heath	34	15	1	1	58	12	5	5	7	20	26	46
4	Newton Heath	34	15	1	1	44	11	5	3	9	19	16	44
5	Leicester Fosse	34	11	5	1	34	8	6	4	7	19	28	43
6	Grimsby Town	34	10	3	4	46	24	7	3	7	21	22	40
7	Chesterfield Town	34	10	4	3	35	24	6	2	9	30	36	38
8	Woolwich Arsenal	34	13	1	3	47	12	3	3	11	14	31	36
9	Lincoln City	34	11	5	1	31	9	3	3	11	15	34	36
10	New Brighton Tower	34	9	4	4	44	22	4	5	8	22	36	35
11	Burslem Port Vale	34	11	2	4	26	16	3	4	10	13	33	34
12	Walsall	34	10	5	2	36	18	2	3	12	15	37	32
13	Gainsborough Trin.	34	8	4	5	37	24	1	3	13	10	61	26
14	Middlesbrough	34	8	4	5	28	15	0	4	13	11	54	24
15	Burton Swifts	34	8	5	4	31	24	1	1	15	12	60	24
16	Barnsley	34	8	5	4	36	23	0	2	15	10	56	23
17	LUTON TOWN	34	5	3	9	25	25	0	5	12	15	50	18
18	Loughborough	34	1	6	10	12	26	0	0	17	6	74	8

Line ups taken from Luton Town team books.
Newspaper reports in the Luton Reporter and Luton News have differences as follows:

Match 12: Garratt at 6, not Barnes
Match 15: Barnes at 5, not J Brown
Match 16: Holdstock at 6, not Ralley
*   Inglis at 8, not Fairgrieve*
Match 17: Garratt at 6, not Holdstock
Match 24: Ellingham at 4, not Barnes

1920/21 — 9th in Division 3 South

#	Date	Opponent	Score	Scorers	Att	Bailey H	Bayliss R	Bookman LO	Bradley JL	Butcher GH	Cockerill HL	Higginbotham H	Hill FWP	Hoar S	Hull F	Lamb JW	Lennon GF	Mathieson A	McKechnie J	Molyneux W	Parker TB	Pett EF	Roe A	Sample J	Shankland J	Sidney H	Simms E	Tirrell A	Walsh W	Watson J
1	Aug 28	Swindon Town	1-9	Simms	10000			11	8							5	2	10			6	7	4	3			9			1
2	30	PORTSMOUTH	2-2	Hoar (p), Simms				11				8		7		5	2	10		4	6						9	3		1
3	Sep 4	SWINDON TOWN	2-0	Hoar (p), Mathieson	11000	1		11		6		8		7			2	10		4	5						9	3		
4	8	Portsmouth	0-3		16000	1		11		6		8		7			2	10		4	5						9	3		
5	11	SWANSEA TOWN	3-0	Simms, Hills 2	9000	1		11				8	10	7			2	6		4	5						9	3		
6	18	Swansea Town	1-1	Hill	14000	1		11		6		8	10	7			2			4	5						9	3		
7	25	Queen's Park Rangers	1-4	Hill	20000	1		11		6		8	10	7			2			4	5						9	3		
8	Oct 2	QUEEN'S PARK RANGERS	2-1	Simms 2	10000			11				8	10	7		6	2			4	5						9	3		1
9	9	GRIMSBY TOWN	3-1	Simms 2, Bookman	10000	1		11				8		7		6	2	10		4	5						9	3		
10	16	Grimsby Town	1-0	Simms	8000	1		11	8					7		6	2	10		4							9	3	5	
11	23	BRIGHTON & HOVE ALB	3-2	Mathieson, Hayes (og), Simms	11000	1		11	8					7		6	2	10		4							9	3	5	
12	30	Brighton & Hove Albion	1-1	Mathieson	11000	1		11						7		6	2	10		4	5			8			9	3		
13	Nov 6	CRYSTAL PALACE	2-2	Simms, Mathieson	11000	1		11						7		6	2	10		4	5			8			9	3		
14	13	Crystal Palace	1-2	Simms	12000	1		11				8		7		6	2	10		4	5						9	3		
15	20	NORWICH CITY	4-0	Bookman, Simms 3	7000	1		11				8		7			2	10		4	6						9	3	5	
16	27	Norwich City	0-3		9000	1		11				8		7			2	10		4	6						9	3	5	
17	Dec 4	BRENTFORD	2-0	Simms, Mathieson	6000	1		11		6		8		7			2	10		4	5						9	3		
18	11	Brentford	0-1		6000	1		11	8	6		5		7			2	10		4							9	3		
19	25	SOUTHAMPTON	1-1	Simms	14000	1		11				8		7		6	2	10		4	5						9	3		
20	27	Southampton	1-1	Mathieson	19793	1		11				8		7		6		10		4	5			2			9	3		
21	28	GILLINGHAM	5-0	Mathieson 2, Higginbotham 2, Hoar	11000	1		11				8		7		6		10		4	5			2			9	3		
22	Jan 1	BRISTOL ROVERS	1-2	Mathieson	9000	1		11		6		8		7				10		4	5			2			9	3		
23	15	Northampton Town	0-1		7000	1		11				8		7		6	2	10			5		4				9	3		
24	22	NORTHAMPTON T	3-1	Bookman, Bradley, Simms	12000	1		11	8			10		7		6	2				5		4				9	3		
25	Feb 5	Reading	1-0	Butcher	6000	1		11		6		8		7			2	10		4	5						9	3		
26	9	READING	6-0	Simms 4, Hoar, Higginbotham		1		11				8		7		6	2	10		4	5						9	3		
27	12	Southend United	1-1	Simms	7000	1		11				8		7		6	2	10		4	5						9	3		
28	26	Merthyr Town	1-4	Simms	15000							8		7		6	2	10		4	5					11	9	3		1
29	Mar 5	MERTHYR TOWN	1-0	Simms	8000	1		11				8		7		6	2	10			5						9	3	4	
30	12	Plymouth Argyle	0-1		10000	1		11				8		7			2	10		4	6			5			9	3		
31	19	PLYMOUTH ARGYLE	1-1	Simms	9000	1		11				8		7			2	10			5			6			9	3	4	
32	25	Watford	0-1		10000	1		11						7		6	2	10		4	5				8		9	3		
33	26	EXETER CITY	3-0	Simms 2, Mathieson	8000	1		11						7		6	2	10		4	5				8		9	3		
34	28	WATFORD	1-0	Mathieson	12000	1		11				8		7		6	2	10		4	5						9	3		
35	29	Bristol Rovers	0-5		6000	1	4	11				5		7		6	2	10						3	8		9			
36	Apr 2	Exeter City	0-1		8000	1		11				8					2	10	7	4	5			3			9		6	
37	9	MILLWALL	0-0		6000	1				6	10	8		7	3		2			4	5					11	9			
38	16	Millwall	0-0		20000	1		11				8		7	3		2	10		4	6						9			
39	23	NEWPORT COUNTY	2-2	Butcher 2	5000	1		11		8				7			2	10			6		4				9	3		
40	30	Newport County	0-2		8000	1		11				8		7			2	10		4	5						9	3	6	
41	May 2	SOUTHEND UNITED	4-0	Simms 2, Hoar, Bookman		1		11				8		7				10		4	5			2			9	3	6	
42	7	Gillingham	0-0		6000	1		11				8		7			2	10		4	5						9	3	6	
					Apps	38	1	40	5	16	8	27	6	39	3	24	37	29	1	36	35	1	11	7	3	2	40	37	10	4
					Goals			4	1	3		4	4	5				10									28	1		

Played at 5 in game 38: JR Walker
Played at 5 in game 39: RM Millar

One own goal

F.A. Cup

#	Date	Opponent	Score	Scorers	Att	Bailey H	Bookman LO	Butcher GH	Higginbotham H	Hoar S	Lamb JW	Lennon GF	Mathieson A	Molyneux W	Parker TB	Simms E	Tirrell A
Q6	Dec 18	Rotherham County	3-1	Simms 3	6000	1	11		8	7	6	2	10	4	5	9	3
R1	Jan 8	BIRMINGHAM	2-1	Simms, Bookman	12700	1	11		8	7	6	2	10	4	5	9	3
R2	Jan 29	South Shields	4-0	Higginbotham, Butcher 2, Simms	21003	1	11	10	8	7	6	2		4	5	9	3
R3	Feb 19	PRESTON NORTH END	2-3	Higginbotham 2	17754	1	11	10	8	7	6	2		4	5	9	3

Final League Table — Division 3 South

		P	W	D	L	F	A	W	D	L	F	A	Pts
1	Crystal Palace	42	15	4	2	45	17	9	7	5	25	17	59
2	Southampton	42	14	5	2	46	10	5	11	5	18	18	54
3	Queen's Park Rgs.	42	14	4	3	38	11	8	5	8	23	21	53
4	Swindon Town	42	14	5	2	51	17	7	5	9	22	32	52
5	Swansea Town	42	9	10	2	32	19	9	5	7	24	26	51
6	Watford	42	14	4	3	40	15	6	4	11	19	29	48
7	Millwall	42	11	5	5	25	8	7	6	8	17	22	47
8	Merthyr Town	42	13	5	3	46	20	2	10	9	14	29	45
9	LUTON TOWN	42	14	6	1	51	15	2	6	13	10	41	44
10	Bristol Rovers	42	15	3	3	51	22	3	4	14	17	35	43
11	Plymouth Argyle	42	10	7	4	25	13	1	14	6	10	21	43
12	Portsmouth	42	10	8	3	28	14	2	7	12	18	34	39
13	Grimsby Town	42	12	5	4	32	16	3	4	14	17	43	39
14	Northampton Town	42	11	4	6	32	23	4	4	13	27	52	38
15	Newport County	42	8	5	8	20	23	6	4	11	23	41	37
16	Norwich City	42	9	10	2	31	14	1	6	14	13	39	36
17	Southend United	42	13	2	6	32	20	1	6	14	12	41	36
18	Brighton & Hove A.	42	11	6	4	28	20	3	2	16	14	41	36
19	Exeter City	42	9	7	5	27	15	1	8	12	12	39	35
20	Reading	42	8	4	9	26	22	4	3	14	16	37	31
21	Brentford	42	7	9	5	27	23	2	3	16	15	44	30
22	Gillingham	42	6	9	6	19	24	2	3	16	15	50	28

1921/22 — 4th in Division 3 South

#	Date	Opponent	Score	Scorers	Att	Bailey H	Bassett EJ	Bookman LO	Butcher G	Foster JH	Graham RC	Higginbotham H	Hoar S	Lennon GF	Mathieson A	Millar RM	Molyneux W	Parker TB	Reid S	Roe A	Simms E	Stephenson J	Tirrell A	Walker JR	Walsh W
1	Aug 27	Norwich City	1-0	Mathieson	12000	1		11	8				7	2	10		4	5			9		3		6
2	29	SOUTHAMPTON	0-0		10000	1		11	8				7	2	10		4				9		3	5	6
3	Sep 3	NORWICH CITY	2-1	Simms, Hoar	11000	1		11	8				7	2	10		4				9		3	5	6
4	5	Southampton	1-2	Simms	11000	1		11					7	2	10	6	4			8	9		3	5	
5	10	NEWPORT COUNTY	4-0	Mathieson 2, Higginbotham, Simms	9000	1		11				8	7	2	10		4			6	9		3	5	
6	14	EXETER CITY	4-0	Simms 3, Hoar	8000	1		11		5	2	8	7		10		4			6	9		3		
7	17	Newport County	2-2	Simms 2	7000	1		11				8	7	2	10		4			6	9		3	5	
8	24	PLYMOUTH ARGYLE	1-0	Higginbotham	10000	1		11				8	7	2	10		4			6	9		3	5	
9	Oct 1	Plymouth Argyle	0-2		19000	1		11	8				7	2	10		6			4	9		3	5	
10	8	MERTHYR TOWN	3-0	Mathieson, Simms, Higginbotham	8000	1		11				8	7	2	10		4			6	9		3	5	
11	15	Merthyr Town	0-2		12000	1		11			3	8	7	2	10		4			6	9			5	
12	22	PORTSMOUTH	1-0	Walsh	9000	1	7		8	4			10	11	2						5		3	6	9
13	29	Portsmouth	1-1	Hoar	16004	1	7	11	8	6			7	2	10					4	9		3	5	
14	Nov 5	SOUTHEND UNITED	3-0	Foster, Tirrell, Simms	6000	1	7		8	4				11	2	10				6	9		3	5	
15	12	Southend United	1-0	Hoar	6000	1	7		8	4			10	11	2					6	9		3	5	
16	19	SWANSEA TOWN	3-0	Hoar 2, Butcher	10000	1	7	11	8				10	9	2		4			6			3	5	
17	26	Swansea Town	1-1	Bassett	15000	1	7		8				10	11	2	9	4			6			3	5	
18	Dec 10	Exeter City	1-0	Butcher	5000	1	7		8	4			11	2						6	9		3	5	
19	17	MILLWALL	1-0	Tirrell	10000	1	7	11	8	4			10	2						6	9		3	5	
20	24	Millwall	1-1	Butcher	11000	1	7	11	10	4			8	2						6	9		3	5	
21	26	Swindon Town	1-1	Walsh	12000	1	7	11	10	5			8	2			4			6			3		9
22	27	SWINDON TOWN	2-1	Higginbotham, Butcher	14000	1	7	11	10			8		2	9		4			6			3		5
23	31	GILLINGHAM	7-0	Simms 3, Bassett, Butcher 2, Higginbotham	8000	1	7	11	10	4		8					6				9	2	3	5	
24	Jan 14	Gillingham	1-0	Simms	7000	1	7	11				8		2	10		4			6	9		3	5	
25	21	Reading	1-2	Simms	5000	1		11	8					2	10		4			6	9		3	5	
26	Feb 4	Bristol Rovers	0-2		8000	1		11	10	4		8	7	2			6			5	9		3	5	
27	11	BRISTOL ROVERS	1-2	Simms	9000	1		11		4		8	7	2	10	6				5	9		3		
28	18	Brentford	2-0	Bassett, Simms	10000	1	7	11	10	4		8		2						6	9		3	5	
29	25	BRENTFORD	3-0	Higginbotham, Bethune (og), Simms	5000	1	7	11	10	4		8		2						6	9		3	5	
30	Mar 6	READING	0-1		5000	1		11	10	4		8	7							6	9	2	3	5	
31	11	ABERDARE ATHLETIC	1-2	Mathieson	8000	1		11	10	4		8	7	2	9					6			3	5	
32	18	Brighton & Hove Albion	1-1	Bassett	8000	1	7		10			8		11	2		6			9		4	3	5	
33	25	BRIGHTON & HOVE ALB	2-0	Butcher, Higginbotham	8000	1	7		10			8		11	2		6			9		4	3	5	
34	Apr 1	WATFORD	1-1	Reid	7000	1	7		10			8		11	2		6		9				3	4	5
35	8	Watford	1-4	Reid	7000	1	7	11		4			8		2	10			9	6			3	5	
36	14	Queen's Park Rangers	0-1		11000	1		11	10				7	2	9		4			8	6		3	5	
37	15	CHARLTON ATHLETIC	2-0	Mathieson, Butcher	7000	1		11	10	5			7	2	9		4			8	6		3		
38	17	QUEEN'S PARK RANGERS	3-1	Higginbotham 3	16000	1		11		5		8	7	2	10		4			9	6		3		
39	22	Charlton Athletic	1-0	Higginbotham	3000	1		11	10	4		8	7	2						9	6		3	5	
40	29	Northampton Town	0-2		7000	1		11		4		8	7	2	10					9	6		3	5	
41	May 1	Aberdare Athletic	0-2		10000	1	7		10	4		8		11	2					9	6	3			5
42	6	NORTHAMPTON T	3-0	Walker 2, Higginbotham		1	7		10	5		8		11	2		6				4		3	9	
		Apps				42	21	32	30	23	2	30	33	39	25	8	20	1	10	35	25	6	39	34	7
		Goals					3		9	1		12	5		6				2		18		2	2	2

Two own goals

F.A. Cup

#	Date	Opponent	Score	Scorers	Att	Bailey H	Bassett EJ	Bookman LO	Butcher G	Foster JH	Graham RC	Higginbotham H	Hoar S	Lennon GF	Mathieson A	Millar RM	Molyneux W	Parker TB	Reid S	Roe A	Simms E	Stephenson J	Tirrell A	Walker JR	Walsh W
R1	Jan 7	Portsmouth	1-1	Bassett	22437	1	7	11	10	4			8	2						6	9		3	5	
rep	Jan 11	PORTSMOUTH	2-1	Higginbotham, Hoar	10600	1	7		10	4		8	11	2						6	9		3	5	
R2	Jan 28	Aston Villa	0-1		53832	1	7		10	4		8	11	2						6	9		3	5	

Final Table

		P	W	D	L	F	A	W	D	L	F	A	Pts
1	Southampton	42	14	7	0	50	8	9	8	4	18	13	61
2	Plymouth Argyle	42	17	4	0	43	4	8	7	6	20	20	61
3	Portsmouth	42	13	5	3	38	18	5	12	4	24	21	53
4	LUTON TOWN	42	16	2	3	47	9	6	6	9	17	26	52
5	Queen's Park Rgs.	42	13	7	1	36	12	5	6	10	17	32	49
6	Swindon Town	42	10	7	4	40	21	6	6	9	32	39	45
7	Watford	42	9	9	3	34	21	4	9	8	20	27	44
8	Aberdare Ath.	42	11	6	4	38	18	6	4	11	19	33	44
9	Brentford	42	15	2	4	41	17	1	9	11	11	26	43
10	Swansea Town	42	11	8	2	40	19	2	7	12	10	28	41
11	Merthyr Town	42	14	2	5	33	15	3	4	14	12	41	40
12	Millwall	42	6	13	2	22	10	4	5	12	16	32	38
13	Reading	42	10	5	6	28	15	4	5	12	12	32	38
14	Bristol Rovers	42	8	8	5	32	24	6	2	13	20	43	38
15	Norwich City	42	8	10	3	29	17	4	3	14	21	45	37
16	Charlton Athletic	42	10	6	5	28	19	3	5	13	15	37	37
17	Northampton Town	42	13	3	5	30	17	0	8	13	17	54	37
18	Gillingham	42	11	4	6	36	20	3	4	14	11	40	36
19	Brighton & Hove A.	42	9	6	6	33	19	4	3	14	12	32	35
20	Newport County	42	8	7	6	22	18	3	5	13	22	43	34
21	Exeter City	42	7	5	9	22	29	4	7	10	16	30	34
22	Southend United	42	7	5	9	23	23	1	6	14	11	51	27

1922/23   5th in Division 3 South

#		Date	Opponent	Score	Scorers	Att	Bailey H	Bird SA	Bonsall C	Brown AC	Butcher G	Clarkson W	Foster JH	Gibbon T	Graham RC	Higginbotham H	Hoar S	Hoten RV	Irvine TB	Jennings W	Lennon GF	Millar RM	Molyneux W	Mosley HT	Reader R	Reid S	Roe A	Stephenson J	Thompson R	Tirrell A	Walker JR
1	Aug	26	CHARLTON ATHLETIC	2-2	Higginbotham, Hoar	12000	1			9	10					8	11			4	2				7		6			3	5
2		28	Brentford	2-3	Thompson 2	10000	1				10	11				8	7			4	2						6		9	3	5
3	Sep	2	Charlton Athletic	1-2	Hoar	8000								1		8	7			5	2			11		10	6		9	3	4
4		4	BRENTFORD	4-0	Higginbotham, Hoar 2, Thompson	11000								1		8	7			4	2	6		11		10			9	3	5
5		9	BRIGHTON & HOVE ALB	1-1	Reid	9000								1		8	7			4	2			11		10	6		9	3	5
6		16	Brighton & Hove Albion	1-0	Butcher	8000					10	11	4	1		8	7				2					9	6			3	5
7		23	SWINDON TOWN	3-2	Reid 2, Foster	5000					10	11	4	1		8					2				7	9	6			3	5
8		30	Swindon Town	1-1	Higginbotham	7000					10	11	4	1		8	7				2					9	6			3	5
9	Oct	7	ABERDARE ATHLETIC	4-1	Higginbotham, Thompson 2, Reid	9000						11	4	1		8	7				2					10	6		9	3	5
10		14	Aberdare Athletic	1-2	Reid	7000						11	4	1		8	7				2					10	6		9	3	5
11		21	PLYMOUTH ARGYLE	2-1	Thompson, Higginbotham	11000						11	4	1		8	7				2					10	6		9	3	5
12		28	Plymouth Argyle	0-4		10000						11	4	1		8	7				2	6				10			9	3	5
13	Nov	4	Newport County	3-0	Higginbotham 2, Butcher	7000					10	11	4	1		8	7				2					9	6			3	5
14		11	NEWPORT COUNTY	1-0	Tirrell	8000					10	11	4	1		8	7				2					9	6			3	5
15		18	Watford	1-2	Clarkson	10000					10	11	4	1		8	7				2					9	6			3	5
16		25	WATFORD	0-1		11000					10	11	4	1		8					2				7	9	6			3	5
17	Dec	2	BRISTOL CITY	1-1	Higginbotham	12000					10	11		1		8				4	2				7	9	6			3	5
18		9	Bristol City	0-1		15000					8			1				10	11		2		4		7	9	6			3	5
19		16	Portsmouth	2-1	Walker, Thompson	10185		1			8							10	11		2		4		7		6		9	3	5
20		23	PORTSMOUTH	0-2		10000					8			1				10	11		2		4		7	9	6			3	5
21		25	Queen's Park Rangers	0-4		16000					8			1				10	11		2		4		7	9	6			3	5
22		26	QUEEN'S PARK RANGERS	1-0	Higginbotham	11000						11		1		8	7	10			2		4			9	6			3	5
23		30	MILLWALL	2-2	Molyneux, Reid	10000					8	11		1			7	10			2		4			9	6			3	5
24	Jan	6	Millwall	0-0		20000					8	11		1	3		7	10		5	2		4			9	6				
25		20	SWANSEA TOWN	6-1	Reid 3, Higginbotham, Hoar, Clarkson	7000					10	11		1		8	7			5	2		4			9	6			3	
26		27	Swansea Town	0-1		20000					8	11		1			7	10		5	2		4			9	6			3	
27	Feb	3	BRISTOL ROVERS	1-0	Reid	7000					10	11		1		8	7			5	2		4			9	6			3	
28		10	Bristol Rovers	1-1	Reid	9000					10	11		1		8	7			5	2		4			9	6			3	
29		17	READING	1-2	Butcher	6000					8	11		1			7	10		5	2		4				6			3	9
30		24	Reading	0-3		7000					8	11		1			7	10			2		4			9	6			3	5
31	Mar	3	SOUTHEND UNITED	2-0	Reid, Hoten	7000					8	11		1			7	10		5	2		4			9	6			3	
32		10	Southend United	3-1	Hoten, Reid 2	7296					8	11		1			7	10		5	2		4			9	6			3	
33		17	Merthyr Town	1-0	Clarkson	6000					8	11		1			7	10					4			9	6	2		3	5
34		24	MERTHYR TOWN	2-1	Hoten, Reid	8000					8	11		1			7	10					4			9	6	2		3	5
35		30	Gillingham	0-1		8000					8	11		1				10		5			4			9	6	2		3	
36		31	Exeter City	2-1	Hoar, Tirrell	7000					8	11		1			7	10		5	2		4			9	6			3	
37	Apr	2	GILLINGHAM	2-0	Reid, Hoten	5000					8	11		1			7	10		5	2		4			9	6			3	
38		7	EXETER CITY	6-0	Roe, Hoten 3, Butcher 2	6000					8	11		1			7	10		5	2		4			9	6			3	
39		14	Northampton Town	0-2		10000					8	11		1			7	10		5	2		4				6			3	9
40		21	NORTHAMPTON T	2-1	Reid 2	8000						11		1			7	10		5	2		4			9	6		8	3	
41		28	Norwich City	2-1	Jennings, Butcher	6000					8	11		1			7	10		5	2		4			9	6			3	
42	May	5	NORWICH CITY	4-0	Butcher, Bonsall, Hoten, Hoar	7000			11		8			1			7	10			2		4			9	6			3	5

Played at 8 in game 5: T Cottingham
Played at 7 in game 35: WJ Henderson

	Bailey H	Bird SA	Bonsall C	Brown AC	Butcher G	Clarkson W	Foster JH	Gibbon T	Graham RC	Higginbotham H	Hoar S	Hoten RV	Irvine TB	Jennings W	Lennon GF	Millar RM	Molyneux W	Mosley HT	Reader R	Reid S	Roe A	Stephenson J	Thompson R	Tirrell A	Walker JR
Apps	2	1	1	1	33	32	14	39	9	23	36	12	8	30	31	2	23	3	7	33	30	4	17	40	29
Goals			1		7	3	1			10	7	8		1			1			18	1		7	2	1

F.A. Cup

R		Date	Opponent	Score	Scorers	Att	Butcher G	Clarkson W	Gibbon T	Higginbotham H	Hoar S	Jennings W	Lennon GF	Molyneux W	Roe A	Tirrell A	Walker JR
R1	Jan	13	Bury	1-2	Tirrell (p)	16327	10	11	1	8	7	5	2	4	6	3	9

			P	W	D	L	F	A	W	D	L	F	A	Pts
1	Bristol City		42	16	4	1	43	13	8	7	6	23	27	59
2	Plymouth Argyle		42	18	3	0	47	6	5	4	12	14	23	53
3	Swansea Town		42	13	6	2	46	14	9	3	9	32	31	53
4	Brighton & Hove A.		42	15	3	3	39	13	5	8	8	13	21	51
5	LUTON TOWN		42	14	4	3	47	18	7	3	11	21	31	49
6	Millwall		42	9	10	2	27	13	5	8	8	18	27	46
7	Portsmouth		42	10	5	6	34	20	9	3	9	24	32	46
8	Northampton Town		42	13	6	2	40	17	4	6	12	14	27	45
9	Swindon Town		42	14	4	3	41	17	3	7	11	21	39	45
10	Watford		42	10	6	5	35	23	7	4	10	22	31	44
11	Queen's Park Rgs.		42	10	4	7	34	24	6	6	9	20	25	42
12	Charlton Athletic		42	11	6	4	33	14	3	8	10	22	37	42
13	Bristol Rovers		42	7	9	5	25	19	6	7	8	10	17	42
14	Brentford		42	9	4	8	27	23	4	8	9	14	28	38
15	Southend United		42	10	6	5	35	18	2	7	12	14	36	37
16	Gillingham		42	13	4	4	38	18	2	3	16	13	41	37
17	Merthyr Town		42	10	4	7	27	17	1	10	10	12	31	36
18	Norwich City		42	8	7	6	29	26	5	3	13	22	45	36
19	Reading		42	9	8	4	24	15	1	6	14	12	40	34
20	Exeter City		42	10	4	7	27	18	3	3	15	20	66	33
21	Aberdare Ath.		42	6	8	7	25	23	3	3	15	17	47	29
22	Newport County		42	8	6	7	28	21	0	5	16	12	49	27

1923/24　　7th in Division 3 South

#	Date	Opponent	Score	Scorers	Att	Anderson R	Bonsall C	Butcher GH	Clarke PR	Danskin C	Foster JH	Gibbon T	Graham RC	Green J	Henderson WJ	Hoar S	Hoten RV	Jennings W	Kerr A	Millar RM	Molyneux W	Orr J	Pearson J	Prentice H	Reid S	Roe A	Shepherd JMV	Till J	Tirrell A	Walker JR
1	Aug 25	Swansea Town	0-1		18000					11	4	1	2	8		7	10	5	9	6									3	
2	27	NORTHAMPTON T	1-1	Green						11	4	1	2	8		7	10	5	9	6			3							
3	Sep 1	SWANSEA TOWN	1-2	Kerr	9000		11	8			4	1				7	10	5	9	6									2	3
4	3	Northampton Town	0-2		9968			8				1	9		7	11	10	5			4					6			2	3
5	8	Brentford	1-2	Reid	8000		7	8			4	1				11	10	5							9	6			2	3
6	15	BRENTFORD	2-1	Kerr 2	8000	4	11									7	10	5	9						8		1	2	3	6
7	22	Portsmouth	0-3		11375	4	11									7	10	5	9						8		1	2	3	6
8	29	PORTSMOUTH	4-1	Kerr 3, Hoten	9000	2		8		11		1				7	10	5	9	6								3		4
9	Oct 6	Exeter City	1-2	Kerr	6000	2		8		11		1				7	10	5	9	6								3		4
10	13	EXETER CITY	1-0	Hoten	8000	2		8		11		1				7	10	5	9	6								3		4
11	20	Aberdare Athletic	1-0	Hoten	6000	2				11		1		8		7	10	5	9	6								3		4
12	27	ABERDARE ATHLETIC	1-0	Hoten	8000	2				11		1		8		7	10	5	9	6								3		4
13	Nov 3	WATFORD	0-0		9000	2				11		1		8		7	10	5	9	6								3		4
14	10	Watford	0-0			2				11		1		8		7	10	5	9	6								3		4
15	17	Millwall	1-0	Kerr	15000	2				11		1		8		7	10	5	9	6								3		4
16	24	MILLWALL	2-0	Hoar, Kerr	7000	2				11		1	3	8		7	10	5	9	6										4
17	Dec 1	BOURNEMOUTH	6-2	Hoar 2, Kerr 4	7000	2				11		1	3	8		7	10	5	9	6										4
18	8	Bournemouth	3-2	Kerr 2, Green		2				11		1		8		7	10	5	9	6								3		4
19	15	READING	2-0	Hoten, Green	8000	2				11		1		8		7	10	5	9	6								3		4
20	22	Reading	1-0	Hoar		2				11				8		7	10	5	9	6		1						3		4
21	25	BRIGHTON & HOVE ALB	0-0		13000	2				11				8		7	10	5	9	6		1						3		4
22	26	Brighton & Hove Albion	0-4		15457	2							5	8			11		9	6		1		7	10			3		4
23	29	SOUTHEND UNITED	4-4	Millar, Kerr, Hoar 2		2			10				5	8		7	11		9	6		1						3		4
24	Jan 5	Southend United	1-1	Foster	7000	2	11				4			8		7	10		9	6		1						3		5
25	19	Gillingham	0-0		5000	2	11							8		7	10	4	9	6		1						3		5
26	26	GILLINGHAM	1-1	Bonsall		2	11							8		7	10	5	9	6		1						3		4
27	Feb 2	Queen's Park Rangers	2-0	Green 2	9000	4	11					1	2	8		7	10		9							6		3		5
28	9	QUEEN'S PARK RANGERS	2-0	Kerr 2	6000	4	11					1	2	8		7	10		9							6		3		5
29	16	Plymouth Argyle	0-0			4					11	1	2	8		7	10		9							6		3		5
30	23	PLYMOUTH ARGYLE	0-2			4					11	1	2	8		7	10		9							6		3		5
31	Mar 1	Newport County	0-1		9000	2	11	8			4	1				7	10		9							6		3		5
32	8	NEWPORT COUNTY		Walker, Hoar	5000	2	11	8			4	1				7	10		9							6		3		5
33	15	MERTHYR TOWN	1-1	Butcher		2	11	8			4	1				7	10		9							6		3		5
34	22	Merthyr Town	0-0		11000	2		8				1		10		11	7	5	9							6		3		4
35	29	CHARLTON ATHLETIC	0-1			2		8				1		10		11	7	5	9							6		3		4
36	Apr 5	Charlton Athletic	1-1	Kerr		2		8				1				7	11	5	9	6					10			3		4
37	12	NORWICH CITY	2-1	Reid, Kerr	4000	2		8				1	3			7	11	5	9	6					10					4
38	18	BRISTOL ROVERS	0-0		11000	2		8				1				7	11	5	9	6					10			3		4
39	19	Norwich City	0-2		7000	2		8				1	3			7	11	5	9	6					10					4
40	21	Bristol Rovers	1-1	Kerr	6000	2		8					3			7	11	5	9	6		1			10					4
41	26	SWINDON TOWN	3-2	Butcher, Reid 2		2		8					3			7	11	5	9	6		1			10					4
42	May 3	Swindon Town	2-3	Reid 2		2		8					6			7	10	5	9			1			11			3		4
		Apps				35	7	30	1	11	10	30	16	26	1	38	41	32	39	29	1	9	1	1	13	11	3	34	6	37
		Goals					1	3			1			5		7	5		20	1					6					1

F.A. Cup

	Date	Opponent	Score	Scorers	Att	Anderson R	Bonsall C	Butcher GH	Clarke PR	Danskin C	Foster JH	Gibbon T	Graham RC	Green J	Henderson WJ	Hoar S	Hoten RV	Jennings W	Kerr A	Millar RM	Molyneux W	Orr J	Pearson J	Prentice H	Reid S	Roe A	Shepherd JMV	Till J	Tirrell A	Walker JR
R1	Jan 12	Arsenal	1-4	Green	37500	2		10						8		7	11	5	9	6		1						3		4

		P	W	D	L	F	A	W	D	L	F	A	Pts
1	Portsmouth	42	15	3	3	57	11	9	8	4	30	19	59
2	Plymouth Argyle	42	13	6	2	46	15	10	3	8	24	19	55
3	Millwall	42	17	3	1	45	11	5	7	9	19	27	54
4	Swansea Town	42	18	2	1	39	10	4	6	11	21	38	52
5	Brighton & Hove A.	42	16	4	1	56	12	5	5	11	12	25	51
6	Swindon Town	42	14	5	2	38	11	3	8	10	20	33	47
7	LUTON TOWN	42	11	7	3	35	19	5	7	9	15	25	46
8	Northampton Town	42	14	3	4	40	15	3	8	10	24	32	45
9	Bristol Rovers	42	11	7	3	34	15	4	6	11	18	31	43
10	Newport County	42	15	4	2	39	15	2	5	14	17	49	43
11	Norwich City	42	13	5	3	45	18	3	3	15	15	41	40
12	Aberdare Ath.	42	9	9	3	35	18	3	5	13	10	40	38
13	Merthyr Town	42	11	8	2	33	19	0	8	13	12	46	38
14	Charlton Athletic	42	8	7	6	26	20	3	8	10	12	25	37
15	Gillingham	42	11	6	4	27	15	1	7	13	16	43	37
16	Exeter City	42	14	4	3	33	17	1	4	16	4	35	37
17	Brentford	42	9	8	4	33	21	5	0	16	21	50	36
18	Reading	42	12	2	7	35	20	1	7	13	16	37	35
19	Southend United	42	11	7	3	35	19	1	3	17	18	65	34
20	Watford	42	8	8	5	35	18	1	7	13	10	36	33
21	Bournemouth	42	6	8	7	19	19	5	3	13	21	46	33
22	Queen's Park Rgs.	42	9	6	6	28	26	2	3	16	9	51	31

1924/25 16th in Division 3 South

#	Date	Opponent	Res	Scorers	Att	Anderson R	Brookes GH	Brown TH	Butcher GH	Cockle ES	Dennis GT	Graham RC	Hoar S	Hoten RV	Jennings W	Johnson J	Keen WJ	Kerr A	Mackey JA	Millar RM	Mills J	Neal S	Reid S	Richards AC	Roe A	Shankly J	Thirlaway WJ	Till J	Tricker RW	Walker JR
1	Aug 30	GILLINGHAM	0-0		8000	2	1	11					7	10	5	3					6		9			8				4
2	Sep 1	MILLWALL	1-1	Hoar	8000	2	1			8	11		7	10	5	3	9				6									4
3	6	Bournemouth	1-2	Cockle		2	1			8	11		7	10	5		9				6							3		4
4	8	EXETER CITY	1-1	Shankly	6000		1			8	11	2	7		5						6					10		3		4
5	13	BRIGHTON & HOVE ALB	3-1	Kerr 2, Mills	7000		1			8	11		7		5	2		9			6					10		3		4
6	15	Northampton Town	0-1		5340		1			8	11	3	7		5	2		9			6					10				4
7	20	Plymouth Argyle	0-4				1			8	11	3			5	2		9	7		6					10				4
8	22	NORTHAMPTON T	2-0	Dennis, Shankly	5000		1	11			10	3				2		9	7	6	4					8				5
9	24	BRISTOL CITY	3-0	Hoar, Dennis, Shankly	11000		1	11			10	3	7			2		9		6	4					8				5
10	27	Swindon Town	1-4	Shankly			1	11			10	3	7			2		9		6	4					8				5
11	Oct 4	Reading	0-3				1	11			10	3	7			2		9		6	4					8				5
12	11	ABERDARE ATHLETIC	0-0				1				9	11	3	7	10	5		2			4			6	8					
13	18	Norwich City	1-1	Dennis	9000	2	1		8		11		3	7	10	5		9			4			6						
14	25	Charlton Athletic	0-2			2	1	7	8		11		3		10	5		9			4			6						
15	Nov 1	QUEEN'S PARK RANGERS	3-0	Mills, Butcher, Dennis	4000	2	1	11	8		10		3	7	5					6	4		9							
16	8	Merthyr Town	0-0			2	1	11	8		10		3	7	5					6	4		9							
17	22	Swansea Town	1-4	Reid	15000	2	1	11	8		10		3	7	5					6	4		9							
18	29	Millwall	2-2	Butcher, Kerr	16000	2	1	7	8		11		3		5			9			4		10							
19	Dec 6	Bristol Rovers	1-1	Kerr	8000	2	1	7	8		11		3		5			9			4		10	6						
20	13	NEWPORT COUNTY	2-2	Shankly, Reid		2	1				11		3		5			9			4		10	7	6	8				
21	20	Southend United	1-2	Reid		2	1		8		11		3		5			9			4		10	7						
22	25	Watford	1-1	Reid	7000	2	1		8		11		3		5				7	6	4		10						9	
23	26	WATFORD	0-3		14000	2	1		8		11		3		5			9	7	6	4		10							5
24	27	Gillingham	1-4	Reid	1000	2	1		8		11				5			9	7	6	4		10					3		5
25	Jan 3	BOURNEMOUTH	0-2		5000		1		8		11						2		7		4	5	10	6				3	9	
26	17	Brighton & Hove Albion	1-2	Mackey	7246	2	1	11			10				5				7		4	6	9			8		3		
27	24	PLYMOUTH ARGYLE	1-1	Shankly		2	1	11			10				5			9	7	6	4					8		3		
28	Feb 7	SWINDON TOWN	2-2	Dennis 2		2	1				11				5			9	7	6	4		10			8		3		
29	14	Aberdare Athletic	1-1	Dennis		2	1	11			10				5			9	7	6	4					8		3		
30	21	NORWICH CITY	0-0		5000	2	1	11			10				5			9		6	4					8	7	3		
31	28	CHARLTON ATHLETIC	1-0	Reid		2	1				11				5			9		6	4		10			8	7	3		
32	Mar 4	Bristol City	0-2		6000	2	1				11				5					6			10			8	7	3	9	4
33	7	Queen's Park Rangers	1-2	Reid	7000	2	1				11				5			9		6			10			8	7	3		4
34	14	MERTHYR TOWN	6-0	Reid, Shankly 2, Jennings, Dennis, Kerr		2	1				11				5			9		6			10			8	7	3		4
35	21	READING	1-0	Reid		2	1				11				5			9		6			10			8	7	3		4
36	28	SWANSEA TOWN	0-0			2	1				11				5			9		6			10			8	7	3		4
37	Apr 4	Exeter City	1-0	Dennis	5000	2	1				11				5			9		6			10			8	7	3		4
38	10	Brentford	0-3		8000	2	1				11				5			9		6			10			8	7	3		4
39	11	BRISTOL ROVERS	1-1	Dennis	6000	2	1				11				5			9		6			10			8	7	3		4
40	13	BRENTFORD	3-1	Dennis 2, Shankly	6000	2	1				11				5			9		6			10			8	7	3		4
41	18	Newport County	1-1	Shankly	7000		1				11	2			5			9		6			10			8	7	3		4
42	25	SOUTHEND UNITED	4-0	Reid 3, Shankly			1				11	2			5					6			10			8	7	3	9	4
		Apps				30	42	15	12	7	41	21	14	6	35	11	3	29	10	28	31	2	26	2	6	28	13	22	4	24
		Goals							2	1	12		2		1			5	1		2		12			11				

F.A. Cup

Rnd	Date	Opponent	Res		Att	Anderson R	Brookes GH	Brown TH	Butcher GH	Cockle ES	Dennis GT	Graham RC	Hoar S	Hoten RV	Jennings W	Johnson J	Keen WJ	Kerr A	Mackey JA	Millar RM	Mills J	Neal S	Reid S	Richards AC	Roe A	Shankly J	Thirlaway WJ	Till J	Tricker RW	Walker JR
R1	Jan 10	West Bromwich Albion	0-4		30287	2	1		10		11		3						7		4	5		6		8			9	

		P	W	D	L	F	A	W	D	L	F	A	Pts
1	Swansea Town	42	17	4	0	51	12	6	7	8	17	23	57
2	Plymouth Argyle	42	17	3	1	55	12	6	7	8	22	26	56
3	Bristol City	42	14	5	2	40	10	8	4	9	20	31	53
4	Swindon Town	42	17	2	2	51	13	3	9	9	15	25	51
5	Millwall	42	12	5	4	35	14	6	8	7	23	24	49
6	Newport County	42	13	6	2	35	12	7	3	11	27	30	49
7	Exeter City	42	13	4	4	37	19	6	5	10	22	29	47
8	Brighton & Hove A.	42	14	3	4	43	17	5	5	11	16	28	46
9	Northampton Town	42	12	3	6	34	18	8	3	10	17	26	46
10	Southend United	42	14	1	6	34	18	5	4	12	17	43	43
11	Watford	42	12	3	6	22	20	5	6	10	16	27	43
12	Norwich City	42	10	8	3	39	18	4	5	12	14	33	41
13	Gillingham	42	11	8	2	25	11	2	6	13	10	33	40
14	Reading	42	9	6	6	28	15	5	4	12	9	23	38
15	Charlton Athletic	42	12	6	3	31	13	1	6	14	15	35	38
16	LUTON TOWN	42	9	10	2	34	15	1	7	13	15	42	37
17	Bristol Rovers	42	10	5	6	26	13	2	8	11	16	36	37
18	Aberdare Ath.	42	13	4	4	40	21	1	5	15	14	46	37
18	Queen's Park Rgs.	42	10	6	5	28	19	4	2	15	14	44	36
20	Bournemouth	42	8	6	7	20	17	5	2	14	20	41	34
21	Brentford	42	8	7	6	28	26	1	0	20	10	65	25
22	Merthyr Town	42	8	3	10	24	27	0	2	19	11	60	21

1925/26   7th in Division 3 South

#	Date	Opponent	Score	Scorers	Att	Agnew W	Anderson R	Bedford SG	Dennis GT	Graham RC	Jennings W	Littlewood SC	Love T	Millar RM	Miller J	Mingay HJ	Moffat H	Neal S	Purdy A	Reid S	Rennie A	Richards D	Robinson F	Shankly J	Thompson JW	Thomson NS	Till J	Walker JR
1	Aug 29	Merthyr Town	1-2	Reid	8057	2			11		5			6	7	1				10					9	8	3	4
2	31	BOURNEMOUTH	4-1	Thompson 2, Shankly, Reid	7880	2			11	3	5			6	7	1				10				8	9			4
3	Sep 5	NEWPORT COUNTY	4-2	Shankly 2, Dennis (p), Thompson	6816	2			11	3	5			6		1	7			10				8	9			4
4	9	Bournemouth	2-2	Thompson, Dennis	5612	2			11	3	5			6		1	7			10				8	9			4
5	12	Watford	0-2		13035	2			11	3	5			6		1	7			10				8	9			4
6	14	READING	0-1		7289	2			11	3	5					1	7		4	9				8	10			6
7	19	Queen's Park Rangers	0-1		5198				11	2	5			6		1	7							8	9	10	3	4
8	26	BRISTOL ROVERS	1-0	Reid	7100					3	5			6		1	7		4	9				8	11	10	2	
9	30	Reading	0-3		5621		4			3	5			6		1	7			9				8	11	10	2	
10	Oct 3	Swindon Town	0-2		7482				11	3	5			6		1	7			10	4			8	9		2	
11	10	EXETER CITY	1-1	Shankly	7046				11	3	5			6	7	1				10	4			8	9		2	
12	17	BRIGHTON & HOVE ALB	3-3	Littlewood, Millar, Shankly	7522	2				6		9		10	7				1		5			8	11		3	4
13	24	Aberdare Athletic	5-2	Graham 2, Till, Thompson, Shankly	4266	2			10	6	5	9			7				1		4			8	11		3	
14	31	CRYSTAL PALACE	3-2	Shankly 3	7980				10	3	5	9		6	7				1		4			8	11		2	
15	Nov 7	Brentford	0-1		7533				6	2	5	9			7				1		4			8	11	10	3	
16	14	NORWICH CITY	3-2	Thompson, Littlewood, Miller	6380				10	3	5	9		6	7				1		4			8	11		2	
17	21	Southend United	0-2		6706				10	3	5	9		6				7	1		4			8	11		2	
18	Dec 5	Bristol City	1-5	Miller	10208				11	2	5		9	6	7				1		4			8	10		3	
19	19	Millwall	0-7		10481		4			3			9	6			7		1		5			10	11	8	2	
20	25	Gillingham	1-2	Thompson	6350	9			10	2				6			7	5	1	8	4					11	3	
21	26	GILLINGHAM	5-3	Dennis 2, Thompson 2, Reid	9898	10			11	2				6			7	5	1	8	4				9		3	
22	28	PLYMOUTH ARGYLE	1-1	Dennis (p)	9717	10			11	2				6			7	5	1	8	4				9		3	
23	Jan 2	MERTHYR TOWN	4-0	Thompson 2, Dennis (p), Agnew	5858	10			11	2				6			7	5	1		4				9	8	3	
24	16	Newport County	1-2	Thompson	4498	10			11	2				6			7	5	1		4				9	8	3	
25	23	WATFORD	5-0	Agnew 2, Dennis, Thompson, Thomson	7233	10			11	2				6			7	5	1		4				9	8	3	
26	30	QUEEN'S PARK RANGERS	4-0	Thompson, Thomson, Moffat, Dennis	6750	10			11	2				6			7	5	1		4				9	8	3	
27	Feb 6	Bristol Rovers	2-2	Thompson 2	5896	10			11	2				6			7	5	1		4				9	8	3	
28	13	SWINDON TOWN	4-1	Thompson, Dennis (p), Agnew	8588	10			11	2				6			7	4	1			5			9	8	3	
29	20	Exeter City	2-2	Thomson, Dennis (p)	6540	10			11	2				6			7	4	1			5			9	8	3	
30	22	NORTHAMPTON T	3-2	Dennis 2 (2p), Moffat	5549	10			11	2				6			7	4	1			5			9	8	3	
31	27	Brighton & Hove Albion	0-2		7721	10			11	2				6			7	4	1			5			9	8	3	
32	Mar 6	ABERDARE ATHLETIC	2-1	Thompson, Thomson	7746	10			11	2				6			7	4	1			5			9	8	3	
33	13	Crystal Palace	0-3		12306	10			11	2				6			7	4	1			5			9	8	3	
34	20	BRENTFORD	4-2	Thompson 2, Agnew, Moffat	6072	10			11	2				6			7	4	1			5			9	8	3	
35	27	Norwich City	0-2		5763	10			11	2				6			7	4	1			5			9	8	3	
36	Apr 2	CHARLTON ATHLETIC	1-0	Miller	8509					2				6	7	1	11	4				5			9	8	3	
37	3	SOUTHEND UNITED	2-0	Robinson, Thomson	7239	10				2				6		1	7	4				5	11		9	8	3	
38	5	Charlton Athletic	1-2	Dennis (p)	4493	10			11	2				6		1	7	4				5			9	8	3	
39	10	Plymouth Argyle	3-4	Dennis, Agnew, Thomson	12641	10			11	2				6		1	7	4				5			9	8	3	
40	17	BRISTOL CITY	4-1	Thompson 2, Moffat, Agnew	7336	10			11	2				6		1	7	4				5			9	8	3	
41	24	Northampton Town	1-0	Dennis	6697	10			11	2				6		1	7	4				5			9	8	3	
42	May 1	MILLWALL	2-2	Thompson 2	9303	10			11	2				6		1	7	4				5			9	8	3	
				Apps		23	9	1	36	41	17	6	2	39	10	18	33	25	24	13	15	18	1	18	42	26	37	8
				Goals		8			16	2		2		1	3		4			4			1	9	24	5	1	

F. A. Cup

#	Date	Opponent	Score	Scorers	Att	Agnew W	Anderson R	Bedford SG	Dennis GT	Graham RC	Jennings W	Littlewood SC	Love T	Millar RM	Miller J	Mingay HJ	Moffat H	Neal S	Purdy A	Reid S	Rennie A	Richards D	Robinson F	Shankly J	Thompson JW	Thomson NS	Till J	Walker JR
R1	Nov 28	FOLKESTONE	3-0	Reid, Littlewood, Shankly	7000				11	3	6	9		4	7				1	8	5			10			2	
R2	Dec 12	Aberdare Athletic	0-1		6500	2			11	6				4			9		1	8	5			10		7	3	

League table

		P	W	D	L	F	A	W	D	L	F	A	Pts
1	Reading	42	16	5	0	49	16	7	6	8	28	36	57
2	Plymouth Argyle	42	16	2	3	71	33	8	6	7	36	34	56
3	Millwall	42	14	6	1	52	12	7	5	9	21	27	53
4	Bristol City	42	14	3	4	42	15	7	6	8	30	36	51
5	Brighton & Hove A.	42	12	4	5	47	33	7	5	9	37	40	47
6	Swindon Town	42	16	2	3	48	22	4	4	13	21	42	46
7	LUTON TOWN	42	16	4	1	60	25	2	3	16	20	50	43
8	Bournemouth	42	10	5	6	44	30	7	4	10	31	61	43
9	Aberdare Ath.	42	11	6	4	50	24	6	2	13	24	42	42
10	Gillingham	42	11	4	6	36	19	6	4	11	17	30	42
11	Southend United	42	13	2	6	50	20	6	2	13	28	53	42
12	Northampton Town	42	13	3	5	47	26	4	4	13	35	54	41
13	Crystal Palace	42	16	1	4	50	21	3	2	16	25	68	41
14	Merthyr Town	42	13	3	5	51	25	1	8	12	18	50	39
15	Watford	42	12	5	4	47	26	3	4	14	26	63	39
16	Norwich City	42	11	5	5	35	26	4	4	13	23	47	39
17	Newport County	42	11	5	5	39	27	3	5	13	25	47	38
18	Brentford	42	12	4	5	44	32	4	2	15	25	62	38
19	Bristol Rovers	42	9	4	8	44	28	6	2	13	22	41	36
20	Exeter City	42	13	2	6	54	25	2	3	16	18	45	35
21	Charlton Athletic	42	9	7	5	32	23	2	6	13	16	45	35
22	Queen's Park Rgs.	42	5	7	9	23	32	1	2	18	14	52	21

#	Date		Opponent	Score	Scorers	Att	Agnew W	Black JR	Clark J	Dennis GT	Fraser CR	Gordon J	Graham RC	Harper WG	Kingham HR	Millar RM	Mingay HJ	Moir RM	Panther FG	Pointon J	Reid S	Rennie A	Richards D	Thompson JW	Thomson NS	Till J	Woods H	Yardley J
1	Aug	28	Bristol Rovers	2-1	Thompson 2	13705	10		11				2			6	1			7	5	4		9	8	3		
2		30	BRENTFORD	2-1	Millar, Thomson	9090	10	11					2			6	1			7	5	4		9	8	3		
3	Sep	4	SWINDON TOWN	1-1	Thompson	11386	10	11					2			6	1			7	5	4		9	8	3		
4		11	Exeter City	2-1	Graham (p), Thompson	8444	10	11					2			6	1			7	5	4		9	8	3		
5		13	NORTHAMPTON T	2-0	Graham (p), Thomson	8856		11					2			6	1			7	5	4		9	8	3	10	
6		18	MERTHYR TOWN	2-1	Thompson, Woods	9920		11				5	2			6	1			7		4		9	8	3	10	
7		25	Southend United	1-2	Thompson	9211			11	7			2			6	1	5				4		9	8	3	10	
8	Oct	2	GILLINGHAM	2-1	Thompson 2	9138			11	7		5	2			6	1					4		9	8	3	10	
9		9	NORWICH CITY	2-2	Clark, Dennis	8775			11	7		5	2			6	1					4		9	8	3	10	
10		16	Newport County	2-3	Woods, Reid	6821			11	7		4	2			6	1				9	5	3		8		10	
11		23	ABERDARE ATHLETIC	3-3	Pointon 2, Dennis	7329				11		4	2			6	1			7	9	5			8	3	10	
12		30	Watford	1-2	Thomson	12199			11			4	2	1		6				7	5			9	8	3	10	
13	Nov	6	CRYSTAL PALACE	1-0	Woods	7343	10	4	11					1		6				7	5	2		9		3	8	
14		13	Coventry City	1-4	Clark	6349		4	11					1		6				7	10	5	2	9		3	8	
15		20	QUEEN'S PARK RANGERS	2-0	Reid, Woods	5075	10	4	11					1		6				7	9	5	2			3	8	
16	Dec	4	BRISTOL CITY	0-0		8601	10	4		11			2	1		6				7	9	5				3	8	
17		18	PLYMOUTH ARGYLE	3-3	Woods 2, Reid	8175		4		11			2	1		6				7	9	5			8	3	10	
18		25	MILLWALL	6-0	Black, Thomson, Reid 3, Woods	9447		4					2	1		6				7	9	5	11		8	3	10	
19		27	Millwall	0-7		20936		4					2	1		6				7	9	5	11		8	3	10	
20		28	Northampton Town	1-2	Woods	8700		4	11				2	1		6				7	5		9		8	3	10	
21	Jan	1	Brentford	2-2	Thomson, Panther	9116	10	4	7				2	1		6			9		5		11		8	3		
22		15	BRISTOL ROVERS	1-1	Panther	6723	10	4	11				2	1		6			9	7	5					3	8	
23		22	Swindon Town	0-2		7567	10	4	11		6		2	1					8	7	9	5				3		
24		26	Bournemouth	0-2		4833	10		11		6	4	2	1					9	7		5				3		8
25		29	EXETER CITY	2-2	Pointon, Graham (p)	5631	10		11		6	4	2	1					9	7	5					3		8
26	Feb	5	Merthyr Town	1-4	Reid	1530			11		6	4	2	1						7	10	5	9			3		8
27		12	SOUTHEND UNITED	0-0		4334	8		11			4	2	1						7	9	5				3		10
28		19	Gillingham	0-0		3979		4	11				3	1	2	6				7	8	5	9					10
29		26	Norwich City	2-3	Reid, Pointon	7270		4	11				2	1		6				7	8	5	9			3	10	
30	Mar	3	Charlton Athletic	2-2	Thompson, Reid	3129		4	11				2	1		6				7	8	5	9			3	10	
31		5	NEWPORT COUNTY	4-1	Reid 2, Woods, Thompson	5240		4	11				2	1		6				7	8	5	3	9			10	
32		12	Aberdare Athletic	1-0	Thompson	2653		4	11				2	1		6				7	8	5	3	9			10	
33		19	WATFORD	2-2	Black, Thompson	10561		4	11				2	1		6				7	8	5	3	9			10	
34		26	Crystal Palace	1-1	Reid	9264		4	7	11				1		6				8	5	2		9		3	10	
35	Apr	2	COVENTRY CITY	4-1	Reid, Dennis 2 (1p), Thompson	6960		4	7	11				1		6				8	5	2		9		3	10	
36		9	Queen's Park Rangers	0-1		4484		4	7	11				1		6				8	5	2		9		3	10	
37		15	Brighton & Hove Albion	1-1	Thompson	12581		4	7	11				1		6				8	5	2		9		3	10	
38		16	CHARLTON ATHLETIC	1-0	Thompson	7502		4	7	11				1		6				8	5	2		9		3	10	
39		18	BRIGHTON & HOVE ALB	4-0	Reid 3, Thompson	7353		4	11					1		6				7	8	5	2	9		3	10	
40		23	Bristol City	0-6		12826		4	11	6				1						7	9	5	2			3	10	8
41		30	BOURNEMOUTH	4-0	Rennie, Reid, Thompson, Dennis	6709		4		11				1		6				7	8	5	2	9		3	10	
42	May	7	Plymouth Argyle	0-1		8142		4	11					1		6				7	8	5	2	9		3	10	
			Apps				12	27	29	19	4	10	30	31	1	38	11	1	5	33	26	35	29	30	17	37	31	6
			Goals					2	2	5			3			1			2	4	17	1		17	5		9	

F.A. Cup

	Date		Opponent	Score	Scorers	Att	Agnew W	Black JR	Clark J	Dennis GT	Fraser CR	Gordon J	Graham RC	Harper WG	Kingham HR	Millar RM	Mingay HJ	Moir RM	Panther FG	Pointon J	Reid S	Rennie A	Richards D	Thompson JW	Thomson NS	Till J	Woods H	Yardley J
R1	Nov	27	LONDON CALEDONIANS	4-2	Reid 2, Clark, Pointon	10923	10	2	11					1		4				7	8	6	5			3	9	
R2	Dec	11	NORTHFLEET UNITED	6-2	Woods 3, Reid 2, Rennie	9641	10		11				2	1		4				7	8	6	5			3	9	
R3	Jan	8	Chelsea	0-4		41441	6						2	1		4				11	9	5		7	10	3	8	

		P	W	D	L	F	A	W	D	L	F	A	Pts
1	Bristol City	42	19	1	1	71	24	8	7	6	33	30	62
2	Plymouth Argyle	42	17	4	0	52	14	8	6	7	43	47	60
3	Millwall	42	16	2	3	55	19	7	8	6	34	32	56
4	Brighton & Hove A.	42	15	4	2	61	24	6	7	8	18	26	53
5	Swindon Town	42	16	3	2	64	31	5	6	10	36	54	51
6	Crystal Palace	42	12	6	3	57	33	6	3	12	27	48	45
7	Bournemouth	42	13	2	6	49	24	5	6	10	29	42	44
8	LUTON TOWN	42	12	9	0	48	19	3	5	13	20	47	44
9	Newport County	42	15	4	2	40	20	4	2	15	17	51	44
10	Bristol Rovers	42	12	4	5	46	28	4	5	12	32	52	41
11	Brentford	42	10	9	2	46	20	3	5	13	24	41	40
12	Exeter City	42	14	4	3	46	18	1	6	14	30	55	40
13	Charlton Athletic	42	13	5	3	44	22	3	3	15	16	39	40
14	Queen's Park Rgs.	42	9	8	4	41	27	6	1	14	24	44	39
15	Coventry City	42	11	4	6	44	33	4	3	14	27	53	37
16	Norwich City	42	10	5	6	41	25	2	6	13	18	46	35
17	Merthyr Town	42	11	5	5	42	25	2	4	15	21	55	35
18	Northampton Town	42	13	4	4	36	23	2	1	18	23	64	35
18	Southend United	42	12	3	6	44	25	2	3	16	20	52	34
20	Gillingham	42	10	5	6	36	26	1	6	15	18	46	32
21	Watford	42	9	6	6	36	27	3	2	16	21	60	32
22	Aberdare Ath.	42	8	2	11	38	48	1	5	15	24	53	25

No	Date	Opponent	Score	Scorers	Att	Abbott H	Banks JA	Black JR	Davies AS	Dennis GT	Fraser CR	Fulton JJ	Galloway SR	Gordon J	Graham RC	Harkins J	Kingham HR	Millar RM	Muir J	Nunn AS	Panther FG	Pointon J	Ramage J	Reid S	Rennie A	Reynolds JW	Richards D	Till J	Woods H	Yardley J
1	Aug 27	Southend United	0-1		11186	1		4		11			9					6				7		8	5			2	3	10
2	29	NORWICH CITY	1-3	Rennie	9157	1		4		11								6			9	7		8	5			2	3	10
3	Sep 3	BRIGHTON & HOVE ALB	2-5	Panther, Banks	9468	1	10	4	11								2	6			9	7		8	5				3	
4	5	Norwich City	0-3		13640		10		11		6	5			4		3	2	1		9	7								8
5	10	Bournemouth	2-2	Yardley, Galloway	6040		10		11		6	5	9		4		3	2	1			7								8
6	17	BRENTFORD	5-2	Yardley 3, Reid, Pointon	9182			4		10	6	5			3		2		1	11		7		9						8
7	24	Watford	0-1		12903	1		4		10	6	5			3		2			11		7		9						8
8	Oct 1	Millwall	2-3	Rennie, Harkins	7645			4			6	5			3	10	2		1	11		7			9					8
9	8	CRYSTAL PALACE	6-1	Black, Rennie 2, Harkins, Pointon, Yardley	8844			4			6	5			3	10	2		1	11		7			9					8
10	15	Exeter City	2-3	Rennie, Nunn	6827			4			6	5			3	10	2		1	11		7			9					8
11	22	NEWPORT COUNTY	1-1	Harkins	5192				11		6	5			3	10	2	4	1			7			9					8
12	29	Swindon Town	2-4	Pointon, Rennie	7580						6	5			3		2	4	1			7			9				10	8
13	Nov 5	QUEEN'S PARK RANGERS	0-1		7695		10				6	5			3		2	4	1			7			9					8
14	12	Coventry City	2-4	Reid, Yardley	10141			4		11	6				3		2		1			7		9	5				10	8
15	19	GILLINGHAM	6-1	Dennis (p), Woods, Reid, Rennie, Pointon, Yardley	4527	1		4		11	6				3		2					7		9	5				10	8
16	Dec 3	MERTHYR TOWN	5-1	Reid 4, Dennis	5040	1		4		11	6				3		2					7		9	5				10	8
17	17	BRISTOL ROVERS	2-0	Pointon, Woods	5946	1		4		11	6				3		2					7		9	5				10	8
18	24	Charlton Athletic	3-4	Yardley, Pointon, Rennie	7265	1		4		11	6				3		2					7		8	5				10	9
19	26	Northampton Town	5-6	Yardley, Reid 4	10153	1		4		11	6				3		2					7		9	5				10	8
20	31	SOUTHEND UNITED	0-0		5402	1		4		11	6				3		2					7		9	5				10	8
21	Jan 7	Brighton & Hove Albion	1-3	Pointon	5707	1	9	4		11	6				3		2					7			5				10	8
22	21	BOURNEMOUTH	3-3	Yardley, Woods, Fraser	6453	1		4		11	6						2					7		9	5		3		10	8
23	28	Brentford	2-4	Yardley 2	3291	1		4		11	6				3		2					7	5	9					10	8
24	Feb 4	WATFORD	3-2	Rennie, Yardley, Woods	8012	1		4		11	6						2					7	5		9			3	10	8
25	11	MILLWALL	1-1	Yardley	8738	1		4			6										11	7	5	9			2	3	10	8
26	18	Crystal Palace	2-3	Rennie 2	13370	1		4		11	6											7	5		9		2	3	10	8
27	25	EXETER CITY	2-1	Rennie, Nunn	8309	1		4			6									11		7	5		9		2	3	10	8
28	Mar 3	Newport County	2-7	Rennie, Woods	3995	1		4			6									11		7	5		9		2	3	10	8
29	10	SWINDON TOWN	2-1	Yardley, Woods	6973	1				11							2	6				7	5		9	4	3		10	8
30	17	Queen's Park Rangers	2-3	Yardley, Dennis	11217	1				11							2	6				7	5		9	4	3		10	8
31	19	NORTHAMPTON T	2-0	Yardley, Woods	8194	1	7	4				5			2			6		11					9		3		10	8
32	24	COVENTRY CITY	3-1	Rennie, Yardley, Nunn	8054	1	7	4				5			2			6		11					9		3		10	8
33	31	Gillingham	4-0	Dennis 2, Rennie 2	4045	1	7	4		11		5			2			6							9		3		10	8
34	Apr 6	TORQUAY UNITED	5-0	Rennie 3, Woods, Dennis	10397	1	7	4		11		5			2			6							9		3		10	8
35	7	PLYMOUTH ARGYLE	1-1	Banks	10451	1	9	4		11		5			2			6				7					3		10	8
36	9	Torquay United	4-0	Yardley 2, Pointon, Dennis	2994	1		4		11		5			2			6				7	8				3		10	9
37	14	Merthyr Town	0-0		2089	1	7	4		11		5			2			6							9		3		10	8
38	21	WALSALL	4-1	Rennie 2, Yardley, Dennis	6118	1	7	4		11		5			2			6							9		3		10	8
39	23	Walsall	1-4	Rennie	3666	1	7	4		11		5			2			6						5	9		3		10	8
40	28	Bristol Rovers	2-1	Woods, Yardley	5639	1		4		11		5			2			6				7			9		3		10	8
41	May 2	Plymouth Argyle	0-4		4719	1				11		5			2			6				7			9		3		10	8
42	5	CHARLTON ATHLETIC	2-1	Rennie, Yardley	5982	1		4		11		5			2			6				7			9		3		10	8

Played at 4 in game 41: R Lumsden
Played at 11 in games 12 and 13: H Briggs

| | | | | | Apps | 32 | 13 | 34 | 4 | 30 | 25 | 21 | 2 | 4 | 33 | 4 | 22 | 16 | 10 | 14 | 3 | 32 | 9 | 13 | 36 | 2 | 21 | 8 | 32 | 39 |
| | | | | | Goals | | 2 | 1 | | 8 | 1 | | 1 | | | 3 | | | | 3 | 1 | 8 | | 11 | 24 | | | | 8 | 23 |

F.A. Cup

Rd	Date	Opponent	Score	Scorers	Att	Abbott H	Black JR	Dennis GT	Fraser CR	Graham RC	Kingham HR	Pointon J	Reid S	Rennie A	Woods H	Yardley J
R1	Nov 30	CLAPTON	9-0	Dennis 2, Woods, Yardley 4, Reid 2	9639	1	4	11	6	3	2	7	9	5	10	8
R2	Dec 10	NORWICH CITY	6-0	Reid 3, Woods, Yardley, Dennis	10750	1	4	11	6	3	2	7	9	5	10	8
R3	Jan 14	Bolton Wanderers	1-2	Reid	20266	1	4	11	6	3	2	7	9	5	10	8

First game with Clapton on Nov. 26th abandoned with Luton leading 5-0 (same 11 players, goals from Yardley, Dennis, Reid 2 and Woods)

		P	W	D	L	F	A	W	D	L	F	A	Pts
1	Millwall	42	19	2	0	87	15	11	3	7	40	35	65
2	Northampton Town	42	17	3	1	67	23	6	6	9	35	41	55
3	Plymouth Argyle	42	17	2	2	60	19	6	5	10	25	35	53
4	Brighton & Hove A.	42	14	4	3	51	24	5	6	10	30	45	48
5	Crystal Palace	42	15	3	3	46	23	3	9	9	33	49	48
6	Swindon Town	42	12	6	3	60	26	7	3	11	30	43	47
7	Southend United	42	14	2	5	48	19	6	4	11	32	45	46
8	Exeter City	42	11	6	4	49	27	6	6	9	21	33	46
9	Newport County	42	12	5	4	52	38	6	4	11	29	46	45
10	Queen's Park Rgs.	42	8	5	8	37	35	9	4	8	35	36	43
11	Charlton Athletic	42	12	5	4	34	27	3	8	10	26	43	43
12	Brentford	42	12	4	5	49	30	4	4	13	27	44	40
13	LUTON TOWN	42	13	5	3	66	27	3	2	16	38	60	39
14	Bournemouth	42	12	6	3	44	24	1	6	14	28	55	38
15	Watford	42	10	5	6	42	34	4	5	12	26	44	38
16	Gillingham	42	10	3	8	33	26	3	8	10	29	55	37
17	Norwich City	42	9	8	4	41	26	1	8	12	25	44	36
18	Walsall	42	9	6	6	52	35	3	3	15	23	66	33
19	Bristol Rovers	42	11	3	7	41	36	1	1	17	26	57	32
20	Coventry City	42	5	8	8	40	36	6	1	14	27	60	31
21	Merthyr Town	42	7	6	8	38	40	2	7	12	15	51	31
22	Torquay United	42	4	10	7	27	36	4	4	13	26	67	30

1928/29   7th in Division 3 South

#	Date	Opponent	Res	Scorers	Att	Abbott H	Banes CS	Bedford L	Black JR	Boylen RH	Clark AW	Curwen W	Daly J	Dennis GT	Forbes AS	Fraser CR	Fulton JJ	Graham RC	Harris B	Kingham HR	Millar RM	Rennie A	Richards D	Roe TW	Vaughan W	Walters AV	Woods H	Yardley J
1	Aug 25	BRIGHTON & HOVE ALB	1-0	Yardley	10526	1			4				7	11			5			6	2	9	3				10	8
2	30	Northampton Town	2-2	Rennie 2	12220	1			4				7	11			5			6	2	9	3				10	8
3	Sep 1	Exeter City	1-1	Yardley	7375	1			4				7	11			5			6	2	9	3				10	8
4	3	NORTHAMPTON T	4-0	Dennis, Rennie 2, Yardley	10931	1			4				7	11			5			6	2	9	3				10	8
5	8	SOUTHEND UNITED	4-2	Millar, Rennie 2, Yardley	10600	1			4				7	11			5			6	2	9	3				10	8
6	15	Merthyr Town	4-3	Rennie 2, Bedford, Yardley	6016	1		11	4				7				5			6	2	9	3				10	8
7	22	BOURNEMOUTH	2-1	Rennie, Black	10675	1		11	4				7		5					6	2	9	3				10	8
8	29	Brentford	1-0	Rennie	13758	1		11	4				7				5			6	2	9	3				10	8
9	Oct 6	BRISTOL ROVERS	4-2	Rennie 2, Woods, Bedford	11650	1		11	4				7				5			6	2	9	3				10	8
10	13	COVENTRY CITY	1-1	Rennie	12509	1		11	4				7				5			6	2	9	3				10	8
11	20	Watford	2-3	Yardley, Bedford	20395	1		11	4				7				5			6	2	9	3				10	8
12	27	WALSALL	3-1	Rennie 2, Woods	10458	1		11	4				7	6			5	3			2	9					10	8
13	Nov 3	Newport County	2-1	Rennie 2	4177	1		11	4				7	6			5	3			2	9					10	8
14	10	CRYSTAL PALACE	5-3	Rennie, Bedford 2, Yardley 2	9606	1		11	4				7	6			5	3			2	9					10	8
15	17	Swindon Town	2-4	Rennie, Yardley	6992	1		11					7	6		5	4	3				9	2				10	8
16	Dec 1	Gillingham	0-1		4661	1		11		5			7	6				4	3		2	9					10	8
17	15	Fulham	2-4	Bedford, Daly	11069	1		11		5			7	6				3	2	4		9	8				10	
18	22	QUEEN'S PARK RANGERS	3-2	Rennie 2, Bedford	9112	1		11	4				7				5	3	2	6		9					10	8
19	25	NORWICH CITY	2-1	Rennie 2	14146	1		11	4				7				5	3	2	6		9					10	8
20	26	Norwich City	0-3		12418	1		11	4				7			5		3	2	6		9					10	8
21	29	Brighton & Hove Albion	0-1		6824	1		11	4				7			6	5	2	3				8		9		10	
22	Jan 5	EXETER CITY	4-0	Clark, Rennie 3	6882	1		11	4		10		7			6	5	2	3			9						8
23	19	Southend United	0-5		6153	1		11	4	5			7					3	2	6		9					10	8
24	26	MERTHYR TOWN	2-0	Roe 2	7485		1	11	4				7				5	2	3	6		9		10				8
25	Feb 2	Bournemouth	3-3	Roe, Rennie, Yardley	3726		1	11	4				7				5	2		6		9	3	10				8
26	9	BRENTFORD	2-1	Yardley, Bedford	8148		1	11	4				7				5	2		6		9	3	10				8
27	16	Bristol Rovers	1-1	Rennie	6749		1	11			4		7				5	2		6		9	3				10	8
28	23	Coventry City	1-1	Rennie	13900		1	11			4		7				5	2	3	6		9					10	8
29	Mar 2	WATFORD	2-2	Bedford, Vaughan	15199		1	11			4		7				5		3	6		9	2		10			8
30	9	Walsall	0-0		6925		1	11			4		7				5	2	3	6		9		8			10	
31	11	PLYMOUTH ARGYLE	2-2	Rennie, Yardley	8289		1	11			4		7			6	5	2	3			9		8				10
32	16	NEWPORT COUNTY	5-2	Roe 3, Bedford, Yardley	8782		1	11			4		7			6	5	3				9	2	8				10
33	23	Crystal Palace	0-3		22981		1	11			4		7			6	5	3				9	2	8				10
34	29	Charlton Athletic	1-4	Rennie	12814		1	11			4		7			6	5	3				9	2	8				10
35	30	SWINDON TOWN	5-3	Yardley 2, Rennie 2, Roe	9772		1	11			4		7				5	3		6		9	2	8				10
36	Apr 1	CHARLTON ATHLETIC	3-0	Rennie, Boylen, Vaughan	13214		1	11		6			7	4			5				2	9	3		10			8
37	6	Torquay United	2-2	Rennie 2	3909		1	11	4	7							5			6	2	9	3		10			8
38	13	GILLINGHAM	8-0	Rennie 5, Yardley, Woods, Bedford	7278		1	11	4				7				5			6	2	9	3				10	8
39	20	Plymouth Argyle	0-2		8484		1	11	4				7				5			6	2	9	3				10	8
40	27	FULHAM	1-3	Rennie	13469		1	11	4				7				5			6	2	9	3				10	8
41	29	TORQUAY UNITED	1-2	Yardley	3155		1	11	4				7			5				6	2	9	3				10	8
42	May 4	Queen's Park Rangers	1-1	Rennie	13449		1	11	4				7				5			6	2	9	3		10			8
		Apps				23	19	36	27	2	16	1	40	13	1	7	36	12	19	27	31	41	27	17	3	1	23	40
		Goals						11		1	1		2	1							1	43		7	2		3	17

F.A. Cup

Rnd	Date	Opponent	Res	Scorers	Att	Abbott H	Banes CS	Bedford L	Black JR	Boylen RH	Clark AW	Curwen W	Daly J	Dennis GT	Forbes AS	Fraser CR	Fulton JJ	Graham RC	Harris B	Kingham HR	Millar RM	Rennie A	Richards D	Roe TW	Vaughan W	Walters AV	Woods H	Yardley J
R1	Nov 24	SOUTHEND UNITED	5-1	Rennie 4, Bedford	12489	1		11					7	4		5	6	3	2			9					10	8
R2	Dec 8	Fulham	0-0		19000	1		11	4				7	6			5	3	2			9					10	8
rep	Dec 13	FULHAM	4-1	Yardley 2, Rennie, Bedford	11250	1		11	4				7	6			5	3	2			9					10	8
R3	Jan 12	CRYSTAL PALACE	0-0		14200	1		11	4		10		7			6	2	5	3			9						8
rep	Jan 16	Crystal Palace	0-7		17000	1			4		10		7	11			5	3		6		9					2	8

Division 3 South — Final Table

		P	W	D	L	F	A	W	D	L	F	A	Pts
1	Charlton Athletic	42	14	5	2	51	22	9	3	9	35	38	54
2	Crystal Palace	42	14	2	5	40	25	9	6	6	41	42	54
3	Northampton Town	42	14	6	1	68	23	6	6	9	28	34	52
4	Plymouth Argyle	42	14	6	1	51	13	6	6	9	32	38	52
5	Fulham	42	14	3	4	60	31	7	7	7	41	40	52
6	Queen's Park Rgs.	42	13	7	1	50	22	6	7	8	32	39	52
7	LUTON TOWN	42	16	3	2	64	28	3	8	10	25	45	49
8	Watford	42	15	3	3	55	31	4	7	10	24	43	48
9	Bournemouth	42	14	4	3	54	31	5	5	11	30	46	47
10	Swindon Town	42	12	5	4	48	27	3	8	10	27	45	43
11	Coventry City	42	9	6	6	35	23	5	8	8	27	34	42
12	Southend United	42	10	7	4	44	27	5	4	12	36	48	41
13	Brentford	42	11	6	4	34	21	3	6	12	22	39	38
14	Walsall	42	11	7	3	47	25	2	5	14	26	54	38
15	Brighton & Hove A.	42	14	2	5	39	28	2	4	15	19	48	38
16	Newport County	42	8	6	7	37	28	5	3	13	32	58	35
17	Norwich City	42	12	3	6	49	29	2	3	16	20	52	34
18	Torquay United	42	10	3	8	46	36	4	3	14	20	48	34
19	Bristol Rovers	42	9	6	6	39	28	4	1	16	21	51	33
20	Merthyr Town	42	11	6	4	42	28	0	2	19	13	75	30
21	Exeter City	42	7	6	8	49	40	2	5	14	18	48	29
22	Gillingham	42	7	8	6	22	24	3	1	17	21	59	29

#	Date	Opponent	Score	Scorers	Att	Baker A	Banes CS	Bedford L	Birch W	Black JR	Boylen RH	Clark AW	Daly J	Drinnan JMcK	Fraser CR	Fulton JJ	Harford GB	Hutchinson A	Kingham HR	McInnes WA	Millar RM	Morgan FG	Rennie A	Richards D	Sheldon W	Smeaton AR	Smith E	Walker R	Woods H	Yardley J	Young JW
1	Aug 31	Exeter City	2-2	Bedford, Drinnan	8520			11				4	7	10	6		1		2				5	9			3			8	
2	Sep 2	NORWICH CITY	1-1	Rennie	11097			7				4		10	6	5	1		2	11				9			3			8	
3	7	SOUTHEND UNITED	0-3		9992			11	4				7		6		1		2				5	9			3		10	8	
4	9	Norwich City	1-1	Bedford	9086			11	4				7		6	5	1		2					9			3		10	8	
5	14	Watford	4-0	Yardley, Rennie 3	16945			11	4				7		6	5	1		2					9			3		10	8	
6	16	GILLINGHAM	2-0	Rennie, Yardley	7168			11					7		6	4	1		2				5	9			3		10	8	
7	21	Bournemouth	1-5	Woods	7268			11			7			10	6	4	1		2				5	9			3			8	
8	28	WALSALL	2-3	Rennie, Yardley	8700			11				5	7		6	4	1		2					9			3		10	8	
9	Oct 5	Queen's Park Rangers	0-1		12273			11				5	7		6	4	1		2					9			3		10	8	
10	12	FULHAM	4-1	Drinnan 2, Yardley, Rennie	10053							5	7	10	6	4	1		2	11				9			3			8	
11	19	NEWPORT COUNTY	4-2	Daly, Clark, Rennie, McInnes	8825							4	7	10	6	5	1		2	11				9			3			8	
12	26	Torquay United	2-2	Yardley, Drinnan	4755							4	7	10		5	1		2	11				9		6	3			8	
13	Nov 2	MERTHYR TOWN	4-0	Drinnan 2, Yardley, Bedford	7988			11	8			4	7	10		5	1		2					3		6				9	
14	9	Plymouth Argyle	1-6	Clark	15073			11				4	7	10	6	5	1		2					3					8	9	
15	16	SWINDON TOWN	1-1	Bedford	2547			11	8			4	7	10	6	5	1							2		3				9	
16	23	Brighton & Hove Albion	1-4	Clark	4827			11	8			4	7	10	6	5	1							2		3				9	
17	Dec 7	Brentford	0-2		7167							9	7	10	5	4	1		2	11	6			3						8	
18	21	Coventry City	1-5	Hutchison	10865	1		8					7		4			9		11	6			3		5	2			10	
19	25	NORTHAMPTON T	1-0	Brett (og)	9473	1							7						2	11				3		5		4	10	9	8
20	26	Northampton Town	1-4	Clark	19251	1						4	7		6					11				3		5	2		10	9	8
21	28	EXETER CITY	0-4		5285	1							7		6				2	11				3		5		4	10	9	8
22	Jan 4	Southend United	1-1	Yardley	5859	1		8			7	5		10	6	4				11				2			3			9	
23	18	WATFORD	2-0	Birch, Yardley	9920	1		8			7	5		10	6	4				11				2			3			9	
24	25	BOURNEMOUTH	1-0	Yardley	6971	1		8			7	5		10	6	4				11				2			3			9	
25	Feb 1	Walsall	0-1		6143	1		8			7	5		10	6	4				11				2			3			9	
26	8	QUEEN'S PARK RANGERS	2-1	Rennie, Fraser	7049	1						5	7	10	6	4				11			9	2			3			8	
27	15	Fulham	1-1	Birch	13739	11		8				5	7		6	4							9	2			3			10	
28	22	Newport County	0-0		3879	1		8				5	7	10	6	4				11			9	2			3				
29	Mar 1	TORQUAY UNITED	3-1	Rennie, Birch, Daly	7239	1		8				5	7	10	6								9	2			3	4		11	
30	8	Merthyr Town	1-3	Drinnan	1838	1		8				5	7	10	6	4							9	2			3			11	
31	10	CLAPTON ORIENT	1-2	Drinnan	2612	1		8				5	7	10	6								9	2			3	4		11	
32	15	PLYMOUTH ARGYLE	5-2	Rennie 3, Yardley 2	9051	1						5	7	10	4					11	6		9	2			3			8	
33	22	Swindon Town	1-1	Rennie	3710	1						5	7	10	4					11	6		9	2			3			8	
34	24	BRISTOL ROVERS	3-0	Drinnan 2, Daly	3589	1						5	7	10	4					11	6		9	2			3			8	
35	29	BRIGHTON & HOVE ALB	1-0	Yardley	7199	1						5	7	10	4					11	6		9	2			3			8	
36	Apr 5	Bristol Rovers	2-2	Rennie, Yardley	4786	1						5	7	10	4				2	11	6		9	3						8	
37	12	BRENTFORD	2-1	Clark, Rennie	11150	1					7	5		10	4				11	2	6		9	3						8	
38	18	CRYSTAL PALACE	2-2	Yardley, Drinnan	9135	1					7	5		10	4				11		6		9	2			3			8	
39	19	Clapton Orient	1-6	Yardley	6228	1				8	7	5		10	4				11	2	6						3			9	
40	21	Crystal Palace	1-4	Rennie	15167	1						5		10	4			7	2	11	6		9				3			8	
41	26	COVENTRY CITY	1-1	Drinnan	4819							5		10	4	1				11	6		9	2	7		3			8	
42	May 3	Gillingham	0-2		4831	1				8	7	5		10					4		6			2	11		3			8	
		Apps				1	24	13	15	3	9	34	30	31	39	24	18	5	21	22	13	4	27	38	2	6	24	5	11	40	3
		Goals						4	3			5	3	12	1			1		1			17						1	15	

One own goal

F.A. Cup

R	Date	Opponent	Score	Scorers	Att	Bedford L	Birch W	Clark AW	Daly J	Drinnan JMcK	Fraser CR	Fulton JJ	Harford GB	Kingham HR	Rennie A	Smith E	Yardley J
R1	Nov 30	QUEEN'S PARK RANGERS	2-3	Yardley 2	9000	11	8	4	7	10	6	5	1	2	9	3	

	Team	P	W	D	L	F	A	W	D	L	F	A	Pts
1	Plymouth Argyle	42	18	3	0	63	12	12	5	4	35	26	68
2	Brentford	42	21	0	0	66	12	7	5	9	28	32	61
3	Queen's Park Rgs.	42	13	5	3	46	26	8	4	9	34	42	51
4	Northampton Town	42	14	6	1	53	20	7	2	12	29	38	50
5	Brighton & Hove A.	42	16	2	3	54	20	5	6	10	33	43	50
6	Coventry City	42	14	3	4	54	25	5	6	10	34	48	47
7	Fulham	42	12	6	3	54	33	6	5	10	33	50	47
8	Norwich City	42	14	4	3	55	28	4	6	11	33	49	46
9	Crystal Palace	42	14	5	2	56	26	3	7	11	25	48	46
10	Bournemouth	42	11	6	4	47	24	4	7	10	25	37	43
11	Southend United	42	11	6	4	41	19	4	7	10	28	40	43
12	Clapton Orient	42	10	8	3	38	21	4	5	12	17	41	41
13	LUTON TOWN	42	13	4	4	42	25	1	8	12	22	53	40
14	Swindon Town	42	10	7	4	42	25	3	5	13	31	58	38
15	Watford	42	10	4	7	37	30	5	4	12	23	43	38
16	Exeter City	42	10	6	5	45	29	2	5	14	22	44	35
17	Walsall	42	10	4	7	45	24	3	4	14	26	54	34
18	Newport County	42	9	9	3	48	29	3	1	17	26	56	34
19	Torquay United	42	9	6	6	50	38	1	5	15	14	56	31
20	Bristol Rovers	42	11	3	7	45	31	0	5	16	22	62	30
21	Gillingham	42	9	5	7	38	28	2	3	16	13	52	30
22	Merthyr Town	42	5	6	10	39	49	1	3	17	21	86	21

1930/31 7th in Division 3 South

#		Date	Opponent	Score	Scorers	Att	Armstrong JW	Banes CS	Brown WI	Bryce RS	Clark AW	Dent F	Edwards GG	Fraser CR	Gale EWA	Hale A	Harford GB	Heslop AS	Hodgson T	Kingham HR	McGinnigle H	McNestry G	Muir JB	Page JE	Rennie A	Richards D	Richmond J	Rickett WJ	Slicer J	Smith E	Yardley J
1	Aug	30	BRENTFORD	1-1	Page	11686		1			5					6				2	4	7		10	9	3			8	11	
2	Sep	3	Exeter City	1-1	Slicer	4627	10	1			5					6				2	4	7			9	3			11		8
3		6	Crystal Palace	1-5	McNestry	15237	10	1			5					6				2	9	7				3	4		11		8
4		8	BRIGHTON & HOVE ALB	2-2	Rennie 2	7849		1		10	5					6				2	4	7			9	3			11		8
5		13	SOUTHEND UNITED	2-1	Yardley, Clark	6347		1		8	5					6				2	4	7			9	3			11		10
6		17	Brighton & Hove Albion	0-2		4088			11		5					6	1			2		7	4	10	9	3					8
7		20	Watford	0-1		8991			9		5			6		4	1			2		7		10		3			11		8
8		27	Bristol Rovers	1-5	McNestry	7930			9		5			6		4	1			2		7		10		3			11		8
9		29	EXETER CITY	3-1	McNestry, Slicer, Dent	1450	8				4	10		6			1			2	5	7			9	3			11		
10	Oct	4	NEWPORT COUNTY	3-1	Dent 2, Slicer	8097	8	1			4	10		6						2	5	7			9	3			11		
11		11	Gillingham	0-4		7491		1			5	10		6						2	4	7			9	3			11		8
12		18	BOURNEMOUTH	2-3	Rennie 2	7367		1			5	10		6						2		7			9	3	4		11		
13		25	Swindon Town	0-0		4671		1	11	4	10			6	5				3	2		7			9						8
14	Nov	1	FULHAM	5-0	Rennie 2, McNestry, Dent 2	8389		1	11	4		10		6	5			7	3	2		8			9						
15		8	Coventry City	2-1	Rennie 2	10542		1	11	4	10			6	5			7	3	2		8			9						
16		15	WALSALL	1-5		7508		1	11	4	10			6	5			7	3	2		8			9						
17		22	Queen's Park Rangers	1-3	Rennie	6388		1	11	4	10			6	5			7	3	2		8			9						
18	Dec	6	Thames	0-1		469	8	1	11			10				4			3	2	5	7	6		9						
19		20	Notts County	0-1		11307	8		10	11				6	4		1			2	5	7			9		3				
20		25	TORQUAY UNITED	3-1	Rennie 2, Bryce	7553			11		10			6	4		1			2	5	8			9				7	3	
21		26	Torquay United	1-1	Armstrong	6619	8		11					6	4		1			2	5	7			9					3	10
22		27	Brentford	1-0	Clark	7353	8		11	5				4			1		3	2		7			9					6	10
23	Jan	3	CRYSTAL PALACE	1-2	Rennie	6051	8		11					6	4		1			2	5	7			9					3	10
24		10	NORWICH CITY	1-0	McNestry	5032	8		11	4	10			6			1		3	2	5	7			9						
25		17	Southend United	2-0	McNestry 2	4857			7	4				6	5		1		3	2		8			10				11		9
26		28	WATFORD	4-1	Rennie, Bryce, McNestry, Yardley	3603			7	4				6			1		3	2	5	8			10				11		9
27		31	BRISTOL ROVERS	4-1	Rennie, Yardley, McNestry 2	7174			7	4				6	1		1		3	2	5	8			10				11		9
28	Feb	7	Newport County	1-3	McNestry	2868			7	4				6	1				3	2	5	8			10				11		9
29		14	GILLINGHAM	4-1	Rennie, McNestry 2, Yardley	5837				4				6			1	7	3	2	5	8			10				11		9
30		21	Bournemouth	0-0		4439				4				6			1	7	3	2	5	8			10				11		9
31		28	SWINDON TOWN	4-0	Rennie, Yardley 2, Heslop	5057				4				6			1	7	3	2	5	8			10				11		9
32	Mar	7	Fulham	1-2	Yardley	7000				4				6			1	7	3	2	5	8			10				11		9
33		14	COVENTRY CITY	2-0	Brown, McNestry	7134			9	11	4			6			1	7	3	2		8			10						
34		21	Walsall	1-0	Brown	3937			9	11	4			6			1	7		2		8			10	5					
35		23	CLAPTON ORIENT	0-1		3284			9	11	4			6			1	7		2		8			10	5				3	
36		28	QUEEN'S PARK RANGERS	5-1	Yardley 2, Heslop 2, Slicer	6035				4				5	6		1	7		2		8			10				11	3	9
37	Apr	4	Norwich City	0-1		7903				4				5	6		1	7	3	2		8			10				11		9
38		6	NORTHAMPTON T	4-0	Rennie, Clark, Slicer, Yardley	12292					5			6			1	7	3	2	4	8			10				11		9
39		7	Northampton Town	0-0		8614					5	8	4	6			1	7	3	2					10				11		9
40		11	THAMES	8-0	* see below	6029			10	4				6			1	7	3	2	5	8							11		9
41		18	Clapton Orient	2-3	Slicer, Clark	5078			11	4				6			1	7	3	2	5	8							10		9
42		25	NOTTS COUNTY	3-0	Yardley, Slicer, Heslop	7312			10	4				6	5		1	7	3	2		8							11		9

Scorers in game 40: McNestry 2, Clark, Yardley 2, Bryce, Heslop, Slicer

	Armstrong JW	Banes CS	Brown WI	Bryce RS	Clark AW	Dent F	Edwards GG	Fraser CR	Gale EWA	Hale A	Harford GB	Heslop AS	Hodgson T	Kingham HR	McGinnigle H	McNestry G	Muir JB	Page JE	Rennie A	Richards D	Richmond J	Rickett WJ	Slicer J	Smith E	Yardley J
Apps	10	14	6	25	37	13	2	30	10	16	26	18	26	39	25	41	4	4	36	14	2	1	27	8	28
Goals			2	3	5	5						6				17		1	18				8		11

F.A. Cup

		Date	Opponent	Score	Scorers	Att	Armstrong JW	Banes CS	Brown WI	Bryce RS	Clark AW	Dent F	Edwards GG	Fraser CR	Gale EWA	Hale A	Harford GB	Heslop AS	Hodgson T	Kingham HR	McGinnigle H	McNestry G	Muir JB	Page JE	Rennie A	Richards D	Richmond J	Rickett WJ	Slicer J	Smith E	Yardley J
R1	Nov	29	CLAPTON ORIENT	2-2	Rennie, Bryce	9244		1	11	4	10			6					3	2	5	7			9						8
rep	Dec	4	Clapton Orient	4-2	McNestry, Rennie 2, Armstrong	8021	8	1	11	4	10			6					3	2	5	7			9						
R2	Dec	13	Watford	1-3	Yardley	17770		1	11		10			6	4				3	2	5	7			9						8

R1 replay at Highbury

		P	W	D	L	F	A	W	D	L	F	A	Pts
1	Notts County	42	16	4	1	58	13	8	7	6	39	33	59
2	Crystal Palace	42	17	2	2	71	20	5	5	11	36	51	51
3	Brentford	42	14	3	4	62	30	8	3	10	28	34	50
4	Brighton & Hove A.	42	13	5	3	45	20	4	10	7	23	33	49
5	Southend United	42	16	0	5	53	26	6	5	10	23	34	49
6	Northampton Town	42	10	6	5	37	20	8	6	7	40	39	48
7	LUTON TOWN	42	15	3	3	61	17	4	5	12	15	34	46
8	Queen's Park Rgs.	42	15	0	6	57	23	5	3	13	25	52	43
9	Fulham	42	15	3	3	49	21	3	4	14	28	54	43
10	Bournemouth	42	11	7	3	39	22	4	6	11	33	51	43
11	Torquay United	42	13	5	3	56	26	4	4	13	24	58	43
12	Swindon Town	42	15	5	1	68	29	3	1	17	21	65	42
13	Exeter City	42	12	6	3	55	35	5	2	14	29	55	42
14	Coventry City	42	11	4	6	55	28	5	5	11	20	37	41
15	Bristol Rovers	42	12	3	6	49	36	4	5	12	26	56	40
16	Gillingham	42	10	6	5	40	29	4	4	13	21	47	38
17	Walsall	42	9	5	7	44	38	5	4	12	34	57	37
18	Watford	42	9	4	8	41	29	5	3	13	31	46	35
19	Clapton Orient	42	12	3	6	47	33	2	4	15	16	58	35
20	Thames	42	12	5	4	34	20	1	3	17	20	73	34
21	Newport County	42	10	5	6	45	31	1	1	19	24	80	28
22	Norwich City	42	10	7	4	37	20	0	1	20	10	56	28

1931/32   6th in Division 3 South

#	Date		Opponent	Score	Scorers	Att.	Black AJ	Bryce RS	Chapman JR	Cupitt WW	Fraser CR	Gale EWA	Hale A	Harford GB	Heslop AS	Hodgson T	Imrie J	Jones VW	Kean FW	Kingham HR	Loasby H	McGinnigle H	McNestry G	Miller W	Rennie A	Rowe DH	Slicer J	Tait T	Turner GW	Wales A	Wilson GG	Yardley J
1	Aug	29	Reading	1-2	Tait	14591					6			1	7	3			4	2			8	5	10			11	9			
2		31	NORTHAMPTON T	1-0	Rennie	11235					6	5				3	1		4	2			7		10			11	9			8
3	Sep	5	SOUTHEND UNITED	1-3	Rennie	9179		11				5				3	1	6	4	2	8		7		10				9			
4		9	Gillingham	3-1	McNestry, Rennie 2	5950					6				7	3	1		4	2			5	8	10				9	11		
5		12	Fulham	2-3	Rennie 2	8510					6				7	3	1		4	2			5	8	10				9	11		
6		14	GILLINGHAM	2-0	Tait 2	6333					6				7	3	1		4	2			5	8	10			11	9			
7		19	THAMES	2-0	Rennie, Heslop	8239					6				7	3	1		4	2			5	8	10				9	11		
8		26	Brentford	0-1		12540					6				7	3	1		4	2			5	8	10			11	9			
9		28	Northampton Town	2-1	Tait, McNestry	6503						6				3	1		4	2			5	7	10			11	8			9
10	Oct	3	EXETER CITY	6-3	Yardley 2, Rennie 3, McNestry	8509						6					1		4	2			5	7	10			11	8		3	9
11		10	Coventry City	2-3	Yardley 2	12371	11				6				3		1		4	2			5	7	10				8			9
12		17	WATFORD	0-1		14765					6					3	1		4	2			5	7	10			11	8			9
13		24	Crystal Palace	1-1	Yardley	15327					6		3				1	4	2				5	7	10			11	8			9
14		31	BOURNEMOUTH	1-0	Slicer	7231					6		3		7		1	4	2				5		10		9	11	8			
15	Nov	7	Queen's Park Rangers	1-3	Tait	10993					6				7	3	1		4	2			5		10			11	9			8
16		14	BRISTOL ROVERS	3-0	Yardley, Heslop, Turner	6244					6				7	3	1		4	2			5	8					9	11		10
17		21	Torquay United	2-1	Rennie, McNestry	3490		8			6					3	1		4	2			5	7	10				11			9
18	Dec	5	Swindon Town	2-3	Loasby, Tait	2532					6					3	1		4	2	9		5	7	10			8	11			
19		19	Brighton & Hove Albion	2-3	Tait, Slicer	6628					6					3	1	4		2			5	7	10		11	8	9			
20		25	CARDIFF CITY	2-1	Tait 2	11609					6					3	1		4	2			5	7	10			8	11			9
21		26	Cardiff City	1-4	Yardley	13515					6					3	1		4				5	7	10			8	11	2		9
22	Jan	2	READING	6-1	Hodgkiss(og), McNestry 2, Yardley 3	5179					6					3	1		4	2			5	7	10			11	8			9
23		11	CLAPTON ORIENT	1-5	Rennie	1716				7	6						1		4	2			5		10			8	11	3		9
24		16	Southend United	1-1	McNestry	5508					6					3	1		4	2			7	5	10			11	8			9
25		23	FULHAM	1-3	Tait	6315					6					3	1		4	2			7	5	10			11	8			9
26		30	Thames	4-2	Loasby 2, Tait, Cuppit	1473				7	6					3	1		4	2	9		5					10	11			8
27	Feb	6	BRENTFORD	1-1	Loasby	7402				7	6					3	1		4	2	9	5			10			8	11			
28		13	Exeter City	1-1	Loasby	6454				7	6					3	1		4	2	9	5						8	11			10
29		20	COVENTRY CITY	3-1	Turner 2, Tait	5412					6					3	1		4	2	9		5	7	10			8	11			9
30	Mar	5	CRYSTAL PALACE	3-0	Loasby, McNestry, Turner	6105					6					3	1		4	2	9	5	7		10			8	11			
31		12	Bournemouth	1-1	Loasby	4277					6					3	1		4	2	9	5	7		10			8	11			
32		19	QUEEN'S PARK RANGERS	4-1	Loasby, Bryce, Tait 2	5768		11		7	6					3	1		4	2	9	5			10			8				
33		25	MANSFIELD TOWN	3-1	Rennie, Loasby, Bryce	7621		11		7	6					3	1		4	2	9	5			10			8				
34		26	Bristol Rovers	1-3	Bryce	4265		11		7	6					3	1		4	2	9	5			10			8				
35		28	Mansfield Town	2-5	Bryce, Loasby	5588		11		7	6					3	1		4	2	9	5			10			8				
36		29	NORWICH CITY	7-1	Tait, Loasby 3, Slicer 2, Rennie	2619				7	6					3	1		4	2	9	5			10			8	11			
37	Apr	2	TORQUAY UNITED	6-1	Slicer, Tait 3, Loasby, Rennie	5778				7	6					3	1		4	2	9	5			10			8	11			
38		9	Clapton Orient	0-0		5979				7	6					3	1		4	2	9	5			10			8	11			
39		13	Watford	1-3	Bryce	4635		7			6						1		4	2	9	5			10			8	11		3	
40		16	SWINDON TOWN	6-0	Tait 5, Kean	3982					6						1		4	2			5	7	10			11	9		8	3
41		23	Norwich City	3-3	McNestry, Rennie, Tait	6247					6						1		4	2			5	7	10	11		9			8	3
42		30	BRIGHTON & HOVE ALB	3-2	Rennie, McNestry, Tait	6328					6						1		4	2			5	7	10	11		9			8	3
			Apps				1	9	1	8	39	1	6	1	9	35	41	3	40	39	15	36	28	3	40	2	18	41	16	3	7	20
			Goals					5		1					2				1		14		9		17		5	25	4			11

One own goal

F.A. Cup

#	Date		Opponent	Score	Scorers	Att.	Fraser CR	Hodgson T	Imrie J	Kean FW	Kingham HR	McNestry G	Miller W	Rennie A	Slicer J	Tait T	Turner GW	Yardley J
R1	Nov	28	Swindon Town	5-0	McNestry 2, Rennie, Yardley 2	8000	6	3	1	4	2	5	7	10		8	11	9
R2	Dec	12	Lincoln City	2-2	Yardley 2	5000	6	3	1	4	2	5	7	10		8	11	9
rep	Dec	16	LINCOLN CITY	4-1	Tait 2, Yardley, Slicer	9500	6	3	1	4	2	5	7	10	11	8		9
R3	Jan	9	WOLVERHAMPTON WAN.	1-2	Yardley	16945	6	3	1	4	2	5	7	10	11	8		9

Division 3 South — Final Table

		P	W	D	L	F	A	W	D	L	F	A	Pts
1	Fulham	42	15	3	3	72	27	9	6	6	39	35	57
2	Reading	42	19	1	1	65	21	4	8	9	32	46	55
3	Southend United	42	12	5	4	41	18	9	6	6	36	35	53
4	Crystal Palace	42	14	7	0	48	12	6	4	11	26	51	51
5	Brentford	42	11	6	4	40	22	8	4	9	28	30	48
6	LUTON TOWN	42	16	1	4	62	25	4	6	11	33	45	47
7	Exeter City	42	16	3	2	53	16	4	4	13	24	46	47
8	Brighton & Hove A.	42	12	4	5	42	21	5	8	8	31	37	46
9	Cardiff City	42	14	2	5	62	29	5	6	10	25	44	46
10	Norwich City	42	12	7	2	51	22	5	5	11	25	45	46
11	Watford	42	14	4	3	49	27	5	4	12	32	52	46
12	Coventry City	42	17	2	2	74	28	1	6	14	34	69	44
13	Queen's Park Rgs.	42	11	6	4	50	30	4	6	11	29	43	42
14	Northampton Town	42	12	3	6	48	26	4	4	13	21	43	39
15	Bournemouth	42	8	8	5	42	32	5	4	12	28	46	38
16	Clapton Orient	42	7	8	6	41	35	5	3	13	36	55	35
17	Swindon Town	42	12	2	7	47	31	2	4	15	23	53	34
18	Bristol Rovers	42	11	6	4	46	30	2	2	17	19	62	34
19	Torquay United	42	9	6	6	49	39	3	3	15	23	67	33
20	Mansfield Town	42	11	5	5	44	45	0	5	16	21	63	32
21	Gillingham	42	8	6	7	26	26	2	2	17	14	56	28
22	Thames	42	6	7	8	35	35	1	2	18	18	74	23

1932/33 — 14th in Division 3 South

#	Date	Opponent	Res	Scorers	Att	Alderson T	Brown WI	Coote SA	Corkindale WJ	Diaper R	Fraser CR	Harford GB	Hayhurst A	Hodgson T	Hutchison D	Imrie J	Kean FW	Kingham HR	Mackey TS	McGinnigle H	Mills AS	Nelson A	Pacey HJ	Rennie A	Roberts J	Rowe DH	Tait T	Weaver RS	Whalley R
1	Aug 27	NORTHAMPTON T	2-1	Mills, Rowe	11414						6			3	8	1	4	2		5	7			10		11	9		
2	29	Clapton Orient	0-0		7528						6			3	8	1	4	2		5	7			10	11		9		
3	Sep 3	Bristol City	2-5	Tait 2	9044						6			3	8	1	4	2		5	7			10		11	9		
4	5	CLAPTON ORIENT	4-1	Tait 2, Mills 2	4496						6	1		3	8		4	2		5	7			10	11		9		
5	10	COVENTRY CITY	4-1	Rennie, Rowe, Fraser, Tait	7829						6	1			8		4	2	3	5	7			10		11	9		
6	17	Brentford	0-1		15409						6	1			8		4	2	3	5	7			10		11	9		
7	24	TORQUAY UNITED	2-1	Hutchison 2	8424						6	1			8		4	2	3	5	7			10		11	9		
8	Oct 1	Exeter City	0-2		6681		9		11		6	1					4	2	3	5	7			10					
9	8	GILLINGHAM	2-1	Mills, Whalley	6244		9				6	1					4	2	3	5	7	8		10					11
10	15	NEWPORT COUNTY	2-2	Kean, Nelson	6504		9				6	1					4	2	3	5	7	8		10					11
11	22	Watford	1-4	Hutchison	12130						6	1			8		4	2	3	5	7			10			9		11
12	29	CARDIFF CITY	8-1	Tait 3, Mills 2, Nelson, Hutchison, Fraser	6002						6				10	1	4	2	3	5	7	8					9		
13	Nov 5	Reading	1-4	Tait	9861						6				10	1	4	2	3	5	7	8					9		
14	12	NORWICH CITY	1-1	Kean	5501						6				10	1	4	2	3	5	7	8					9		
15	19	Brighton & Hove Albion	0-2		4102						6		5			1	4	2	3		7	8		10			9		
16	Dec 3	Aldershot	2-2	Tait 2	3993						6					1	4	2	3	5		8		10	7	11	9		
17	17	Southend United	1-2	Roberts	6057						6					1	4	2	3	5	7	8		10	11		9		
18	24	CRYSTAL PALACE	1-1	Rennie	7042	9					6					1	4	2	3	5	7	8		10	11				
19	26	Bournemouth	2-0	Alderson 2	7342	9					6					1	4	2	3	5	7	8		10	11				
20	27	BOURNEMOUTH	1-2	Alderson	10428	9					6					1	4	2	3	5	7	8		10	11				
21	31	Northampton Town	0-1		8321	8					6					1	4	2	3	5			7	10	11		9		
22	Jan 7	BRISTOL CITY	5-4	Rennie 3, Mills, Tait	6080	10					6			3		1	4	2		5	7			9	11		8		
23	21	Coventry City	0-4		11010	10					6	1					4	2	3	5	7	8			11		9		
24	Feb 1	BRENTFORD	5-5	Nelson 2, Tait 3	3044	10					6	1					4	2	3	5	7	8			11		9		
25	4	Torquay United	1-3	Nelson	2745	10	4				6	1						2	3	5	7	8			11		9		
26	11	EXETER CITY	4-0	Alderson, Mills, Tait 2	6388	10					6	1					4	2	3	5	7	8			11		9		
27	22	Gillingham	1-1	Roberts	2152	10	6			4		1						2	3	5	7			9	11		8		
28	Mar 11	Cardiff City	2-3	Nelson, Tait	5919	10					6	1					4	2	3	5	7	8			11		9		
29	13	BRISTOL ROVERS	1-1	Hutchison	2272	10	6					1		2	8		4		3	5	7				11		9		
30	18	READING	1-1	Rennie	6219	10					6	1			8		4	2	3	5	7			9	11				
31	25	Norwich City	1-2	Weaver	14098						6	1			8		4	2	3	5	11	10	7					9	
32	Apr 1	BRIGHTON & HOVE ALB	0-0		4240					4	6	1			8			2	3	5		10	7		11			9	
33	5	Newport County	2-3	Rowe, Hutchison	2344					4	6	1			8			2	3	5		7		10		11		9	
34	8	Bristol Rovers	0-0		6127		4				6				8	1		2	3	5	7	10		9		11			
35	14	SWINDON TOWN	6-2	Rennie 3, Nelson, Mills 2	5535		4				6				8	1		2	3	5	7	10		9		11			
36	15	ALDERSHOT	2-1	Alderson, Rennie	5128	10	4				6				8	1		2	3	5	7			9		11			
37	17	Swindon Town	1-1	Rennie	4693		4				6				8	1		2	3	5	7			9		11			10
38	18	QUEEN'S PARK RANGERS	3-1	Mills, Rowe 2	2402		4				6				10	1		2	3	5	7			9		11	8		
39	22	Queen's Park Rangers	1-3	Hutchison	2837		4				6				10	1		2	3	5	7			9		11	8		
40	26	WATFORD	3-2	Hutchison, Rowe 2	4140						6				8	1	4	2	3	5	7			10		11	9		
41	29	SOUTHEND UNITED	3-3	Rowe, Mills 2	2969						6				8	1	4	2	3	5	7			10		11	9		
42	May 6	Crystal Palace	0-3		6554			2			6	1			8		4		3	5	7			10		11	9		
		Apps				14	12	1	1	3	40	20	1	6	26	22	32	40	38	40	37	21	4	31	17	21	28	3	4
		Goals				5					2				9		2				14	5		11	2	8	18	1	1

F.A. Cup

Rd	Date	Opponent	Res	Scorers	Att	Alderson T	Brown WI	Coote SA	Corkindale WJ	Diaper R	Fraser CR	Harford GB	Hayhurst A	Hodgson T	Hutchison D	Imrie J	Kean FW	Kingham HR	Mackey TS	McGinnigle H	Mills AS	Nelson A	Pacey HJ	Rennie A	Roberts J	Rowe DH	Tait T	Weaver RS	Whalley R
R1	Nov 26	KINGSTONIAN	2-2	Rennie, Tait	7701			7			6		5		8	1	4	2	3					9		11	10		
rep	Nov 30	Kingstonian	3-2	McGinnigle, Rennie, Tait	6227		7				6					1	4	2	3	5		8		9			10		11
R2	Dec 10	Stockport County	3-2	Kean, Rennie, Tait	7500		7				6					1	4	2	3	5		8		9			10		
R3	Jan 14	Barnsley	0-0		12500	10					6	1					4	2	3	5	7			9	11		8		
rep	Jan 18	BARNSLEY	2-0	Rennie 2	11000	10					6	1					4	2	3	5	7			9	11		8		
R4	Jan 28	TOTTENHAM HOTSPUR	2-0	Alderson, Tait	17213	9					6	1					4	2	3	5	7	8			11		10		
R5	Feb 18	Halifax Town	2-0	Nelson, Tait	29325	8					6	1					4	2	3	5	7			9	11		10		
R6	Mar 4	Everton	0-6		55431						6	1					4	2	3	5	7	8		9	11		10		

		P	W	D	L	F	A	W	D	L	F	A	Pts
1	Brentford	42	15	4	2	45	19	11	6	4	45	30	62
2	Exeter City	42	17	2	2	57	13	7	8	6	31	35	58
3	Norwich City	42	16	3	2	49	17	6	10	5	39	38	57
4	Reading	42	14	5	2	68	30	5	8	8	35	41	51
5	Crystal Palace	42	14	4	3	51	21	5	4	12	27	43	46
6	Coventry City	42	16	1	4	75	24	3	5	13	51	53	44
7	Gillingham	42	14	4	3	54	24	4	4	13	18	37	44
8	Northampton Town	42	16	5	0	54	11	2	3	16	22	55	44
9	Bristol Rovers	42	13	5	3	38	22	2	9	10	23	34	44
10	Torquay United	42	12	7	2	51	26	4	5	12	21	41	44
11	Watford	42	11	8	2	37	22	5	4	12	29	41	44
12	Brighton & Hove A.	42	13	3	5	42	20	4	5	12	24	45	42
13	Southend United	42	11	5	5	39	27	4	6	11	26	55	41
14	LUTON TOWN	42	12	8	1	60	32	1	5	15	18	46	39
15	Bristol City	42	11	5	5	59	37	1	8	12	24	53	37
16	Queen's Park Rgs.	42	9	8	4	48	32	4	3	14	24	55	37
17	Aldershot	42	11	6	4	37	21	2	4	15	24	51	36
18	Bournemouth	42	10	7	4	44	27	2	5	14	16	54	36
19	Cardiff City	42	12	4	5	48	30	0	3	18	21	69	31
20	Clapton Orient	42	7	8	6	39	35	1	5	15	20	58	29
21	Newport County	42	9	4	8	42	42	2	3	16	19	63	29
22	Swindon Town	42	7	9	5	36	29	2	2	17	24	76	29

1933/34   6th in Division 3 South

#		Date	Opponent	Score	Scorers	Att	Anderson SJ	Bell S	Bell T	Brown WI	Fraser CR	Gibson JR	Harford GB	Holbeach F	Hutchison D	Kean FW	Kingham HR	Kirkwood D	Kitchen H	Lawson H	Mackey TS	Martin GS	McGinnigle H	Mittel JL	Pearson GW	Pease WH	Reece HJ	Rennie A	Rennie J	Tait T
1	Aug	26	Northampton Town	3-2	Tait 3	16823					6	3				4	2					8	5	1	11	7		10		9
2		28	CHARLTON ATHLETIC	2-1	Rennie, Tait	11904					6					4	2				3	8	5	1	11	7		10		9
3	Sep	2	TORQUAY UNITED	10-2	Rennie 4,T Bell 2,Martin 2,Kean,Pease	10475			9		6					4	2				3	8	5	1	11	7		10		
4		4	Charlton Athletic	0-2		8089			9		6					4	2				3	8	5	1	11	7		10		
5		9	Queen's Park Rangers	1-2	Pease	10110					6				10	4	2				3	8	5	1	11	7		9		
6		13	Crystal Palace	2-2	Pease 2	9457			9		6					4	2				3	8	5	1	11	7		10		
7		16	NEWPORT COUNTY	1-1	T Bell	10072			9		6					4	2				3	8	5	1	11	7		10		
8		23	Norwich City	0-4		12599					6					4	2				3	8	5	1	11	7		10		9
9		30	BRISTOL CITY	3-0	T Bell 2, Martin	8831	11		9	4	6		1				2				3	8	5			7		10		
10	Oct	7	Clapton Orient	1-1	Martin	10182	11		9		6	3	1			4	2					5	8			7		10		
11		14	SWINDON TOWN	2-3	Anderson, Tait	7756	11				6	3	1			4	2					5	8			7		10		9
12		21	WATFORD	2-1	Anderson, Martin	10674	11				6		1			4	2				3	8	5			7		10		9
13		28	Reading	1-4	Kirkwood	8110					6		1			4	2	8			3	9	5		11	7		10		
14	Nov	4	COVENTRY CITY	0-1		7690					6		1			4	2			8	3		5		11	7		10		9
15		11	Southend United	1-0	Hutchison	5828	11		9		6		1		8	4	2				3	10	5			7				
16		18	BRISTOL ROVERS	2-2	T Bell, Anderson	6778	11		9		6		1		8	4	2				3	10	5							7
17	Dec	2	GILLINGHAM	4-2	Rennie 2, Anderson, McGinnigle	5447	11				6		1			4	2				3	8	5			7		10		9
18		9	Exeter City	2-4	Rennie 2	4257	11			4	6		1		10		2	7			3		5					9		8
19		16	CARDIFF CITY	3-1	McGinnigle, Rennie, Martin	5984				4	6		1		10		2					8	5		11	7	3	9		
20		23	Bournemouth	3-4	Pease, Martin, Pearson	4081							1		10	4	2				3	8	5		11	7		9	6	
21		25	Aldershot	0-0		4668				4			1		10		2				3	8	5		11	7		9	6	
22		26	ALDERSHOT	1-1	Rennie	8301							1		8	4	2				3		5		11	7		10	6	9
23		30	NORTHAMPTON T	3-1	Hutchison 2, Martin	7696			9				1	7	10	4	2				3	8	5				11		6	
24	Jan	6	Torquay United	1-0	Rennie	2548			9		6		1			4	2				3	8	5			7	11	10		
25		20	QUEEN'S PARK RANGERS	4-2	Martin, T Bell 2, Hutchison	8096			9		6		1		11	4	2				3	8	5			7		10		
26		27	Newport County	2-1	T Bell, Hutchison	5524			9		6		1		11	4	2				3	8	5			7		10		
27	Feb	3	NORWICH CITY	2-3	Pease 2	7651			9	6			1		11	4	2				3	8	5			7		10		
28		10	Bristol City	0-0		8697			9		6		1		11	4	2				3	8	5			7		10		
29		17	CLAPTON ORIENT	2-0	Martin, T Bell	7106			9		6		1		11	4	2				3	8	5			7		10		
30		24	Swindon Town	1-3	Hutchison	7689			9		6		1		11	4	2				3	8	5			7		10		
31	Mar	3	Watford	1-0	Pease	10204			9		6		1		11	4					2	8	5			7	3	10		
32		10	READING	3-1	Rennie, T Bell, Hutchison	7568			9		6		1		11	4					2	8	5			7	3	10		
33		17	Coventry City	2-2	Kean, Rennie	12455			9		6		1		11	4					2	8	5			7	3	10		
34		24	SOUTHEND UNITED	3-1	Rennie 2, Hutchison	6313			9		6		1		11	4					2	8	5			7	3	10		
35		30	Brighton & Hove Albion	1-1	Martin	10134			9		6		1		11	4					2	8	5			7	3	10		
36		31	Bristol Rovers	1-0	Hutchison	8234			9		6		1		11	4					2	8	5			7	3	10		
37	Apr	2	BRIGHTON & HOVE ALB	1-2	Rennie	10133			9		6		1	7	11	4					2	8	5				3	10		
38		7	CRYSTAL PALACE	2-1	Tait, T Bell	6841			9		6		1		11	4					2	8	5				3	10		7
39		14	Gillingham	1-1	Kitchen	4729	11		9		6		1		10	4			8		2		5				3			7
40		21	EXETER CITY	3-2	Anderson, Tait, Hutchison	5836	11		9	7	6		1		10	4					2		5				3			8
41		28	Cardiff City	4-0	Hutchison 2, Brown, Martin	3080			9	7	6		1		11	4					2	10	5				3			8
42	May	5	BOURNEMOUTH	2-0	S Bell 2	5614		10	9	7	6		1		11	4					2		5				3			8
			Apps				10	1	28	8	37	3	34	2	27	38	29	2	1	1	41	36	40	8	14	33	15	35	4	15
			Goals				5	2	12	1					13	2		1	1			12	2		1	8		16		7

F.A. Cup

		Date	Opponent	Score	Scorers	Att	Bell T	Fraser CR	Harford GB	Hutchison D	Kean FW	Kingham HR	Mackey TS	Martin GS	McGinnigle H	Pease WH	Rennie A
R3	Jan	13	ARSENAL	0-1		18641	9	6	1	11	4	2	3	8	5	7	10

Division 3 (South) Cup

		Date	Opponent	Score	Scorers	Bell T	Brown WI	Fraser CR	Harford GB	Hutchison D	Kean FW	Kingham HR	Mackey TS	Martin GS	McGinnigle H	Rennie A
R2	Feb	28	Aldershot	3-4	Bell T 2, Martin	9	7	6	1	11	4	2	3	8	5	10

		P	W	D	L	F	A	W	D	L	F	A	Pts
1	Norwich City	42	16	4	1	55	19	9	7	5	33	30	61
2	Coventry City	42	16	3	2	70	22	5	9	7	30	32	54
3	Reading	42	17	4	0	60	13	4	8	9	22	37	54
4	Queen's Park Rgs.	42	17	2	2	42	12	7	4	10	28	39	54
5	Charlton Athletic	42	14	5	2	53	27	8	3	10	30	29	52
6	LUTON TOWN	42	14	3	4	55	28	7	7	7	28	33	52
7	Bristol Rovers	42	14	4	3	49	21	6	7	8	28	26	51
8	Swindon Town	42	13	5	3	42	25	4	6	11	22	43	45
9	Exeter City	42	12	5	4	43	19	4	6	11	25	38	43
10	Brighton & Hove A.	42	12	7	2	47	18	3	6	12	21	42	43
11	Clapton Orient	42	14	4	3	60	25	2	6	13	15	44	42
12	Crystal Palace	42	11	6	4	40	25	5	3	13	31	42	41
13	Northampton Town	42	10	6	5	45	32	4	6	11	26	46	40
14	Aldershot	42	8	6	7	28	27	5	6	10	24	44	38
15	Watford	42	12	4	5	43	16	3	3	15	28	47	37
16	Southend United	42	9	6	6	32	27	3	4	14	19	47	34
17	Gillingham	42	8	8	5	49	41	3	3	15	26	55	33
18	Newport County	42	6	9	6	25	23	2	8	11	24	47	33
19	Bristol City	42	7	8	6	33	22	3	5	13	25	63	33
20	Torquay United	42	10	4	7	32	28	3	3	15	21	65	33
21	Bournemouth	42	7	7	7	41	37	2	2	17	19	65	27
22	Cardiff City	42	6	4	11	32	43	3	2	16	25	62	24

1934/35   4th in Division 3 South

No	Date	Opponent	Score	Scorers	Att	Ball JT	Beck W	Bell S	Bell T	Brown WI	Coen JL	Colquhoun DM	Cook C	Crompton W	Fraser CR	Hutchison D	Kean FW	Kidd GI	Kingham HR	Mackey TS	Martin GS	McGinnigle H	Payne J	Pready CJF	Reece HJ	Rennie A	Roberts F	Russell CJ	Smith TS	Stephenson GH	Thayne W
1	Aug 25	SOUTHEND UNITED	1-1	S Bell	12255			7	9						6		4			2	8	5			1	3			11	10	
2	27	Cardiff City	0-1		18608			7	9						6		4			2	8	5			1	3			11	10	
3	Sep 1	Bristol Rovers	1-1	S Bell	11980			7					9		6		4			2	8	5			1	3			11	10	
4	3	CARDIFF CITY	4-0	Martin 2, S Bell, Cook	9392			7					9		6		4			2	8	5			1	3			11	10	
5	8	CHARLTON ATHLETIC	1-2	Russell	11226			7					9		6		4		2	3	8	5			1				11	10	
6	15	Crystal Palace	1-2	S Bell	13416			7			1		9		6		4			2	8	5				3	10		11		
7	22	QUEEN'S PARK RANGERS	1-1	Rennie	7233			7			1				6	11	4			2	8	5				3	10		9		
8	29	Torquay United	2-6	T Bell, Stephenson	3612		6	8	9	4	1							7		2						3			11	10	5
9	Oct 6	SWINDON TOWN	2-0	S Bell, Stephenson	7801			7	9	4	1				6					2	8					3			11	10	5
10	13	Aldershot	1-0	Stephenson	4931			7	9	4	1				6					2	8					3			11	10	5
11	20	Exeter City	2-1	T Bell 2	4040			7	9	4	1				6					2	8					3			11	10	5
12	27	BRISTOL CITY	1-1		8956	9		8		4	1				6					2	7					3			11	10	5
13	Nov 3	Bournemouth	3-1	Martin, Stephenson, Brown	5939	9		8		4	1				6					2	7					3			11	10	5
14	10	WATFORD	2-2	Stephenson, Ball	11260	9		8		4	1				6					2	7					3			11	10	5
15	17	Clapton Orient	1-1	S Bell	8455	9		8		4	1				6					3	7				2		10		11		5
16	24	MILLWALL	2-1	Martin, Ball	8936	9		8		4	1				6						7				2		10	3	11		5
17	Dec 1	Reading	0-1		9513	9				4	1			7	6					3	8				2		10		11		5
18	15	Millwall	4-1	Ball 2, Roberts, S Bell	5279	9		8		4	1			7	6					3							10	2	11		5
19	22	COVENTRY CITY	4-0	Ball 2, Crompton, S Bell	9231	9		8		4	1			7	6					3							10	2	11		5
20	25	BRIGHTON & HOVE ALB	4-0	S Bell 3, Ball	12964	9		8		4	1			7	6					3	5						10	2	11		
21	26	Brighton & Hove Albion	1-4	Ball	13577	9	6	8		4	1			7						3	5						10	2	11		
22	29	Southend United	3-3	S Bell, Crompton, Roberts	5394	9		8		4	1			7						3	5	6					10	2	11		
23	Jan 5	BRISTOL ROVERS	6-2	S Bell 3, Ball 2, Roberts	8574	9		8		4	1			7	6					3							10	2	11		5
24	19	Charlton Athletic	2-4	Ball, Roberts	12222	9		8		4	1			7	6			2			5						10	3	11		
25	30	CRYSTAL PALACE	2-2	S Bell, Wilde (og)	3410	9		8		4	1			7	6			2	3								10		11		5
26	Feb 2	Queen's Park Rangers	0-3		6201	9		8		4	1			7	6			2	3								10		11		5
27	9	TORQUAY UNITED	3-1	Stephenson, Crompton, Ball	6886	9		8		4	1			7						3		6					10	2	11		5
28	16	Swindon Town	1-0	S Bell	5428	9		8		4	1			7	6					3							10	2	11		5
29	23	ALDERSHOT	6-1	Roberts, S Bell, Ball 2, Stephenson 2	6536	9		8		4	1			7	6												10	3	11		5
30	Mar 2	EXETER CITY	4-0	Ball 3, Stephenson	8383	9		8		4	1			7						3	5						10	2		11	6
31	9	Bristol City	2-0	Ball, Roberts	6749	9					1	4		7					2	3	8						10		6	11	5
32	16	BOURNEMOUTH	4-0	Roberts 2, Crompton, Ball	8497	9					1	4		7					2	3	8						10		6	11	5
33	23	Watford	2-2	Ball 2	10828	9					1	4		7					2	3	8						10		6	11	5
34	30	CLAPTON ORIENT	3-0	Ball 2, Stephenson	7966	9					1	4		7					2	3	8						10		6	11	5
35	Apr 6	Gillingham	1-1	Ball	4139	9					1	4		7					2	3	8						10		6	11	5
36	13	READING	2-4	Crompton, Stephenson	11960	9					1	4		7					2	3	8						10		6	11	5
37	19	Newport County	4-2	Martin, Crompton, Stephenson, Ball	4052	9					1	4		7					2		8					3	10		6	11	5
38	20	Northampton Town		7240	9					1	4		7					2		8					3	10		6	11	5
39	22	NEWPORT COUNTY	4-1	Crompton 3, Martin	8759	9					1	4		7					2		8					3	10		6	11	5
40	23	NORTHAMPTON T	2-2	Ball 2	8168	9					1	4		7				6	2		8					3	10			11	5
41	May 1	GILLINGHAM	2-2	Ball, Martin	3996	9					1	4		7					2		8	5					10	3		11	
42	4	Coventry City	0-1		6843	9					1	4		7					2		8	5					10	3		11	
		Apps				31	2	29	6	23	37	12	4	26	25	2	7	2		33	28	14	2	5	14	11	25	8	23	40	29
		Goals				30		18	3	1			1	9							7					1	8	1		12	

Played at 6 in game 41: JT Taylor

One own goal

F.A. Cup

Rd	Date	Opponent	Score	Scorers	Att	Ball JT	Beck W	Bell S	Bell T	Brown WI	Coen JL	Colquhoun DM	Cook C	Crompton W	Fraser CR	Hutchison D	Kean FW	Kidd GI	Kingham HR	Mackey TS	Martin GS	McGinnigle H	Payne J	Pready CJF	Reece HJ	Rennie A	Roberts F	Russell CJ	Smith TS	Stephenson GH	Thayne W
R3	Jan 12	Chelsea	1-1	Bell S	46492	9		8		4	1			7	6					3							10	2	11		5
rep	Jan 16	CHELSEA	2-0	Ball, Roberts	23041	9		8		4	1			7	6							5			3		10	2	11		
R4	Jan 26	Burnley	1-3	Stephenson	26727	9		8		4	1			7	6					3							10	2	11		5

Division 3 (South) Cup

Rd	Date	Opponent	Score	Scorers	Ball JT	Beck W	Bell S	Bell T	Brown WI	Coen JL	Colquhoun DM	Cook C	Crompton W	Fraser CR	Hutchison D	Kean FW	Kidd GI	Kingham HR	Mackey TS	Martin GS	McGinnigle H	Payne J	Pready CJF	Reece HJ	Rennie A	Roberts F	Russell CJ	Smith TS	Stephenson GH	Thayne W
R1	Sep 26	Gillingham	3-1	Bell S, Pease, one unknown		6	8	9	4	1									3						2			11	10	5
R2	Oct 18	Queen's Park Rangers	1-2	Bell S			7	9	4	1				6				2	3	8				10				11		5

Played at 7 in R1: WH Pease

		P	W	D	L	F	A	W	D	L	F	A	Pts
1	Charlton Athletic	42	17	2	2	62	20	10	5	6	41	32	61
2	Reading	42	16	5	0	59	23	5	6	10	30	42	53
3	Coventry City	42	14	5	2	56	14	7	4	10	30	36	51
4	LUTON TOWN	42	12	7	2	60	23	7	6	9	32	37	50
5	Crystal Palace	42	15	3	3	51	14	4	7	10	35	50	48
6	Watford	42	14	2	5	53	19	5	7	9	23	30	47
7	Northampton Town	42	14	4	3	40	21	5	4	12	25	46	46
8	Bristol Rovers	42	14	6	1	54	27	3	4	14	19	50	44
9	Brighton & Hove A.	42	15	4	2	51	16	2	5	14	18	46	43
10	Torquay United	42	15	2	4	60	22	3	4	14	21	53	42
11	Exeter City	42	11	5	5	48	29	5	4	12	22	46	41
12	Millwall	42	11	4	6	33	26	6	3	12	24	36	41
13	Queen's Park Rgs.	42	14	6	1	49	22	2	3	16	14	50	41
14	Clapton Orient	42	13	3	5	47	21	2	7	12	18	44	40
15	Bristol City	42	14	3	4	37	18	1	6	14	15	50	39
16	Swindon Town	42	11	7	3	46	22	2	5	14	22	56	38
17	Bournemouth	42	10	5	6	36	26	5	2	14	18	45	37
18	Aldershot	42	12	6	3	35	20	1	4	16	15	55	36
19	Cardiff City	42	11	6	4	42	27	2	3	16	20	55	35
20	Gillingham	42	10	7	4	36	25	1	6	14	19	50	35
21	Southend United	42	10	4	7	40	29	1	5	15	25	49	31
22	Newport County	42	7	4	10	36	40	3	1	17	18	72	25

1935/36 Second in Division 3 South

Player columns (left to right): Ball JT, Beresford FE, Booton H, Boyd WG, Coen JL, Colquhoun DM, Cook C, Crompton W, Crook MS, Dolman HW, Fellowes WJ, Finlayson J, Godfrey W, Gooney WH, Hodge J, Kidd GI, Kingham HR, Mackey TS, Martin GS, Nelson JH, Payne J, Rich LT, Roberts F, Smith TS, Stephenson GH, Turner GW

League — fixtures and results

#	Date		Opponent	Score	Scorers	Att
1	Aug	31	Clapton Orient	0-3		12494
2	Sep	4	Bournemouth	1-2	Crompton	9018
3		7	SOUTHEND UNITED	1-2	Ball	14379
4		9	BOURNEMOUTH	0-0		9350
5		14	Northampton Town	0-0		13595
6		16	QUEEN'S PARK RANGERS	2-0	Beresford, Stephenson	8220
7		21	CRYSTAL PALACE	6-0	Turner, Stephenson, Crook, Cook3	13206
8		28	Reading	1-2	Ball	11254
9	Oct	5	CARDIFF CITY	2-2	Ball, Finlayson	12288
10		12	Gillingham	1-0	Roberts	8252
11		19	BRIGHTON & HOVE ALB	2-1	Fellowes, Martin	10679
12		26	Exeter City	2-1	Ball, Crompton	4902
13	Nov	2	NEWPORT COUNTY	7-0	Crompton 2, Roberts 2, Ball 2, Finlayson	10085
14		9	Watford	3-1	Crompton, Roberts, Ball	14906
15		16	SWINDON TOWN	2-1	Finlayson, Stephenson	12213
16		23	Aldershot	1-0	Stephenson	5019
17	Dec	7	Millwall	0-0		3449
18		14	BRISTOL CITY	1-0	Roberts (og)	11134
19		25	Notts County	3-0	Boyd, Martin, Stephenson	12186
20		26	NOTTS COUNTY	1-0	Roberts	18100
21		28	CLAPTON ORIENT	5-3	Boyd 5	13545
22	Jan	4	Southend United	1-0	Boyd	8585
23		18	NORTHAMPTON T	3-3	Boyd, Martin, Roberts	12781
24		29	Crystal Palace	1-5	Ball	6804
25	Feb	1	READING	2-1	Crompton, Roberts	15852
26		8	Cardiff City	3-2	Stephenson, Boyd 2	12142
27		15	GILLINGHAM	1-2	Martin	12276
28		22	Brighton & Hove Albion	1-1	Martin	10111
29		29	WATFORD	2-1	Stephenson 2	13226
30	Mar	7	Bristol City	2-1	Rich, Stephenson	8173
31		14	EXETER CITY	3-1	Rich 2, Stephenson	12710
32		21	Swindon Town	0-3		7839
33		25	TORQUAY UNITED	1-0	Martin	9693
34		28	ALDERSHOT	2-2	Roberts, Boyd	12777
35	Apr	4	Torquay United	1-2	Cook	3675
36		10	Bristol Rovers	2-2	Martin, Rich	16030
37		11	MILLWALL	0-0		12527
38		13	BRISTOL ROVERS	12-0	Payne 10, Roberts, Martin	14296
39		18	Newport County	2-0	Payne 2	6356
40		25	COVENTRY CITY	1-1	Payne	23559
41		27	Coventry City	0-0		42809
42	May	2	Queen's Park Rangers	0-0		17951

Player appearances (shirt numbers)

#	Ball	Bere	Boot	Boyd	Coen	Colq	Cook	Crmp	Crok	Dolm	Fell	Finl	Godf	Goon	Hodg	Kidd	King	Mack	Mart	Nels	Payn	Rich	Robe	Smit	Step	Turn
1	9	8			1	4		7								6	2	3		5			10		11	
2	9	8			1	4		7								6	2			5			10		11	
3	9				1			7			5	2				6				4			10		11	
4	9	8			1				7			4				6	2			5			10	3	11	
5	9	8			1				7			4				6	2			5			10	3	11	
6		8			1		9		7			4				6	2			5			10	3	11	
7					1	4	9		7							6	2			5			8	3	10	11
8	9	8			1				7		5	4					2						10	3	11	
9	9	8			1			7			5	4					2						10	3	11	
10	9				1			7			6	4						2	8	5			10	3	11	
11	9				1			7			6	4						2	8	5			10	3	11	
12	9				1			7			6	4						2	8	5			10	3	11	
13	9				1			7			6	4						2	8	5			10	3	11	
14	9				1			7			6	4						2	8	5			10	3	11	
15	9				1			7			6	4						2	8	5			10	3	11	
16	9				1			7			6	4						2	8	5			10	3	11	
17	9				1			7			6	4						2	8	5			10	3	11	
18					1			7			6	4						2	8	5			10	3	11	
19				9	1			7			6	4						2	8	5			10	3	11	
20		7		9	1						6	4						2	8	5			10	3	11	
21				9	1	4		7			6							2	8	5			10	3	11	
22				9	1			7			6	4						2	8	5			10	3	11	
23		7		9	1						6	4					2		8	5			10	3	11	
24	9				1			7			6	4						2	8	5			10	3	11	
25				9	1			7			6	4						2	8	5			10	3	11	
26		7		9	1						6	4						2	8	5			10	3	11	
27				9	1			7			6	4						2	8				10	3	11	
28		2	7	9	1						6	4							8	5			10	3	11	
29		2	7	9	1						6	4							8	5			10	3	11	
30	9	2			1						6	4							8	5		7	10	3	11	
31	9	2			1						6	4							8	5		7	10	3	11	
32	9	2			1						5	4	6						8			7	10	3	11	
33		2		9	1						6	4	7						8	5			10	3	11	
34		2		9	1						6	4	7							5			10	3	11	
35					1		9				6	4	7					2	8	5	11		10	3		
36					1		9				6	4						2	8	5		7	10	3	11	
37				9	1						6	4						2	8	5		7	10	3	11	
38					1					6		4						2	8	5	9	7	10	3	11	
39		7			1					6		4						2	8	5	9		10	3	11	
40					1					6		4		7				2	8	5	9		10	3	11	
41					1					6		4		7				2	8	5	9		10	3	11	
42		7			1					6		4						2		5	9		10	3	11	
Apps	19	12	7	13	36	4	4	21	5	6	31	33	5	4	4	7	9	25	31	37	9	9	39	39	40	4
Goals	9	1		11			4	6	1		1	3							8		13	3	9		10	1

Played at 8 in game 3: H Andrews. Played at 8 in games 34 and 42: FJ Sloan
Played at 9 in game 18: W Thayne
Played at 3 in games 2 and 3: AA Hubbard
Played at 6 in games 8 and 9, and at 5 in game 27: H McGinnigle

One own goal

F.A. Cup

	Date		Opponent	Score	Scorers	Att	Ball	Coen	Crmp	Fell	Finl	Mack	Mart	Nels	Robe	Smit	Step
R3	Jan	11	West Ham United	2-2	Ball, Roberts	42000	9	1	7	6	4	2	8	5	10	3	11
rep	Jan	15	WEST HAM UNITED	4-0	Ball, Crompton, Roberts, Stephenson	17527	9	1	7	6	4	2	8	5	10	3	11
R4	Jan	25	Manchester City	1-2	Martin	65978	9	1	7	6	4	2	8	5	10	3	11

Division 3 (South) Cup

	Date		Opponent	Score	Scorers	Att	Coen	Colq	Cook	Crmp	Kidd	King	Nels	Robe	Step	Turn
R1	Sep	25	Swindown Town	3-5	Stephenson 3	3057	1	4	9	7	6	2	5	8	10	11

Played at 3: AA Hubbard

League table

		P	W	D	L	F	A	W	D	L	F	A	Pts
1	Coventry City	42	19	1	1	75	12	5	8	8	27	33	57
2	LUTON TOWN	42	13	6	2	66	20	9	6	6	25	25	56
3	Reading	42	18	0	3	52	20	8	2	11	35	42	54
4	Queen's Park Rgs.	42	14	4	3	55	19	8	5	8	29	34	53
5	Watford	42	12	3	6	47	29	8	6	7	33	26	49
6	Crystal Palace	42	15	4	2	64	20	7	1	13	32	54	49
7	Brighton & Hove A.	42	13	4	4	48	25	6	4	12	22	38	44
8	Bournemouth	42	9	6	6	36	26	7	5	9	24	30	43
9	Notts County	42	10	5	6	40	25	5	7	9	20	32	42
10	Torquay United	42	14	4	3	41	27	2	5	14	21	35	41
11	Aldershot	42	9	6	6	29	21	5	6	10	24	40	40
12	Millwall	42	9	8	4	33	21	5	4	12	25	50	40
13	Bristol City	42	11	5	5	32	21	4	5	12	16	38	40
14	Clapton Orient	42	13	2	6	34	15	3	4	14	21	46	38
15	Northampton Town	42	12	5	4	38	24	3	3	15	24	66	38
16	Gillingham	42	9	5	7	34	25	4	4	12	32	52	37
17	Bristol Rovers	42	11	6	4	48	31	3	3	15	21	64	37
18	Southend United	42	8	7	6	38	21	5	3	13	23	41	36
19	Swindon Town	42	10	5	6	43	33	4	3	14	21	40	36
20	Cardiff City	42	11	5	5	37	23	2	5	14	23	50	36
21	Newport County	42	8	4	9	36	44	3	5	13	24	67	31
22	Exeter City	42	7	5	9	38	41	1	6	14	21	52	27

1936/37 — Champions of Division 3 South: Promoted

Appearance numbers shown are the shirt (position) numbers worn by each player. Player columns (left to right): Ball JT, Coen JL, Dawes AG, Dolman HW, Fellowes WJ, Finlayson J, Godfrey W, Hancock E, Hodge J, Hubbard AA, King TP, Lutterloch BR, Mackey TS, Martin GS, McGinnigle H, Mills HM, Nelson JH, Parris JE, Payne J, Rich LT, Roberts F, Sloan FJ, Smith TS, Stephenson GH, Stevens RF.

#	Date	Opponent	Result	Scorers	Att	Ball JT	Coen JL	Dawes AG	Dolman HW	Fellowes WJ	Finlayson J	Godfrey W	Hancock E	Hodge J	Hubbard AA	King TP	Lutterloch BR	Mackey TS	Martin GS	McGinnigle H	Mills HM	Nelson JH	Parris JE	Payne J	Rich LT	Roberts F	Sloan FJ	Smith TS	Stephenson GH	Stevens RF
1	Aug 29	SOUTHEND UNITED	1-0	Payne	14461				1		4	6						2		9		5		8		10		3	11	
2	Aug 31	Walsall	1-0	Stephenson	9025				1	6	4			7			9	2				5		8		10		3	11	
3	Sep 5	Cardiff City	0-3		17915				1	6	4			7			9	2				5		8		10		3	11	
4	Sep 7	WALSALL	2-0	Ball, Payne	11395	9			1	6	4			7				2				5		8		10		3	11	
5	Sep 12	CRYSTAL PALACE	5-2	Fellowes, Ball, Payne 3	14187	9			1	6	4			7				2				5		8		10		3	11	
6	Sep 16	Torquay United	2-2	Stephenson, Payne	5075	9			1	6	4			7				2				5		8		10		3	11	
7	Sep 19	Exeter City	4-2	Payne 2, Ball, Stephenson	6550	9			1	6	4			7				2				5		8		10		3	11	
8	Sep 26	READING	4-0	Payne 3, Stephenson	16717	9			1	6	4			7				2				5		8		10		3	11	
9	Oct 3	Queen's Park Rangers	1-2	Payne	20437	9			1	6	4			7				2				5		8		10		3	11	
10	Oct 10	BRISTOL CITY	4-0	Stephenson, Ball 2, Hodge	13616	9			1	6	4			7				2				5		8		10		3	11	
11	Oct 17	WATFORD	4-1	Payne 3, Ball	20955	9			1	6	4			7				2				5		8		10		3	11	
12	Oct 24	Brighton & Hove Albion	1-2	Payne	14652	9			1	6	4			7				2				5		8		10		3	11	
13	Oct 31	BOURNEMOUTH	1-0	Payne	11581	9			1	6	4			7				2				5		8		10		3	11	
14	Nov 7	Northampton Town	1-3	Payne	18885	9			1	6	4			7				2				5		8		10		3	11	
15	Nov 14	BRISTOL ROVERS	2-0	Payne, Ball	13138	9			1	6	4			7				2				5		8		10		3	11	
16	Nov 21	Millwall	2-0	Payne, Roberts	32629	9			1	6	4							2				5		8	7	10		3	11	
17	Dec 5	Aldershot	3-2	Rich, Payne, Ball	3884	9			1	6	4							2				5		8	7	10		3	11	
18	Dec 19	Newport County	1-2	Stephenson	7654	9			1	6	4							2				5		8	7	10		3	11	
19	Dec 25	NOTTS COUNTY	2-1	Roberts, Payne	17569			8	1	6	4							2				5		9	7	10		3	11	
20	Dec 26	Southend United	0-3		11869			8	1	6	4							2				5		9	7	10		3		11
21	Dec 28	Notts County	1-2	Rich	16987			8	1	6	4							2				5		9	7	10		3	11	
22	Jan 2	CARDIFF CITY	8-1	Payne 4, Dawes, Stephenson 3	12368			8	1	6	4		7					2				5		9		10		3	11	
23	Jan 9	Crystal Palace	4-0	Payne 2, Dawes, Roberts	15211			8	1	6	4		7					2				5		9		10		3	11	
24	Jan 23	EXETER CITY	2-2	Payne, Stephenson	10208			8	1	6	4		7					2				5		9		10		3	11	
25	Feb 6	QUEEN'S PARK RANGERS	0-1		13767			8	1	6	4		7					2				5		9		10		3	11	
26	Feb 10	Reading	2-2	Payne 2	8210			8	1	6	4		7					2				5		9		10		3	11	
27	Feb 13	Bristol City	3-2	Dawes, Payne 2	17193			8	1	6	4		7					2				5		9		10		3	11	
28	Feb 20	Watford	3-1	Dawes, Payne, Roberts	27632			8	1	6	4		7					2				5		9		10		3	11	
29	Feb 27	BRIGHTON & HOVE ALB	2-1	Payne, Stephenson	19488			8	1	6	4		7					2				5		9		10		3	11	
30	Mar 6	Bournemouth	1-2	Stephenson	9432			8	1	6	4		7					2				5		9		10		3	11	
31	Mar 13	NORTHAMPTON T	3-2	Payne 2, Roberts	19579		1	8		6	4		7					2				5		9		10		3	11	
32	Mar 20	Bristol Rovers	0-4		13517		1	8		6	4		7					2				5		9		10		3	11	
33	Mar 26	Clapton Orient	2-0	Payne, Stephenson	17430		1	8		6	4		7					2				5		9		10		3	11	
34	Mar 27	MILLWALL	5-0	*see below	18523		1	8		6	4		7					2				5		9		10		3	11	
35	Mar 29	CLAPTON ORIENT	2-0	Payne, Roberts	18279		1	8		6	4		7					2				5		9		10		3	11	
36	Apr 3	Swindon Town	2-2	Payne, Stephenson	10432		1	8		6	4		7					2				5		9		10		3	11	
37	Apr 7	GILLINGHAM	5-2	Payne 4, Finlayson	13386		1	8		6	4		7					2				5		9		10		3	11	
38	Apr 10	ALDERSHOT	5-2	Dawes 2, Payne 2, Roberts	15505		1	8		6	4		7					2				5		9		10		3	11	
39	Apr 17	Gillingham	0-1		7327		1	8		6	4		7					2				5		9		10		3	11	
40	Apr 21	SWINDON TOWN	5-1	Payne 3, Dawes, Stephenson	11668		1	8		6	4		7					2				5		9		10		3	11	
41	Apr 24	NEWPORT COUNTY	5-0	Payne 3, Stephenson, Dawes	14469		1	8		6	4		7					2				5		9		10		3	11	
42	May 1	TORQUAY UNITED	2-0	Payne 2	20755		1	8		6	4		7					2				5		9		10		3	11	
		Apps				15	12	21	30	41	40	1	18	16	2	11	2	29	3	1	2	41	2	39	10	42	2	42	37	2
		Goals				8		8		1	2		1	1										55	2	8			17	

Scorers in game 34: Hancock, Payne, Roberts, Stephenson, Finlayson
Played at 7 in game 1: W Crompton

F.A. Cup

Rd	Date	Opponent	Result	Scorers	Att	Dolman HW	Fellowes WJ	Finlayson J	Hancock E	Mackey TS	Dawes AG	Nelson JH	Payne J	Rich LT	Roberts F	Sloan FJ	Smith TS	Stephenson GH
R3	Jan 16	BLACKPOOL	3-3	Payne 2, Stephenson	13892	1	6	4	7	2	8	5	9		10		3	11
rep	Jan 20	Blackpool	2-1	Sloan, Roberts	20000	1	6	4	7	2	8	5	9		10	3		11
R4	Jan 30	SUNDERLAND	2-2	Roberts 2	20134	1	6	4	7	2	8	5	9		10		3	11
rep	Feb 3	Sunderland	1-3	Payne	53235	1	6	4		2	8	5	9	7	10		3	11

Division 3 (South) Cup

Rd	Date	Opponent	Result	Scorers	Att	Ball JT	Coen JL	Dolman HW	Fellowes WJ	Finlayson J	Hodge J	King TP	Mackey TS	Nelson JH	Parris JE	Roberts F	Smith TS	Stephenson GH	Stevens RF
R1	Sep 30	BOURNEMOUTH	3-1	Beresford, Roberts, Stephenson	2527	9		1	6	4	7	3	2	5		10		11	
R2	Oct 28	ALDERSHOT	1-0	Stephenson		9		1	6	4	7			5		10	3	11	
R3	Nov 11	NOTTS COUNTY	2-4	Beresford, Stephens	1500				6	4	7			5	8				11

FE Beresford played in all three games, at 8 (R1, R2) and 10 (R3)
Played at 2 in R2 and R3: H Booton. Played at 3 in R3: HR Kingham.

Final Division 3 (South) Table

		P	W	D	L	F	A	W	D	L	F	A	Pts
1	LUTON TOWN	42	19	1	1	69	16	8	3	10	34	37	58
2	Notts County	42	15	3	3	44	23	8	7	6	30	29	56
3	Brighton & Hove A.	42	15	5	1	49	16	9	0	12	25	27	53
4	Watford	42	14	4	3	53	21	5	7	9	32	39	49
5	Reading	42	14	5	2	53	23	5	6	10	23	37	49
6	Bournemouth	42	17	3	1	45	20	3	6	12	20	39	49
7	Northampton Town	42	15	4	2	56	22	5	2	14	29	46	46
8	Millwall	42	12	4	5	43	24	6	6	9	21	30	46
9	Queen's Park Rgs.	42	12	2	7	51	24	6	7	8	22	28	45
10	Southend United	42	10	8	3	49	23	7	3	11	29	44	45
11	Gillingham	42	14	5	2	36	18	4	3	14	16	48	44
12	Clapton Orient	42	10	8	3	29	17	4	7	10	23	39	43
13	Swindon Town	42	12	4	5	52	24	2	7	12	23	49	39
14	Crystal Palace	42	11	7	3	45	20	2	5	14	17	41	38
15	Bristol Rovers	42	14	3	4	49	20	2	1	18	22	60	36
16	Bristol City	42	13	3	5	42	20	2	3	16	16	50	36
17	Walsall	42	11	3	7	38	34	2	7	12	25	51	36
18	Cardiff City	42	10	5	6	35	24	4	2	15	19	63	35
19	Newport County	42	7	7	7	37	28	5	3	13	30	70	34
20	Torquay United	42	9	5	7	42	32	2	5	14	15	48	32
21	Exeter City	42	9	5	7	36	37	1	7	13	23	51	32
22	Aldershot	42	5	6	10	29	29	2	3	16	21	60	23

1937/38 12th in Division Two

League — Division Two

No	Date		Opponent	Score	Scorers	Att.
1	Aug	28	Stockport County	1-2	Dawes	19077
2	Sep	1	ASTON VILLA	3-2	Dawes, Payne, Hancock	25349
3		4	MANCHESTER UNITED	1-0	Dawes	20610
4		6	Aston Villa	1-4	Stephenson	30439
5		11	Sheffield United	0-2		20283
6		15	Newcastle United	3-1	Payne, Stevens, Griffiths	17622
7		18	TOTTENHAM HOTSPUR	2-4	Redfern 2	23788
8		25	Burnley	2-3	Payne 2	14073
9	Oct	2	BURY	0-1		17650
10		9	Coventry City	1-2	Roberts	30549
11		16	Bradford Park Avenue	1-1	Dawes	15397
12		23	WEST HAM UNITED	2-2	Dawes, Vinall	17757
13		30	Southampton	6-3	Parris, Ferguson, Vinall 2, Roberts 2	20544
14	Nov	6	BLACKBURN ROVERS	4-1	Ferguson 2, Parris, Dawes (p)	16776
15		13	Sheffield Wednesday	0-4		16815
16		20	CHESTERFIELD	1-1	Fellowes	17088
17		27	Plymouth Argyle	4-2	Roberts 2, Payne, Vinall	18969
18	Dec	4	FULHAM	4-0	Payne 2, Dawes, Vinall	13529
19		11	Swansea Town	1-1	Payne	7454
20		18	Norwich City	1-1	Vinall	14492
21		25	BARNSLEY	4-0	Roberts 2, Dawes 2	15829
22		27	Barnsley	1-3	Roberts	8242
23	Jan	1	STOCKPORT COUNTY	6-4	Vinall 2, Dawes 2, Stephenson, Roberts	14138
24		15	Manchester United	2-4	Ferguson, Redfern	16845
25		29	Tottenham Hotspur	0-3		29806
26	Feb	2	SHEFFIELD UNITED	2-3	Vinall, Payne	8414
27		5	BURNLEY	3-1	Stephenson, Mackey 2	14957
28		16	Bury	4-3	Payne 3, Redfern	4689
29		19	COVENTRY CITY	1-4	Payne (p)	17188
30		26	BRADFORD PARK AVE.	4-2	Vinall 2, Payne 2 (1p)	14494
31	Mar	5	West Ham United	0-0		22955
32		12	SOUTHAMPTON	1-3	Ferguson	14428
33		19	Blackburn Rovers	2-2	Hancock, Stephenson	11957
34		26	SHEFFIELD WEDNESDAY	2-2	Roberts, Connelly	13216
35	Apr	2	Chesterfield	2-5	Stephenson, Ferguson	9212
36		9	PLYMOUTH ARGYLE	1-1	Ferguson	11516
37		15	Nottingham Forest	0-1		17644
38		16	Fulham	1-4	Smith	17226
39		18	NOTTM. FOREST	2-2	Vinall, Finlayson	13561
40		23	SWANSEA TOWN	5-1	Stephenson, Connelly 2, Ferguson 2	12433
41		30	Norwich City	4-0	Roberts 2, Finlayson, Vinall	10071
42	May	7	NEWCASTLE UNITED	4-1	Redfern 2, Finlayson, Stephenson	15344

Played at 5 in game 26: G Dreyer
Played at 2 in game 37: J Strathie

Player appearances (shirt numbers)

No	Carte R	Coen JL	Connelly E	Dawes AG	Dolman HW	Fellowes WJ	Ferguson C	Finlayson J	Griffiths EO	Hancock E	Hogg F	King TP	Lewis J	Loughran JL	Lutterloch BR	Mackey TS	Nelson JH	Parris JE	Payne J	Redfern WJ	Roberts F	Smith TS	Stephenson GH	Stevens RF	Vinall EJ
1		1		9		6	4			8		2					5	7			10	3	11		
2		1		8		6	4			7		2					5		9		10	3	11		
3		1		8		6	4			7		2					5		9		10	3	11		
4		1		8		6	4			7		2					5		9		10	3	11		
5		1		8		6	4			7		2					5		9		10	3	11		
6		1		8		6	4		7	10		2					5		9			3		11	
7		1				6	4		7	10		2					5		9	8		3		11	
8		1				6	4		7	10		2					5		9	8		3		11	
9		1				6			7	10		2		4			5		9	8		3	11		
10		1		8		6	4		7			2					5		9		10	3	11		
11				8	1		4	7				2		6			5				10	3	11		9
12				8	1	5	4	7						6	2						10	3	11		9
13			8		1	6	4	7							2		5	11			10	3			9
14				8	1	6	4	7							2		5	11			10	3			9
15			8		1	6	4	7							2		5	11			10	3			9
16			8		1	6	4								2		5	11	9		10	3			7
17					1	6	4	7							2		5		8		10	3	11		9
18					1	6	4	7							2		5		8		10	3	11		9
19					1	6	4	7							2		5		8		10	3	11		9
20					1	6	4	7				2					5		8		10	3	11		9
21				8	1	6	4	7				2					5				10	3	11		9
22				8	1	6	4	7				2					5				10	3	11		9
23			8	8	1	6	4	7				2					5				10	3	11		9
24					1		4	7				2		6			5			8	10	3	11		9
25			8		1		4	7				2		6			5				10	3	11		9
26					1	6	4	7							2				8		10	3	11		9
27		1	8			6	4	7				2				9	5				10	3	11		
28	2	1		10		6	4	7								3	5		9	8			11		
29	2	1				6	4	7								3	5		9	8	10		11		
30		1				6	4	7				2		6		3	5		8		10		11		9
31		1				6	4	7				2	5	6		3			8		10		11		9
32		1				6	4	7				2	5	6		3			8		10		11		9
33		1	8			6	4		7			2					5				10	3	11		9
34		1	8			6	4		7			2					5				10	3	11		9
35		1	8			6	4	7				2					5				10	3	11		9
36	2	1	8			6	4	7									5				10	3	11		9
37	2	1	8			6	4	7									5				10	3	11		9
38	2	1	7			6								4	3		5				10	9	11		8
39		1	8			6	4	7	2								5				10	3	11		9
40		1	8			6	4	7	2								5				10	3	11		9
41		1	8			6	4	7	2								5				10	3	11		9
42		1				6	4	7	2								5			8	10	3	11		9
Apps	4	26	9	23	16	38	20	39	6	8	4	18	2	9	8	17	37	5	22	8	37	37	35	3	29
Goals			3	10	1	1	9	3	1	2						2		2	15	6	12	1	8	1	13

F.A. Cup

Rd	Date		Opponent	Score	Scorers	Att.	Coen JL	Connelly E	Fellowes WJ	Ferguson C	Finlayson J	Hancock E	Nelson JH	Payne J	Roberts F	Smith TS	Stephenson GH	Vinall EJ
R3	Jan	8	Scarborough	1-1	Ferguson	11162	1	8	6	7	4		5		10	3	11	9
rep	Jan	12	SCARBOROUGH	5-1	Vinall 2, Ferguson, Dawes, Stephenson	11750	1	8	6	7	4		5		10	3	11	9
R4	Jan	22	SWINDON TOWN	2-1	Ferguson, Stephenson	27546	1	8	6	7	4		5		10	3	11	9
R5	Feb	12	MANCHESTER CITY	1-3	Payne	21290	1		6	7	4	2	5	9	10	3	11	8

Division Two — Final Table

		P	W	D	L	F	A	W	D	L	F	A	Pts
1	Aston Villa	42	17	2	2	50	12	8	5	8	23	23	57
2	Manchester United	42	15	3	3	50	18	7	6	8	32	32	53
3	Sheffield United	42	15	4	2	46	19	7	5	9	27	37	53
4	Coventry City	42	12	5	4	31	15	8	7	6	35	30	52
5	Tottenham Hotspur	42	14	3	4	46	16	5	3	13	30	38	44
6	Burnley	42	15	4	2	35	11	2	6	13	19	43	44
7	Bradford Park Ave.	42	13	4	4	51	22	4	5	12	18	34	43
8	Fulham	42	10	7	4	44	23	6	4	11	17	34	43
9	West Ham United	42	13	5	3	34	16	1	9	11	19	36	42
10	Bury	42	12	3	6	43	26	6	2	13	20	34	41
11	Chesterfield	42	12	2	7	39	24	4	7	10	24	39	41
12	LUTON TOWN	42	10	6	5	53	36	5	4	12	36	50	40
13	Plymouth Argyle	42	10	7	4	40	30	4	5	12	17	35	40
14	Norwich City	42	11	5	5	35	28	3	6	12	21	47	39
15	Southampton	42	12	6	3	42	26	3	3	15	13	51	39
16	Blackburn Rovers	42	13	6	2	51	30	1	4	16	20	50	38
17	Sheffield Wed.	42	10	5	6	27	21	4	5	12	22	35	38
18	Swansea Town	42	12	6	3	31	21	1	6	14	14	52	38
18	Newcastle United	42	12	4	5	38	18	2	4	15	13	40	36
20	Nottingham Forest	42	12	3	6	29	21	2	5	14	18	39	36
21	Barnsley	42	7	11	3	30	20	4	3	14	20	44	36
22	Stockport County	42	8	6	7	24	24	3	3	15	19	46	31

1938/39   7th in Division Two

No	Date	Opponent	Score	Scorers	Att	Billington HJR	Burgess WW	Carroll JT	Carte R	Clark C	Coen JL	Connelly E	Dolman HW	Dreyer G	Dunsmore TH	Ferguson C	Finlayson J	King TP	Loughran JL	Mayberry S	Nelson JH	Redfern WJ	Roberts F	Smith TS	Stephenson GH	Stevens RF	Strathie J	Vinall EJ
1	Aug 27	West Bromwich Albion	0-3		24377			7				8	1		3		4		6		5		10	2	11			9
2	31	NEWCASTLE UNITED	2-1	Stephenson, Nelson	17689							8	1		3	7	4		6		5		10	2	11			9
3	Sep 3	NORWICH CITY	2-1	Vinall (p), Ferguson	16547							8	1		3	7	4		6		5		10	2	11			9
4	5	Coventry City	0-1		19844				2				1			7	4		6		5	8	10	3	11			9
5	10	Manchester City	2-1	Connelly, Vinall	31316				2			8	1			7	4		6		5		10	3	11			9
6	17	Plymouth Argyle	1-4	Connelly	15083							8	1		3	7	4		6		5		10	2	11			9
7	24	SHEFFIELD UNITED	2-0	Vinall, Connelly	17436							8	1		3	7	4		6		5		10	2	11			9
8	Oct 1	Burnley	2-3	Vinall 2	11699							8	1		3	7	4		6		5		10	2	11			9
9	8	TOTTENHAM HOTSPUR	0-0		21061							8	1		3	7	4		6		5		10	2	11			9
10	15	BRADFORD PARK AVE.	2-2	Connelly 2	14955							8	1		3	7	4		6		5		10	2	11			9
11	22	Swansea Town	3-2	Clark 2, Connelly	8658					7	1	10			3		4		6		5	8	11	2				9
12	29	BLACKBURN ROVERS	1-1	Clark	16819					7	1	10			3		4		6		5	8		2	11			9
13	Nov 5	Tranmere Rovers	3-2	Billington 2, Redfern	11409	9				7	1	10			3		4		6		5	8		2	11			
14	12	WEST HAM UNITED	1-2	Stephenson	18331	9				7	1	10			3		4		6		5	8		2	11			
15	19	Bury	5-2	Billington 2, Stephenson 2, Redfern	8658	9				7	1	10			3		4		6		5	8		2	11			
16	26	SHEFFIELD WEDNESDAY	1-5	Billington	15936	9				7	1	10			3		4		6		5	8		2	11			
17	Dec 3	Fulham	1-2	Redfern	19443	9				7	1	10			3		4	2			5	8	6			11		
18	10	CHESTERFIELD	5-0	Billington 4, Stephenson	12744	9				7	1	10			3		4	2			5	8	6		11			
19	17	Millwall	1-2	Billington	19733	9				7	1	10			3		4	2			5	8	6		11			
20	24	WEST BROMWICH ALB.	3-1	Redfern 2, Stephenson	8887	9				7	1	10		5	3		4	2				8	6		11			
21	26	Nottingham Forest	4-2	Billington, Connelly, Clark, Redfern	12688	9				7	1	10		5	3		4	2				8	6		11			
22	27	NOTTM. FOREST	1-0	Redfern (p)	17125	9				7	1	10		5	3		4	2				8	6		11			
23	31	Norwich City	1-2	Clark	9336	9				7	1	10		5	3		4	2				8	6		11			
24	Jan 14	MANCHESTER CITY	3-0	Billington, Connelly 2	16163	9		7			1	10		5	3		4	2				8	6		11			
25	21	PLYMOUTH ARGYLE	3-4	Connelly, Billington 2	13120	9		7			1	10		5	3		4	2				8	6		11			
26	28	Sheffield United	2-2	Billington 2	25315	9		7			1	10		5	3		4	2				8	6		11			
27	Feb 4	BURNLEY	1-0	Marshall (og)	13547	9		7			1	10		5	3		4	2				8	6		11			
28	11	Tottenham Hotspur	1-0	Stephenson	30704	9		7			1	10		5	3		4	2				8	6		11			
29	18	Bradford Park Avenue	1-2	Stephenson	8215	9		7			1	10		5	3		4	2				8	6		11			
30	25	SWANSEA TOWN	6-3	Billington 4, Clark, Stephenson	11264	9				7	1	10		5	3		4	2				8	6		11			
31	Mar 11	TRANMERE ROVERS	3-0	Stephenson, Roberts, Billington	12788	9	7				1	10		5	3		4	2				8	6		11			
32	16	Blackburn Rovers	0-2		8872	9	7				1	10		5	3		4	2				8	6		11			
33	18	West Ham United	1-0	Redfern	18628		7				1	10		5	3		4	2				8	6		11			9
34	25	Bury	2-1	Redfern, Connelly	11943		7				1	10		5	3		4	2				8	6		11			9
35	Apr 1	Sheffield Wednesday	1-4	Finlayson	28051						1	10		5	3		4	2				8	6		11	7		9
36	7	SOUTHAMPTON	6-2	Billington 3, Redfern 2, Connelly	15946	9		7			1	10		5	3		4	2				8	6		11			
37	8	FULHAM	2-1	Connelly, Billington	16322	9		7			1	10		5	3		4	2				8	6		11			
38	10	Southampton	4-0	Stephenson, Billington 3	15114	9		7			1	10		5	3		4	2				8	6		11			
39	15	Chesterfield	2-1	Redfern 2	14925	9		7			1	10		5	3		4	2				8	6		11			
40	22	MILLWALL	0-0		20109	9		7			1	10		5	3		4	2				8	6		11			
41	29	Newcastle United	0-2		10341	9		7			1	10		5	3		4	2				8	6		11			
42	May 6	COVENTRY CITY	1-3	Stephenson	13128	9	7					10			3		4	2		1		8	6		11		5	
		Apps				27	5	13	2	14	31	41	10	22	40	9	42	26	16	1	19	33	37	16	40	2	1	15
		Goals				28				6		13				1	1					13	1		12			5

Two own goals

F.A. Cup

Round	Date	Opponent	Score		Att	Billington HJR	Burgess WW	Carroll JT	Carte R	Clark C	Coen JL	Connelly E	Dolman HW	Dreyer G	Dunsmore TH	Ferguson C	Finlayson J	King TP	Loughran JL	Mayberry S	Nelson JH	Redfern WJ	Roberts F	Smith TS	Stephenson GH	Stevens RF	Strathie J	Vinall EJ
R3	Jan 7	Liverpool	0-3		40341	9				7	1	10		5	3		4	2				8	6		11			

1939/40 season: cancelled on outbreak of WW2

No	Date	Opponent	Score	Scorers	Att	Billington HJR	Burgess WW	Coen JL	Dreyer G	Finlayson J	King TP	Roberts F	Stephenson GH
1	Aug 26	SHEFFIELD WEDNESDAY	3-0	Billington 2, Stockill	12357	9	7	1	5	4	2	6	11
2	30	Bradford Park Avenue	3-0	Billington 2, Stockill	7319	9	7	1	5	4	2	6	11
3	Sep 2	Fulham	1-1	Billington	6805	9	7	1	5	4	2	6	11

Played in all three games: BR Lutterloch (3), RR Stockill (8) and HE Gager (10)

1938/39 table:

		P	W	D	L	F	A	W	D	L	F	A	Pts
1	Blackburn Rovers	42	17	1	3	59	23	8	4	9	35	37	55
2	Sheffield United	42	9	9	3	35	15	11	5	5	34	26	54
3	Sheffield Wed.	42	14	4	3	47	18	7	7	7	41	41	53
4	Coventry City	42	13	4	4	35	13	8	4	9	27	32	50
5	Manchester City	42	13	3	5	56	35	8	4	9	40	37	49
6	Chesterfield	42	16	1	4	54	20	4	8	9	15	32	49
7	LUTON TOWN	42	13	4	4	47	27	9	1	11	35	39	49
8	Tottenham Hotspur	42	13	6	2	48	27	6	3	12	19	35	47
9	Newcastle United	42	13	3	5	44	21	5	7	9	17	27	46
10	West Bromwich Alb.	42	15	3	3	54	22	3	6	12	35	50	45
11	West Ham United	42	10	5	6	36	21	7	5	9	34	31	44
12	Fulham	42	12	5	4	35	20	5	5	11	26	35	44
13	Millwall	42	12	6	3	44	18	2	8	11	20	35	42
14	Burnley	42	13	3	5	32	20	2	6	13	18	36	39
15	Plymouth Argyle	42	9	7	5	24	13	6	1	14	25	42	38
16	Bury	42	9	5	7	48	36	3	8	10	17	38	37
17	Bradford Park Ave.	42	8	6	7	33	35	4	5	12	28	47	35
18	Southampton	42	9	6	6	35	34	4	3	14	21	48	35
19	Swansea Town	42	8	6	7	33	30	3	6	12	17	53	34
20	Nottingham Forest	42	8	6	7	33	29	2	5	14	16	53	31
21	Norwich City	42	10	5	6	39	29	3	0	18	11	62	31
22	Tranmere Rovers	42	6	4	11	26	38	0	1	20	13	61	17

1946/47   13th in Division Two

#	Date	Opponent	Score	Scorers	Att	Bates WH	Beach DF	Billington HJR	Brice GHJ	Bywater NL	Connelly E	Cooke WH	Daniel MJ	Driver A	Duggan EJ	Duke GE	Duncan D	Gager HE	Gardiner D	Goodyear GW	Hacking R	Kettley SC	Lake LE	Sanderson JR	Shanks WG	Soo FC	Steen AW	Streten BR	Wallbanks WH	Waugh WL
1	Aug 31	SHEFFIELD WEDNESDAY	4-1	Daniel 3, Waugh	21105		2	9			10	6	8			1		5						3		4	7			11
2	Sep 4	Bradford Park Avenue	1-2	Daniel	16931		2	9			10	6	8			1		5						3		4	7			11
3	7	Fulham	1-2	Billington	26038			9			10	6	8			1		5					2	3		4	7			11
4	11	MILLWALL	3-0	Billington 2, Connelly	15676		3	9			10	6	8			1		5						2		4	7			11
5	14	BURY	2-0	Connelly, Billington	17864		3	9			10	6	8			1		5						2		4	7			11
6	21	Nottingham Forest	2-4	Billington 2	24237		3	9			10	6	8			1		5						2		4	7			11
7	28	Plymouth Argyle	1-2	Gager	27535		2	9			10	6	8			1		5						3		4	7			11
8	Oct 5	LEICESTER CITY	1-2	Gager	18073		2		5		10	6				1		9					8	3		4	7			11
9	7	Millwall	0-2		9845	7	3				10	4	9			1		5					8	2			6			11
10	12	Chesterfield	1-2	Driver	13190		3			1		6	9	10				5	7				8	2		4				11
11	19	SOUTHAMPTON	2-2	Connelly, Daniel	17668		3			1	10	6	9					5					8	2		4	7			11
12	26	Newport County	3-1	Duggan 2, Daniel	11480		3	9	5	1			4	10	8		11		6				2							7
13	Nov 2	BARNSLEY	3-1	Billington 2, Duggan	21723		3	9	5	1			4	10	8		11		6				2							7
14	9	Burnley	1-1	Driver	26007		3	9		1			4	10	8		11	5	6				2							7
15	16	TOTTENHAM HOTSPUR	3-2	Duggan, Duncan, Billington	26362		3	9		1			4	10	8		11	5	6				2							7
16	23	Swansea Town	0-2		11768		3	9		1			2	10	8		11	5	6							4				7
17	30	NEWCASTLE UNITED	4-3	Waugh, Driver, Billington, Daniel	25410		3	9		1			2	10	8		11	5	6							4				7
18	Dec 7	West Bromwich Albion	2-1	Duncan, Billington	20685			9		1			2	10	8		11	5	6					3		4				7
19	14	BIRMINGHAM CITY	1-3	Billington	21760		3	9		1			2	10	8		11	5	6							4				7
20	21	Coventry City	0-0		13047		3	9		1			2	10			11	5	6	8						4				7
21	25	West Ham United	1-2	Duncan	19948			9		1			2	10	8		11	5	6					3		4				7
22	26	WEST HAM UNITED	2-1	Billington, Waugh	22320		3	9		1			2	10	8		11	5	6	4										7
23	28	Sheffield Wednesday	1-1	Daniel	29497		3	9		1			2	10	8		11	5	6							4				7
24	Jan 4	FULHAM	2-0	Billington, Cooke (p)	17341			9	5			2		10	8	1	11		6				3			4				7
25	18	Bury	0-3		16083			9		1		2		10	8			5	6				3		11	4				7
26	29	NOTTM. FOREST	3-2	Billington, Duncan, Driver	4209			9		1		2		10			11	5	6	8			3			4				7
27	Feb 1	PLYMOUTH ARGYLE	3-4	Billington, Connelly, Cooke (p)	15165			9		1	10	2			8		11	5	6				3			4				7
28	15	CHESTERFIELD	1-1	Daniel	15175			9	5				2	10	8				6				3		7	4		1		11
29	22	Southampton	3-1	Duggan 2, Driver	11710			9					2	10	8			5	6				3		7	4		1		11
30	Mar 15	BURNLEY	1-3	Driver	18462			9					2	10	8			5	6				3		7	4		1		11
31	22	Tottenham Hotspur	1-2	Duggan	36160		2	9			10				8		11	5	6				3			4		1		7
32	29	SWANSEA TOWN	3-0	Duggan 2, Billington	13486		3	9			10		2		8		11	5	6						7	4		1		
33	Apr 4	Manchester City	0-2		53692		3	9			10		2		8		11	5								4	6	1		7
34	5	Newcastle United	2-7	Driver 2	40372		5				10	6	2	9			11			8			3			4		1		7
35	7	MANCHESTER CITY	0-0		22976		5	10			8	6	2	9			11			4			3					1		7
36	12	WEST BROMWICH ALB.	2-0	Connelly, Billington	14920		5	10			8	6	2	9						4			3		7			1		11
37	19	Birmingham City	0-1		27316		5	10			8	6	2	9						4			3		7			1		11
38	26	COVENTRY CITY	1-1	Waugh	13686			10			8		2	9			11	5	6				3			4		1		7
39	May 3	Leicester City	1-2	Driver	18578			9	5	1	8		2	10			11		6				3			4				7
40	10	Barnsley	0-4		15264			9	5		8		2	10			11		6				3			4				7
41	24	BRADFORD PARK AVE.	3-0	Billington 2, Driver	10805			9	5	1	8		2	10					6				3		7	4				11
42	31	NEWPORT COUNTY	6-3	Connelly, Wallbanks, Waugh, Billington 3	7814		5	9			8		2	10					6				3			4		1	7	11
				Apps		1	23	36	13	19	23	33	29	29	10	10	23	34	22	10	1	1	28	6	8	38	10	12	1	41
				Goals				23			6	2	9	10	9		4	2											1	5

Played at 1 in game 40: M Morrison

F.A. Cup

Rnd	Date	Opponent	Score	Scorers	Att	Beach DF	Billington HJR	Brice GHJ	Bywater NL	Connelly E	Cooke WH	Daniel MJ	Driver A	Duggan EJ	Duncan D	Gager HE	Gardiner D	Lake LE	Soo FC	Waugh WL
R3	Jan 11	NOTTS COUNTY	6-0	Billington 5, Daniel	21842		9		1			2	10	8	11	5	6	3	4	7
R4	Jan 25	SWANSEA TOWN	2-0	Daniel, Roberts (og)	24327		9		1			2	10	8	11	5	6	3	4	7
R5	Feb 8	BURNLEY	0-0		22640	3	9		1			2	10	8	11	5	6		4	7
rep	Feb 11	Burnley	0-3		28330	3	9		1	8	7	2	10		11	5	6		4	

		P	W	D	L	F	A	W	D	L	F	A	Pts
1	Manchester City	42	17	3	1	49	14	9	7	5	29	21	62
2	Burnley	42	11	8	2	30	14	11	6	4	35	15	58
3	Birmingham City	42	17	2	2	51	11	8	3	10	23	22	55
4	Chesterfield	42	12	6	3	37	17	6	8	7	21	27	50
5	Newcastle United	42	11	4	6	60	32	8	6	7	35	30	48
6	Tottenham Hotspur	42	11	8	2	35	21	6	6	9	30	32	48
7	West Bromwich Alb.	42	12	4	5	53	37	8	4	9	35	38	48
8	Coventry City	42	12	8	1	40	17	4	5	12	26	42	45
9	Leicester City	42	11	4	6	42	25	7	3	11	27	39	43
10	Barnsley	42	13	2	6	48	29	4	6	11	36	57	42
11	Nottingham Forest	42	13	5	3	47	20	2	5	14	22	54	40
12	West Ham United	42	12	4	5	46	31	4	4	13	24	45	40
13	LUTON TOWN	42	13	4	4	50	29	3	3	15	21	44	39
14	Southampton	42	11	5	5	45	24	4	4	13	24	52	39
15	Fulham	42	12	4	5	40	25	3	5	13	23	49	39
16	Bradford Park Ave.	42	7	6	8	29	28	7	5	9	36	49	39
17	Bury	42	11	6	4	62	34	1	6	14	18	44	36
18	Millwall	42	7	7	7	30	30	7	1	13	26	49	36
19	Plymouth Argyle	42	11	3	7	45	34	3	2	16	34	62	33
20	Sheffield Wed.	42	10	5	6	39	28	2	3	16	28	60	32
21	Swansea Town	42	9	1	11	36	40	2	6	13	19	43	29
22	Newport County	42	9	1	11	41	52	1	2	18	20	81	23

1947/48   13th in Division Two

Player columns (left to right): Billington HJR, Brennan RA, Collins WH, Connelly E, Cooke WH, Daniel MJ, Driver A, Duggan EJ, Duncan D, Gager HE, Gardiner D, Hall LF, Hughes WM, Lake LE, Nelson SE, O'Brien J, Ottewell S, Owen SW, Shanks WG, Small PV, Soo FC, Streten BR, Wallbanks WH, Waugh WL, Wilson JA

#	Date	Opponent	Score	Scorers	Att.	Bil	Bre	Col	Con	Coo	Dan	Dri	Dug	Dun	Gag	Gar	Hal	Hug	Lak	Nel	O'Br	Ott	Owe	Sha	Sma	Soo	Str	Wal	Wau	Wil
1	Aug 23	Coventry City	1-4	Driver	25550	9			10			8	11	5	6		3	2								4	1		7	
2	27	Brentford	3-0	Billington 3	17022	9			10			8	11	5			3	2					6			4	1	7		
3	30	NEWCASTLE UNITED	2-1	Driver, Connelly	24570	9			10			8	11	5			3	2					6			4	1		7	
4	Sep 3	BRENTFORD	3-0	Billington 3	20921	9			10			8	11	5			3	2					6			4	1		7	
5	6	Birmingham City	1-2	Soo (p)	40032	9			10			8	11	5			3	2					6			4	1		7	
6	8	Leicester City	2-3	Duggan 2	22573	9					7	10	8	5			3	2					6			4	1			11
7	13	WEST BROMWICH ALB.	1-1	Connelly	21019				8	2		9	10	11	5		3						6			4	1		7	
8	17	LEICESTER CITY	2-1	Duggan 2	17597				8	2		9	10	11	5		3						6			4	1		7	
9	20	Barnsley	0-3		17670	9			10	2			8	11	5		3						6			4	1			11
10	27	PLYMOUTH ARGYLE	0-0		19244	9				2		10	8			5		3					6	7		4	1			11
11	Oct 4	Bradford Park Avenue	2-2	Billington, Daniel	21568	9				2	10		8			5		3					6	7		4	1			11
12	11	Cardiff City	0-1		39505	9			10	2			8			5		3					6	7		4	1			11
13	18	Sheffield Wednesday	0-1		40299	9			10	2			8		7	5		3					6			4	1			11
14	25	TOTTENHAM HOTSPUR	0-0		26496	9	10			2			8	11		5		3					6			4	1			7
15	Nov 1	Millwall	1-3	Daniel	25290		7		10	2	8	9				5		3					6			4	1			11
16	8	CHESTERFIELD	2-1	Daniel 2	18352		7			2	10	9				5	4	3					6		8		1			11
17	15	West Ham United	0-0		30535		7			2	10	9				5		3					6			4	1			11
18	22	BURY	1-1	Duggan	17249	8	7			2	10	9			6	5		3								4	1			11
19	29	Southampton	1-3	Soo	20133		7		10	2		9	8		6	5		3								4	1			11
20	Dec 6	DONCASTER ROVERS	2-1	Brennan, Driver	15556	9	7			2		8				5	6	3			11	10				4	1			
21	13	Nottingham Forest	2-1	Brennan, Soo (p)	12977	9	8			2						5	6	3			11	10			7	4	1			
22	20	COVENTRY CITY	2-3	Brennan, Billington	15687	9	8			2						5	6	3			11	10	4		7		1			
23	26	Leeds United	2-0	O'Brien, Billington	28597	9	8			2						5	6	3			11	10			7	4	1			
24	27	LEEDS UNITED	6-1	* see below	16964		8			2			9			5	6	3			11	10			7	4	1			
25	Jan 3	Newcastle United	1-4	O'Brien	64931		8			2			9			5	6	3			11	10			7	4	1			
26	17	BIRMINGHAM CITY	0-1		19697	9	8			2					6	5		3	7		11	10				4	1			
27	31	West Bromwich Albion	0-1		27047	9	10			2						5		3			11	8	6			4	1		7	
28	Feb 14	Plymouth Argyle	3-1	Ottewell, Daniel, Billington	22175	9	7			2	8				6	5		3				10				4	1			11
29	21	BRADFORD PARK AVE.	3-3	Billington, Brennan, Ottewell	11418	9	7			2	8				6	5		3				10				4	1			11
30	28	CARDIFF CITY	2-1	Daniel	22112	9	7			2	8				6	5		3				10				4	1			11
31	Mar 6	SHEFFIELD WEDNESDAY	1-1	Billington	16888	9	7			2	8				6	5		3				10				4	1			11
32	20	MILLWALL	1-2	Daniel	14128		8				3	11			6	5		2				10	9			4	1			7
33	26	FULHAM	0-3		18033				10		8	9			6	5		3			11					4	1		7	2
34	27	Chesterfield	0-2		10682						11	9			4	5		3			10	6	7		8		1			2
35	29	Fulham	1-1	Daniel	20151	10				2	8	9			4	5		3					6	7			1			11
36	Apr 3	WEST HAM UNITED	0-0		15059	10				2	8	9			4	5		3					6	7			1			11
37	5	Tottenham Hotspur	1-0	Daniel	23807		8			2	10	9			4	5		3					6	7			1			11
38	10	Bury	2-2	Brennan, Ottewell	15648		8			2	10				4	5		3				9	6	7			1			11
39	14	BARNSLEY	2-1	Daniel, Duggan	13594		8			2	10		9		6			3					5	7		4	1			11
40	17	SOUTHAMPTON	0-2		17202		8			2	10	9			4	5		3					6	7			1			11
41	24	Doncaster Rovers	2-0	Brennan 2	7263		8		10	2		9			4	5		3					6				1		7	11
42	May 1	NOTTM. FOREST	2-1	Brennan 2 (1p)	15126		8	4	10			9				5		3		2			6				1		7	11
				Apps		23	27	1	15	33	22	12	24	9	25	26	16	31	17	1	9	15	27	10	5	33	42	3	33	3
				Goals		12	11		2		10	3	7									3	4			4				

Scorers in game 24: O'Brien, Ottewell, Duggan, Brennan 2, Soo (p)

F.A. Cup

Rnd	Date	Opponent	Score	Scorers	Att.	Bil	Bre	Coo	Dan	Gag	Gar	Hug	Lak	O'Br	Ott	Soo	Str	Wau
R3	Jan 10	Plymouth Argyle	4-2	Brennan 2, Billington 2	34689	9	8			6	5	3	2	11	10	4	1	7
R4	Jan 24	COVENTRY CITY	3-2	Soo, Waugh, Ottewell	23982	9	8	2		6	5	3		11	10	4	1	7
R5	Feb 7	Queen's Park Rangers	1-3	Waugh	30564	9	8	2		6	5	3		11	10	4	1	7

Division Two — Final Table

	Team	P	W	D	L	F	A	W	D	L	F	A	Pts
1	Birmingham City	42	12	7	2	34	13	10	8	3	21	11	59
2	Newcastle United	42	18	1	2	46	13	6	7	8	26	28	56
3	Southampton	42	15	3	3	53	23	6	7	8	18	30	52
4	Sheffield Wed.	42	13	6	2	39	21	7	5	9	27	32	51
5	Cardiff City	42	12	6	3	36	18	6	5	10	25	40	47
6	West Ham United	42	10	7	4	29	19	6	7	8	26	34	46
7	West Bromwich Alb.	42	11	4	6	37	29	7	5	9	26	29	45
8	Tottenham Hotspur	42	10	6	5	36	24	5	8	8	20	19	44
9	Leicester City	42	10	5	6	36	29	6	6	9	24	28	43
10	Coventry City	42	10	5	6	33	16	4	8	9	26	36	41
11	Fulham	42	6	9	6	24	19	9	1	11	23	27	40
12	Barnsley	42	10	5	6	31	22	5	5	11	31	42	40
13	LUTON TOWN	42	8	8	5	31	25	6	4	11	25	34	40
14	Bradford Park Ave.	42	11	3	7	45	30	5	5	11	23	42	40
15	Brentford	42	10	6	5	31	26	3	8	10	13	35	40
16	Chesterfield	42	8	4	9	32	26	8	3	10	22	29	39
17	Plymouth Argyle	42	8	9	4	27	22	1	11	9	13	36	38
18	Leeds United	42	12	5	4	44	20	2	3	16	18	52	36
19	Nottingham Forest	42	10	5	6	32	23	2	6	13	22	37	35
20	Bury	42	6	8	7	27	28	3	8	10	31	40	34
21	Doncaster Rovers	42	7	8	6	23	20	2	3	16	17	46	29
22	Millwall	42	7	7	7	27	28	2	4	15	17	46	29

35

1948/49   10th in Division Two

#	Date		Opponent	Result	Scorers	Att	Aherne T	Arnison JW	Brennan RA	Burtenshaw CE	Collins WH	Cooke WH	Daniel MJ	Duggan EJ	Duke GE	Gardiner D	Gripton EW	Hall LF	Kiernan T	Lake LE	Lindsay D	Morton RH	Mulvaney J	Nelson SE	Owen SW	Shanks WG	Small PV	Streten BR	Taylor JE	Watkins C	Waugh WL	Wilson JA
1	Aug	21	QUEEN'S PARK RANGERS	0-0		23764		9	8			2				4	6	5			3			7				1			11	
2		23	Cardiff City	3-3	Duggan, Nelson, Arnison	35687		9	8		4	2		10		6		5			3			7				1			11	
3		28	Leeds United	0-2		25463		9	8		4	2		10		6		5			3			7				1			11	
4		30	CARDIFF CITY	3-0	Arnison 3	20185		9	8			2		10		4		5			3				6	7		1			11	
5	Sep	4	Bradford Park Avenue	1-4	Arnison	18697		9	10			2		8		4		5			3				6	7		1			11	
6		6	BLACKBURN ROVERS	2-0	Brennan, Duggan	18642		9	8					10		4		5			3				6	7		1			11	2
7		11	SOUTHAMPTON	1-1	Small	20257		9	8		4			10		6		5			3					7		1			11	2
8		18	Barnsley	2-1	Small, Arnison	20922		9	8		4	3		10		6		5								7		1			11	2
9		20	Blackburn Rovers	1-4	Duggan	18478		9	8		4	3		10		6		5								7		1			11	2
10		25	GRIMSBY TOWN	1-1	Arnison	18173		9	8		4	3		10		6		5									7	1			11	2
11	Oct	2	Nottingham Forest	0-2		22695		9	8			3		10		4		5							6		7	1			11	2
12		9	LEICESTER CITY	1-1	Duggan	16663		9	7			3		10	8	4		5							6			1			11	2
13		16	Brentford	0-2		23211		9	7			3		10		4		5							6	8		1			11	2
14		23	TOTTENHAM HOTSPUR	1-1	Arnison (p)	24859		9	7			3		10		4		5							6	8		1			11	2
15		30	West Ham United	1-0	Arnison	28132		9	7			3				6		5	8						4			1		10	11	2
16	Nov	6	BURY	1-0	Arnison	16764		9	7			3				6		5	8						4			1		10	11	2
17		13	West Bromwich Albion	1-2	Watkins	32589		9	7			3			8	6		5							4			1		10	11	2
18		20	CHESTERFIELD	1-0	Arnison	17808		9	7			3			8	6		5							4			1		10	11	2
19		27	Lincoln City	4-4	Waugh 2, Kiernan 2	10817		9	7			3			8	6		5							4			1		10	11	2
20	Dec	4	SHEFFIELD WEDNESDAY	2-1	Kiernan, Arnison	18558		9	7			3			8	6		5							4			1		10	11	2
21		11	Coventry City	0-2		19951		9	10			3			8	6		5							4			1	7		11	2
22		18	Queen's Park Rangers	3-0	Arnison 2, Brennan	16557		9	7			3			8	6		5							4			1		10	11	2
23		25	PLYMOUTH ARGYLE	3-1	Arnsion 2, Kiernan	17109		9	7			3			8	6		5							4			1		10	11	2
24		27	Plymouth Argyle	1-1	Wilson	32241		9	7			3			8	6		5							4			1		10	11	2
25	Jan	1	LEEDS UNITED	0-0		15310			7			3			9	6		5	8						4			1		10	11	2
26		15	BRADFORD PARK AVE.	0-1		16071		9	7			3				6		5	8						4			1		10	11	2
27		22	Southampton	1-1	Kiernan	24815			9			3				6		5	8						4		7	1		10	11	2
28	Feb	5	BARNSLEY	1-0	Small	16386			9	11		3				6		5	8						4		7	1		10		
29		26	NOTTM. FOREST	4-3	Brennan, Arnison, Small, Thomas(og)	17777		9	10			3				6		5	8			2					7	1		4	11	
30	Mar	5	Leicester City	1-1	Owen	26321		9	10			3						5	8			2			6		7	1		4	11	
31		12	BRENTFORD	2-1	Brennan 2	16682		9	10			3						5	8			2			6		7	1		4	11	
32		19	Tottenham Hotspur	1-2	Brennan	41839	3	9	10			2						5	8						6		7	1		4	11	
33		26	WEST HAM UNITED	0-1		15587		9	10			2						5	8			2			6		7	1		4	11	
34	Apr	2	Bury	1-3	Brennan	11461	3		9			2						5	8						6		7	1		10		
35		9	WEST BROMWICH ALB.	0-1		16651	3		9	7		2				4		5	8						6			1		10	11	
36		15	Fulham	1-4	Owen	35622			9	7		2				1	4			3					6					10	11	
37		16	Chesterfield	0-1		10938			9	7		2				1	4	5		8	3				6					10	11	
38		18	FULHAM	1-3	Brennan	20125			9	7		2				1	4	5		8	3				6					10	11	
39		23	LINCOLN CITY	6-0	* see below	12643			10	7		3				1	6					9			5					8	4	11	2
40		30	Sheffield Wednesday	0-0		18228			9	7						1	6					3	4		5					8	10	11	2
41	May	3	Grimsby Town	1-2	Brennan	13809			9	7						1	6					3	4		5					8	10		2
42		7	COVENTRY CITY	2-0	Daniel, Morton	13705			9				11			1	6					8	3		4			5	7		10		2
			Apps				3	30	42	8	6	37	2	14	6	37	3	36	23	6	7	17	5	3	20	6	16	36	3	27	38	27
			Goals					17	11	1			1	4					5			1	2	1	2		4		1	1	2	1

Scorers in game 39: C Burtenshaw, Mulvaney 2, Brennan 2, Taylor
Played at 4 in game 34: RD Ruffett
Played at 10 in game 1: WF Burtenshaw
Played at 11 in games 34 and 41: J O'Brien

One own goal

F.A. Cup

Rd	Date		Opponent	Result	Scorers	Att	Arnison JW	Brennan RA	Cooke WH	Gardiner D	Hall LF	Kiernan T	Morton RH	Owen SW	Small PV	Streten BR	Taylor JE	Watkins C	Waugh WL	Wilson JA
R3	Jan	8	WEST HAM UNITED	3-1	Kiernan, Arnison, Watkins	22229	9	7	3	6	5	8		4		1		10	11	2
R4	Jan	29	WALSALL	4-0	Brennan 3, Watkins	26422		9	3	6	5	8		4	7	1		10	11	2
R5	Feb	12	LEICESTER CITY	5-5	Kiernan 2, Small, Brennan, Watkins	26280		9	3	6	5	8		4	7	1		10	11	2
rep	Feb	19	Leicester City	3-5	Brennan 2, Arnison	38322	9	10	3	6	5	8	2	4		1	7		4	11

R5 (first game) a.e.t.

		P	W	D	L	F	A	W	D	L	F	A	Pts
1	Fulham	42	16	4	1	52	14	8	5	8	25	23	57
2	West Bromwich Alb.	42	16	3	2	47	16	8	5	8	22	23	56
3	Southampton	42	16	4	1	48	10	7	5	9	21	26	55
4	Cardiff City	42	14	4	3	45	21	5	9	7	17	26	51
5	Tottenham Hotspur	42	14	4	3	50	18	3	12	6	22	26	50
6	Chesterfield	42	9	7	5	24	18	6	10	5	27	27	47
7	West Ham United	42	13	5	3	38	23	5	5	11	18	35	46
8	Sheffield Wed.	42	12	6	3	36	17	3	7	11	27	39	43
9	Barnsley	42	10	7	4	40	18	4	5	12	22	43	40
10	LUTON TOWN	42	11	6	4	32	16	3	6	12	23	41	40
11	Grimsby Town	42	10	5	6	44	28	5	5	11	28	48	40
12	Bury	42	12	5	4	41	23	5	1	15	26	53	40
13	Queen's Park Rgs.	42	11	4	6	31	26	3	7	11	13	36	39
14	Blackburn Rovers	42	12	4	4	41	23	3	3	15	12	40	38
15	Leeds United	42	11	6	4	36	21	1	7	13	19	42	37
16	Coventry City	42	12	3	6	35	20	3	4	14	20	44	37
17	Bradford Park Ave.	42	8	8	5	37	26	5	3	13	28	52	37
18	Brentford	42	7	10	4	28	21	4	4	13	14	32	36
19	Leicester City	42	6	10	5	41	38	4	6	11	21	41	36
20	Plymouth Argyle	42	9	6	6	33	25	1	8	12	16	39	36
21	Nottingham Forest	42	9	6	6	22	14	1	5	15	28	40	35
22	Lincoln City	42	6	7	8	31	35	2	5	14	22	56	28

#	Date	Opponent	Score	Scorers	Att	Aherne T	Amison JW	Burtenshaw CE	Cooke WH	Gardiner D	Glover A	Hall LF	Hughes I	James PGB	Jinks JT	Kiernan T	Lake LE	Morton RH	Mulvaney J	Northover SC	Owen SW	Shanks WG	Slatter LAH	Small PV	Stobbart GC	Streten BR	Taylor JE	Walsh P	Watkins C	Waugh WL	Wilson JA	Wyldes JR
1	Aug 20	WEST HAM UNITED	2-2	Owen, Taylor	17003	3	9		2	6											5	8		7		1	10		4	11		
2	24	COVENTRY CITY	2-0	Watkins, Arnison	16070	3	9		2	6											5	8		7		1	10		4	11		
3	27	Sheffield United	2-2	Waugh, Arnison	27572	3	9		2	6											5	8		7		1	10		4	11		
4	29	Coventry City	0-1		22338	3	9	11	2	6											5	8		7		1	10		4			
5	Sep 3	GRIMSBY TOWN	0-0		16717	3			2	6									4		5	9	11	7		1	10		8			
6	7	Bradford Park Avenue	0-1		11201	3	9	11	2	6				8							5	7				1	10		4			
7	10	Queen's Park Rangers	0-3		20674	3	9	11	2	6											5	8				1	10		4	7		
8	17	PRESTON NORTH END	1-1	Waters (og)	20135	3	8		2	6	7									9	5					1	10		4	11		
9	24	Swansea Town	0-0		24297	3	8		2	6	7	5								9						1	10		4	11		
10	Oct 1	LEEDS UNITED	1-0	Taylor	15291	3			2	6	7	5								9		8				1	10		4	11		
11	8	LEICESTER CITY	1-0	Walsh	20816		8		2	6	7										5				10	1		9	4	11	3	
12	15	Bury	2-5	James, Walsh	17651	3	8		2	6	7				11						5				10	1		9	4			
13	22	TOTTENHAM HOTSPUR	1-1	Stobbart	27319	3	8		2	6	7				11						5				10	1		9	4			
14	29	Cardiff City	0-0		24011	3	8		2	6	7										5				10	1	11	9	4			
15	Nov 5	BLACKBURN ROVERS	5-2	Stobbart 4, Bell (og)	9513	3			2	6	7										5				8	1	10	9	4			11
16	12	Brentford	0-1		20520				2		7								4		5	10			8	1		9	6		3	11
17	19	HULL CITY	0-3		22269	3			2	6	10										5	8				1		9	4	7		11
18	26	Sheffield Wednesday	1-1	Watkins	29432	3			2	6	7								4		5	8			9	1			10			11
19	Dec 3	PLYMOUTH ARGYLE	1-1	Waugh	13273	3			2	6	7								4		5	8			9	1			10	11		
20	10	Chesterfield	1-0	Stobbart	7937	3			2	6	7					8					5	10			9	1			4			11
21	17	West Ham United	0-0		16445	3			2	6	7					8					5	10			9	1			4			11
22	24	SHEFFIELD UNITED	1-3	Stobbart	15594	3			2	6	7					8					5	10			9	1			4			11
23	26	SOUTHAMPTON	1-1	Cooke (p)	18765	3			2	6	7					8					5	10			9	1			4			11
24	27	Southampton	1-2	Kiernan	26928	3	10		2							8		6			5				9	1	7		4			11
25	31	Grimsby Town	1-6	Morton	15991	3			2		7					8		6			5	10			9	1			4			11
26	Jan 14	QUEEN'S PARK RANGERS	1-2	Watkins	16291	3			2	6	7	5	1			8					4							9	10	11		
27	21	Preston North End	1-0	Shanks	23532	3			2	6	7		1			8					5	9					10		4	11		
28	Feb 4	SWANSEA TOWN	1-2	Stobbart	15205	3			2	6			1			8		10			5	9		7					4	11		
29	18	Leeds United	1-2	Small	37263	3			2	6			1			8			4		5	10		9	7							11
30	25	Leicester City	2-3	Watkins, Wyldes	26385	3			2	6	7		1			8			4		5				9				10			11
31	Mar 4	BURY	2-1	Glover, Wyldes	14365	3			2	6	7		1	9		8					5				10				4			11
32	11	Tottenham Hotspur	0-0		53145	3			2		7		1	9		8					5	6			10				4			11
33	18	CARDIFF CITY	0-0		15071	3			2		7		1	9		8					5	6			10				4			11
34	25	Blackburn Rovers	0-0		17255	3			2		7		1	9		8					5	6			10				4			11
35	Apr 1	SHEFFIELD WEDNESDAY	0-0		15273	3			2		7	11	1			8					5	6			9				10	4		
36	7	BARNSLEY	3-1	Kiernan 2, Gardiner	15149	3			2	6	7	11	1			8					5				9				10	4		
37	8	Plymouth Argyle	0-0		16977	3			2		7		1			8					5	6			9				10	4		11
38	10	Barnsley	0-1		9476				2		7		1			8	3				5	6			9				10	4		11
39	15	BRENTFORD	1-0	Stobbart	13991	3			2		7	11	1			8					5	6			9				10	4		
40	22	Hull City	1-1	Glover	28205	3			2		7	11	1			8					5	6			9				10	4		
41	29	CHESTERFIELD	1-1	Kiernan	7420				2		7		1			8					5	6			9				10	4	3	11
42	May 6	BRADFORD PARK AVE.	3-1	Cooke (p), Taylor, Farr (og)	11232				2		7		1			8					5	6			9		10			4	3	11
		Apps				37	13	3	42	33	32	3	17	2	4	24	1	10	3	1	40	30	1	7	30	25	21	8	39	23	4	9
		Goals					2		2	1	2			1		4		1				1		1	9		3	2	4	2		2

Three own goals

F.A. Cup

Rd	Date	Opponent	Score	Scorers	Att	Aherne T	Cooke WH	Gardiner D	Glover A	Hall LF	Kiernan T	Owen SW	Stobbart GC	Streten BR	Watkins C	Waugh WL
R3	Jan 7	GRIMSBY TOWN	3-4	Kiernan 2, Waugh	18843	3	2	10	7	5	8	6	9	1	4	11

		P	W	D	L	F	A	W	D	L	F	A	Pts
1	Tottenham Hotspur	42	15	3	3	51	15	12	4	5	30	20	61
2	Sheffield Wed.	42	12	7	2	46	23	6	9	6	21	25	52
3	Sheffield United	42	9	10	2	36	19	10	4	7	32	30	52
4	Southampton	42	13	4	4	44	25	6	10	5	20	23	52
5	Leeds United	42	11	8	2	33	16	6	5	10	21	29	47
6	Preston North End	42	12	5	4	37	21	6	4	11	23	28	45
7	Hull City	42	11	8	2	39	25	6	3	12	25	47	45
8	Swansea Town	42	11	3	7	34	18	6	6	9	19	31	43
9	Brentford	42	11	5	5	21	12	4	8	9	23	37	43
10	Cardiff City	42	13	3	5	28	14	3	7	11	13	30	42
11	Grimsby Town	42	13	5	3	53	25	3	3	15	21	48	40
12	Coventry City	42	8	6	7	32	24	5	7	9	23	31	39
13	Barnsley	42	11	6	4	45	28	2	7	12	19	39	39
14	Chesterfield	42	12	3	6	28	16	3	6	12	15	31	39
15	Leicester City	42	8	9	4	30	25	4	6	11	25	40	39
16	Blackburn Rovers	42	10	5	6	30	15	4	5	12	25	45	38
17	LUTON TOWN	42	8	9	4	28	22	2	9	10	13	29	38
18	Bury	42	10	8	3	37	19	4	1	16	23	46	37
19	West Ham United	42	8	7	6	30	25	4	5	12	23	36	36
20	Queen's Park Rgs.	42	6	5	10	21	30	5	7	9	19	27	34
21	Plymouth Argyle	42	6	6	9	19	24	2	10	9	25	41	32
22	Bradford Park Ave.	42	7	6	8	34	34	3	5	13	17	43	31

1950/51 — 19th in Division Two

#	Date	Opponent	Score	Scorers	Att	Aherne T	Amison JW	Cooke WH	Davie WC	Gardiner D	Glover A	Hall LF	Havenga WS	Hughes I	Jinks JT	Jones LC	Kiernan T	Lake LE	McAuley PJ	Moore BJ	Morton RH	Owen SW	Pemberton JT	Shanks WG	Stobbart GC	Streten BR	Taylor JE	Turner GR	Watkins C	Whent JR	Wilson JA	Wyldes JR
1	Aug 19	BRENTFORD	2-0	Taylor, Whent	17721	3		2			7			1								5		6	9		8		4	10		11
2	24	West Ham United	1-2	Glover	20560	3		2			7			1								5		6	9		8		4	10		11
3	26	Blackburn Rovers	0-1		25114	3		2			7			1								5		6	9		8		4	10		11
4	30	WEST HAM UNITED	1-1	Wyldes	12366	3		2			7			1							4	5		6	9		8			10		11
5	Sep 2	SOUTHAMPTON	0-1		16942	3		2			7			1								5		6	9		8		4	10		11
6	6	Hull City	1-2	Jinks	14905			2			7			1	9		3					5		6	8		10		4			11
7	9	Barnsley	1-6	Jinks	22052			2			7			1	9		3					5		6	8		10		4			11
8	16	SHEFFIELD UNITED	0-0		14768	3		2			11			1	9			8				5		6	7		10		4			
9	23	Manchester City	1-1	Taylor	42312	3		2			11		5	1	9			8						6	7		10		4			
10	30	Leeds United	1-2	Kiernan	21209	3		2			11		5	1	9			8						6	7		10		4			
11	Oct 7	PRESTON NORTH END	1-2	Glover	16637	3		2			11			1				8			9	5		6	7		10		4			
12	14	Notts County	2-2	Morton, Stobbart	34054	3		2			7			1				8			9	5		6	10				4			11
13	21	QUEEN'S PARK RANGERS	2-0	Stobbart, Wyldes	15692	3		2			7			1				8			9	5		6	10				4			11
14	28	Bury	1-4	Wyldes	13486	3	10	2			7			1				8			4	5			9				6			11
15	Nov 4	LEICESTER CITY	0-2		12967	3							5	1			8	2			4	6		7	9		10					11
16	11	Chesterfield	1-1	Wyldes	10996	3		2			7			1							4	5		6	8		10			9		11
17	18	GRIMSBY TOWN	4-0	Whent 2, Shanks, Taylor	12144	3		2			7			1							4	5		6	8		10			9		11
18	25	Birmingham City	0-3		18606			2			7			1			3				4	5		6	8		10			9		11
19	Dec 2	CARDIFF CITY	1-1	Havenga	13062	3		2					11	1							4	5		8	7		10		6	9		
20	9	Coventry City	1-4	Stobbart	22044	3		2					11								6	5		8	7	1	9		4			10
21	16	Brentford	0-1		9808	3		2	10	6			11								4	5		8	7	1	9					
22	23	BLACKBURN ROVERS	1-1	Davie	11632	3		2	10	7			11						6		4	5		8	9	1						
23	25	Swansea Town	2-0	Shanks, Havenga	16862	3		2	10	7			11								4	5		8	9	1			6			
24	26	SWANSEA TOWN	3-1	Havenga 3 (1p)	17245	3		2	10		7		11								4	5		8	9	1			6			
25	30	Southampton	1-1	Stobbart	21094	3		2	10		7		11								4	5		8	9	1			6			
26	Jan 13	BARNSLEY	1-1	Shanks	15032	3		2	10		7		11								4	5		8	9	1			6			
27	20	Sheffield United	1-2	Glover	26364	3		2	10		7		11								4	5		8	9	1			6			
28	Feb 3	MANCHESTER CITY	2-2	Davie, Moore	12087	3		2	10		7		11							9	4	5		8		1			6			
29	17	LEEDS UNITED	2-3	Stobbart, Glover	13323	3		2	10		7		11						6			5		8		1	9		4			
30	24	Preston North End	0-1		31096	3		2	10		7		11						6		4	5		8		1	9					
31	Mar 3	NOTTS COUNTY	1-1	Moore	17398	3		2	10		7		11						6	9	4	5		8		1						
32	10	Queen's Park Rangers	1-1	Davie	13708	3		2	10										6	9	4	5			11	1	7		8			
33	17	BURY	4-2	Moore 2, Watkins, McAuley	11576	3		2	10			11							6	9	4	5				1	7		8			
34	23	Doncaster Rovers	2-5	Moore, Davie	22613	3		2	10			11							6	9	4	5				1	7		8			
35	24	Leicester City	1-3	Stobbart	23560	3		2	10										6	9		5			7	1	8		4			11
36	26	DONCASTER ROVERS	3-1	Stobbart, Moore, Davie (p)	14486	3		2	10											9		5	11	6	7	1	8		4			
37	31	CHESTERFIELD	3-0	Taylor, Moore, Davie	13055			2	10								3			9		5	11	6	7	1	8		4			
38	Apr 7	Grimsby Town	2-0	Taylor, Pemberton	12435			2	10								3			9		5	11	6	7	1	8		4			
39	14	BIRMINGHAM CITY	1-1	Pemberton	16324			2	10								3			9		5	11	6	7	1	8		4			
40	21	Cardiff City	1-2	Stobbart	28022	3		2	10											9		5	11	6	7	1	8		4			
41	28	COVENTRY CITY	1-1	Davie	11336			3	10							2				9		5	11	6	7	1	8		4			
42	May 5	Hull City	3-5	Stobbart, Davie, Wyldes	17478			3	10				5			2				9				6	7	1	8		4			11
		Apps				34	1	36	22	3	24	4	16	19	5	2	8	7	8	13	24	39	7	34	39	23	25	2	35	11	5	16
		Goals							8		4		5		2		1		1	7	1		2	3	9		5		1	3		5

F.A. Cup

Rnd	Date	Opponent	Score	Scorers	Att	Aherne T	Amison JW	Cooke WH	Davie WC	Gardiner D	Glover A	Hall LF	Havenga WS	Hughes I	Jinks JT	Jones LC	Kiernan T	Lake LE	McAuley PJ	Moore BJ	Morton RH	Owen SW	Pemberton JT	Shanks WG	Stobbart GC	Streten BR	Taylor JE	Turner GR	Watkins C	Whent JR	Wilson JA	Wyldes JR
R3	Jan 6	PORTSMOUTH	2-0	Davie, Havenga	21631	3		2	10	7			11								4	5		8	9	1			6			
R4	Jan 27	BRISTOL ROVERS	1-2	Watkins	26586	3		2	10	7											4	5		8	9	1			6			11

Division Two final table

		P	W	D	L	F	A	W	D	L	F	A	Pts
1	Preston North End	42	16	3	2	53	18	10	2	9	38	31	57
2	Manchester City	42	12	6	3	53	25	7	8	6	36	36	52
3	Cardiff City	42	13	7	1	36	20	4	9	8	17	25	50
4	Birmingham City	42	12	6	3	37	20	8	3	10	27	33	49
5	Leeds United	42	14	4	3	36	17	6	4	11	27	38	48
6	Blackburn Rovers	42	13	3	5	39	27	6	5	10	26	39	46
7	Coventry City	42	15	3	3	51	25	4	4	13	24	34	45
8	Sheffield United	42	11	4	6	44	27	5	8	8	28	35	44
9	Brentford	42	13	3	5	44	25	5	5	11	31	49	44
10	Hull City	42	12	5	4	47	28	4	6	11	27	42	43
11	Doncaster Rovers	42	9	6	6	37	32	6	7	8	27	36	43
12	Southampton	42	10	9	2	38	27	5	4	12	28	46	43
13	West Ham United	42	10	5	6	44	33	6	5	10	24	36	42
14	Leicester City	42	10	4	7	42	28	5	7	9	26	30	41
15	Barnsley	42	9	5	7	42	22	6	5	10	32	46	40
16	Queen's Park Rgs.	42	13	5	3	47	25	2	5	14	24	57	40
17	Notts County	42	7	7	7	37	34	6	6	9	24	26	39
18	Swansea Town	42	14	1	6	34	25	2	3	16	20	52	36
19	LUTON TOWN	42	7	9	5	34	23	2	5	14	23	47	32
20	Bury	42	9	4	8	33	27	3	4	14	27	59	32
21	Chesterfield	42	7	7	7	30	28	2	5	14	14	41	30
22	Grimsby Town	42	6	8	7	37	38	2	4	15	24	57	28

1951/52 8th in Division Two

Player columns (left → right): Aherne T · Cooke WH · Cullen MJ · Davie WC · Davies RA · Dunne S · Hall LF · Havenga WS · Jones LC · McJarrow H · Mitchell AJ · Moore BJ · Morton RH · Owen SW · Pemberton JT · Sexton DJ · Shanks WG · Smith RS · Stobbart GC · Stone PJ · Streten BR · Taylor JE · Turner GR · Watkins C · Wyldes JR

#	Date	Opponent	Res	Scorers	Att	Ah	Co	Cu	DaW	DaR	Du	Ha	Hv	Jo	Mc	Mi	Mo	Mr	Ow	Pe	Sx	Sh	Sm	St	Sn	Sr	Ta	Tu	Wa	Wy
1	Aug 18	SWANSEA TOWN	2-2	Taylor, Mitchell	15606	3	2		10	7						11			5			6		9		1	8		4	
2	20	Sheffield United	0-3		24012	3	2		10	7						11			5			6		9		1	8		4	
3	25	Bury	1-0	Stobbart	11196	3	2		10	7						11			5			6		9		1	8		4	
4	29	SHEFFIELD UNITED	2-1	Stobbart, Taylor	16642	3	2		10	7						11			5			6		9		1	8		4	
5	Sep 1	Leicester City	3-3	Taylor 3	25735	3	2		10	7						11			5			6		9		1	8		4	
6	5	Barnsley	2-1	Taylor, Mitchell	13109	3	2		10	7						11			5			6		9		1	8		4	
7	8	NOTTS COUNTY	6-0	Taylor 2, Mitchell, Davie, Stobbart 2	24511	3	2		10	7						11			5			6		9		1	8		4	
8	15	Queen's Park Rangers	0-0		17391	3	2		10	7						11			5			6		9		1	8		4	
9	22	BLACKBURN ROVERS	1-1	Mitchell	20022	3	2		10	7						11			5			6		9		1	8		4	
10	29	Hull City	2-1	Stobbart, Mitchell	29646	3	2		10	7		5				11						6		9		1	8		4	
11	Oct 6	Nottingham Forest	0-2		31257	3	2		10	7		5				11						6		9		1	8		4	
12	13	BRENTFORD	0-2		18521	3	2		10	7						11			5			6		9		1	8		4	
13	20	Doncaster Rovers	1-1	Davies	18801	3	2		10	7						11	8		5			6		9		1			4	
14	27	EVERTON	1-1	Davies	16667	3	2		10	7						11	8		5			6		9		1			4	
15	Nov 3	Southampton	3-2	Taylor 2, Mitchell	20002	3	2		10	7						11		4	5					9		1	8		6	
16	10	SHEFFIELD WEDNESDAY	5-3	Mitchell 2, Davies, Taylor, Morton	19091	3	2		10	7						11		4	5					9		1	8		6	
17	17	Leeds United	1-1	Stobbart	27405	3	2		10	7						11		4	5					9		1	8		6	
18	24	ROTHERHAM UNITED	1-1	Taylor	23565	3	2		10	7						11		4	5					9		1	8		6	
19	Dec 1	Cardiff City	0-3		26106	3	2		10							11	9	4	5					7		1	8		6	
20	8	BIRMINGHAM CITY	2-4	Taylor, Stobbart	15937	3	2		10	7						11	9	4	5					7		1	8		6	
21	15	Swansea Town	3-0	Stobbart 2, Havenga	14896	3	2						7			11		4	5					9		1	8	10	6	
22	22	BURY	2-1	Taylor, Stobbart	12931	3	2						7			11		4	5					9		1	8	10	6	
23	25	West Ham United	0-3		20403	3	2			7						11		4	5					9		1	8	10	6	
24	26	WEST HAM UNITED	6-1	Mitchell, Taylor, Turner 3, Stobbart	19476	3					2					11	9	4	5					7		1	8	10	6	
25	29	LEICESTER CITY	1-2	Watkins	17992	3					2					11	9	4	5					7		1	8	10	6	
26	Jan 5	Notts County	4-5	Taylor 2, Turner, Moore	22808	3					2					11	9	4	5					7		1	8	10	6	
27	19	QUEEN'S PARK RANGERS	0-1		15242	3				7	2					11		4	5					9		1	8	10	6	
28	26	Blackburn Rovers	1-2	Mitchell	25156	3				7	2					11		4	5					9		1	8	10	6	
29	Feb 9	HULL CITY	1-1	Moore	16550	3	2					8				11	9	4	5	7						1		10	6	
30	16	NOTTM. FOREST	3-3	McJarrow 2, Mitchell	18369	3	2								9	11		4	5	7						1	8	10	6	
31	Mar 1	Brentford	3-3	Taylor 2, Davies	21218	3	2			7						11	9	4	5							1	8	10	6	
32	12	DONCASTER ROVERS	1-4	Morton	5635	3				7	2			5		11	9	4								1	8	10	6	
33	15	Everton	3-1	Mitchell 2, Taylor	37889	3					2					11	9		5		10	4		7		1	8		6	
34	22	SOUTHAMPTON	2-1	Moore, Mitchell (p)	15551	3					2					11	9		5		10	4		7		1	8		6	
35	Apr 2	Sheffield Wednesday	0-4		23862	3					2			8		11	9		5		10	4		7		1			6	
36	5	LEEDS UNITED	2-1	Moore 2	11460	3	2									11	9	4	5		10			7		1	8		6	
37	12	Rotherham United	1-0	Mitchell	17309	3	2									11	9	4	5		10			7		1	8		6	
38	14	COVENTRY CITY	2-1	Moore, Sexton	15216	3	2									11	9	4	5		10			7		1	8		6	
39	15	Coventry City	2-5	Moore, Wyldes	26160	3	2										9	4	5					7		1	8	10	6	11
40	19	CARDIFF CITY	2-2	McJarrow, Moore	14186	3								2	10	11	9	4	5					7		1	8		6	
41	26	Birmingham City	1-3	Warhurst (og)	28816	3		7						2	10	11	9	4	5		6			8		1				
42	May 3	BARNSLEY	4-2	Stobbart, Mitchell, McJarrow 2	8789	3		7						2	10	11	9	4	5					8		1			6	
	Apps					41	27	2	20	25	13	3	2	3	5	41	20	28	35	2	6	18	1	38	1	42	36	11	41	1
	Goals								3	2			1		5	16	8	2			1			12			20	4	1	1

One own goal

F.A. Cup

Rd	Date	Opponent	Res	Scorers	Att	Ah	Co	Cu	DaW	DaR	Du	Ha	Hv	Jo	Mc	Mi	Mo	Mr	Ow	Pe	Sx	Sh	Sm	St	Sn	Sr	Ta	Tu	Wa	Wy
R3	Jan 12	CHARLTON ATHLETIC	1-0	Turner	25554	3				7	2					11		4	5					9		1	8	10	6	
R4	Feb 2	BRENTFORD	2-2	Turner, Taylor	25320	3	2		9							11		4	5					7		1	8	10	6	
rep	Feb 6	Brentford	0-0		31143	3	2		9							11		4	5					7		1	8	10	6	
rep2	Feb 18	Brentford	3-2	Taylor, Moore, Morton	37269	3	2			7						11	9	4	5		10					1	8		6	
R5	Feb 23	SWINDON TOWN	3-1	Taylor 2, Davies	27553	3	2		10	7						11	9	4	5							1	8		6	
R6	Mar 8	ARSENAL	2-3	Moore, Mitchell (p)	28433	3	2		10	7						11	9	4	5							1	8		6	

Both R4 replays a.e.t. Replay 2 at Highbury.

Division Two final table

	Club	P	W	D	L	F	A	W	D	L	F	A	Pts
1	Sheffield Wed.	42	14	4	3	54	23	7	7	7	46	43	53
2	Cardiff City	42	18	2	1	52	15	2	9	10	20	39	51
3	Birmingham City	42	11	6	4	36	21	10	3	8	31	35	51
4	Nottingham Forest	42	12	6	3	41	22	6	7	8	36	40	49
5	Leicester City	42	12	6	3	48	24	7	3	11	30	40	47
6	Leeds United	42	13	7	1	35	15	5	4	12	24	42	47
7	Everton	42	12	5	4	42	25	5	5	11	22	33	44
8	LUTON TOWN	42	9	7	5	46	35	7	5	9	31	43	44
8	Rotherham United	42	11	4	6	40	25	6	4	11	33	46	42
10	Brentford	42	11	7	3	34	20	4	5	12	20	35	42
11	Sheffield United	42	13	2	6	57	28	5	3	13	33	48	41
12	West Ham United	42	13	5	3	48	29	2	6	13	19	48	41
13	Southampton	42	11	6	4	40	25	4	5	12	21	48	41
14	Blackburn Rovers	42	11	3	7	35	30	6	3	12	19	33	40
15	Notts County	42	11	5	5	45	27	5	2	14	26	41	39
16	Doncaster Rovers	42	9	4	8	29	28	4	8	9	26	32	38
17	Bury	42	13	2	6	43	22	2	5	14	24	47	37
18	Hull City	42	11	5	5	44	23	2	6	13	16	47	37
19	Swansea Town	42	10	4	7	45	26	2	8	11	27	50	36
20	Barnsley	42	8	7	6	39	33	3	7	11	20	39	36
21	Coventry City	42	9	5	7	36	33	5	1	15	23	49	34
22	Queen's Park Rgs.	42	8	8	5	35	35	3	4	14	17	46	34

1952/53 3rd in Division Two

#		Date	Opponent	Score	Scorers	Att	Aheme T	Baynham RL	Cooke WH	Cullen MJ	Davies RA	Dunne S	Hall LF	Jones LC	McJarrow H	Mitchell AJ	Moore BJ	Morton RH	Owen SW	Pemberton JT	Pye J	Scott JC	Sexton DJ	Shanks WG	Smith RS	Streten BR	Taylor AA	Turner GR	Watkins C
1	Aug	23	Plymouth Argyle	1-2	Moore	28836	3					2		8		11	9	4	5		10	7				1			6
2		27	BIRMINGHAM CITY	0-1		20231	3		2	11				8			9	4	5		10	7				1			6
3		30	ROTHERHAM UNITED	2-1	Turner 2	14427	3		2	7	11		5				9	4						10		1		8	6
4	Sep	3	Birmingham City	2-2	Turner, Moore	17478	3			7	11	2	5				9	4						10		1		8	6
5		6	Fulham	0-2		28680	3			7	11	2						4	5		9			10		1		8	6
6		10	SWANSEA TOWN	3-1	Turner 2, Pye	13218	3	1		7	11	2						4	5		9			10				8	6
7		13	WEST HAM UNITED	0-0		16009	3			7	11	2					10	4	5		9					1		8	6
8		18	Swansea Town	2-4	Scott, Moore	17358	3			7		2				11	9	4	5		10	8				1			6
9		20	Leicester City	1-1	Turner	24052	3				7	2				11		4	5		9			10		1		8	6
10		27	NOTTS COUNTY	5-1	Moore 2, Pye 2, Mitchell	13557	3				7	2				11	8	4	5		9					1			10
11	Oct	4	Southampton	3-1	Moore, Pye 2	17539	3				7	2				11	8	4	5		9					1			10
12		11	Huddersfield Town	0-3		26345	3				7	2				11	8	4	5		9					1			10
13		18	SHEFFIELD UNITED	4-1	Moore, Pye, Mitchell, Watkins	18185	3				7	2				11	8	4	5		9					1			10
14		25	Barnsley	3-2	Pye 2, Watkins	11423	3				7	2				11	8	4	5		9					1			10
15	Nov	1	LINCOLN CITY	4-0	Pye 2, Moore 2	17538	3				7	2				11	8	4	5		9					1			10
16		8	Hull City	2-0	Pye, Mitchell	22484	3				7	2				11	8	4	5		9					1			10
17		15	BLACKBURN ROVERS	6-0	Pye 3, Mitchell, Davies, Moore	16276					7			2		11	8	4	5	3	9					1			10
18		22	Nottingham Forest	3-4	Mitchell 2, Pye	22924	3				7	2				11	8	4	5		9					1			10
19		29	EVERTON	4-2	Moore, Pye, Mitchell, Clinton (og)	15160	3				7	2				11	8	4	5		9					1			10
20	Dec	13	DONCASTER ROVERS	1-2	Mitchell	15258	3	1			7	2				11	8	4	5		9								10
21		20	PLYMOUTH ARGYLE	1-0	Davies	13055	3	1			7			2		11	8	4	5		9								10
22		26	LEEDS UNITED	2-0	McCabe (og), Pye	19480	3	1			7			2		11	8	4	5		9								10
23		27	Leeds United	2-2	Pye, Pemberton	31634	3	1			7			2			8	4	5	11	9								6
24	Jan	3	Rotherham United	3-1	Moore, Pye 2	16850	3	1			7			2		11	8	4	5		9								10
25		17	FULHAM	2-0	Jones, Moore	21409	3	1			7			2			8	4	5		9			6			11		10
26		24	West Ham United	1-0	Mitchell	23667	3	1		7				2		11	8	4	5		9			6					10
27	Feb	7	LEICESTER CITY	2-0	Turner, Mitchell (p)	22489	3	1		7			5	2		11	8	4			9							10	6
28		19	Notts County	2-1	Pye 2	8648	3	1		7		2			10	11	8	4	5		9								6
29		21	SOUTHAMPTON	1-2	Cullen	19424	3	1		7					9	11	8	4	5									10	6
30		28	HUDDERSFIELD T	0-2		25841					7	2	3				8	4	5	11	9		10		1				6
31	Mar	7	Sheffield United	1-1	Turner	38839		1		7			5	2		11		4	6	3	9							8	10
32		14	BARNSLEY	6-0	Watkins, Yeull (og), Cullen 2, Turner 2	15315		1		7			5	2		11		4	6	3	9							8	10
33		21	Lincoln City	2-1	Turner, Pye	15510		1		7			5	2	10	11		4	6	3	9							8	
34		28	HULL CITY	3-2	McJarrow 2, Turner	13747		1		7			5	2	10	11		4	6	3	9							8	
35	Apr	3	Bury	0-1		15648		1		7			2	5	10	11		4	6	3	9							8	
36		4	Blackburn Rovers	1-1	Mitchell	23920		1			7	2	5			11	8	4	6	3	9								10
37		6	BURY	4-1	Turner, McJarrow 2, Hart (og)	16360		1			7	2	5		10	11		4		3	9							8	6
38		11	NOTTM. FOREST	3-0	Davies, Watkins, Mitchell	18599		1			7			2		11		4	5	3	9			6				8	10
39		16	Everton	1-1	Davies	32948		1			7			2		11		4	5	3	9			6				8	10
40		22	Brentford	1-1	Pye	16347		1			7	2				11		4	5	3	9			6				8	10
41		25	BRENTFORD	0-1		15826		1		7		2				11	9	4	5	3	10			6				8	
42		30	Doncaster Rovers	0-1		9415		1				2			10	11	7	4	5	3	9			6				8	
			Apps				28	22	2	16	29	25	10	16	9	33	30	42	38	15	39	1	3	26	1	20	1	21	35
			Goals							3	4			1	4	12	13			1	24	1						13	4

Four own goals

F.A. Cup

			Opponent	Score	Scorers	Att	Aheme T	Baynham RL	Cooke WH	Cullen MJ	Davies RA	Dunne S	Hall LF	Jones LC	McJarrow H	Mitchell AJ	Moore BJ	Morton RH	Owen SW	Pemberton JT	Pye J	Scott JC	Sexton DJ	Shanks WG	Smith RS	Streten BR	Taylor AA	Turner GR	Watkins C
R3	Jan	10	BLACKBURN ROVERS	6-1	Taylor 2, Pye 3, Moore	21034	3	1			7			2			8	4	5		9			6			11		10
R4	Jan	31	Manchester City	1-1	Pye	38411	3	1		7			5	2		11	8	4			9			6					10
rep	Feb	4	MANCHESTER CITY	5-1	Turner 3, Mitchell, Little (og)	21991	3	1		7			5	2		11	8	4			9							10	6
R5	Feb	14	BOLTON WAN.	0-1		23735	3	1		7				2		11	8	4	5		9							10	6

		P	W	D	L	F	A	W	D	L	F	A	Pts
1	Sheffield United	42	15	3	3	60	27	10	7	4	37	28	60
2	Huddersfield Town	42	14	4	3	51	14	10	6	5	33	19	58
3	LUTON TOWN	42	15	1	5	53	17	7	7	7	31	32	52
4	Plymouth Argyle	42	12	5	4	37	24	8	4	9	28	36	49
5	Leicester City	42	13	6	2	55	29	5	6	10	34	45	48
6	Birmingham City	42	11	3	7	44	38	8	7	6	27	28	48
7	Nottingham Forest	42	11	5	5	46	32	7	3	11	31	35	44
8	Fulham	42	14	1	6	52	28	3	9	9	29	43	44
9	Blackburn Rovers	42	12	4	5	40	20	6	4	11	28	45	44
10	Leeds United	42	13	4	4	42	24	1	11	9	29	39	43
11	Swansea Town	42	10	9	2	45	26	5	3	13	33	55	42
12	Rotherham United	42	9	7	5	41	30	7	2	12	34	44	41
13	Doncaster Rovers	42	9	9	3	26	17	3	7	11	32	47	40
14	West Ham United	42	9	5	7	38	28	4	8	9	20	32	39
15	Lincoln City	42	9	3	9	41	26	2	8	11	23	45	39
16	Everton	42	9	8	4	38	23	3	6	12	33	52	38
17	Brentford	42	8	8	5	38	29	5	3	13	21	47	37
18	Hull City	42	11	6	4	36	19	3	2	16	21	50	36
18	Notts County	42	11	5	5	41	31	3	3	15	19	57	36
20	Bury	42	10	6	5	33	30	3	3	15	20	51	36
21	Southampton	42	5	7	9	45	44	6	6	10	23	41	33
22	Barnsley	42	4	4	13	31	46	1	4	16	16	62	18

#	Date	Opponent	Score	Scorers	Att	Adam J	Aherne T	Baynham RL	Bennett EW	Cullen MJ	Cummins GP	Davies RA	Downie JD	Dunne S	Groves J	Hall LF	Jones LC	MacEwan MP	McJarrow H	Mitchell AJ	Moore BJ	Morton RH	Owen SW	Pemberton JT	Pye J	Scott JC	Shanks WG	Streten BR	Taylor AA	Turner GR	Watkins C
1	Aug 19	OLDHAM ATHLETIC	4-4	Downie 3, Pemberton	22822	11	2	1			10	7	8			5					9	4		3			6				
2	22	EVERTON	1-1	McJarrow	20217		3				10	7	8	2					9			5					6		1	11	4
3	26	NOTTM. FOREST	0-1		17522		3				10	7	8	2							9	5					6		1	11	4
4	29	Plymouth Argyle	2-2	Turner, Moore	22574					7	10		8	2				3			9	4	5				6		1	11	
5	Sep 2	Nottingham Forest	1-2	Turner	17172					7	10		8	2				3			9	4	5				6		1	11	
6	5	SWANSEA TOWN	2-0	Downie, Mitchell	17479		3				10		8	2						11	9	4	5				6	1		7	
7	9	Birmingham City	1-5	Downie	18881		3				10		8	2						11	9	4	5				6	1		7	
8	12	Rotherham United	1-2	Mitchell	15726		3				10		8	2		5				11	9						6	1		7	4
9	16	BIRMINGHAM CITY	2-0	Cummins, Downie (p)	12231		3	1		7	10		8	2						11	9	4	5				6				
10	19	LEICESTER CITY	2-2	Downie, Dunn (og)	19138		3	1			10	7	8	2						11	9	4	5				6				
11	26	Stoke City	1-1	Scott	24083		3	1			10		8	2						11	9	4	5		7		6				
12	Oct 3	FULHAM	1-2	Cummins	18619			1			10		8	2						11			5	3	9	7	6				4
13	10	HULL CITY	3-1	Turner 2, Watkins	14754		3				10			2						11	9	4	5			7		1		8	6
14	17	Notts County	2-1	Cummins, Mitchell	12208		3		7		10			2						11		4	5		9		6	1		8	
15	24	LINCOLN CITY	1-0	Davies	15578		3				10	7	8	2						11		4	5		9		6	1			
16	31	Bristol Rovers	3-3	Pye 2, Mitchell	20021		3				10	7	8	2		5				11		4			9		6	1			
17	Nov 7	BRENTFORD	1-1	Mitchell	15167		3				10	7	8	2						11			5		9		6	1			4
18	14	Derby County	2-1	Mitchell 2	15934		3				10	7		2						11			5		9		6	1		8	4
19	21	BLACKBURN ROVERS	2-1	Watkins, Mitchell	16269		3				10	7		2						11		4	5		9		6	1		8	6
20	28	Doncaster Rovers	3-1	Pye, Mitchell, Graham (og)	18273		3				10	7		2						11		4	5		9		6	1		8	6
21	Dec 5	BURY	3-2	Morton, Turner, Pye	15309		3				10	7		2						11		4	5		9		6	1		8	6
22	12	Oldham Athletic	2-1	Turner 2	14128		3				10	7		2						11		4	5		9		6	1		8	6
23	19	Everton	1-2	Cummins	33544		3				10	7		2						11		4	5		9		6	1		8	6
24	25	West Ham United	0-1		19721		3				10	7		2						11		4	5		9		6	1		8	6
25	26	WEST HAM UNITED	3-1	Turner 2, Mitchell	20133		3				10	7		2						11	9	4	5				6	1		8	6
26	Jan 2	PLYMOUTH ARGYLE	2-1	Moore, Turner	9694		3				10	7		2						11	9	4	5				6	1		8	6
27	16	Swansea Town	1-1	Moore	16785		3				10	7		2						11	9	4	5				6	1		8	6
28	23	ROTHERHAM UNITED	1-1	Mitchell	17300		3				10	7		2						11	9	4	5				6	1		8	6
29	Feb 6	Leicester City	1-2	Turner	31892		3				10	7		2			9			11		4						1		8	6
30	13	STOKE CITY	0-1		17055		3				10	7		2			9			11		4	5					1		8	6
31	20	Fulham	1-5	Downie	26982		3				10	7	9	2						11		4	5					1		8	6
32	27	Hull City	2-1	Shanks, Downie	21555		3				10	7	9	2			5			11		4					6	1		8	
33	Mar 6	NOTTS COUNTY	2-1	Downie, Davies	14623		3				10	7	9	2			5			11		4					6	1		8	
34	13	Lincoln City	1-1	Turner	11195		3				10	7	9	2						11		4	5				6	1		8	
35	20	BRISTOL ROVERS	1-1	Downie	12195	11	3				10	7	9	2								4	5				6	1		8	
36	27	Blackburn Rovers	0-2		24331		3				10	7	8	2						11		4	5				6	1		9	
37	Apr 3	DONCASTER ROVERS	2-0	Turner, Davies	10838		3				10	7	8	2						11		4	5				6	1		9	
38	10	Brentford	1-0	Turner	14204		3				10	7	8	2						11		4	5				6	1		9	
39	16	LEEDS UNITED	1-1	Mitchell	16129		3				10	7	8	2						11		4	5				6	1		9	
40	17	DERBY COUNTY	2-1	Morton, Downie	12874		3				10	7	8	2						11		4	5				6	1		9	
41	19	Leeds United	1-2	Turner	13930	11	3				10	7		2	9							4	5				6	1		8	
42	24	Bury	1-0	Mitchell	11018		3				10	7		2						11		4	5		9		6	1		8	
		Apps				3	35	5	1	8	33	31	26	25	1	4	22	3	1	30	11	40	25	4	14	12	25	37	4	32	30
		Goals									4	3	12				1			12	3	2			1	4	1			16	2

Two own goals

F.A. Cup

Rd	Date	Opponent	Score	Scorers	Att	Aherne T	Cummins GP	Davies RA	Dunne S	Mitchell AJ	Moore BJ	Morton RH	Owen SW	Streten BR	Turner GR	Watkins C
R3	Jan 9	Blackpool	1-1	Cummins	25242	3	10	7	2	11	9	4	5	1	8	6
rep	Jan 13	BLACKPOOL	0-0		23472	3	10	7	2	11	9	4	5	1	8	6
rep 2	Jan 18	Blackpool	1-1	Cummins	31663	3	10	7	2	11	9	4	5	1	8	6
rep 3	Jan 25	Blackpool	0-2		25855	3	10	7	2	11	9	4	5	1	8	6

First and second replays a.e.t. Replay 2 at Villa Park, replay 3 at Molineux.

		P	W	D	L	F	A	W	D	L	F	A	Pts
1	Leicester City	42	15	4	2	63	23	8	6	7	34	37	56
2	Everton	42	13	6	2	55	27	7	10	4	37	31	56
3	Blackburn Rovers	42	15	4	2	54	16	8	5	8	32	34	55
4	Nottingham Forest	42	15	5	1	61	27	5	7	9	25	32	52
5	Rotherham United	42	13	4	4	51	26	8	3	10	29	41	49
6	LUTON TOWN	42	11	7	3	36	23	7	5	9	28	36	48
7	Birmingham City	42	12	6	3	49	18	6	5	10	29	40	47
8	Fulham	42	12	3	6	62	39	5	7	9	36	46	44
9	Bristol Rovers	42	10	7	4	32	19	4	9	8	32	39	44
10	Leeds United	42	12	5	4	56	30	3	8	10	33	51	43
11	Stoke City	42	8	8	5	43	28	4	9	8	28	32	41
12	Doncaster Rovers	42	9	5	7	32	28	7	4	10	27	35	41
13	West Ham United	42	11	6	4	44	20	4	3	14	23	49	39
14	Notts County	42	8	6	7	26	29	5	7	9	28	45	39
15	Hull City	42	14	1	6	47	22	2	5	14	17	44	38
16	Lincoln City	42	11	6	4	46	23	3	3	15	19	60	37
17	Bury	42	9	7	5	39	32	2	7	12	15	40	36
18	Derby County	42	9	5	7	38	35	3	6	12	26	47	35
19	Plymouth Argyle	42	6	12	3	38	31	3	4	14	27	51	34
20	Swansea Town	42	11	5	5	34	25	2	3	16	24	57	34
21	Brentford	42	9	5	7	25	26	1	6	14	15	52	31
22	Oldham Athletic	42	6	7	8	26	31	2	2	17	14	58	25

1954/55   Second in Division 2: Promoted

#	Date	Opponent	Score	Scorers	Att	Adam J	Aheme T	Allen DS	Baynham RL	Cullen MJ	Cummins GP	Davies RA	Dunne S	Groves J	Hall LF	Jones LC	Kelly TWJ	MacEwan MP	Mitchell AJ	Morton RH	Owen SW	Pearce RS	Pemberton JT	Pye J	Shanks WG	Smith RS	Streten BR	Turner GR	Watkins C
1	Aug 21	NOTTM. FOREST	3-0	Davies, Turner, Pye	19832	11	3					7	2	10						4	5			9	6		1	8	
2	24	Bury	1-2	Turner	15545	11	3				9	7	2	10						4	5				6		1	8	
3	28	Ipswich Town	1-3	Adam	20665	11	3			7			2	10						4	5			9		6	1	8	
4	Sep 1	BURY	3-2	Mitchell (p), Turner, Adam	13654	11	3				10		2						7	4	5			9	6		1	8	
5	4	BIRMINGHAM CITY	1-0	Adam	16347	11	3				10		2						7	4	5			9		6	1	8	
6	8	Lincoln City	2-1	Pye 2	13450	11	3			7	10		2							4	5			9	6		1	8	
7	11	Middlesbrough	2-0	Davies, Turner	16071	11	3				10	7	2							4	5			9	6		1	8	
8	15	LINCOLN CITY	2-1	Turner 2	11972	11	3				10	7	2					9		4	5				6		1	8	
9	18	STOKE CITY	3-1	Adam 2, Watkins	17325	11	3			7			2					9		4	5				6		1	8	10
10	25	Rotherham United	0-2		17114	11	3			7			2							4	5			9	6		1	8	10
11	Oct 2	DERBY COUNTY	2-0	Turner, Pye	17156	11	3					7	2							4	5			9	6		1	8	10
12	9	Bristol Rovers	2-3	Turner, Kelly	30654	11	3					7	2				9			4	5				6		1	8	10
13	16	PLYMOUTH ARGYLE	3-1	Davies, Turner, Adam	15059	11	3					7	2		5			9		4					6		1	8	10
14	23	Fulham	1-3	Turner	30632	11	3					7	2	10	5		9			4					6		1	8	
15	30	Swansea Town	1-2	Turner	15555	11	3					7	2	10	5		9			4					6		1	8	
16	Nov 6	Notts County	3-3	Morton 2, Adam	10395	11	3					7	2	10						9	5		4		6		1	8	
17	13	LIVERPOOL	3-2	Morton 2, Adam	15887	11	3		1		10	7	2							9	5		4		6			8	
18	20	West Ham United	1-2	Morton	23034	11	3		1		10	7	2							9	5		4		6			8	
19	27	BLACKBURN ROVERS	7-3	Pemberton, Adam, Turner 3, Davies 2	17314	11	3		1		10	7	2							9	5		4		6			8	
20	Dec 4	Port Vale	1-1	Davies	14052	11	3		1		10	7	2							9	5		4		6			8	
21	11	DONCASTER ROVERS	3-0	Turner 2, Morton	14541		3		1	11	10	7	2							9	5		4		6			8	
22	18	Nottingham Forest	5-1	Pemberton, Cummins, Turner 2, Davies	11943		3		1	11	10	7	2							9	5		4		6			8	
23	25	HULL CITY	1-1	Turner	15853		3		1	11	10	7	2							9	5		4		6			8	
24	27	Hull City	4-0	Morton 2, Cullen, Turner	39890		3		1	11	10	7	2							9	5		4		6			8	
25	Jan 1	IPSWICH TOWN	3-2	Davies, Morton, Cummins	16581		3		1	11	10	7	2							9	5		4		6			8	
26	22	MIDDLESBROUGH	2-0	Turner, Davies	13372		3		1	11	10	7	2							9	5		4		6			8	
27	Feb 5	Stoke City	0-0		21156		3		1	11	10	7	2							9	5		4		6			8	
28	12	ROTHERHAM UNITED	4-0	Turner 2, Groves, Williams (og)	18450		3		1	11		7	2	10						9	5		4		6			8	
29	Mar 2	Derby County	0-0		5987		3	7	1	11	10		2							9	5		4		6			8	
30	5	Plymouth Argyle	1-2	Morton	25975	11	3		1		10	7	2			5				9			4		6			8	
31	12	FULHAM	3-0	Turner 2, Groves	17966		3		1	11	10	7	2	9							5		4		6			8	
32	19	Swansea Town	1-2	Turner	19422		3			11	10	7	2	9							5		4		6		1	8	
33	26	NOTTS COUNTY	3-1	Morton 2, Cummins	16917	11	3				10	7	2							9	5		4		6		1	8	
34	Apr 2	Liverpool	4-4	Turner 2, Morton 2	30710	11	3				10	7	2							9	5		4		6		1	8	
35	8	LEEDS UNITED	0-0		25775	11	3		1		10	7	2							9	5		4					8	6
36	9	WEST HAM UNITED	2-0	Turner, Cummins	27148		3		1		10		2							9	5	7	4		11			8	6
37	11	Leeds United	0-4		29583		3		1		10	7	2							9	5		4		11			8	6
38	16	Blackburn Rovers	0-0		35912	11	3		1		10	7	2							9	5		4		6			8	
39	20	Birmingham City	1-2	Turner	34612		3		1		10	7	2	11						9	5		4		6			8	
40	23	PORT VALE	4-2	Turner 2, Davies, MacEwan	16704		3		1			7	2					9		4	5		11		6			8	10
41	27	BRISTOL ROVERS	2-0	Watkins 2	20120		3		1			7	2					9		4	5		11		6			8	10
42	30	Doncaster Rovers	3-0	MacEwan 2, Pemberton	12585		3		1			7	2					9		4	5		11		6			8	10
				Apps		25	42	1	23	16	28	33	42	13	3	1	3	6	2	39	36	1	27	8	39	2	19	42	11
				Goals		9				1	4	10		2			1	3	1	14			3	4				32	3

One own goal

F.A. Cup

Rd	Date	Opponent	Score	Scorers	Att	Aheme T	Baynham RL	Cullen MJ	Cummins GP	Davies RA	Dunne S	Morton RH	Owen SW	Pemberton JT	Shanks WG	Turner GR
R3	Jan 8	WORKINGTON TOWN	5-0	Turner 2, Cummins, Cullen 2	18853	3	1	11	10	7	2	9	5	4	6	8
R4	Jan 29	Rotherham United	5-1	Turner 3, Cummins, Cullen	21231	3	1	11	10	7	2	9	5	4	6	8
R5	Feb 19	MANCHESTER CITY	0-2		23104	3	1	11	10	7	2	9	5	4	6	8

		P	W	D	L	F	A	W	D	L	F	A	Pts
1	Birmingham City	42	14	4	3	56	22	8	6	7	36	25	54
2	LUTON TOWN	42	18	2	1	55	18	5	6	10	33	35	54
3	Rotherham United	42	17	1	3	59	22	8	3	10	35	42	54
4	Leeds United	42	14	4	3	43	19	9	3	9	27	34	53
5	Stoke City	42	12	5	4	38	17	9	5	7	31	29	52
6	Blackburn Rovers	42	14	4	3	73	31	8	2	11	41	48	50
7	Notts County	42	14	3	4	46	27	7	3	11	28	44	48
8	West Ham United	42	12	4	5	46	28	6	6	9	28	42	46
9	Bristol Rovers	42	15	4	2	52	23	4	3	14	23	47	45
10	Swansea Town	42	15	3	3	58	28	2	6	13	28	55	43
11	Liverpool	42	11	7	3	55	37	5	3	13	37	59	42
12	Middlesbrough	42	13	1	7	48	31	5	5	11	25	51	42
13	Bury	42	10	5	6	44	35	5	6	10	33	37	41
14	Fulham	42	10	5	6	46	29	4	6	11	30	50	39
15	Nottingham Forest	42	8	4	9	29	29	8	3	10	29	33	39
16	Lincoln City	42	8	6	7	39	35	5	4	12	29	44	36
17	Port Vale	42	10	6	5	31	21	2	5	14	17	50	35
18	Doncaster Rovers	42	10	5	6	35	34	4	2	15	23	61	35
19	Hull City	42	7	5	9	30	35	5	5	11	14	34	34
20	Plymouth Argyle	42	10	4	7	29	26	2	3	16	28	56	31
21	Ipswich Town	42	10	3	8	37	28	1	3	17	20	64	28
22	Derby County	42	6	6	9	39	34	1	3	17	14	48	23

1955/56 — 10th in Division One

No		Date	Opponent	Score	Scorers	Att	Adam J	Aherne T	Baynham RL	Cullen MJ	Cummins GP	Davies RA	Dunne S	Gregory AC	Groves J	Jones LC	Kelly TWJ	MacEwan MP	McGuffie AS	McLeod GJ	Morton RH	Owen SW	Pearce RS	Pemberton JT	Pounder JA	Shanks WG	Streten BR	Taylor AA	Turner GR
1	Aug	20	Charlton Athletic	2-2	Turner, MacEwan	28460		3	1		10	7	2					9			4	5				6		11	8
2		24	Preston North End	1-2	MacEwan	30770		3	1		10	7	2					9			4	5				6		11	8
3		27	TOTTENHAM HOTSPUR	2-1	Cummins, Taylor	21143		3	1		10		2					9			4	5	7			6		11	8
4		31	PRESTON NORTH END	2-1	Cullen, MacEwan	24174		3	1	7	10		2		11			9			4	5				6			8
5	Sep	3	Everton	1-0	MacEwan	44237		3	1	7	10		2		11			9			4	5				6			8
6		5	Burnley	1-3	Turner	19350		3	1	7	10		2		11			9			4	5				6			8
7		10	NEWCASTLE UNITED	4-2	Turner, MacEwan, Morton, Lackenby (og)	25814	11	3	1	7	10		2					9			4	5				6			8
8		17	Birmingham City	0-0		31013	11	3	1	7	10		2					9			4	5				6			8
9		24	WEST BROMWICH ALB.	0-2		24440	11	3	1	7	10		2					9			4	5				6			8
10	Oct	1	Manchester United	1-3	Cummins	34661	11	3	1	7	10		2	8				9			4	5				6			
11		8	BLACKPOOL	3-1	Turner 2, MacEwan	24493	11	3	1	7	10		2					9			4	5				6			8
12		15	Huddersfield Town	2-0	Turner, Adam	19621	11	3	1	7	10		2					9				5			4	6			8
13		22	ARSENAL	0-0		24009	11	3	1	7	10		2					9			4	5				6			8
14		29	Bolton Wanderers	0-4		26794	11	3	1	7	10	9	2								4	5				6			8
15	Nov	5	WOLVERHAMPTON W.	5-1	Morton 2, Cullen, Turner 2	27911	11	3	1	7	10		2								9	5		4		6			8
16		12	Aston Villa	0-1		29761	11		1	7	10		2			3					9	5		4		6			8
17		19	SUNDERLAND	8-2	Cullen 2, Adam, Morton 3, Turner 2	25802	11	3	1	7	10		2								9	5		4		6			8
18		26	Portsmouth	0-0		27758	11	3	1	7	10		2								9	5		4		6			8
19	Dec	3	CARDIFF CITY	3-0	Turner, Morton, Adam	21827	11	3	1	7			2								9	5	10	4		6			8
20		10	Manchester City	2-3	Morton, Ewing (og)	15499	11	3	1	7			2					9			8	5	10	4		6			
21		17	CHARLTON ATHLETIC	2-1	MacEwan, Hammond (og)	19686	11	3	1	7			2					9			8	5	10	4		6			
22		24	Tottenham Hotspur	1-2	Turner	41168	11	3	1	7			2								9	5	10	4		6			8
23		26	Sheffield United	4-0	Cullen, Turner, Pearce, Morton	29563		3	1	7			2		11						9	5	10	4		6			8
24		27	SHEFFIELD UNITED	2-1	Pearce, Davies	23522		3	1	7			2		11						9	5	10	4		6			8
25		31	EVERTON	2-2	Turner, Adam	23226	11	3	1	7	10		2								9	5		4		6			8
26	Jan	14	Newcastle United	0-4		21464		3	1	7	10		2				5				9		11	4		6			8
27		21	BIRMINGHAM CITY	0-1		18970		3	1	7	10		2				5				9		11	4		6			8
28	Feb	4	West Bromwich Albion	1-3	Turner	25190	11	3	1	7	10		2				5				9			4		6			8
29		11	MANCHESTER UNITED	0-2		16368			1	7	10		2		11	3	5				9			4		6			8
30		18	Blackpool	2-3	MacEwan, Davies	18562	11				10	7	2			3	5	9			4					6	1		8
31		25	HUDDERSFIELD T	1-2	Turner	15431	11		1			7	2			3	5	9			4		10			6			8
32	Mar	7	Sunderland	2-1	Davies, Daniel (og)	21317	11		1			7	2	9		3	5				4		10			6			8
33		10	BOLTON WANDERERS	0-0		20432	11		1			7	2	9		3	5				4		10			6			8
34		17	Wolverhampton Wan.	2-1	Davies, Gregory	32339	11		1			7	2	9		3	5				4		10			6			8
35		24	ASTON VILLA	2-1	Pearce 2	17126	11		1			7	2	9		3	5				4		10	8		6			
36		30	CHELSEA	2-2	Davies, Gregory	24276	11		1	8		7	2	9		3	5				4		10			6			
37		31	Arsenal	0-3		45968	11		1	8		7	2	9		3	5				4		10			6			
38	Apr	2	Chelsea	0-0		26364	11		1	7			2	9		3	5				4		10	8		6			
39		7	PORTSMOUTH	1-0	Turner	17839	11		1				2			3	5				4	9	10	7		6			8
40		14	Cardiff City	0-2		16086	11		1	7			2	8		3			4	9		5	10			6			
41		21	MANCHESTER CITY	3-2	Turner (p), Ewing (og), Groves	18074	11	3	1	7			2		9				4			5	10			6			8
42		28	BURNLEY	2-3	Morton, Adam	15999	11	3	1	7			2		9						4	5	10			6			8

| | | | | | | Apps | 30 | 29 | 41 | 30 | 24 | 16 | 40 | 7 | 12 | 15 | 14 | 17 | 3 | 1 | 39 | 27 | 19 | 20 | 1 | 40 | 1 | 3 | 33 |
| | | | | | | Goals | 5 | | | 6 | 2 | 5 | | | 2 | 1 | | 8 | | | 10 | | 3 | | | | | | 19 |

Five own goals

F.A. Cup

		Date	Opponent	Score		Att	Adam J	Aherne T	Baynham RL	Cullen MJ	Cummins GP	Davies RA	Dunne S	Gregory AC	Groves J	Jones LC	Kelly TWJ	MacEwan MP	McGuffie AS	McLeod GJ	Morton RH	Owen SW	Pearce RS	Pemberton JT	Pounder JA	Shanks WG	Streten BR	Taylor AA	Turner GR
R3	Jan	11	LEICESTER CITY	0-4		23221		3	1	7	10		2								9	5	11	4		6			8

		P	W	D	L	F	A	W	D	L	F	A	Pts
1	Manchester United	42	18	3	0	51	20	7	7	7	32	31	60
2	Blackpool	42	13	4	4	56	27	7	5	9	30	35	49
3	Wolverhampton Wan.	42	15	2	4	51	27	5	7	9	38	38	49
4	Manchester City	42	11	5	5	40	27	7	5	9	42	42	46
5	Arsenal	42	13	4	4	38	22	5	6	10	22	39	46
6	Birmingham City	42	12	4	5	51	26	6	5	10	24	31	45
7	Burnley	42	11	3	7	37	20	7	5	9	27	34	44
8	Bolton Wanderers	42	13	3	5	50	24	5	4	12	21	34	43
9	Sunderland	42	10	8	3	44	36	7	1	13	36	59	43
10	LUTON TOWN	42	12	4	5	44	27	5	4	12	22	37	42
11	Newcastle United	42	12	4	5	49	24	5	3	13	36	46	41
12	Portsmouth	42	9	8	4	46	38	7	1	13	32	47	41
13	West Bromwich Alb.	42	13	3	5	37	25	5	2	14	21	45	41
14	Charlton Athletic	42	13	2	6	47	26	4	4	13	28	55	40
15	Everton	42	11	5	5	37	29	4	5	12	18	40	40
16	Chelsea	42	10	4	7	32	26	4	7	10	32	51	39
17	Cardiff City	42	11	4	6	36	32	4	5	12	19	37	39
18	Tottenham Hotspur	42	9	4	8	37	33	6	3	12	24	38	37
19	Preston North End	42	6	5	10	32	36	8	3	10	41	36	36
20	Aston Villa	42	9	6	6	32	29	2	7	12	20	40	35
21	Huddersfield Town	42	9	4	8	32	30	5	3	13	22	53	35
22	Sheffield United	42	8	6	7	31	35	4	3	14	32	42	33

1956/57   16th in Division One

No		Date	Opponent	Score	Scorers	Att	Adam J	Aherne T	Baynham RL	Brown AD	Cullen MJ	Cummins GP	Davies RA	Dunne S	Gregory AC	Groves J	Jones LC	Kelly TWJ	Legate RA	McLeod GJ	McNally JB	Morton RH	Owen SW	Pearce RS	Pemberton JT	Pounder JA	Shanks WG	Smith RS	Streten BR	Thompson A	Turner GR
1	Aug 18	SUNDERLAND	6-2	Turner 4, Groves, Cullen	23049	11	3			7			2		10						9	5		4		6		1		8
2	22	WOLVERHAMPTON W.	1-0	Morton	26715	11	3			7			2		10						9	5		4		6		1		8
3	25	Charlton Athletic	2-1	Morton, Cullen	19014	11	3			7			2		10						9	5		4		6		1		8
4	29	Wolverhampton Wan.	4-5	Cullen, Turner 3	46781	11	3			7			2								9	5	10	4		6		1		8
5	Sep 1	MANCHESTER CITY	3-2	Pemberton, Turner, Adam	21648	11	3			7	10		2								9	5		4		6		1		8
6	5	ASTON VILLA	0-0		21171	11	3			7	10		2								9	5		4		6		1		8
7	8	Blackpool	0-4		32112	11	3			7			2								9	5	10	4		6		1		8
8	15	EVERTON	2-0	Turner, Pearce	18076	11	3			7			2								9	5	10	4		6		1		8
9	22	Tottenham Hotspur	0-5		58960	11	3			7			2								9	5	10	4		6		1		8
10	29	LEEDS UNITED	2-2	Turner 2	20949			1		11	10	7	2	9	6	3					4	5								8
11	Oct 6	Newcastle United	2-2	Turner 2	36941	11		1		10		7	2		6	3			9		4	5								8
12	13	SHEFFIELD WEDNESDAY	2-0	Turner (p), Legate	19202			1		10		7	2	9		3		11			4	5				6				8
13	20	Birmingham City	0-3		31783			1		10		7	2	9		3		11			4	5				6				8
14	27	WEST BROMWICH ALB.	0-1		16786	11				10		7		9		3				2	4	5				6		1		8
15	Nov 3	Burnley	1-1	Groves	22891					7	10		2	8	11	3					9	5		4		6		1		
16	10	PRESTON NORTH END	1-1	Cullen	18721					7	10		2	8		3		11			9	5		4		6		1		
17	17	Chelsea	1-4	Gregory	30823					7	10		2	11		3					9	5	8	4		6		1		
18	24	CARDIFF CITY	3-0	Morton 2, Gregory	13674		3	1		10		7	2	11							9	5		4		6				8
19	Dec 1	Manchester United	1-3	Gregory	34954		3	1		10		7	2	11			5				9			4		6				8
20	8	ARSENAL	1-2	Groves	19792								2	11	10	3					9	5	7	4		6		1		8
21	15	Sunderland	0-1		28473	11	3						2		10						9	5	7	4		6		1		8
22	22	CHARLTON ATHLETIC	4-2	Turner 3 (1p), Cullen	9922		3	1		7			2	11					9		10	5		4		6				8
23	29	Manchester City	2-3	Turner 2	27253		3	1		7			2	11					9		10	5		4		6				8
24	Jan 12	BLACKPOOL	0-2		16589			1		7		11	2						9	3	4	5	10			6				8
25	19	Everton	1-2	Shanks	29017						10		2						9	3	4	5	7			6	11	1		8
26	Feb 2	TOTTENHAM HOTSPUR	1-3	Turner (p)	22586						10	11	2						9	3	4	5	7			6		1		8
27	9	Leeds United	2-1	Brown, McLeod	25646		3	1	8				2	9					10		11	4	5	6	7					
28	16	NEWCASTLE UNITED	4-1	Turner 3, Groves	21007		3	1	10				2		9						11	4	5	6	7					8
29	23	West Bromwich Albion	0-4		21835		3	1	10				2	9							11	4	5	6	7					8
30	Mar 9	Arsenal	3-1	Brown 2, Turner (p)	41288			1	10				2	9						3	11	4	5	6	7					8
31	13	Portsmouth	2-2	Turner, Morton	22438			1	10				2	9						3	11	4	5	6	7					8
32	16	BURNLEY	0-2		16420			1	8	7	10		2	9						3	11	4	5			6				
33	20	PORTSMOUTH	1-0	Brown	14601			1	8	7	10		2	9						3	11	4	5			6				
34	23	Preston North End	0-2		23361			1	8	7	10		2	9							11	4	5				6		3	
35	30	CHELSEA	0-4		15083					6	10		2	9						3	11	4	5			7		1		8
36	Apr 3	BIRMINGHAM CITY	0-0		12881			1	10	11			2	9		3					4	5	6	7						8
37	6	Cardiff City	0-0		18730	11		1	10				2	9		3					4	5	6	7						8
38	13	MANCHESTER UNITED	0-2		21244	11		1	10	7	9					3	5			2	4		6							8
39	19	Bolton Wanderers	2-2	Turner 2	18666	11		1	10	7	9					3	5			2	4		6							8
40	20	Sheffield Wednesday	0-3		21794	11		1	10	7	9					3	5			2			6				4			8
41	22	BOLTON WANDERERS	1-0	Turner	13396	11		1	10	7				9		3	5			2	4		6							8
42	27	Aston Villa	3-1	Turner 2, Brown	28524	11		1	10	7	9					3	5			2	4		6							8
		Apps				18	18	23	16	23	17	16	29	13	18	20	8	3	15	16	40	34	26	17	2	28	8	19	1	34
		Goals				1			5	5				3	3			1	1		5		1	1		1				30

One own goal

F.A. Cup

		Date	Opponent	Score	Scorers	Att	Cullen MJ	Davies RA	Dunne S	Kelly TWJ	McLeod GJ	McNally JB	Pearce RS	Pemberton JT	Shanks WG	Streten BR	Turner GR
R3	Jan 5	ASTON VILLA	2-2	Davies, Turner (p)	20108	7	11	2	5	9	3	10	4	6	1	8
rep	Jan 7	Aston Villa	0-2		28356	7	11	2	5	9	3	10	4	6	1	8

Southern Professional Floodlit Cup

		Date	Opponent	Score	Scorers	Adam J	Baynham RL	Cullen MJ	Cummins GP	Davies RA	Dunne S	Gregory AC	Groves J	Jones LC	Kelly TWJ	McLeod GJ	McNally JB	Morton RH	Owen SW	Pearce RS	Pemberton JT	Shanks WG	Smith RS	Streten BR	Turner GR
R1	Sep 26	CHELSEA	4-2	Turner 3, Cummins		1	7	10		2	11	6	3				4	5	9					8
R2	Nov 7	WATFORD	4-3	Cummins 2, Groves, Morton			7	10		2		11	3				9	5		4	6		1	8
SF	Mar 26	Brentford	4-0	Pemberton 2, Davies, Smith		1	7		11				3		9	2	10	5		4	6	8		
F	Apr 15	Reading	2-1	Adam, Turner	11	1	7	9					3	5	10	2	4		6					8

Division One Final Table

		P	W	D	L	F	A	W	D	L	F	A	Pts
1	Manchester United	42	14	4	3	55	25	14	4	3	48	29	64
2	Tottenham Hotspur	42	15	4	2	70	24	7	8	6	34	32	56
3	Preston North End	42	15	4	2	50	19	8	6	7	34	37	56
4	Blackpool	42	14	3	4	55	26	8	6	7	38	39	53
5	Arsenal	42	12	5	4	45	21	9	3	9	40	48	50
6	Wolverhampton Wan.	42	17	2	2	70	29	3	6	12	24	41	48
7	Burnley	42	14	5	2	41	21	4	5	12	15	29	46
8	Leeds United	42	10	8	3	42	18	5	6	10	30	45	44
9	Bolton Wanderers	42	13	6	2	42	23	3	6	12	23	42	44
10	Aston Villa	42	10	8	3	46	25	4	7	10	20	30	43
11	West Bromwich Alb.	42	8	8	5	31	25	6	6	9	28	36	42
12	Chelsea	42	7	8	6	43	36	6	5	10	30	37	39
13	Birmingham City	42	12	5	4	52	25	3	4	14	17	44	39
14	Sheffield Wed.	42	14	3	4	55	29	2	3	16	27	59	38
15	Everton	42	10	5	6	34	28	4	5	12	27	51	38
16	LUTON TOWN	42	10	4	7	32	26	4	5	12	26	50	37
17	Newcastle United	42	10	5	6	43	31	4	3	14	24	56	36
18	Manchester City	42	10	2	9	48	42	3	7	11	30	46	35
19	Portsmouth	42	8	6	7	37	35	2	7	12	25	57	33
20	Sunderland	42	9	5	7	40	30	3	3	15	27	58	32
21	Cardiff City	42	7	6	8	35	34	3	3	15	18	54	29
22	Charlton Athletic	42	7	3	11	31	44	2	1	18	31	76	22

1957/58 8th in Division One

						Adam J	Baynham RL	Brown AD	Cullen MJ	Cummins GP	Dunne S	Gregory AC	Groves J	Hawkes KK	Jones LC	Kelly TWJ	Marsh WE	McGuffie AS	McLeod GJ	McNally JB	Morton RH	Owen SW	Pacey D	Pearce RS	Rowlands DC	Turner GR	Whitby BK
1	Aug 24	BOLTON WANDERERS	1-0	Turner	17591	11	1	10	7		2		9		3						4	5		6		8	
2	26	Blackpool	2-1	Turner 2	21099	11	1	10	7		2		9		3						4	5		6		8	
3	31	Arsenal	0-2		49914	11	1	10	7		2		9		3						4	5		6		8	
4	Sep 4	BLACKPOOL	2-0	Brown, Cullen	19567	11	1	10	7		2		9		3						4	5		6		8	
5	7	WOLVERHAMPTON W.	3-1	Turner 2, Cullen	22030		1	10	7		2		4		3				11		9	5		6		8	
6	11	Leeds United	2-0	Morton, Turner	21972		1	10	7		2		4		3				11		9	5		6		8	
7	14	Aston Villa	0-2		28962		1	10	7		2		4		3				11		9	5		6		8	
8	18	LEEDS UNITED	1-1	Morton	16887		1	10	7		2		4		3				11		9	5		6		8	
9	21	EVERTON	0-1		19797		1	10	7		2		4						11	3	9	5		6		8	
10	28	Sunderland	0-3		36724	7	1	10			2		4		3				11		9	5		6		8	
11	Oct 5	BURNLEY	3-2	Turner 2, Brown	15179	7	1	9		10	2				3				11		4	5		6		8	
12	12	Preston North End	0-1		25403	7	1	9		10	2				3				11		4	5		6		8	
13	19	SHEFFIELD WEDNESDAY	2-0	McLeod, Brown	14473	7	1	9		10	2				3				11		4	5		6		8	
14	26	Manchester City	2-2	Pearce, Turner	30654	7	1	9		10	2				3				11		4	5		6		8	
15	Nov 2	BIRMINGHAM CITY	3-0	Turner 2, MacLeod	17316	7	1	9		10					3				11	2	4	5		6		8	
16	9	Chelsea	3-1	Turner 3	34102	7	1	9		10	2				3				11		4	5		6		8	
17	16	NEWCASTLE UNITED	0-3		19703	7	1	9		10	2				3				11		4	5		6		8	
18	23	Tottenham Hotspur	1-3	Cummins	41242	7	1	9		10	2				3				11		4	5		6		8	
19	30	NOTTM. FOREST	3-1	Turner 3	18391	7	1	9		10	2				3				11		4	5		6		8	
20	Dec 7	Portsmouth	0-5		17782	7	1	9		10	2				3				11		4	5		6		8	
21	14	WEST BROMWICH ALB.	5-1	Turner 2,Adam,Brown,Kennedy(og)	15365	7	1	9			2		10	3					11		4	5		6		8	
22	21	Bolton Wanderers	2-1	Turner, Groves	16754	7	1	9			2		10	3					11		4	5		6		8	
23	25	Manchester United	0-3		39594	7	1	9			2	8	10	3		5			11				4	6			
24	26	MANCHESTER UNITED	2-2	Brown, Groves	26478	7		9	10		2		8	3		5	1		11				4	6			
25	28	ARSENAL	4-0	Brown 3, Groves	27493	7	1	9			2		10	3					11		4	5		6		8	
26	Jan 11	Wolverhampton Wan.	1-1	Brown	30805	7	1	9			2		10	3					11		4	5		6		8	
27	18	ASTON VILLA	3-0	Adam, Turner, MacLeod	16619	7	1	9			2		10	3					11		4	5		6		8	
28	Feb 1	Everton	2-0	Gregory, Turner	26908	7	1				2	9	10	3					11		4	5	6			8	
29	8	SUNDERLAND	7-1	Turner 4, Groves, Brown 2	15932	7	1	9			2		10	3					11			5	4	6		8	
30	15	Burnley	2-1	Turner, Brown	16869	7	1	9			2		10	3					11			5	4	6		8	
31	22	PRESTON NORTH END	1-3	Adam	22549	7	1	9			2		10	3		5			11		4		6			8	
32	Mar 1	Sheffield Wednesday	1-2	Turner	17747	7	1	9		10	2		4	3		5			11				6			8	
33	8	MANCHESTER CITY	1-2	Pacey	16019	7	1	9			2		4	3					11			5	6		10	8	
34	15	Birmingham City	1-1	Turner (p)	25225	7	1		10		2		9	3				4	11			5	6			8	
35	22	TOTTENHAM HOTSPUR	0-0		22384	7	1		10		2		9	3				4	11			5	6			8	
36	29	Newcastle United	2-3	Whitby, Turner	16775		1		10		2		9	3				4	11			5	6			8	7
37	Apr 5	CHELSEA	0-2		15285		1	9			2		10	3				4	11			5	6			8	7
38	7	LEICESTER CITY	2-1	Gregory 2	14795	11	1			10	2	9	6	3				4				5				8	7
39	8	Leicester City	1-4	Gregory	32480	11	1		7	10	2	9	6	3		5		4								8	
40	12	Nottingham Forest	0-1		22085		1		11	10	2	9		3		4		6				5				8	7
41	19	PORTSMOUTH	2-1	McLeod, Turner	12942		1		7		2		10	3		4		6	9			5				8	11
42	26	West Bromwich Albion	2-4	Turner 2	20158		1		7	10	2	9	4	3		5		6								8	11
					Apps	32	41	33	17	15	41	6	31	22	19	8	1	9	34	2	27	36	12	29	1	40	6
					Goals	3		12	2	1		4	4						4		2		1	1		33	1

One own goal

F.A. Cup

						Adam J	Baynham RL	Brown AD	Cullen MJ	Cummins GP	Dunne S	Gregory AC	Groves J	Hawkes KK	Jones LC	Kelly TWJ	Marsh WE	McGuffie AS	McLeod GJ	McNally JB	Morton RH	Owen SW	Pacey D	Pearce RS	Rowlands DC	Turner GR	Whitby BK
R3	Jan 4	Stockport County	0-3		18200	7	1	9			2		10	3					11		4	5		6		8	

Southern Professional Floodlit Cup

						Adam J	Baynham RL	Brown AD	Cullen MJ	Cummins GP	Dunne S	Gregory AC	Groves J	Hawkes KK	Jones LC	Kelly TWJ	Marsh WE	McGuffie AS	McLeod GJ	McNally JB	Morton RH	Owen SW	Pacey D	Pearce RS	Rowlands DC	Turner GR	Whitby BK
R1	Oct 28	Southampton	2-0	Turner, Cummins			1		7	10	2	11	6		3						4	5		9		8	
R2	Dec 10	Brentford	0-0				1			10		11	6								4	5		9		8	
rep	Jan 29	BRENTFORD	7-1	Turner 2,McLeod 2,Groves,Adam,Brown			1			10		11	6								4	5		9		8	
SF	Mar 25	Reading	3-3	Turner 2, Brown			1			10		11							9	6		5				8	
rep	31	READING	0-1				1			11						7			9	6		5				8	

R2 game with Brentford on Dec. 3rd abandoned.

Played in R2 onwards: BR Streten (at 2), JT Pemberton (at 3), RS Smith (at 7, but 10 in SF replay)
Played at 4 in SF and SF replay: RA Davies.

		P	W	D	L	F	A	W	D	L	F	A	Pts
1	Wolverhampton Wan.	42	17	3	1	60	21	11	5	5	43	26	64
2	Preston North End	42	18	2	1	63	14	8	5	8	37	37	59
3	Tottenham Hotspur	42	13	4	4	58	33	8	5	8	35	44	51
4	West Bromwich Alb.	42	14	4	3	59	29	4	10	7	33	41	50
5	Manchester City	42	14	4	3	58	33	8	1	12	46	67	49
6	Burnley	42	16	2	3	52	21	5	3	13	28	53	47
7	Blackpool	42	11	2	8	47	35	8	4	9	33	32	44
8	LUTON TOWN	42	13	3	5	45	22	6	3	12	24	41	44
9	Manchester United	42	10	4	7	45	31	6	7	8	40	44	43
10	Nottingham Forest	42	10	4	7	41	27	6	6	9	28	36	42
11	Chelsea	42	10	5	6	47	34	5	7	9	36	45	42
12	Arsenal	42	10	4	7	48	39	6	3	12	25	46	39
13	Birmingham City	42	8	6	7	43	37	6	5	10	33	52	39
14	Aston Villa	42	12	4	5	46	26	4	3	14	27	60	39
15	Bolton Wanderers	42	9	5	7	38	35	5	5	11	27	52	38
16	Everton	42	5	9	7	34	35	8	2	11	31	40	37
17	Leeds United	42	10	6	5	33	23	4	3	14	18	40	37
18	Leicester City	42	11	4	6	59	41	3	1	17	32	71	33
19	Newcastle United	42	6	4	11	38	42	6	4	11	35	39	32
20	Portsmouth	42	10	6	5	45	34	2	2	17	28	54	32
21	Sunderland	42	7	7	7	32	33	3	5	13	22	64	32
22	Sheffield Wed.	42	12	2	7	45	40	0	5	16	24	52	31

1958/59   17th in Division One

#		Date	Opponent	Score	Scorers	Att	Adam J	Baynham RL	Bingham WL	Brown AD	Collier AS	Cummins GP	Daniel AW	Dixon MJ	Dunne S	Gregory AC	Groves J	Hawkes B	Hawkes KK	Kelly TWJ	Kilgannon J	Marsh WE	McGuffie AS	McLeod GJ	McNally JB	Morton RH	Owen SW	Pacey D	Turner GR	Whitby BK
1	Aug	23	WEST BROMWICH ALB.	1-1	Turner (p)	24425	11	1	7	9					2		10		3							4	5	6	8	
2		26	Leeds United	1-1	Turner	25498	11	1	7	9					2		10		3							4	5	6	8	
3		30	Birmingham City	1-0	Groves	31943	11	1	7	9					2		10		3							4	5	6	8	
4	Sep	3	LEEDS UNITED	1-1	Brown	13497	11	1	7	9					2		10		3							4	5	6	8	
5		6	WEST HAM UNITED	4-1	Turner 2, Brown, Pacey	25715	11	1	7	9					2		10		3							4	5	6	8	
6		10	Manchester City	1-1	Groves	30771	11	1	7	9					2		10		3							4	5	6	8	
7		13	BOLTON WANDERERS	0-0		19699	11	1	7	9					2		10		3							4	5	6	8	
8		17	MANCHESTER CITY	5-1	Turner 2, Adam, Brown 2	18160	11	1	7	9		10			2				3							4	5	6	8	
9		20	Burnley	2-2	Cummins, Turner	23760	11	1	7	9		10			2				3							4	5	6	8	
10		27	PRESTON NORTH END	4-1	Adam 2, Cummins, Bingham	23056	11	1	7	9		10			2				3							4	5	6	8	
11	Oct	4	Leicester City	1-3	McLeod	32019	11	1		8		10			2	7			3	4				9			5	6		
12		11	Nottingham Forest	1-3	Turner	30337	11		7	9		10			2				3		1					4	5	6	8	
13		18	CHELSEA	2-1	Brown, Cummins	24864	11	1	7	9		10			2				3							4	5	6	8	
14		25	Portsmouth	2-2	Hawkes, Brown	24831	11	1	7	9		10			2				3							4	5	6	8	
15	Nov	1	ASTON VILLA	2-1	Turner 2	18714	11	1	7	9		10			2				3							4	5	6	8	
16		8	Newcastle United	0-1		53488	11	1	7	9		10			2				3							4	5	6	8	
17		15	TOTTENHAM HOTSPUR	1-2	Bingham	23592	11	1	7	8		10			2	9			3							4	5	6		
18		22	Manchester United	1-2	Cummins	42428	11	1	7	9		10			2				3							4	5	6	8	
19		29	WOLVERHAMPTON W.	0-1		20648	11	1	7	9		10			2		6		3							4	5		8	
20	Dec	6	Blackpool	0-3		14140	11	1	7	9		10			2		6		3	4							5		8	
21		13	BLACKBURN ROVERS	1-1	Bingham	13475		1	7	11		8			2		6		3						9	4	5		10	
22		26	ARSENAL	6-3	Adam, Gregory, Bingham 2, Brown 2	21870	11	1	7	8		10			2	9	4		3								5	6		
23		27	Arsenal	0-1		56277	11	1	7	8		10			2	9	4		3	5								6		
24	Jan	3	BIRMINGHAM CITY	0-1		15538	11	1	7	9		10					4		3	5			2					6	8	
25		31	Bolton Wanderers	2-4	Bingham, Brown	27787		1	7	8		10				11			3	4					9	2	5	6		
26	Feb	7	BURNLEY	6-2	Brown 3, Pacey, Morton 2	15753		1	7	8		10				11			3	4					9	2	5	6		
27		21	LEICESTER CITY	4-3	Gregory, Morton, Brown, Cummins	15786		1	7	8		10				11			3	4					9	2	5	6		
28	Mar	7	Chelsea	3-3	Turner 2, McGuffie	29175			7		1					11		4	3	5			8		2	9		6	10	
29		21	Aston Villa	1-3	Bingham	27401	11	1	7	8		10			2				3	4					9		5	6		
30		27	EVERTON	0-1		22954		1	7	8		10				11			3	4					9	2	5	6		
31		28	NEWCASTLE UNITED	4-2	Brown 2, Gregory, Pacey	20880			7	9	1	10				11			3	4						2	5	6	8	
32		30	Everton	1-3	Morton	32620				9	1				2	11	6		3	5						4			8	7
33	Apr	4	Tottenham Hotspur	0-3		37093		1	7			10			2	11			3	4					9		5	6	8	
34		6	Preston North End	0-0		10548	11	1	7			10							3	4					9	2	5	6	8	
35		9	NOTTM. FOREST	5-1	Brown 4, Bingham	22352		1	7	8		10				11			3	4					9	2	5	6		
36		11	MANCHESTER UNITED	0-0		27025		1	7	8		10							3	4		11			9	2	5	6		
37		13	West Ham United	0-0		26784	11	1	7	8		10							3	4					9	2	5	6		
38		15	West Bromwich Albion	0-2		19173	11	1	7			10	3	9	2								4				5	6	8	
39		18	Wolverhampton Wan.	0-5		40981		1	7			10			11				3				4		9	2	5	6	8	
40		20	Blackburn Rovers	1-3	Brown	18092	11	1		8		10					6	7	3	5					2			4	9	
41		22	PORTSMOUTH	3-1	Pacey, Turner, Cummins	11592	11	1	7			10			2				3	4					9		5	6	8	
42		25	BLACKPOOL	1-1	Turner	17720		1	7	8						11			3	4					9	2	5	6	10	
			Apps				29	38	36	39	3	31	1	1	29	15	30	3	40	12	1	1	3	1	15	35	31	36	31	1
			Goals				4		8	20		6				3	2		1				1		1	4		4	14	

F.A. Cup

		Date	Opponent	Score	Scorers	Att	Baynham	Bingham	Brown	Cummins	Gregory	Hawkes KK	Kelly	McNally	Morton	Owen	Pacey
R3	Jan	10	LEEDS UNITED	5-1	Bingham 2, Morton, Gregory 2	18534	1	7	8	10	11	3	4	9	2	5	6
R4	Jan	24	Leicester City	1-1	Bingham	36984	1	7	8	10	11	3	4	9	2	5	6
rep	Jan	28	LEICESTER CITY	4-1	Brown 3, Gregory	27277	1	7	8	10	11	3	4	9	2	5	6
R5	Feb	14	Ipswich Town	5-2	Pacey, Morton 2, Bingham, Gregory	26700	1	7	8	10	11	3	4	9	2	5	6
R6	Feb	28	Blackpool	1-1	Bingham	30634	1	7	8	10	11	3	4	9	2	5	6
rep	Mar	4	BLACKPOOL	1-0	Brown	30069	1	7	8	10	11	3	4	9	2	5	6
SF	Mar	14	Norwich City	1-1	Brown	65000	1	7	8	10	11	3	4	9	2	5	6
rep	Mar	18	Norwich City	1-0	Bingham	49500	1	7	8	10	11	3	4	9	2	5	6
F	May	2	Nottingham Forest	1-2	Pacey	100000	1	7	8	10	11	3	4	9	2	5	6

SF at White Hart Lane, replay at St. Andrews. Final at Wembley Stadium.

Southern Professional Floodlit Cup

		Date	Opponent	Score	Scorers	Adam	Baynham	Brown	Collier	Cummins	Dixon	Dunne	Gregory	Groves	Hawkes KK	Kelly	Kilgannon	McNally	Morton	Owen	Pacey	Turner	Whitby
R1	Nov	3	Portsmouth	2-0	Turner 2,	11	1	9		10		2	7	6	3				4	5		8	
R2	Feb	18	SOUTHAMPTON	4-0	Morton 2, Cummins, Gregory		1	9		10		2	7	6	3			11	4	5		8	
SF	Apr	1	Crystal Palace	0-1					1	10	9	2				5	11	4	6			8	7

Played in SF: AS Collier (at 1), Walker (at 3).

Division One — Final Table

		P	W	D	L	F	A	W	D	L	F	A	Pts
1	Wolverhampton Wan.	42	15	3	3	68	19	13	2	6	42	30	61
2	Manchester United	42	14	4	3	58	27	10	3	8	45	39	55
3	Arsenal	42	14	3	4	53	29	7	5	9	35	39	50
4	Bolton Wanderers	42	14	3	4	56	30	6	7	8	23	36	50
5	West Bromwich Alb.	42	8	7	6	41	33	10	6	5	47	35	49
6	West Ham United	42	15	3	3	59	29	6	3	12	26	41	48
7	Burnley	42	11	4	6	41	29	8	6	7	40	41	48
8	Blackpool	42	12	7	2	39	13	6	4	11	27	36	47
9	Birmingham City	42	14	1	6	54	35	6	5	10	30	33	46
10	Blackburn Rovers	42	12	3	6	48	28	5	7	9	28	42	44
11	Newcastle United	42	11	3	7	40	29	6	4	11	40	51	41
12	Preston North End	42	9	3	9	40	39	8	4	9	30	38	41
13	Nottingham Forest	42	9	4	8	37	32	8	2	11	34	42	40
14	Chelsea	42	13	2	6	52	37	5	2	14	25	61	40
15	Leeds United	42	8	7	6	28	27	7	2	12	29	47	39
16	Everton	42	11	3	7	39	38	6	1	14	32	49	38
17	LUTON TOWN	42	11	6	4	50	26	1	7	13	18	45	37
18	Tottenham Hotspur	42	10	3	8	56	42	3	7	11	29	53	36
19	Leicester City	42	7	6	8	34	36	4	4	13	33	62	32
20	Manchester City	42	8	7	6	40	32	3	2	16	24	63	31
21	Aston Villa	42	8	5	8	31	33	3	3	15	27	54	30
22	Portsmouth	42	5	4	12	38	47	1	5	15	26	65	21

#	Date	Opponent	Score	Scorers	Att	Baynham RL	Bingham WL	Brown AD	Collier AS	Collins MJA	Cummins GP	Daniel AW	Dixon MJ	Dunne S	Gregory AC	Groves J	Hawkes B	Hawkes KK	Kelly TWJ	Kilgannon J	McBride J	McCann A	McCreadie WH	McNally JB	Morton RH	Noake DJ	Pacey D	Tracey MG	Turner GR	Warner J
1	Aug 22	Everton	2-2	Brown, Bingham	38539	1	7	9			10			2	11	6			3						4		5		8	
2	26	BLACKPOOL	0-1		19095	1	7	9			10			2	11	6			3						4		5		8	
3	29	LEEDS UNITED	0-1		15822	1	7	9			10			2	11	6			3						4		5		8	
4	31	Blackpool	0-0		22008	1	7	8			10			2		6			3						4	9	5		11	
5	Sep 5	BOLTON WANDERERS	0-0		15604	1	7	8			10			2		6			3						4	9	5		11	
6	9	MANCHESTER CITY	1-2	Brown	13122	1	7	8			10			2		6			3						4	9	5		11	
7	12	Fulham	2-4	Bingham 2	30012	1	7	8			10			2		6			3						4	9	5		11	
8	16	Manchester City	2-1	Bingham 2	29309	1	7	9			10			2	11	6			3						4		5		8	
9	19	NOTTM. FOREST	1-0	Brown	16634	1	7	9						2	11	6		10	3						4		5		8	
10	26	Sheffield Wednesday	0-2		24775	1	7	9			10			2	11	6			3						4		5		8	
11	Oct 3	WOLVERHAMPTON W.	1-5	Dixon	22908	1					10		9	2	11	6	7		3						4		5		8	
12	10	West Ham United	1-3	Turner	23266	1	7	10			11			2		6			3						4	9	5		8	
13	17	CHELSEA	1-2	Brown	18831	1	7	9			10			2	11	6			3						4		5		8	
14	24	West Bromwich Albion	0-4		22352	1	7	9			10			2		6		11	3						4		5		8	
15	31	BURNLEY	1-1	Brown	15638		7	4	1			3		2		6				8					10	9	5	11		
16	Nov 7	Birmingham City	1-1	Bingham	19007	1	7	4			10	3		2	11	6				8						9	5			
17	14	TOTTENHAM HOTSPUR	1-0	Cummins	22528	1	7	6			10	3		2	11	4				8						9	5			
18	21	Manchester United	1-4	Kilgannon	40807	1	7	6			10	3		2	11	4				8						9	5			
19	28	PRESTON NORTH END	1-3	Bingham	17174		7	6	1		10	3		2	11	4				8					9		5			
20	Dec 5	Leicester City	3-3	Bingham, Pacey, Brown	16682		7	9	1		10	3		2	11	6				8					4		5			
21	12	NEWCASTLE UNITED	3-4	Bingham 2, Gregory	14524	1	7	9			10	3		2	11	6				8					4		5			
22	19	EVERTON	2-1	Gregory 2	9799	1	7	9				3		2	11	6		4		8					10		5			
23	26	Arsenal	3-0	Gregory 2, Turner	31331	1	7	9				3		2	11	6		4							10		5		8	
24	26	ARSENAL	0-1		27055	1	7	9				3		2	11	6		4		8					10		5			
25	Jan 2	Leeds United	1-1	Turner	19921	1	7	9				3		2	11	6		4							10		5		8	
26	23	FULHAM	4-1	Morton, Brown, Bingham, Turner	17876	1	7	9				3		2	11	6		4							10		5		8	
27	Feb 6	Nottingham Forest	0-2		22808	1	7	9				3		2	11	6		4		8					10		5			
28	13	SHEFFIELD WEDNESDAY	0-1		14392	1	7	4			10			2		6			5					3	9			11	8	
29	23	Wolverhampton Wan.	2-3	Bingham, Groves	30059	1	7	4						2	11	6		10						3	9		5		8	
30	27	LEICESTER CITY	2-0	Turner, McBride	18691	1	7	4			11			2		6		10			9			3			5		8	
31	Mar 5	Chelsea	0-3		33679		7	4	1		10			2		6					9			3			5	11	8	
32	9	Bolton Wanderers	2-2	McBride, Turner	14791	1	7	6			10			2							9			3	4		5	11	8	
33	12	WEST BROMWICH ALB.	0-0		18285	1	7	6			10			2							9			3	4		5	11	8	
34	19	Newcastle United	2-3	Bingham 2	29269	1	7	6			10			2					3		9				4		5	11	8	
35	26	BIRMINGHAM CITY	1-1	McBride (p)	13620	1	7	6			10			2					3		9				4		5	11	8	
36	Apr 2	Tottenham Hotspur	1-1	McBride	39462	1	7	6			10			2					3		9				4		5	11	8	
37	9	MANCHESTER UNITED	2-3	Cummins 2	21242	1	7	6			10			2					3		9				4		5	11	8	
38	15	Blackburn Rovers	2-0	McBride, Bingham	22714	1	7	6			10			2					3		9				4		5	11	8	
39	16	Burnley	0-3		20893	1	7	6			10			2					3		9				4		5	11	8	
40	18	BLACKBURN ROVERS	1-1	Bingham	14167	1	11			4	10	3		2		6	7		5		9								8	
41	23	WEST HAM UNITED	3-1	McBride, Cummins, Lansdowne(og)	11404	1	11				10	3		2		6	7		5		9				4				8	
42	30	Preston North End	0-2		29781	1	7	6			10	3		2					5		9				4			11	8	
				Apps		37	40	39	5	1	30	16	1	41	18	33	5	22	31	12	13	1	1	6	33	7	32	6	31	1
				Goals			16	7			4		1		5	1				1	6						1		6	

One own goal

F.A. Cup

#	Date	Opponent	Score	Scorers	Att	Baynham RL	Bingham WL	Brown AD	Collier AS	Collins MJA	Cummins GP	Daniel AW	Dixon MJ	Dunne S	Gregory AC	Groves J	Hawkes B	Hawkes KK	Kelly TWJ	Kilgannon J	McBride J	McCann A	McCreadie WH	McNally JB	Morton RH	Noake DJ	Pacey D	Tracey MG	Turner GR	Warner J
R3	Jan 9	Exeter City	2-1	Turner 2	20193	1	7	9				3		2	11	6		4							10		5		8	
R4	Jan 30	Huddersfield Town	1-0	Gregory	22500	1	7	9				3		2	11	6		4							10		5		8	
R5	Feb 20	WOLVERHAMPTON WAN.	1-4	Turner	25619	1	7	4						2	11	6		10						3	9		5		8	

Southern Professional Floodlit Cup

#	Date	Opponent	Score	Scorers	Bingham WL	Brown AD	Collier AS	Collins MJA	Cummins GP	Daniel AW	Dunne S	Groves J	Kilgannon J	Morton RH	Noake DJ	Pacey D	Tracey MG	Turner GR	Warner J
R2	Oct 26	FULHAM	1-1	Warner	7	4	1			3	2	6	8	10	9	5			11
rep	Nov 23	Fulham	0-1		6		1	1	10	3	2	4	11		9	5	7	8	

Replay at Griffin Park

		P	W	D	L	F	A	W	D	L	F	A	Pts
1	Burnley	42	15	2	4	52	28	9	5	7	33	33	55
2	Wolverhampton Wan.	42	15	3	3	63	28	9	3	9	43	39	54
3	Tottenham Hotspur	42	10	6	5	43	24	11	5	5	43	26	53
4	West Bromwich Alb.	42	12	4	5	48	25	7	7	7	35	32	49
5	Sheffield Wed.	42	12	7	2	48	20	7	4	10	32	39	49
6	Bolton Wanderers	42	12	5	4	37	27	8	3	10	22	24	48
7	Manchester United	42	13	3	5	53	30	6	4	11	49	50	45
8	Newcastle United	42	10	5	6	42	32	8	3	10	40	46	44
9	Preston North End	42	10	6	5	43	34	6	6	9	36	42	44
10	Fulham	42	12	4	5	42	28	5	6	10	31	52	44
11	Blackpool	42	9	6	6	32	32	6	4	11	27	39	40
12	Leicester City	42	8	6	7	38	32	5	7	9	28	43	39
13	Arsenal	42	9	5	7	39	38	6	4	11	29	42	39
14	West Ham United	42	12	3	6	47	33	4	3	14	28	58	38
15	Everton	42	13	3	5	50	20	0	8	13	23	68	37
16	Manchester City	42	11	2	8	47	34	6	1	14	31	50	37
17	Blackburn Rovers	42	12	3	6	38	29	4	2	15	22	41	37
18	Chelsea	42	7	5	9	44	50	7	4	10	32	41	37
19	Birmingham City	42	9	5	7	37	36	4	5	12	26	44	36
20	Nottingham Forest	42	8	6	7	30	28	5	3	13	20	46	35
21	Leeds United	42	7	5	9	37	46	5	5	11	28	46	34
22	LUTON TOWN	42	6	5	10	25	29	3	7	11	25	44	30

Match results

#	Month	Date	Opponent	Score	Scorers	Att.
1	Aug	20	Huddersfield Town	1-1	Turner	18156
2		24	PORTSMOUTH	1-0	Turner	17514
3		27	SUNDERLAND	3-3	Pacey, McBride, Bingham	17632
4		31	Portsmouth	2-3	Turner, Bingham	15176
5	Sep	3	Plymouth Argyle	1-1	Brown	21408
6		7	Liverpool	2-2	Turner, Bingham	27339
7		10	NORWICH CITY	0-2		22252
8		14	LIVERPOOL	2-1	Brown, McBride	10055
9		17	Charlton Athletic	1-4	Brown	11778
10		24	SHEFFIELD UNITED	1-4	Turner	13726
11	Oct	1	Stoke City	0-3		9395
12		8	BRISTOL ROVERS	4-2	Tracey, McBride, Turner, Sampson(og)	9373
13		15	Derby County	1-4	Ashworth	13447
14		22	LEYTON ORIENT	0-1		11037
15		29	Scunthorpe United	0-1		8643
16	Nov	5	IPSWICH TOWN	3-2	Turner 2, Ashworth	11221
17		12	Brighton & Hove Albion	0-1		14186
18		19	MIDDLESBROUGH	6-1	* see below	12579
19	Dec	3	SOUTHAMPTON	4-1	Turner 2, Tracey, Brown	12927
20		10	Rotherham United	2-5	Turner 2	6297
21		17	HUDDERSFIELD T	1-0	Turner	11219
22		26	LINCOLN CITY	3-0	Fleming 2, Ashworth	15283
23		27	Lincoln City	1-1	Ashworth	10345
24		31	Sunderland	1-7	Turner	28695
25	Jan	14	PLYMOUTH ARGYLE	3-2	Turner, Brown, Williams (og)	13873
26		21	Norwich City	1-2	Turner	21290
27	Feb	11	Sheffield United	1-2	Turner	16716
28		23	STOKE CITY	4-1	Turner 4 (1p)	12142
29		25	Bristol Rovers	1-4	Mabbutt (og)	13105
30	Mar	4	DERBY COUNTY	1-1	Fleming	13001
31		8	Leeds United	2-1	Ashworth, Turner	9995
32		11	Leyton Orient	1-2	McGuffie	11918
33		18	ROTHERHAM UNITED	2-1	McGuffie, Fleming	10179
34		25	Ipswich Town	1-0	McGuffie	21744
35		31	SWANSEA TOWN	2-2	Turner (p), Nurse (og)	14286
36	Apr	1	LEEDS UNITED	1-1	Turner (p)	11137
37		3	Swansea Town	1-3	Groves	14884
38		8	Middlesbrough	1-2	Legate	13017
39		15	BRIGHTON & HOVE ALB	3-1	McGuffie, Legate, Ashworth	9104
40		22	Southampton	2-3	Morton, Fairchild	7016
41		26	CHARLTON ATHLETIC	4-1	Ashworth 2, Legate 2	7149
42		29	SCUNTHORPE UNITED	0-0		8373

Scorers in game 18: Brown 2, Spencer, Tracey, Turner 2 (2p).
Played at 1 in games 11 and 14: MJ O'Hara
Played at 1 in games 12 and 13: AS Collier
Played at 7 in games 37 and 41: RAS Chandler
Played at 9 in game 42: MJ Dixon. Played at 7 in 4 games, 26, 28, 29 and 30: HB Walden.

Appearances and goals

Player	Apps	Goals
Ashworth A	25	8
Baynham RL	25	
Bingham WL	11	3
Bramwell J	30	
Brogan D	4	
Brown AD	24	7
Collins MJA	4	
Cummins GP	6	
Daniel AW	7	
Dunne S	16	
Fairchild MP	1	1
Fleming JP	18	4
Groves J	37	1
Hawkes KK	6	
Imlach JJS	8	
Kelly TWJ	17	
Legate RA	5	4
McBride J	12	3
McCann A	5	
McGuffie AS	24	4
McNally JB	26	
Morton RH	27	1
Noake DJ	10	
Pacey D	29	1
Spencer L	7	1
Standen JA	13	
Tracey MG	17	3
Turner GR	37	26

Four own goals

F.A. Cup

Rd	Month	Date	Opponent	Score	Scorers	Att.
R3	Jan	7	NORTHAMPTON TOWN	4-0	Turner 2, Brown, Ashworth	26220
R4	Feb	1	MANCHESTER CITY	3-1	Ashworth 2, Fleming	15583
R5	Feb	18	Barnsley	0-1		32923

First game with Manchester City on Jan. 28th abandoned with score 2-6 (Ashworth 2)

F.L. Cup

Rd	Month	Date	Opponent	Score	Scorers	Att.
R2	Oct	19	Liverpool	1-1	Brogan	10502
rep	Oct	25	LIVERPOOL	2-5	Turner, Brogan	6125

Played at 1 in both games: MJ O'Hara

Division Two table

		P	W	D	L	F	A	W	D	L	F	A	Pts
1	Ipswich Town	42	15	3	3	55	24	11	4	6	45	31	59
2	Sheffield United	42	16	2	3	49	22	10	4	7	32	29	58
3	Liverpool	42	14	5	2	49	21	7	5	9	38	37	52
4	Norwich City	42	15	3	3	46	20	5	6	10	24	33	49
5	Middlesbrough	42	13	6	2	44	20	5	6	10	39	54	48
6	Sunderland	42	12	5	4	47	24	5	8	8	28	36	47
7	Swansea Town	42	14	4	3	49	26	4	7	10	28	47	47
8	Southampton	42	12	4	5	57	35	6	4	11	27	46	44
9	Scunthorpe United	42	9	8	4	39	25	5	7	9	30	39	43
10	Charlton Athletic	42	12	3	6	60	42	4	8	9	37	49	43
11	Plymouth Argyle	42	13	4	4	52	32	4	4	13	29	50	42
12	Derby County	42	9	6	6	46	35	6	4	11	34	45	40
13	LUTON TOWN	42	13	5	3	48	27	2	4	15	23	52	39
14	Leeds United	42	7	7	7	41	38	7	3	11	34	45	38
15	Rotherham United	42	9	7	5	37	24	3	6	12	28	40	37
16	Brighton & Hove A.	42	9	6	6	33	26	5	3	13	28	49	37
17	Bristol Rovers	42	13	4	4	52	35	2	3	16	21	57	37
18	Stoke City	42	9	6	6	34	26	3	6	12	17	33	36
19	Leyton Orient	42	10	6	5	31	29	4	3	14	24	49	36
20	Huddersfield Town	42	7	5	9	33	33	6	4	11	29	38	35
21	Portsmouth	42	10	6	5	38	27	1	5	15	26	64	33
22	Lincoln City	42	5	4	12	30	43	3	4	14	18	52	24

1961/62 — 13th in Division Two

#	Date	Opponent	Score	Scorers	Att	Ashworth A	Baynham RL	Bramwell J	Chandler RAS	Clarke A	Collins MJA	Cope R	Daniel AW	Fleming JP	Groves J	Jardine F	Kelly TWJ	Legate RA	Lornie J	Lownds MU	McGuffie AS	McKechnie TS	McNally JB	Morton RH	Pacey D	Reed BEF	Standen JA	Turner GR	Walden HB
1	Aug 19	PRESTON NORTH END	4-1	Ashworth 2, Turner, Groves	14109	10	1	3				5		11	6				9				2	4				8	7
2	23	Derby County	0-2		18705	10	1	3				5		11	6				9				2	4				8	7
3	26	Plymouth Argyle	3-0	Turner 2, Walden	15299	8	1	3						11	6	5						10	2	4				9	7
4	30	DERBY COUNTY	4-2	McKechnie 2, Walden, Ashworth	15380	8	1	3						11	6	5						10	2	4				9	7
5	Sep 2	HUDDERSFIELD T	3-4	McKechnie, Lornie, Coddington(og)	14436	8	1	3							6	5			11			10	2	4				9	7
6	9	Swansea Town	2-3	Turner (p), Fleming	11813	8	1	3				5		11	6							10	2	4				9	7
7	16	SOUTHAMPTON	1-4	Turner	13209	8	1	3				5		11	6							10		4		2		9	7
8	20	Middlesbrough	4-2	McKechnie 2, Turner 2 (1p)	15878	8	1	3				5		11	6							10	2	4				9	7
9	23	Charlton Athletic	1-0	Turner	10176	8	1	3				5		11	6							10	2	4				9	7
10	27	MIDDLESBROUGH	3-2	Ashworth, Turner, McKechnie	11276	8	1	3				5		11	6							10	2	4				9	7
11	30	Newcastle United	1-4	McGuffie	22452	8	1	3				5		11	6						10		2	4				9	7
12	Oct 7	BURY	4-0	Turner 2, Ashworth 2	10315	8	1	3			5			11	6							10	2	4				9	7
13	14	Brighton & Hove Albion	1-2	Lornie	14186	8		3			5			11	6				10				2	4			1	9	7
14	21	SCUNTHORPE UNITED	1-2	Ashworth	9766	8		3			5			11	6							10	2	9	4		1		7
15	28	Norwich City	4-0	Ashworth 2, Legate, Scott (og)	18845	9		3				5		7	10			11				8	2	4	6		1		
16	Nov 4	LEEDS UNITED	3-2	Legate 2, Fleming	10341	10		3				5		7	6			11				8	2	4			1	9	
17	11	Liverpool	1-1	Turner	34924	10		3				5		7	6			11				8	2	4			1	9	
18	18	STOKE CITY	0-0		15163	8		3				5			6			11				10	2	4			1	9	7
19	25	Sunderland	2-2	Ashworth, Pacey	32763	8		3				5			6			11				10	2		4		1	9	7
20	Dec 2	ROTHERHAM UNITED	4-3	Ashworth, McKechnie, Walden, McGuffie	9886	9		3				5		11	6						8	10	2		4		1		7
21	9	Bristol Rovers	0-1		9688	9		3				5		11	8							10	2	4	6		1		7
22	16	Preston North End	0-2		8702	8		3				5		11	10				9				2	4	6		1		7
23	23	PLYMOUTH ARGYLE	0-2		8410	8	1	3	9			5		11	6							10	2	4					7
24	26	Walsall	0-2		9609	9	1	3				5		10	11							8	2	4	6				7
25	Jan 13	Huddersfield Town	2-1	McKechnie, Morton	11140	8	1	3	9								5	11				10	2	4	6				7
26	20	SWANSEA TOWN	5-1	Fleming, Lownds, Turner 2, Pacey	8107		1	3						11				5		10	4	8	2		6			9	7
27	Feb 3	Southampton	0-3		13037	8	1	3				5		11	10						4		2		6			9	7
28	10	CHARLTON ATHLETIC	1-6	Turner	9827	8	1	3				5		7	4							10	2		6			9	7
29	17	NEWCASTLE UNITED	1-0	Turner	9040		1	3				5		7	4					10	9		2		6			8	11
30	24	Bury	1-2	McNally	6133		1	3				5		7	4					10	9		2		6			8	11
31	Mar 3	BRIGHTON & HOVE ALB	2-1	McKechnie, Pacey	7005		1	3	7			5	2	6							11	10			4		8	9	
32	10	Scunthorpe United	0-2		7911	8	1	3	7			5										10	2	4	6			9	11
33	17	NORWICH CITY	1-2	McKechnie	9736	8	1	3				5							11			10	2	4	6			9	7
34	24	Leeds United	1-2	McNally	13078	8		3						11	4		5					10	2		6		1	9	7
35	31	LIVERPOOL	1-0	Pacey	9086	9		3						11	4		5					10	2	7	6		1		8
36	Apr 7	Stoke City	1-2	Morton	7530	9		3						11	4		5					10	2	7	6		1		8
37	11	WALSALL	2-0	Turner 2	6123	9		3		7				11	4		5					10	2		6		1	8	
38	14	SUNDERLAND	1-2	Pacey	9571	9		3		7				11	4		5					10	2		6		1		8
39	20	Leyton Orient	0-0		21312	9		3		7				11			5					10	2	4	6		1		8
40	21	Rotherham United	1-1	Turner	3492	8		3						11			5				10		2	4	6		1	9	7
41	23	LEYTON ORIENT	1-3	Morton	13681	8	1	3		7				11			5					10	2	4	6				7
42	28	BRISTOL ROVERS	2-0	Turner, Ashworth	6555	8		3		7				11	6		5						2	4	10		1	9	
		Apps				38	23	42	4	5	3	25	1	33	34	3	14	7	5	3	7	33	40	27	30	1	20	33	31
		Goals				12								3	1			3	2	1	2	10		2	3	5			20	3

Two own goals

F.A. Cup

	Date	Opponent	Score	Scorers	Att	Ashworth A	Baynham RL	Bramwell J	Chandler RAS	Clarke A	Collins MJA	Cope R	Daniel AW	Fleming JP	Groves J	Jardine F	Kelly TWJ	Legate RA	Lornie J	Lownds MU	McGuffie AS	McKechnie TS	McNally JB	Morton RH	Pacey D	Reed BEF	Standen JA	Turner GR	Walden HB
R3	Jan 6	Ipswich Town	1-1	Chandler	18450	8	1	3	9			5						11				10	2	4	6				7
rep	Jan 10	IPSWICH TOWN	1-1	Pacey	23818	8	1	3	9			5						11				10	2	4	6				7
rep 2	Jan 15	Ipswich Town	1-5	Ashworth	29348	8	1	3	9								5	11				10	2	4	6				7

Replay a.e.t. Replay 2 at Highbury

F.L. Cup

	Date	Opponent	Score	Scorers	Att	Ashworth A	Baynham RL	Bramwell J	Chandler RAS	Clarke A	Collins MJA	Cope R	Daniel AW	Fleming JP	Groves J	Jardine F	Kelly TWJ	Legate RA	Lornie J	Lownds MU	McGuffie AS	McKechnie TS	McNally JB	Morton RH	Pacey D	Reed BEF	Standen JA	Turner GR	Walden HB
R1	Sep 13	NORTHAMPTON TOWN	2-1	Turner, Foley (og)	7482		1	3				5		11	6						9	10	2	4				8	7
R2	Oct 4	ROTHERHAM UNITED	0-0		6544	8		3			5				10	11					9		2	4	6		1		
rep	Oct 10	Rotherham United	0-2		5176	8		3			5			11	6							10	2	4			1	9	7

Played at 7 in R2: MP Fairchild

Final Table

		P	W	D	L	F	A	W	D	L	F	A	Pts
1	Liverpool	42	18	3	0	68	19	9	5	7	31	24	62
2	Leyton Orient	42	11	5	5	34	17	11	5	5	35	23	54
3	Sunderland	42	17	3	1	60	16	6	6	10	25	34	53
4	Scunthorpe United	42	14	4	3	52	26	7	3	11	34	45	49
5	Plymouth Argyle	42	12	4	5	45	30	7	4	10	30	45	46
6	Southampton	42	13	3	5	53	28	5	6	10	24	34	45
7	Huddersfield Town	42	11	5	5	39	22	6	7	9	28	37	44
8	Stoke City	42	13	4	4	34	17	4	4	13	21	40	42
9	Rotherham United	42	9	6	6	36	30	7	3	11	34	46	41
10	Preston North End	42	11	4	6	34	23	4	6	11	21	34	40
11	Newcastle United	42	10	5	6	40	27	5	4	12	24	31	39
12	Middlesbrough	42	11	3	7	45	29	5	4	12	31	43	39
13	LUTON TOWN	42	12	1	8	44	37	5	4	12	25	34	39
14	Walsall	42	11	7	3	42	23	3	4	14	28	52	39
15	Charlton Athletic	42	10	5	6	38	30	5	4	12	31	45	39
16	Derby County	42	10	7	4	42	27	4	4	13	26	48	39
17	Norwich City	42	10	6	5	36	28	4	5	12	25	42	39
18	Bury	42	9	4	8	32	36	8	1	12	20	40	39
19	Leeds United	42	9	6	6	24	19	3	6	12	26	42	36
20	Swansea Town	42	10	5	6	38	30	2	7	12	23	53	36
21	Bristol Rovers	42	11	3	7	36	31	2	4	15	17	50	33
22	Brighton & Hove A.	42	7	7	7	24	32	3	4	14	18	54	31

1962/63 Bottom of Division Two: Relegated

Player columns (left to right): Baynham RL, Bramwell J, Brennan MH, Chandler RAS, Clapton DR, Clarke A, Cope R, Daniel AW, Davies RT, Fairchild MP, Fleming JP, Goldie J, Groves J, Jardine F, Kelly TWJ, Lornie J, Lownds MU, McGuffie AS, McKechnie TS, McNally JB, Morton RH, Pacey D, Riddick GG, Standen JA, Turner GR, Walden HB

#	Date	Opponent	Score	Scorers	Att.	Bay	Bra	Bre	Cha	Cla	Clk	Cop	Dan	Dav	Fai	Fle	Gol	Gro	Jar	Kel	Lor	Low	McG	McK	McN	Mor	Pac	Rid	Sta	Tur	Wal
1	Aug 18	Bury	0-1		8313	1	3									11				5	9		10				2	4	6	8	7
2	22	Southampton	2-2	Fleming, Pacey	14863	1	3									11	9			5	10						2	4	6	8	7
3	25	ROTHERHAM UNITED	2-3	Lornie 2	8615	1	3				4					11	9			5	10						2		6	8	7
4	29	SOUTHAMPTON	3-2	Walden, Goldie, Fleming	7124	1	3									11	9			5	10		4	8			2		6		7
5	Sep 1	Charlton Athletic	0-2		14012	1	3					2	8				9		11	5	10							4	6		7
6	5	PRESTON NORTH END	0-2		6702	1	3									11	9			5	10						2	4	6	8	7
7	8	STOKE CITY	0-0		6819	1	3						8							5	11		10				2	4	6	9	7
8	11	Preston North End	1-3	Turner	12216	1	3			7			8							5			10				2	4	6	9	11
9	15	Sunderland	1-3	Turner	36399	1	3			7			8							5			10				2	4	6	9	11
10	22	LEEDS UNITED	2-2	Turner, McNally	8916	1	3			7	5		8												10		2	4	6	9	11
11	29	Swansea Town	0-1		9441	1	3			7			8							5			6		10		2	4		9	11
12	Oct 6	PORTSMOUTH	3-3	Lornie, McKechnie, Walden	8078	1	3			7			8							5	9		6		10		2	4			11
13	13	Cardiff City	0-1		15901	1	3			7			8							5	9		6		10		2	4			11
14	27	Middlesbrough	2-0	Turner, McGuffie	13835	1	3						8			11		6		5			10				2	4		9	7
15	Nov 3	DERBY COUNTY	1-2	Turner	7582	1	3						8			11				5		6	10				2	4		9	7
16	10	Newcastle United	1-3	McGuffie	27428	1	3						8		7			6		5			10				2	4		9	11
17	17	WALSALL	4-3	Davies 2, Walden, Jardine	5489	1	3							9				6	11	5			10	8			2	4			7
18	24	Norwich City	3-3	Davies 2, Jardine	16376	1	3							9				6	11	5			10	8			2	4			7
19	Dec 1	GRIMSBY TOWN	2-2	Davies 2	7202	1	3							9				6	11	5			10	8			2	4			7
20	8	Plymouth Argyle	1-3	McGuffie	9029	1	3							9				6	11	5			10				2	4		8	7
21	15	BURY	2-1	Turner, Davies	6042	1	3					5		9		11							10				2	4	6	8	7
22	21	Rotherham United	1-2	Walden	8198	1	3					5		9		11									10		2	4	6	8	7
23	26	CHELSEA	0-2		11867	1	3							9		11				5					10		2	4	6	8	7
24	Feb 23	Portsmouth	1-3	Turner	12428	1	3							9						5	11		4	10			2		6	8	7
25	Mar 9	Huddersfield Town	0-2		10279	1				7			3	9					4		11	6			10		2		6	8	
26	16	HUDDERSFIELD T	3-2	Jardine, Turner, Bettam (og)	5428	1		9					3	8					11	5		6			10		2		4		7
27	23	Derby County	0-1		10756	1		9					3	8					11	5		6			10		2		4		7
28	25	MIDDLESBROUGH	4-3	Goldie, Turner 2, Lornie	6431	1	3						2	8			9			5	11	6					4			10	7
29	30	NEWCASTLE UNITED	2-3	Davies 2	7163	1	3						2	8	7		9			5	11	6					4			10	
30	Apr 1	Chelsea	1-3	Turner	21211	1	3		7				2	8						5	11	6					4			9	10
31	6	Walsall	1-1	Morton	8960	1	3			7			2	9				10		5						11	4		6	8	
32	12	Scunthorpe United	0-2		7739	1	3						2	9	7					5	11				10		4		6	8	
33	13	NORWICH CITY	4-2	Davies 4	9536	1	3						2	9	7					5	11				10		4		6	8	
34	15	SCUNTHORPE UNITED	1-0	Turner	9091	1	3						2	9	7					5	11				10		4		6	8	
35	20	Grimsby Town	1-3	Davies	9504	1	3						2	9	7					5	11				10		4		6	8	
36	24	CARDIFF CITY	2-3	Daniel (p), Davies	7237	1	3	10					2	9	7					5					11		4		6	8	
37	27	PLYMOUTH ARGYLE	3-0	Pacey, Brennan, Davies	6853	1	3	8		7			2	9						5			10				4		6		11
38	May 1	SWANSEA TOWN	3-1	Davies 3	7642	1	3	8		7			2	9						5	11		10				4		6		
39	4	Leeds United	0-3		23900	1	3	8		7			2	9						5	11	6	10				4				
40	11	CHARLTON ATHLETIC	4-1	Davies 2, Turner 2	10867	1	6			7			2	9						5			10		3		4			8	
41	13	SUNDERLAND	0-3		16419	1	6			7			2	9						5			10	11	3		4			8	
42	18	Stoke City	0-2		34168	1	3							9				6	11	5			10	7			2		4	8	
Apps						39	38	4	3	10	4	3	19	29	7	15	7	9	18	29	14	7	21	20	29	34	38	3	3	32	27
Goals							1						1	21			2	2		3	4				3	1	1	1	2		14	4

One own goal

F.A. Cup

Rd	Date	Opponent	Score	Scorers	Att.	Bay	Bra	Cla	Dav	Fle	Kel	Pac	Rid	Sta	McN	Tur
R3	Jan 26	SWINDON TOWN	0-2		10840	1	3	7	9	11	5	2	4	6	10	8

F.L. Cup

Rd	Date	Opponent	Score	Scorers	Att.	Bay	Bra	Cop	Dan	Fai	Fle	Gol	Kel	McG	McK	Pac	Rid	Sta	Tur	Wal
R2	Sep 24	Southport	3-1	Fleming, Turner, Walden	5375		3		7	8	10		5	6		2	4	1	9	11
R3	Oct 16	Barnsley	2-1	Turner, Fairchild	10335	1	3		7	8			5	6	10	2	4		9	11
R4	Nov 14	Manchester City	0-1		8682	1	3				11	6		10	8	2	4		9	7

League table

		P	W	D	L	F	A	W	D	L	F	A	Pts
1	Stoke City	42	15	3	3	49	20	5	10	6	24	30	53
2	Chelsea	42	15	3	3	54	16	9	1	11	27	26	52
3	Sunderland	42	14	5	2	46	13	6	7	8	38	42	52
4	Middlesbrough	42	12	4	5	48	35	8	5	8	38	50	49
5	Leeds United	42	15	2	4	55	19	4	8	9	24	34	48
6	Huddersfield Town	42	11	6	4	34	21	6	8	7	29	29	48
7	Newcastle United	42	11	8	2	48	23	7	3	11	31	36	47
8	Bury	42	11	6	4	28	20	7	5	9	23	27	47
9	Scunthorpe United	42	12	7	2	35	18	4	5	12	22	41	44
10	Cardiff City	42	12	5	4	50	29	6	2	13	33	44	43
11	Southampton	42	15	3	3	52	23	2	5	14	20	44	42
12	Plymouth Argyle	42	13	4	4	48	24	2	8	11	28	49	42
13	Norwich City	42	11	6	4	53	33	6	2	13	27	46	42
14	Rotherham United	42	11	3	7	34	30	6	3	12	33	44	40
15	Swansea Town	42	13	5	3	33	17	2	4	15	18	55	39
16	Portsmouth	42	9	5	7	33	27	4	6	11	30	52	37
17	Preston North End	42	11	6	4	43	30	2	5	14	16	44	37
18	Derby County	42	10	5	6	40	29	2	7	12	21	43	36
19	Grimsby Town	42	8	6	7	34	26	3	7	11	21	40	35
20	Charlton Athletic	42	8	4	9	33	38	5	1	15	29	56	31
21	Walsall	42	7	7	7	33	37	4	2	15	20	52	31
22	LUTON TOWN	42	10	4	7	45	40	1	3	17	16	44	29

#		Date	Opponent	Score	Scorers	Att	Baynham RL	Bramwell J	Caleb GS	Daniel AW	Davies RT	Fairchild MP	Fincham GR	Jardine F	Lownds MU	McBain A	McGuffie AS	McKechnie TS	Morton RH	O'Rourke J	Pacey D	Reid J	Riddick GG	Salisbury G	Smith HR	Tinsley C	Turner GR	Walden HB	Weir J	Whittaker RH
1	Aug	24	WALSALL	1-0	Turner	9046	1	3		2	9		5	11					4		6			10			8	7		
2		28	Crewe Alexandra	0-1		8909	1	3		2	9		5	11					4		6			10			8	7		
3		31	Reading	1-1	Salisbury	7751	1	3		2	9		5	11					4		6			10			8	7		
4	Sep	6	Barnsley	1-3	Riddick	5388	1	3		2		9	5	11					4		6		10				8	7		
5		11	CREWE ALEXANDRA	3-3	Turner 2, Daniel	5865	1	3		2		9	5	11					4		6		10				8	7		
6		14	COVENTRY CITY	1-3	Daniel	14511	1	6		2		9	5			3	4				10						8	7	11	
7		18	CRYSTAL PALACE	0-4		6152	1	3				9	5			2	10		4		6						8	7	11	
8		21	Mansfield Town	1-1	Gill (og)	9565	1	3					5			6		8	2		4			10			9	7	11	
9		28	BRENTFORD	0-2		7379	1	3				7	5			6			2		4			10	8		9		11	
10	Oct	2	Crystal Palace	1-1	Jardine	16304	1	3				7	5	11		6		9	2		4			10	8					
11		5	Shrewsbury Town	0-1		5887	1	3				7	5	11		6		9	2		4			10	8					
12		9	PORT VALE	1-0	McKechnie	5914	1	3					5	10		6		9	2		4				8			7	11	
13		12	BOURNEMOUTH	1-0	Salisbury	6361	1	3				7	5	11		6		9	2		4			10	8					
14		14	Port Vale	0-1		11449	1	3				7	5	11		6		9	2		4			10	8					
15		19	Watford	0-2		13239	1	3					5			6		9	2		4			10	8			7	11	
16		23	BRISTOL CITY	1-4	Walden	5107	1	3					5			6		10	2		4				8		9	7	11	
17		26	SOUTHEND UNITED	4-1	Turner 3, Weir	5337	1	3				7	5			6		10	2		4				8		9		11	
18		29	Bristol City	1-5	Turner	10269	1	3					5			6		10	2		4				8		9	7	11	
19	Nov	2	Peterborough United	0-0		10687	1	3					5	11		6		9	2		4							7	10	
20		9	OLDHAM ATHLETIC	1-2	Turner	6222	1	3					5	11		6			2		4		8	10			9	7		
21		23	QUEEN'S PARK RANGERS	4-4	Turner 2, McKechnie, Smith	6598	1	3				7	5	11		6		10	2		4				8		9			
22		30	Wrexham	0-2		6381	1	3					5	11		6	4	7	2					10	8		9			
23	Dec	14	Walsall	0-4		3893	1	3				7	5	11		6			2		4		8				9			
24		21	READING	2-1	McKechnie, Turner	4346		3					5			6		10	2	9	4		11		8	1	7			
25		26	Millwall	0-3		7625		3				7	5	11		6		10	2	9	4				8	1				
26		28	MILLWALL	1-3	Jardine	7180		3					5	11		6		10	2	9	4				8	1	7			
27	Jan	11	BARNSLEY	2-3	Turner, O'Rourke	4555	1	6					5			3		10	2	9	4						8	7	11	
28		18	Coventry City	3-3	McKechnie 2, Turner	20921	1	3					5		6			8	2	9	4						10	7	11	
29		25	COLCHESTER UNITED	3-1	Walden, O'Rourke, Turner	4726	1	3					5		6			8	2	9	4						10	7	11	
30	Feb	1	MANSFIELD TOWN	0-2		6307	1	3					5		6			8	2	9	4						10	7	11	
31		8	Brentford	6-2	O'Rourke 4, Walden 2	9003	1	3	5						6			8	2	9	4			10				7	11	
32		15	SHREWSBURY TOWN	2-0	McKechnie, O'Rourke	6282	1	3	5						6			8	2	9	4			10				7	11	
33		22	Bournemouth	1-3	Reid	9298	1	3	5						6			8	2	9	4	10						7	11	
34		29	HULL CITY	2-1	McKechnie, O'Rourke	5267	1	3	5						6			8	2	9	4	10					7		11	
35	Mar	7	Southend United	1-0	O'Rourke	5486	1	3	5						6			8	2	9	4	10					7			11
36		14	PETERBOROUGH UTD.	2-3	Pacey, O'Rourke	6279	1	3	5						6			8	2	9	4		10				7			11
37		21	Hull City	0-2		3576	1	3	5						6			8	2	9	4	10					7			11
38		26	Notts County	1-1	McKechnie	4406	1	3	5						6			8	2	9	4	10					7			11
39		28	BRISTOL ROVERS	4-2	O'Rourke 3, Turner	6612	1	3					5		6				2	9	4	10					8	7		11
40		30	NOTTS COUNTY	2-0	O'Rourke 2	8387	1	3					5		6				2	9	4	10					8	7		11
41	Apr	11	WREXHAM	3-1	Turner (p), Lownds, O'Rourke	7094	1	3					5		6				2	9	4	10					8	7		11
42		13	Bristol Rovers	2-1	O'Rourke 2	8094	1	3					5		6			8	2	9	4	10						7		11
43		18	Colchester United	1-1	O'Rourke	3913	1	3					5		6			8	2	9	4	10						7		11
44		22	Oldham Athletic	1-0	Lownds	6367	1	3					5		6			8	2	9	4	10						7		11
45		25	WATFORD	2-1	O'Rourke 2	19799	1	3					5		6				2	9	4	10					8	7		11
46		29	Queen's Park Rangers	1-1	O'Rourke	5005	1	3					5		6			8	2	9	4	10						7		11
			Apps				43	46	8	6	3	13	35	16	29	22	12	32	33	23	42	22	11	12	10	3	27	34	12	12
			Goals							2				2	2			8		22	1	1	1	2	1		16	4	1	

One own goal

F.A. Cup

		Date	Opponent	Score	Scorers	Att	Baynham RL	Bramwell J	Caleb GS	Daniel AW	Davies RT	Fairchild MP	Fincham GR	Jardine F	Lownds MU	McBain A	McGuffie AS	McKechnie TS	Morton RH	O'Rourke J	Pacey D	Reid J	Riddick GG	Salisbury G	Smith HR	Tinsley C	Turner GR	Walden HB	Weir J	Whittaker RH
R1	Nov	16	Bridgwater Town	3-0	McKechnie 2, Turner	4453	1	3				7	5	11		6		10	2		4				8		9			
R2	Dec	7	READING	2-1	Fairchild, Turner	9090	1	3				7	5			6		10	2		4				8		9		11	
R3	Jan	4	Fulham	1-4	Smith	18089	1	6					5			3		11	2	9	4			10	8		7			

F.L. Cup

		Date	Opponent	Score	Scorers	Att	Baynham RL	Bramwell J	Caleb GS	Daniel AW	Davies RT	Fairchild MP	Fincham GR	Jardine F	Lownds MU	McBain A	McGuffie AS	McKechnie TS	Morton RH	O'Rourke J	Pacey D	Reid J	Riddick GG	Salisbury G	Smith HR	Tinsley C	Turner GR	Walden HB	Weir J	Whittaker RH
R2	Sep	25	COVENTRY CITY	3-4	Salisbury 2, Fincham	3821	1	3				7	5			6		9	2		4			10	8				11	

		P	W	D	L	F	A	W	D	L	F	A	Pts
1	Coventry City	46	14	7	2	62	32	8	9	6	36	29	60
2	Crystal Palace	46	17	4	2	38	14	6	10	7	35	37	60
3	Watford	46	16	6	1	57	28	7	6	10	22	31	58
4	Bournemouth	46	17	4	2	47	15	7	4	12	32	43	56
5	Bristol City	46	13	7	3	52	24	7	8	8	32	40	55
6	Reading	46	15	5	3	49	26	6	5	12	30	36	52
7	Mansfield Town	46	15	8	0	51	20	5	3	15	25	42	51
8	Hull City	46	11	9	3	45	27	5	8	10	28	41	49
9	Oldham Athletic	46	13	3	7	44	35	7	5	11	29	35	48
10	Peterborough Utd.	46	13	6	4	52	27	5	5	13	23	43	47
11	Shrewsbury Town	46	13	6	4	43	19	5	5	13	30	61	47
12	Bristol Rovers	46	9	6	8	52	34	10	2	11	39	45	46
13	Port Vale	46	13	6	4	35	13	3	8	12	18	36	46
14	Southend United	46	9	10	4	42	26	6	5	12	35	52	45
15	Queen's Park Rgs.	46	13	4	6	47	34	5	5	13	29	44	45
16	Brentford	46	11	4	8	54	36	4	10	9	33	44	44
17	Colchester United	46	10	8	5	45	26	2	11	10	25	42	43
18	LUTON TOWN	46	12	2	9	42	41	4	8	11	22	39	42
19	Walsall	46	7	9	7	34	35	6	5	12	25	41	40
20	Barnsley	46	9	9	5	34	29	3	6	14	34	65	39
21	Millwall	46	9	4	10	33	33	5	6	12	20	38	38
22	Crewe Alexandra	46	10	5	8	29	26	1	7	15	21	51	34
23	Wrexham	46	9	4	10	50	42	4	2	17	25	65	32
24	Notts County	46	7	8	8	29	26	2	1	20	16	66	27

1964/65   21st in Division Three: Relegated

Match results

No	Date	Opponent	Score	Scorers	Att
1	Aug 22	Brentford	2-2	O'Rourke, McKechnie	10883
2	26	COLCHESTER UNITED	3-1	McKechnie 2, Riddick	9897
3	29	BRISTOL ROVERS	0-2		9985
4	31	Colchester United	1-0	Whittaker	5115
5	Sep 5	Oldham Athletic	2-0	Reid 2	10793
6	9	PORT VALE	1-1	Pleat	11649
7	12	EXETER CITY	1-2	O'Rourke	10461
8	14	Port Vale	0-1		6381
9	19	Bournemouth	0-4		8763
10	26	PETERBOROUGH UTD.	1-1	O'Rourke	9339
11	Oct 1	CARLISLE UNITED	1-1	O'Rourke	7745
12	3	Grimsby Town	2-2	O'Rourke, Cockerill (og)	8410
13	7	Carlisle United	1-1	Whittaker	9038
14	9	Workington	0-1		6007
15	12	Mansfield Town	0-2		8083
16	17	HULL CITY	1-3	Riddick	6020
17	21	MANSFIELD TOWN	1-1	Pleat	2874
18	24	Gillingham	0-5		9424
19	28	SCUNTHORPE UNITED	1-1	McKechnie	3876
20	31	BRISTOL CITY	0-0		5385
21	Nov 6	Queen's Park Rangers	1-7	Pleat	5175
22	21	Reading	2-1	Harber, Riddick	7568
23	28	SOUTHEND UNITED	0-1		5020
24	Dec 12	BRENTFORD	4-2	McKechnie 2, Whittaker, Riddick	6104
25	19	Bristol Rovers	2-3	Whittaker 2	10624
26	26	WATFORD	2-4	Riddick, Whittaker	11020
27	28	Watford	0-2		6867
28	Jan 2	OLDHAM ATHLETIC	2-0	Pacey, McKechnie	5290
29	16	Exeter City	1-5	McKechnie	4686
30	30	Barnsley	0-3		2989
31	Feb 6	Peterborough United	0-2		12946
32	13	GRIMSBY TOWN	1-1	O'Rourke	5160
33	17	BOURNEMOUTH	0-1		4554
34	27	Hull City	1-3	O'Rourke	22986
35	Mar 10	SHREWSBURY TOWN	2-7	O'Rourke, Phillips	4914
36	13	Bristol City	1-0		11001
37	20	QUEEN'S PARK RANGERS	2-0	Pleat, Phillips	3998
38	26	Shrewsbury Town	2-0	Harber, Phillips	4800
39	Apr 3	READING	3-1	Harber, Phillips, Pleat	5479
40	7	BARNSLEY	5-1	O'Rourke, McKechnie 2, Phillips 2	6112
41	10	Southend United	0-5		4968
42	16	WALSALL	1-3	Phillips	9353
43	17	GILLINGHAM	0-2		6102
44	19	Walsall	1-0	Phillips	7482
45	24	Scunthorpe United	1-8	O'Rourke	2755
46	29	WORKINGTON	0-0		2915

Appearances grid (shirt numbers)

No	Barton KR	Baynham RL	Bramwell J	Caleb GS	Chandler RAS	Edwards R	Fincham GR	Gibson J	Hails W	Harber WH	Jardine F	Knights AF	Lownds MU	McBain A	McKechnie TS	O'Rourke J	Pacey D	Phillips EJ	Pleat DJ	Reid J	Riddick GG	Rioch BD	Tinsley C	Whittaker RH
1		1	3				5						6	2	8	9	4		7	10				11
2		1	3				5						6	2	8		4		7	10	9			11
3		1	3				5						6	2	8		4		7	10	9			11
4		1	3				5						6	2	8		4		7	10	9			11
5		1	3				5						6	2	8	9	4		7	10				11
6		1	3				5						6	2	8		4		7	10	9			11
7		1	3				5						6	2	8	9	4		7	10				11
8		1	3				5						6	2	8	9	4		7	10				11
9		1	3				5						6	2	8	9	4		7	10				11
10		1	3				5					6		2	8	9	4		7	10				11
11		1	3				5					6		2	8	9	4		7	10				11
12		1	3				5						6	2		9	4		7	10	8			11
13		1	6				5			3			4	2		9			7	10	8			11
14		1	6				5			3			4	2	8	9			7	10				11
15		1	6				5			3			4	2		9			7	10	8			11
16		1	6		9		5			3			4	2					7	10	8			11
17		1	6	5							3			2	7		4		8	10	9			11
18		1	6	5	9						3			2	7		4		8	10				11
19			6	5					7		3			2	9		4		8	10			1	11
20			6	5					7		3			2	9		4		8	10			1	11
21			6		9		5		7	11	3			2			4		8	10			1	
22		1	6	5						8	3		4	2					7	10	9			11
23		1	6	5						8	3		4	2					7	10	9			11
24		1	3	5										2	9		4		7	6	8	10		11
25		1	3				5							2	9		4		7	6	8	10		11
26		1	3				5							2	9		4		7	6	8	10		11
27	3	1		5									6	2	9		4		7	10	8			11
28	3	1		5						11				2	9		4		7	6	8	10		
29	3	1		5	9					11				2	10		4		7	6	8			
30	6	1		4						11	3			2	9		5			10	7	8		
31		1					5	4		7	3			2	8				9		6	10		11
32		1	6				5	8		7	3			2	10	9	4							11
33		1	6					4			3			2	7	9	5				8	10		11
34		1						4			3			2	11	9	5	8	7	6		10		
35		1						4			3			2	11	9	5	8	7	6		10		
36	2						5	4		11	3				8	9		10	7	6			1	
37	2						5	4		11	3					9		10	7	6		8	1	
38	2						5	4		11	3				10			9	7	6		8	1	
39	2						5	4		11	3				10			9	7	6		8	1	
40	2						5	4		11	3				10	8		9	7	6			1	
41	2						5	4		11	3				10	8		9	7	6			1	
42	2						5	4		11	3				8			9	7	6	10		1	
43			3	5				4		7			6	2					8	10	9		1	11
44			3				5		7					2	4	10			8		6	9	1	11
45			6				5		7		3		4	2		9			8	10			1	11
46			3		2		5	4		7	9								8		6	10	1	11
Apps	11	28	31	12	4	1	29	16	3	15	29	2	20	38	36	21	27	12	37	46	28	11	18	31
Goals										3					10	10	1	8	5	2	5			6

One own goal

F.A. Cup

Rd	Date	Opponent	Score	Scorers	Att
R1	Nov 14	SOUTHEND UNITED	1-0	Bramwell	6892
R2	Dec 5	GILLINGHAM	1-0	Riddick	5964
R3	Jan 9	SUNDERLAND	0-3		16834

Rd	Barton KR	Baynham RL	Caleb GS	Fincham GR	Harber WH	Jardine F	Lownds MU	McBain A	McKechnie TS	O'Rourke J	Pacey D	Pleat DJ	Reid J	Riddick GG	Rioch BD	Whittaker RH
R1		1	5		8	3	4	2				7	10	9		11
R2		1	5			3		2	9		4	7	6	8	10	11
R3	3	1	5		11			2	9		4	7	6	8	10	

F.L. Cup

Rd	Date	Opponent	Score	Scorers	Att
R1	Sep 7	Port Vale	1-0	McKechnie	5111
R2	Sep 23	ASTON VILLA	0-1		9011

Rd	Baynham RL	Bramwell J	Fincham GR	Lownds MU	McBain A	McKechnie TS	O'Rourke J	Pacey D	Pleat DJ	Reid J	Riddick GG	Whittaker RH
R1	1	3	5	6	2	8	9			10		11
R2	1	3	5	6	2	8	9	4	7	10		11

Played in R1: R Riley at 4, A Clarke at 7

Final table — Division Three

		P	W	D	L	F	A	W	D	L	F	A	Pts
1	Carlisle United	46	14	5	4	46	24	11	5	7	30	29	60
2	Bristol City	46	14	6	3	53	18	10	5	8	39	37	59
3	Mansfield Town	46	17	4	2	61	23	7	7	9	34	38	59
4	Hull City	46	14	6	3	51	25	9	6	8	40	32	58
5	Brentford	46	18	4	1	55	18	6	5	12	28	37	57
6	Bristol Rovers	46	14	7	2	52	21	6	8	9	30	37	55
7	Gillingham	46	16	5	2	45	13	7	4	12	25	37	55
8	Peterborough Utd.	46	16	3	4	61	33	6	4	13	24	41	51
9	Watford	46	13	8	2	45	21	4	8	11	26	43	50
10	Grimsby Town	46	11	10	2	37	21	5	7	11	31	46	49
11	Bournemouth	46	12	4	7	40	24	6	7	10	32	39	47
12	Southend United	46	14	4	5	48	24	5	4	14	30	47	46
13	Reading	46	12	8	3	45	26	4	6	13	25	44	46
14	Queen's Park Rgs.	46	15	5	3	48	23	2	7	14	24	57	46
15	Workington	46	11	7	5	30	22	6	5	12	28	47	46
16	Shrewsbury Town	46	10	6	7	42	38	5	6	12	34	46	42
17	Exeter City	46	8	7	8	33	27	4	10	9	18	25	41
18	Scunthorpe United	46	9	8	6	42	27	5	4	14	23	45	40
19	Walsall	46	9	4	10	34	36	6	3	14	21	44	37
20	Oldham Athletic	46	10	3	10	40	39	3	7	13	21	44	36
21	LUTON TOWN	46	6	8	9	32	36	5	3	15	19	58	33
22	Port Vale	46	7	6	10	27	33	2	8	13	14	43	32
23	Colchester United	46	7	6	10	30	34	3	4	16	20	55	30
24	Barnsley	46	8	5	10	33	31	1	6	16	21	59	29

1965/66 6th in Division Four

#	Mon	Date	Opponent	Score	Scorers	Att	Edwards R	French GE	Fry B	Gibson J	Harber WH	Jardine F	Long C	McKechnie TS	Moore J	O'Rourke J	Pleat DJ	Ramage G	Read JA	Reid J	Riddick GG	Rioch BD	Rivers AD	Slough AP	Stark WR	Thomson R	Tinsley C	Whittaker RH	Woods M
1	Aug	21	BRADFORD PARK AVE.	3-1	McKechnie 2, Reid	6182			7	4		3		8	6	9				10						2	1	11	5
2		23	Wrexham	0-2		5466			7	4		3		8	6	9				10						2	1	11	5
3		28	Aldershot	1-3	O'Rourke	5310				4	7	3		8	6	9				10		12				2	1	11	5
4	Sep	4	NEWPORT COUNTY	2-1	Reid (p), Moore	4899	4			8		3		11	6				9	10			5	7		2	1		
5		11	Torquay United	0-2		5156	4			9		3		11	6					10	7		5		8	2	1		
6		16	WREXHAM	1-0	Whittaker	4780				7		3			6	9				4	10	5		8		2	1	11	
7		18	CHESTERFIELD	1-2	Stark	4905						3			6	9				4	7	8	5		10	2	1	11	
8		24	Rochdale	2-1	Read, O'Rourke	3692					7	3			6	9			8	4			5		10	2	1	11	
9	Oct	7	DONCASTER ROVERS	4-3	O'Rourke 3, Whittaker	5020					7	3			6	9			8	4			5		10	2	1	11	
10		9	BARNSLEY	5-4	Read 2, O'Rourke, Whittaker, Stark	5948					7	3			6	9			8	4			5		10	2	1	11	
11		16	Bradford City	2-2	Moore, O'Rourke	2635		7			10	3			6	9			8	4			5		12		1	11	
12		23	CREWE ALEXANDRA	4-0	Leigh (og), O'Rourke 3	6299		7			10	3			6	9			8	4			5				1	11	
13		30	Port Vale	2-1	O'Rourke, Whittaker	6058		7	10			3			6	9			8	4			5				1	11	
14	Nov	3	Tranmere Rovers	0-2		9278		7	10			3			6	9			8	4			5				1	11	
15		6	HALIFAX TOWN	4-1	Moore, Whittaker, O'Rourke, Read	7879		7	10			3			6	9			8	4		12					1	11	5
16		20	NOTTS COUNTY	5-1	Read 3, O'Rourke, Whittaker	6486	3	10			7				6	9			8	4							1	11	5
17		23	Doncaster Rovers	1-1	Whittaker (p)	4134	3	10			7				6	9			8	4							1	11	5
18		27	Lincoln City	2-2	Read, Whittaker	2941	3	10			7				6	9			8	4							1	11	5
19	Dec	10	Stockport County	1-4	Stark	7778		10				3			6	9	7		8	4					12		1	11	5
20		18	BRADFORD CITY	2-3	Read, Rioch	5550						3				9	7		8		4	6			10	2	1	11	5
21		27	Southport	2-3	Whittaker 2	6638		7	8		10	3				9					4	2	6				1	11	5
22		28	SOUTHPORT	2-0	Read, French	7307		7			10	3				9			8		4	2	6				1	11	5
23	Jan	1	Barnsley	0-3		5053		7				3		10		9			8		4	2					1	11	5
24		8	CHESTER	5-2	French, Read, O'Rourke 3	6670		7				3			6	9			8		4	2	10				1	11	5
25		15	Crewe Alexandra	0-2		3534		7				3			6	9			8		4	2	10				1	11	5
26		29	Bradford Park Avenue	3-1	O'Rourke, Whittaker, Moore	6451		7				3			6	9			8		4	2	10				1	11	5
27	Feb	5	ALDERSHOT	3-1	Read, O'Rourke 2	6822	12	7				3			6	9			8		4	2	10				1	11	5
28		12	HARTLEPOOLS UNITED	2-1	O'Rourke 2	6131		7				3			6	9			8		4	2	10				1	11	5
29		26	TORQUAY UNITED	3-2	O'Rourke 2, Rioch	9271		7				3		8	6	9					4	2	10				1	11	5
30	Mar	5	Hartlepools United	0-2		4896						3		8	6	9	7	12			4	2	10				1	11	5
31		12	Chesterfield	3-1	O'Rourke, Riddick, Jardine	4264		7				3			6	9		1	8		4	10				2		11	5
32		19	ROCHDALE	4-1	O'Rourke 3, Riddick	7381		7				3			6	9		1	8		4	10				2		11	5
33		26	TRANMERE ROVERS	2-1	Moore, O'Rourke	8076	8	7		4		3			6	9		1				10	2					11	5
34	Apr	8	Colchester United	2-2	Edwards, Whittaker (p)	10200	8			4	7	3			6	9		1				10	2					11	5
35		9	DARLINGTON	2-0	O'Rourke, Whittaker	9774	8			4	7	3			6	9		1	12			10	2					11	5
36		11	COLCHESTER UNITED	1-1	Riddick	15309	8			4		3		12	6	9		1				10	2					11	5
37		16	Notts County	1-1	Reid	4740	3	7		4					6	9		1	10	8		2		12				11	5
38		23	LINCOLN CITY	0-0		9621	10	7						9	6				8		4	2		12		3	1	11	5
39		25	Barrow	1-0	French	5186	3	7			11				6				10	8		9	4			2	1		
40		30	Darlington	0-1		11155	3	7							6				10	8		9	4			2	1		
41	May	7	STOCKPORT COUNTY	2-0	Rioch, Whittaker (p)	9524		7				3			6	9		1	8		4	10		12		2		11	5
42		14	PORT VALE	5-0	O'Rourke 2, Whittaker, Riddick 2	12054		7							6	9		1	8		4	10		3		2		11	5
43		16	Halifax Town	0-3		3002	12	7							6	9		1	8		4	10		3		2		11	
44		19	BARROW	3-2	French, Riddick, O'Rourke	10647		7		4	11				6	9		1	8		4	10		3		2			5
45		25	Newport County	1-3	Reid	2073		7		12	11				6	9		1	8		4	10		3		2			5
46		28	Chester	1-1	Stark	4740	8	7		4				12	6			1		9	10	5		3	11	2			
			Apps				16	32	6	16	13	34	1	10	43	40	3	7	33	43	29	20	17	9	10	31	33	40	34
			Goals				1	4				1		2	5	32			12	4	6	3			4			15	

One own goal

F.A. Cup

#	Mon	Date	Opponent	Score	Scorers	Att	Edwards R	French GE	Fry B	Gibson J	Harber WH	Jardine F	Long C	McKechnie TS	Moore J	O'Rourke J	Pleat DJ	Ramage G	Read JA	Reid J	Riddick GG	Rioch BD	Rivers AD	Slough AP	Stark WR	Thomson R	Tinsley C	Whittaker RH	Woods M
R1	Nov	13	Romford	1-1	Harris (og)	9592		10	7			3			6	9			8	4						2	1	11	5
rep	Nov	18	ROMFORD	1-0	O'Rourke	11061	3	10	7						6	9			8	4						2	1	11	5
R2	Dec	4	Corby Town	2-2	O'Rourke, Whittaker (p)	6421	3	10	7						6	9			8	4						2	1	11	5
rep	Dec	7	CORBY TOWN	0-1		13284	3	10	7						6	9			8	4						2	1	11	5

F.L. Cup

#	Mon	Date	Opponent	Score	Scorers	Att	Edwards R	French GE	Fry B	Gibson J	Harber WH	Jardine F	Long C	McKechnie TS	Moore J	O'Rourke J	Pleat DJ	Ramage G	Read JA	Reid J	Riddick GG	Rioch BD	Rivers AD	Slough AP	Stark WR	Thomson R	Tinsley C	Whittaker RH	Woods M
R1	Sep	1	BRIGHTON & HOVE ALB.	1-1	Gibson	3758	4			8	11	3			6				9	10			5	7		2	1		
rep	Sep	7	Brighton & Hove Albion	0-2		11745	4			8				11	6				9	10	3		5	7		2	1		

		P	W	D	L	F	A	W	D	L	F	A	Pts
1	Doncaster Rovers	46	15	6	2	49	21	9	5	9	36	33	59
2	Darlington	46	16	3	4	41	17	9	6	8	31	36	59
3	Torquay United	46	17	2	4	43	20	7	8	8	29	29	58
4	Colchester United	46	13	7	3	45	21	10	3	10	25	26	56
5	Tranmere Rovers	46	15	1	7	56	32	9	7	7	37	34	56
6	LUTON TOWN	46	19	2	2	65	27	5	6	12	25	43	56
7	Chester	46	15	5	3	52	27	5	7	11	27	43	52
8	Notts County	46	9	8	6	32	25	10	4	9	29	28	50
9	Newport County	46	14	6	3	46	24	4	6	13	29	51	48
10	Southport	46	15	6	2	47	20	3	6	14	21	49	48
11	Bradford Park Ave.	46	14	2	7	59	31	7	3	13	43	61	47
12	Barrow	46	12	8	3	48	31	4	7	12	24	45	47
13	Stockport County	46	12	4	7	42	29	6	2	15	29	41	42
14	Crewe Alexandra	46	12	4	7	42	23	4	5	14	19	40	41
15	Halifax Town	46	11	6	6	46	31	4	5	14	21	44	41
16	Barnsley	46	11	6	6	43	24	4	4	15	31	54	40
17	Aldershot	46	12	6	5	47	27	3	4	16	28	57	40
18	Hartlepools United	46	13	4	6	44	22	3	4	16	19	53	40
19	Port Vale	46	12	7	4	38	18	3	2	18	10	41	39
20	Chesterfield	46	8	9	6	37	35	5	4	14	25	43	39
21	Rochdale	46	12	1	10	46	27	4	4	15	25	60	37
22	Lincoln City	46	9	7	7	37	29	4	4	15	20	53	37
23	Bradford City	46	10	5	8	37	34	2	8	13	26	60	37
24	Wrexham	46	10	4	9	43	43	3	5	15	29	61	35

#	Date		Opponent	Res	Scorers	Att	Adamson T	Allen K	Conboy FJ	Dougan MS	French GE	Jardine F	Johnson B	Kevan DT	King GH	Lunnis RE	Moore J	Pleat DJ	Read JA	Riddick GG	Rioch BD	Rivers AD	Slough AP	Swan RM	Thear AC	Thomson R	Whittaker RH	Yardley G
1	Aug	20	HALIFAX TOWN	2-0	King, Rioch	6149						3			10		6	9	1	7	8	5	2			4	11	
2		27	Brentford	0-1		6769						3			10		5	7	1	9	8	4	2			6	11	
3	Sep	3	NEWPORT COUNTY	3-1	Rivers, Whittaker, Rioch	5377					8	3					4	7	1	9	10	5	2			6	11	
4		6	Rochdale	0-3		2472					8	3					6	7	1	9	10	5	2		12	4	11	
5		10	Barnsley	1-2	Moore	2188					8	3		12			6	7	1	9	10	5	2			4	11	
6		17	STOCKPORT COUNTY	0-3		5887					8	3			11		6	7	1	5	10	9	4			2		
7		24	ALDERSHOT	4-0	Whittaker, Slough, Thear 2	4471					7	3			11		6		1	5	10		4		9	2	8	
8		29	ROCHDALE	3-1	Rioch, Thear 2	6435					7	3			11		6		1	5	10		4		9	2	8	
9	Oct	1	Wrexham	0-2		6887					7	3			11		6	12	1	5	10		4		9	2	8	
10		8	Southport	1-4	Rioch	4485					7	3			11		6		1	5	10		4		9	2	8	
11		15	NOTTS COUNTY	2-5	Pleat, Thear	5743			4		7	3			11		6	8	1	5	10		12		9	2	11	
12		20	BRADFORD CITY	0-0		4150					7	3			10		5	8	1	6			4		9	2	11	
13		22	Chester	0-0		5751			4			3	7					8	1	5	10		6		9	2	11	
14		24	Newport County	0-2		3456			4			3					6	7	1	5	10		6		9	2	11	
15		29	BRADFORD PARK AVE.	2-2	Conboy, Whittaker	4566			4		7	3					5	8	1		10		6			2	11	9
16	Nov	5	Port Vale	0-1		3502			4		7	3					5	8	1	9	10		6			2	11	
17		12	CREWE ALEXANDRA	2-1	Riddick 2	4785			4			3					5	7	1	9	10		6		8	2	11	
18		16	Bradford City	1-2	Pleat	3097			4			3					5	7	1	9	10		6		8	2	11	
19		19	Barrow	0-3		5061			4			3					5	7	1	12	10	8	6		9	2	11	
20	Dec	3	Lincoln City	1-8	Rioch	3893						3	7		11		5	9	1	4	10		6		8	2		
21		10	CHESTERFIELD	3-2	Whittaker, Rioch 2	5096					5	3	7		11		6	8	1	9	10		4			2	11	
22		17	Halifax Town	1-1	Kevan	3622					5	3	7	8			6		1	9	10		4			2	11	
23		26	Tranmere Rovers	0-1		6806					5	3	7	9			6		1	8	10		4			2	11	
24		27	TRANMERE ROVERS	2-0	Whittaker, Kevan	9123					5	3	7	9			6	12	1	8	10		4			2	11	
25		31	BRENTFORD	3-0	French, Whittaker, Pleat	8531					5	3	7	8		2	6	9	1	4	10	12					11	
26	Jan	14	BARNSLEY	1-1	Pleat	8287					5	3	7	8			6	9		4	10			1		2	11	
27		20	Stockport County	0-1		9555					5	3	7	8			6	9		4	10			1		2	11	
28	Feb	4	Aldershot	1-4	Rioch	5378					5	3	7	8			6			9	10		4	1		2	11	
29		11	WREXHAM	3-1	Slough, Kevan 2	6551					5	3	7	8			6			9	10		4	1		2	11	
30		18	Exeter City	1-2	Riddick	3744					5	3	7	8	11		6	12		9	10		4	1		2		
31		25	SOUTHPORT	0-0		6903					5	3	7		9			8		10	4		6	1		2	11	
32	Mar	4	Notts County	2-1	King, Upton (og)	3909					5	3	7	8	10		9			4			6	1		2	11	
33		11	EXETER CITY	4-0	Riddick, King, French, Allen	6046	8	4			5	3	7		9		12	10		4			6	1		2	11	
34		18	CHESTER	1-0	Allen	6982	8	4				3	7		10		6			9			5	1		2	11	
35		24	Hartlepools United	1-2	French	8442	8	4				3	7		10		6			9			5	1		2	11	
36		25	York City	1-5	French	1912	8	9	4			3	7		10		6						5	1		2	11	
37		27	HARTLEPOOLS UNITED	0-2		7370	8	2	4			3	7		10		6			9	12		5	1			11	
38	Apr	1	PORT VALE	1-1	Moore	5410	2	9	4	5		3			11	10	6	8				12		1		7		
39		8	Crewe Alexandra	1-3	King	5124		9	4	5		3			7		6	8						1		2	11	
40		12	SOUTHEND UNITED	1-0	Allen	4666	8	4		5	7	3			11		6						9	1		2	10	
41		15	BARROW	3-1	Whittaker 2 (1p), Allen	5710	8	4		5	7	3			11		6						9	1		2	10	
42		22	Bradford Park Avenue	0-0		3760	8	4		5	7	3			11		6						9	1		2	10	
43		24	Southend United	0-2		7303	3	8	4	5	7						6	11					9	1		2	10	
44		29	LINCOLN CITY	2-1	Allen, Whittaker (p)	5382	8	4		5	7	3			11		6						9	1		2	10	
45	May	6	Chesterfield	0-0		3055	8	4		5	7	3			11	10	6						9	1		2		
46		13	YORK CITY	5-1	Allen, Baker (og), Jardine, Rioch 2	5196	9	4		5	7	3			11	10	6				8			1		2		
			Apps				2	14	19	26	36	45	8	11	22	1	44	30	36	31	37	13	30	14	13	43	41	1
			Goals					6	1		4	1		4	4		2	4		4	10	1	2		5		9	

Two own goals

F.A. Cup

	Date		Opponent	Res	Scorers	Att	Allen K	French GE	Jardine F	Johnson B	Kevan DT	Moore J	Pleat DJ	Read JA	Riddick GG	Rioch BD	Slough AP	Thomson R	Whittaker RH
R1	Nov	26	Exeter City	1-1	Whittaker	4704	4		3	7		5	8	1	9	10	6	2	11
rep	Dec	1	EXETER CITY	2-0	Rioch, Pleat	7078	4		3	7	12	5	8	1	9	10	6	2	11
R2	Jan	7	Bristol Rovers	2-3	Kevan 2	8480		5	3	7	8	6	9	1	4	10		2	11

F.L. Cup

	Date		Opponent	Res	Scorers	Att	French GE	Jardine F	Kevan DT	King GH	Moore J	Pleat DJ	Read JA	Riddick GG	Rioch BD	Rivers AD	Slough AP	Thear AC	Thomson R	Whittaker RH
R1	Aug	24	Aldershot	2-2	Whittaker, Jardine	3677		3	8		6	7	1	4	10	5	2	9		11
rep	Aug	29	ALDERSHOT	1-2	King	4832		3	8		6	7	1	9	10	5	2		12 4	11

		P	W	D	L	F	A	W	D	L	F	A	Pts
1	Stockport County	46	16	5	2	41	18	10	7	6	28	24	64
2	Southport	46	19	2	2	47	15	4	11	8	22	27	59
3	Barrow	46	12	8	3	35	18	12	3	8	41	36	59
4	Tranmere Rovers	46	14	6	3	42	20	8	8	7	24	23	58
5	Crewe Alexandra	46	14	5	4	42	26	7	7	9	28	29	54
6	Southend United	46	15	5	3	44	12	7	4	12	26	37	53
7	Wrexham	46	11	12	0	46	20	5	8	10	30	42	52
8	Hartlepools United	46	15	3	5	44	29	7	4	12	22	35	51
9	Brentford	46	13	7	3	36	19	6	6	12	22	37	49
10	Aldershot	46	14	4	5	48	19	4	8	11	24	38	48
11	Bradford City	46	13	4	6	48	31	6	6	11	26	31	48
12	Halifax Town	46	10	11	2	37	27	5	3	15	22	41	44
13	Port Vale	46	9	7	7	33	27	5	8	10	22	31	43
14	Exeter City	46	11	6	6	30	24	3	9	11	20	36	43
15	Chesterfield	46	13	6	4	33	16	4	2	17	27	47	42
16	Barnsley	46	8	7	8	30	28	5	8	10	30	36	41
17	LUTON TOWN	46	11	5	3	47	23	1	4	18	12	50	41
18	Newport County	46	9	9	5	35	23	3	7	13	21	40	40
19	Chester	46	8	5	10	24	32	7	5	11	30	46	40
20	Notts County	46	10	7	6	31	25	3	4	16	22	47	37
21	Rochdale	46	10	4	9	30	27	3	7	13	23	48	37
22	York City	46	11	5	7	45	31	1	6	16	20	48	35
23	Bradford Park Ave.	46	7	6	10	30	34	4	7	12	22	45	35
24	Lincoln City	46	7	8	8	39	39	2	5	16	19	43	31

1967/68   Champions of Division Four: Promoted

						Allen K	Bevan K	Branston TG	Brown MJ	Buxton IR	Denton PR	Dougan MS	French GE	Green HR	Hare T	Jardine F	Johnson B	McDermont W	McLeish H	Moore J	Potter GR	Read JA	Rioch BD	Ryan JO	Slough AP	Taylor WD	Tinsley C	Walker DG	Whittaker RH
1	Aug 19	Wrexham	1-1	Green	9514	8		5					7	9	2	3	12				6			1	10		4				11
2	26	BARNSLEY	2-0	Rioch, Allen	7887	8		5	9				7		2	3		4					1	10		6			12	11
3	Sep 2	Swansea Town	2-2	Brown, Rioch	6674	10		5	8			12	7	9				2			4		1	6		3				11
4	4	Southend United	0-3		11355	8	7	5	11					9	2	3		4			6			10		12		1		
5	9	HARTLEPOOLS UNITED	1-0	Rioch	8347	9		5	8				7		2	3		4			6		1	10						11
6	16	Newport County	1-1	Slough	4625	8		5	7			9			2	3		4			6		1	10		12				11
7	23	YORK CITY	3-1	Rioch 2, Whittaker	7977	8		5					4	7	2	3		9			6		1	10						11
8	27	SOUTHEND UNITED	3-1	Moore, Branston, French	13332	9		5		8			4	7	2	3					6		1	10						11
9	30	Rochdale	2-2	Buxton, Rioch	1884	9		5		8			4	7	2	3					6		1	10						11
10	Oct 3	Doncaster Rovers	0-2		5529	9		5		8			4		2	3		7			6		1	10		12				11
11	7	Chester	3-1	Buxton, Allen 2	3967	9		5	12	8			2			3		7			6		1	10		4				11
12	14	CHESTERFIELD	1-0	Buxton	10441	9		5		8			2	7		3					6		1	10		4				11
13	21	Exeter City	5-0	Buxton, Slough, Allen 2, Whittaker	3434	9		5		8			2			3					6		1	10	7	4				11
14	25	DONCASTER ROVERS	5-3	Buxton 2, Slough, Rioch, Allen	13925	9		5		8			2			3					6		1	10	7	4				11
15	Nov 11	WORKINGTON	4-0	Whittaker 2, Rioch, Slough	10935	9		5		8			2			3					6		1	10	7	4				11
16	15	SWANSEA TOWN	4-0	Buxton 2, Rioch, French	14981	9		5		8			2	7		3					6		1	10		4				11
17	18	Lincoln City	3-2	Whittaker (p), French, Allen	6052	9		5		8			2	7		3		12			6		1	10		4				11
18	25	HALIFAX TOWN	2-0	Buxton, Moore	11572	9		5		8			2	11		3					6		1	10	7	4				11
19	Dec 2	Bradford City	0-2		7957			5		8			2	7		3			9		6		1	10		4				11
20	16	WREXHAM	2-1	Rioch, Branston	9598	9		5		8			2			3					6		1	10	7	4				11
21	23	Barnsley	2-2	Rioch, Ryan	8704	9		5		8			2			3		12			6		1	10	7	4				11
22	26	BRADFORD PARK AVE.	2-0	Branston, Whittaker	16699	9		5		8			2			3		10			6	12			7	4	1			11
23	30	Bradford Park Avenue	1-2	Green	3674	10		5		8			2		9	3	11		12	6				7	4	1			
24	Jan 13	Hartlepools United	1-2	Branston	4766	9		5		8			4		2	3					6			10	7		1			11
25	20	NEWPORT COUNTY	1-1	Allen	10992	9		5		8	7		4	11	2	3					6		1	10						
26	26	Port Vale	0-0		5970	9		5	12	8	7	2				3					6		1	10		4				11
27	Feb 3	York City	1-1	Allen	2747	9		5			7	2		9		3					6		1	10		4				11
28	10	ROCHDALE	4-1	Rioch, Branston, Allen, Buxton	10040	9		5		8			2	7	12	3					6		1	10		4				11
29	17	Brentford	2-0	Slough, Rioch	7726	9		5		8			2	7		3					6		1	10		4				11
30	24	LINCOLN CITY	4-2	Whittaker 2 (1p), Allen, Rioch	11159	9		5	12	8			2	7		3					6		1	10		4				11
31	26	DARLINGTON	3-1	Ricoh, Allen, Moore	13948	9		5		8			2	7		3		12			6		1	10		4				11
32	Mar 2	Chesterfield	0-0		14075	9		5		8			2	7				3			6		1	10		4				11
33	9	PORT VALE	2-0	Buxton, Rioch	12749	9		5		8			2	7		3		12			6		1	10		4				11
34	16	EXETER CITY	0-0		12409	9		5		8			2	7		3		4		6	12		1	10						11
35	20	Aldershot	1-0	Buxton	9724	9		5	12	8			2	11				3		6	4		1	10	7				
36	23	Darlington	2-1	Rioch, Green	4336	10		5	7	8	12	2		9				3		6	4		1	11					
37	30	ALDERSHOT	3-1	Rioch 2, Brown	10618	9		5	7	8			2	11		3				6	4		1	10					
38	Apr 6	Workington	1-0	French	2195	4		5		7			2	8	9	3				6			1	11						10
39	12	NOTTS COUNTY	2-0	Allen, French	16631	9		5		8			2	7		3				6			1	10		4				11
40	13	CHESTER	0-0		13266	9		5		8			2	7	12	3				6			1	10		4				11
41	15	Notts County	2-2	Allen, Buxton	7920	9		5		8			2	7		3				6			1	10		4				11
42	20	Halifax Town	1-0	Rioch	5091	9		5	7	8			2	11		3		12		6			1	10		4				11
43	24	CREWE ALEXANDRA	4-0	Rioch 2, Moore, Slough	18904	9		5		8			2	7		3		12		6			1	10		4				11
44	27	BRADFORD CITY	1-3	Whittaker (p)	14147	9		5		8			2	7		3				6			1	10		4				11
45	May 4	Crewe Alexandra	1-2	Rioch	8634	8		5					2	7	9	3				6	12		1	10		4				11
46	11	BRENTFORD	2-1	Rioch, Whittaker	14643	8		5					2	7	9	3				6			1	10		4				11

				Apps	45	1	46	12	36	4	42	31	11	12	41	2	19	2	45	5	43	44	10	35	3	1	1	38
				Goals	14		5	2	13			5	3						4			24	1	6				10

F.A. Cup

R1	Dec 14	OXFORD CITY	2-1	Rioch, Buxton	13394	9			8			2	7		12	3		5		6		1	10		4				11
R2	Jan 6	Swindon Town	2-3	Allen, Whittaker (p)	18203	9		5	12	10			7		2	3				6			8	4	1				11

F.L. Cup

R1	Aug 23	CHARLTON ATHLETIC	1-1	Allen	9001	8		5					7	9	2	3		4		6		1	10						11
rep	Aug 30	Charlton Ath	2-1	Rioch 2	7659	4		5	8				7	9				2		6		1	10	3					11
R2	Sep 13	Leeds United	1-3	Whittaker	11473	8		5	7			9			2	3		4		6		1	10						11

R1 replay a.e.t.

		P	W	D	L	F	A	W	D	L	F	A	Pts
1	LUTON TOWN	46	19	3	1	55	16	8	9	6	32	28	66
2	Barnsley	46	17	6	0	43	14	7	7	9	25	32	61
3	Hartlepools United	46	15	7	1	34	12	10	3	10	26	34	60
4	Crewe Alexandra	46	13	10	0	44	18	7	8	8	30	31	58
5	Bradford City	46	14	5	4	41	22	9	6	8	31	29	57
6	Southend United	46	12	8	3	45	21	8	6	9	32	37	54
7	Chesterfield	46	15	4	4	47	20	6	7	10	24	30	53
8	Wrexham	46	17	3	3	47	12	3	10	10	25	41	53
9	Aldershot	46	10	11	2	36	19	8	6	9	34	36	53
10	Doncaster Rovers	46	12	8	3	36	16	6	7	10	30	40	51
11	Halifax Town	46	10	6	7	34	24	5	10	8	18	25	46
12	Newport County	46	11	7	5	32	22	5	6	12	26	41	45
13	Lincoln City	46	11	3	9	41	31	6	6	11	30	37	43
14	Brentford	46	13	4	6	41	24	5	3	15	20	40	43
15	Swansea Town	46	11	8	4	38	25	5	2	16	25	52	42
16	Darlington	46	6	11	6	31	27	6	6	11	16	26	41
17	Notts County	46	10	7	6	27	27	5	4	14	26	52	41
18	Port Vale	46	10	5	8	41	31	2	10	11	20	41	39
19	Rochdale	46	9	8	6	35	32	3	6	14	16	40	38
20	Exeter City	46	9	7	7	30	30	2	9	12	15	35	38
21	York City	46	9	6	8	44	30	2	8	13	21	38	36
22	Chester	46	6	6	11	35	38	3	8	12	22	40	32
23	Workington	46	8	8	7	35	29	2	3	18	19	58	31
24	Bradford Park Ave.	46	3	7	13	18	35	1	8	14	12	47	23

1968/69   Third in Division Three

#	Date	Opponent	Score	Scorers	Att	Allen K	Bannister J	Branston TG	Brown MJ	Buxton IR	Davie AG	Denton PR	Dougan MS	French GE	Harrison MJ	Jardine F	Keen MT	Lewis B	McDerment W	Moore J	Potter GR	Read JA	Rioch BD	Ryan JO	Sheffield LJ	Slough AP	Stevenson M	Taylor WD	Whittaker RH
1	Aug 10	OLDHAM ATHLETIC	4-0	Harrison (p), Allen, Jardine, Lewis	14747	4		5					2	7	11	3		8		12		1	10		9	6			
2	17	Barrow	0-0		6628	4		5	7				2			3		8				1	10		9	6			11
3	24	ROTHERHAM UNITED	3-1	Ricoh 2, Lewis	14163	4		5					2	7	11	3		8		12		1	10		9	6			
4	28	BARNSLEY	5-1	Rioch, Lewis 2, Allen, Branston	15899	4		5					2	7	11	3		8		12		1	10		9	6			
5	31	Gillingham	3-1	Lewis 2, Sheffield	8227	4		5					2	11				8	3	12		1	10	7	9	6			
6	Sep 7	Orient	0-0		13719	4							2	11		3		8	12	6		1	10	7	9	5			
7	14	TRANMERE ROVERS	3-1	Sheffield, Lewis, Branston	12965			5					2	7	11	3		8		6		1	10		9	4			
8	18	MANSFIELD TOWN	4-2	Harrison(p), Sheffield, French, Lewis	19315			5					2	7	11	3		8	12	6		1	10		9	4			
9	21	Brighton & Hove Albion	0-1		11930	4		5						12	11	3		8	2			1	10	7	9	6			
10	28	TORQUAY UNITED	1-0	Lewis	14936	12		5					2	7	11	3		8	6			1	10		9	6			
11	Oct 5	Watford	0-1		22133	12		5					2		11	3		8	6			1	10	7	9	4			
12	8	Barnsley	1-3	Sheffield	13019	4		5		8			2		11	3			12				10	7	9	6		1	
13	12	HARTLEPOOL	3-0	Sheffield, Rioch, Lewis	13145	4		5					2	7		3		8	2				10		9	6		1	11
14	19	Plymouth Argyle	0-2		12659	4		5	12	7						3		8	2				10		9	6		1	11
15	26	NORTHAMPTON T	2-1	Allen, Sheffield	17818	4	6				1		3	7				8	5				10		9	2			11
16	Nov 5	Walsall	0-2		5381	4	6				1	7	2					8	3	12			10		9	5			11
17	9	SWINDON TOWN	2-0	Sheffield, Lewis	17250	4	6	5			1		2	7	11			8	3				10		9	4			
18	23	BOURNEMOUTH	1-1	Branston	14150	9	6	5			1		2	7				8	3				10		12	4			11
19	29	Stockport County	0-2		13246	10	3	5			1		6	7				8	2				11		9	4			
20	Dec 14	Hartlepool	0-1		3887	4	3	5		9	1		2	7	11			8								6	10		
21	21	PLYMOUTH ARGYLE	2-0	Lewis, Allen	10971	9	3	5			1		2	7	11			8					10			4			
22	28	Northampton Town	2-0	Rioch 2	15161	9	3	5			1		2	7	11			8		6			10			4			
23	Jan 8	Shrewsbury Town	1-3	Slough	4729	9	3	5			1		2	7	11			8	12	6			10			4			
24	18	Swindon Town	0-0		19105	9	3	5			1		2		11			8		6			10	7		4			
25	25	WALSALL	1-0	Rioch	15205	9	3	5			1		2	7			8	9		6			10			4			11
26	29	Crewe Alexandra	0-2		5053	10	3	5			1		2			11	8	7		6						4			
27	Feb 1	READING	2-1	Slough, Lewis (p)	11871	9	3	5			1		2	7	11			10	12	6						4			
28	8	Bournemouth	2-0	Jardine, Sheffield	9253	10	3	5			1		2	7		11		8		6					9	4			
29	26	CREWE ALEXANDRA	2-0	Slough, Allen	13384	9	3	5			1		2	7		11	8	10		6						4			
30	Mar 1	Oldham Athletic	1-0	Lawason (og)	3946						1		2	7		11	8	12		6					9	4			
31	5	SHREWSBURY TOWN	2-1	Allen, Keen	14337	10	3	5			1		2	7		11	8	12		6					9	4			
32	12	Reading	1-1	Sheffield	6146	10	3				1		2	7		11	8	4		6					9	5			
33	15	Rotherham United	2-2	French, Lewis	9873	8	3				1		2	7		11	10	4		6				12	9	5			
34	19	BRISTOL ROVERS	3-0	Sheffield, Allen, Lewis	14506	8	3	5			1		2	7				10		6			11		9	4			
35	22	GILLINGHAM	1-1	Sheffield	14562	8	3	5			1		2	7				10		6			11		9	4			
36	26	BARROW	5-1	Slough, Allen, Rioch, Lewis 2	14244	8	3	5			1		2	7		12		10		6			11		9	4			
37	29	ORIENT	2-1	Branston, Sheffield	13915	8	3	5			1		2					10		6	12		11	7	9	4			
38	31	Bristol Rovers	0-0		8112	8	3				1		2			11	4	10	12	6			7		9	5			
39	Apr 4	Torquay United	1-1	McDerment	11427	9	3				1		2			11	4	8	7	6	12		10			5			
40	7	Mansfield Town	0-1		8681	9					1		2	7	12	3	4	8	11	6			10			5			
41	8	SOUTHPORT	0-0		15693			5		12	1		2	7	11	3	10	8		6			9			4			
42	12	BRIGHTON & HOVE ALB	3-0	French, Lewis, Slough	11965		3	5		9			2	7			10	8		6		1	11			4			12
43	14	Southport	1-1	Lewis	3392		3	5		9			2	7			10	8		6		1	11			4			
44	18	Tranmere Rovers	2-0	Moore, Rioch	6723	4	3			9			2	7			10	8		6		1	11			5			
45	25	STOCKPORT COUNTY	4-1	Lewis 3, Rioch	12055	10	3			9			2	7			4	8		6		1	11			5			
46	30	WATFORD	2-1	Buxton, Allen	25523	10	3			9			2	7			4	8		6		1	11			5			
	Apps					40	30	35	2	11	27	1	43	36	19	24	14	45	21	33	3	16	37	8	29	46	1	3	8
	Goals					9		4		1				3	2	2	1	22	1	1			10		12	5			

One own goal

F.A. Cup

R	Date	Opponent	Score	Scorers	Att	Allen K	Bannister J	Branston TG	Brown MJ	Buxton IR	Davie AG	Denton PR	Dougan MS	French GE	Harrison MJ	Jardine F	Keen MT	Lewis B	McDerment W	Moore J	Potter GR	Read JA	Rioch BD	Ryan JO	Sheffield LJ	Slough AP
R1	Nov 16	WARE TOWN	6-1	Potter, Slough 2, Allen 3	10952	12	6	5			1		2	7				8	3		10		11		9	4
R2	Dec 7	GILLINGHAM	3-1	French, Harrison 2	12035		4	5		9	1		2	7	11			8	3				10			6
R3	Jan 4	Manchester City	0-1		37120	9	3	5			1		2	7	11			8	12	6			10			4

F.L. Cup

R	Date	Opponent	Score	Scorers	Att	Allen K	Branston TG	Brown MJ	Dougan MS	French GE	Harrison MJ	Jardine F	Lewis B	McDerment W	Moore J	Read JA	Rioch BD	Ryan JO	Sheffield LJ	Slough AP
R1	Aug 14	WATFORD	3-0	Harrison 2, Lewis	20167	4	5		2		11	3	8	12		1	10	7	9	6
R2	Sep 4	Brighton & Hove Albion	1-1	Sheffield	15200	4			2	11			8	3	6	1	10	7	9	5
rep	Sep 11	BRIGHTON & HOVE ALB	4-2	Slough 2, Sheffield, Rioch	18679		5		2	7	11	3	8		6	1	10		9	4
R3	Sep 24	Everton	1-5	Sheffield	30405		5	10	2	7	11	3	8	6		1	12		9	4

	P	W	D	L	F	A	W	D	L	F	A	Pts
1 Watford	46	16	5	2	35	7	11	5	7	39	27	64
2 Swindon Town	46	18	4	1	38	7	9	6	8	33	28	64
3 LUTON TOWN	46	20	3	0	57	14	5	8	10	17	24	61
4 Bournemouth	46	16	2	5	41	17	5	7	11	19	28	51
5 Plymouth Argyle	46	10	8	5	34	25	7	7	9	19	24	49
6 Torquay United	46	13	4	6	35	18	6	5	10	19	28	48
7 Tranmere Rovers	46	12	3	8	36	31	7	7	9	34	37	48
8 Southport	46	14	8	1	52	20	3	5	15	19	44	47
9 Stockport County	46	14	5	4	49	25	2	9	12	18	43	46
10 Barnsley	46	13	6	4	37	21	3	8	12	21	42	46
11 Rotherham United	46	12	6	5	40	21	4	7	12	16	29	45
12 Brighton & Hove A.	46	12	7	4	49	21	4	6	13	23	44	45
13 Walsall	46	10	9	4	34	18	4	7	12	16	31	44
14 Reading	46	13	3	7	41	25	2	10	11	26	41	43
15 Mansfield Town	46	14	5	4	37	18	2	6	15	21	44	43
16 Bristol Rovers	46	12	6	5	41	27	4	5	14	22	44	43
17 Shrewsbury Town	46	11	8	4	28	17	5	3	15	23	50	43
18 Orient	46	10	8	5	31	19	4	6	13	20	39	42
19 Barrow	46	11	6	6	30	23	6	2	15	26	52	42
20 Gillingham	46	10	10	3	35	20	3	5	15	19	43	41
21 Northampton Town	46	9	8	6	37	30	5	4	14	17	31	40
22 Hartlepool	46	6	12	5	25	29	4	7	12	16	41	39
23 Crewe Alexandra	46	11	4	8	40	31	2	5	16	12	45	35
24 Oldham Athletic	46	9	6	8	33	27	4	3	16	17	66	35

1969/70   Second in Division Three: Promoted

#	Date		Opponent	Score	Scorers	Att	Allen K	Bannister J	Branston TG	Busby VD	Collins JW	Davie AG	Dougan MS	French GE	Harrison MJ	Jardine F	Keen MT	Lewis B	MacDonald M	Moore J	Nicholl CJ	Phillips PS	Read JA	Ryan JG	Sheffield LJ	Slough AP	Starling AW	Tees M
1	Aug	9	BARROW	3-0	Allen, Collins, Keen	12080	10	3	5		7			12			4	8	11	6				1	2	9		
2		16	Bournemouth	1-0	MacDonald	9578	10	3	5					11			4		8	6				1	2	9		
3		23	ORIENT	3-2	Collins, MacDonald, French	13761	10	3	5		7			11			4	12	8	6				1	2	9		
4		26	HALIFAX TOWN	1-1	MacDonald	12759	10	3			7			11			4	9	8	6				1	2	12	5	
5		30	Gillingham	2-0	MacDonald (p), Green (og)	7792	10	3			7			11			4		8		6			1	2		6	9
6	Sep	6	BRISTOL ROVERS	4-0	MacDonald, Allen, Collins, Tees	15198	10	3			7		2	11			4		8		6			1			6	9
7		13	Bradford City	1-1	Allen	10851	10	3			7	1	2	11			4		8		6						6	9
8		16	Southport	3-0	MacDonald, French, Nicholl	4003	10	3			7	1	2	11			4		8		6						6	9
9		20	SHREWSBURY TOWN	2-2	Collins, Slough	15396	10	3			7	1	2	11			4		8		6						6	9
10		27	Plymouth Argyle	3-1	Tees 2, French	14111	10	3			7	1	2	11			4		8		6						6	9
11		30	Walsall	3-1	Tees 2, Collins	7557	10	3			7	1	2	11		12	4		8		6						6	9
12	Oct	4	STOCKPORT COUNTY	2-0	Nicholl, MacDonald (p)	15944	10	3			7	1		11		2	4		8		6						6	9
13		7	BOURNEMOUTH	0-0		18065	10	3			7	1		11		2	4		8		6					12	6	9
14		11	Doncaster Rovers	0-2		17380	10	3			7	1		11		2	4		8		6					12	6	9
15		18	Brighton & Hove Albion	2-1	Collins 2	20016	10	3			7	1		11		2	4		8		6	12					6	9
16		25	TORQUAY UNITED	1-1	Tees	16087	10	3			7	1		11			4	12	8		6					2	6	9
17	Nov	1	Rotherham United	1-1	Allen	8911	10	3			7	1		11			4		8		6					2	6	9
18		8	BARNSLEY	1-1	MacDonald	17422	10	3	5			1		7	11		4		8							2	6	9
19		22	ROCHDALE	2-0	Collins, Allen	15876	10	3	5		7	1		11	12		4		8							2	6	9
20		25	FULHAM	1-0	MacDonald	16485	10	3				1		7	11		4		8		6					2	6	9
21	Dec	13	BRADFORD CITY	5-0	MacDonald 3 (1p), Tees, Collins	11857	10	3			8	1			11		4		7		6	12				2	6	
22		26	Orient	0-1		17619	10	3			7	1		11			4	12	8		6	9				2	6	
23		27	GILLINGHAM	1-2	Keen	17402	10	3			8	1		11			4		7		6	9				2	6	
24	Jan	10	Shrewsbury Town	1-5	Harrison	4406	10	3			8	1			11		4		7	12	6					2	6	9
25		17	PLYMOUTH ARGYLE	0-2		12358	10	3			7	1		11			12		8	6	6					2	4	9
26		24	Bury	3-1	MacDonald, Tees 2	6813	12	3			7	1		11			10		8	4	6					2	6	
27		31	Stockport County	1-1	Tees	3922		3			7	1		11			10		9	4	6					2	6	
28	Feb	7	DONCASTER ROVERS	4-0	Slough, MacDonald 2, Tees	12828	9	3			7	1		11			4		10		6					2	6	
29		10	Bristol Rovers	0-3		13304	10	3			12	1		11			4		8	7	6					2	6	9
30		14	Barrow	1-2	French	3843	10	3	12		8	1		11			4		7		6					2	6	9
31		21	Torquay United	2-2	Harrison, MacDonald	6964						1		7	11	3	10		8	6	6					2	4	9
32		28	BRIGHTON & HOVE ALB	1-1	MacDonald (p)	17584					8	1		7	11	3	10		9	6	6					2	4	12
33	Mar	3	TRANMERE ROVERS	2-0	MacDonald, Ryan	11368				5	8	1			11	3	10		7	6						2	4	9
34		11	Reading	1-0	MacDonald	18929				5	7	1		11		3	10		8	6						2	4	
35		14	MANSFIELD TOWN	2-2	Ryan, Harrison	12690					8	1			11	3	10		7	6	6					2	4	9
36		17	BURY	0-0		12751	12	3	5		8	1			11		10		7	6						2	4	9
37		21	Tranmere Rovers	2-3	Allen, Slough	4035	8	3	5		7	1			11		10		9	6						2	4	12
38		27	ROTHERHAM UNITED	2-1	Slough, Allen	14315	8	3	5		7	1			11	12	10		9	6						2	4	
39		28	READING	5-0	MacDonald 3, Harrison, Busby	14401		3	5	8	7				11		10		9	6						2	4	1
40		31	Barnsley	1-2	Keen	9988		3	5	8	7				11		10		9	6						2	4	1
41	Apr	4	Halifax Town	0-0		3482		3	5	8	7				11		10		9	6			12			2	4	1
42		8	Fulham	1-0	MacDonald	18987	10	3	5	8					11		4		9	6						2	7	1
43		11	WALSALL	3-0	Busby, Colliins, MacDonald	17193	12	3	5	8	7				11		10		9	6						2	4	1
44		14	SOUTHPORT	1-0	Busby	16756			5	8	7		2	11			10		9	6			1	3		4		
45		20	Mansfield Town	0-0		10301	10	3	5	8				11			4		9	6			1	2		7		
46		25	Rochdale	2-1	Busby, MacDonald	5886	12	3	5	8	7				11				9	6			1	2		4		10
					Apps		38	40	19	9	40	31	7	39	12	10	46	5	46	23	27	5	9	36	6	45	6	32
					Goals		7			4	10			4	4		3		25		2			2		4		11

One own goal

F.A. Cup

	Date		Opponent	Score	Scorers	Att	Allen K	Bannister J	Branston TG	Busby VD	Collins JW	Davie AG	Dougan MS	French GE	Harrison MJ	Jardine F	Keen MT	Lewis B	MacDonald M	Moore J	Nicholl CJ	Phillips PS	Read JA	Ryan JG	Sheffield LJ	Slough AP	Starling AW	Tees M
R1	Nov	15	Bournemouth	1-1	Collins	7362	10	3	5		7	1		11		12	4		8							2	6	9
rep	Nov	18	BOURNEMOUTH	3-1	Collins, Tees, MacDonald	13384	10	3	5		7	1		11			4		8							2	6	9
R2	Dec	6	Hillingdon Borough	1-2	Tees	9330	10	3			7	1		11	12		4		8		6					2	6	9

F.L. Cup

	Date		Opponent	Score	Scorers	Att	Allen K	Bannister J	Branston TG	Busby VD	Collins JW	Davie AG	Dougan MS	French GE	Harrison MJ	Jardine F	Keen MT	Lewis B	MacDonald M	Moore J	Nicholl CJ	Phillips PS	Read JA	Ryan JG	Sheffield LJ	Slough AP	Starling AW	Tees M
R1	Aug	13	Peterborough	1-1	Sheffield	10249	10	3	5					11			4		8	6				1	2	9	7	
rep	Aug	19	PETERBOROUGH UNITED	5-2	Branston, Allen, Lewis 2, MacDonald	13105	10	3	5					11			4	7	8					1	2	9	6	
R2	Sep	2	MILLWALL	2-2	MacDonald, Sheffield	17372	10	3	5		7		2	11			4	12	8					1	9	6		
rep	Sep	8	Millwall	1-0	Allen	14125	10	3	5		7	1	2	11			4		8						9	6		
R3	Sep	23	Sheffield United	0-3		16884	10	3	5		7	1	2	11			4		8						12	6		9

R2 replay a.e.t.

		P	W	D	L	F	A	W	D	L	F	A	Pts
1	Orient	46	16	5	2	43	15	9	7	7	24	21	62
2	LUTON TOWN	46	13	8	2	46	15	10	6	7	31	28	60
3	Bristol Rovers	46	15	5	3	51	26	5	11	7	29	33	56
4	Fulham	46	12	9	2	43	26	8	6	9	38	29	55
5	Brighton & Hove A.	46	16	4	3	37	16	7	5	11	20	27	55
6	Mansfield Town	46	14	4	5	46	22	7	7	9	24	27	53
7	Barnsley	46	14	6	3	43	24	5	9	9	25	35	53
8	Reading	46	16	3	4	52	29	5	8	10	35	48	53
9	Rochdale	46	11	6	6	39	24	7	4	12	30	36	46
10	Bradford City	46	11	6	6	37	22	6	6	11	20	28	46
11	Doncaster Rovers	46	13	4	6	31	19	4	8	11	21	35	46
12	Walsall	46	11	4	8	33	31	6	8	9	21	36	46
13	Torquay United	46	9	9	5	36	22	5	8	10	26	37	45
14	Rotherham United	46	10	8	5	36	19	5	6	12	26	35	44
15	Shrewsbury Town	46	10	12	1	35	17	3	6	14	27	46	44
16	Tranmere Rovers	46	10	8	5	38	29	4	8	11	18	43	44
17	Plymouth Argyle	46	10	7	6	32	23	6	4	13	24	41	43
18	Halifax Town	46	10	9	4	31	25	4	6	13	16	38	43
18	Bury	46	13	4	6	47	29	2	7	14	28	51	41
20	Gillingham	46	7	6	10	28	33	6	7	10	24	31	39
21	Bournemouth	46	8	9	6	28	27	4	6	13	20	44	39
22	Southport	46	11	5	7	31	23	3	5	15	17	44	38
23	Barrow	46	7	9	7	28	27	1	5	17	18	54	30
24	Stockport County	46	4	7	12	17	30	2	4	17	10	41	23

1970/71 — 6th in Division Two

#		Date	Opponent	Score	Scorers	Att	Anderson PT	Bannister J	Barber K	Branston TG	Busby VD	Collins JW	Court DJ	Givens DJ	Godeve KGA	Guild A	Hoy RE	Keen MT	MacDonald M	Moore J	Nicholl CJ	Read JA	Ryan J	Ryan JG	Slough AP	Starling AW	Tees M
1	Aug	15	Bolton Wanderers	2-4	Keen, MacDonald (p)	11350				5	11			8			4	10	9	6			7	3	2	1	
2		22	NORWICH CITY	0-0		16110					12		8	11			4	10	9	6	5	1	7	2	3		
3		29	Birmingham City	1-1	MacDonald (p)	30141		12					8	11			4	10	7	6	5	1		2	3		9
4	Sep	1	OXFORD UNITED	4-0	Tees 2, MacDonald 2	16173							8	11			4	10	7	6	5	1	12	2	3		9
5		5	MIDDLESBROUGH	1-0	Givens	16018							8	11	4			10	7	6	5	1	12	2	3		9
6		12	Leicester City	0-1		23397		12					8	11			4	10	9	6	5	1	7	2	3		
7		19	ORIENT	4-0	Slough 2, MacDonald 2	16711					11			8			4	10	9	6	5	1	7	2	3		
8		26	Swindon Town	0-0		18698					11			8		12	4	10	9	6	5	1	7	2	3		
9		29	Queen's Park Rangers	1-0	Keen	19268					12		8	11			4	10	9	6	5	1	7	2	3		
10	Oct	3	BRISTOL CITY	3-0	MacDonald 2, Slough	15992					12		8	11			4	10	9	6	5	1	7	2	3		
11		10	Sheffield Wednesday	5-1	MacDonald 3, Givens 2	15189							8	11			4	10	9	6	5	1	7	2	3		
12		17	BOLTON WANDERERS	2-0	Nicholl, Givens	19055							8	11			4	10	9	6	5	1	7	2	3		
13		20	BLACKBURN ROVERS	2-0	Givens, MacDonald	16372					12		8	11			4	10	9	6	5	1	7	2	3		
14		24	Charlton Athletic	1-1	Givens	12928					12		8	11			4	10	9	6	5	1	7	2	3		
15		31	SUNDERLAND	1-2	MacDonald	19202					12		8	11			4	10	9	6	5	1	7	2	3		
16	Nov	7	Hull City	2-0	Givens, MacDonald	18343							8	11			4	10	9	6	5	1	7	2	3		
17		14	CARLISLE UNITED	3-3	Jim Ryan, Slough, MacDonald	14837					12		8	11			4	10	9	6	5	1	7	2	3		
18		21	PORTSMOUTH	2-1	John Ryan, Givens	16876		12			11			8			4	10	9	6	5	1	7	2	3		
19		28	Cardiff City	0-0		26689		3					8	11			4	10	9		5	1	7	2	6		
20	Dec	5	SHEFFIELD UNITED	2-1	MacDonald, Jim Ryan	19665		3					8	11			4	10	9		5	1	7	2	6		
21		12	Watford	1-0	Keen	24456		3				12	8	11			4	10	9		5	1	7	2	6		
22		19	Norwich City	1-1	MacDonald	17438		3				4	8	11				10	9		5	1	7	2	6		
23	Jan	9	QUEEN'S PARK RANGERS	0-0		22024		3				12	8	11			4	10	9		5	1	7	2	6		
24		16	Blackburn Rovers	0-1		8385		3				12	8	11			4	10	9		5	1	7	2	6		
25	Feb	6	Sheffield United	1-2	Jim Ryan	30386							8	11			4	10	9	6	5	1	7	2	3		
26		13	WATFORD	1-0	MacDonald	20099	11							8			4	10	9	6	5	1	7	2	3		
27		20	Portsmouth	1-0	Givens	13661	11							8			4	10	9	6	5	1	7	2	3		
28		27	Sunderland	0-0		12471	11							8			4	10	9	6	5	1	7	2	3		
29	Mar	6	CHARLTON ATHLETIC	1-1	Busby	15262	11						12	8			4	10	9	6	5	1	7	2	3		
30		13	Carlisle United	0-1		13681	11						12	8			4	10	9	6	5	1	7	2	3		
31		20	HULL CITY	3-1	Moore, Busby, MacDonald	19566	11							8			4	10	9	6	5	1	7	2	3		
32		27	Middlesbrough	1-2	MacDonald	19579	11							8			4	10	9	6	5	1	7	2	3		
33		30	MILLWALL	1-1	Keen	17578	11	3						8			4	10	9	6		1	7	2	5		
34	Apr	3	BIRMINGHAM CITY	3-2	Busby 2, Slough	25172	11							8			4	10	9	6	5	1	7	2	3		
35		9	Bristol City	2-3	Busy, MacDonald	18846	11						12	8			4	10	9	6	5	1	7	2	3		
36		10	Millwall	0-4		13864	11	3						8	12		4	10	9	6		1	7	2	5		
37		12	LEICESTER CITY	1-1	Sjoberg (og)	24405	11	12						8			4	10	9	6	5	1	7	2	3		
38		17	SHEFFIELD WEDNESDAY	2-2	Anderson, Givens	12308	7	3	1					8	11		4	10	9	6				2	5		
39		24	Orient	2-1	Busby 2	6339	12		1		7			8			4	10	9	6	5			2	3		
40		28	Oxford United	1-2	Busby	9531			1		7			8			4	10	9	6	5		12	2	3		
41	May	1	SWINDON TOWN	1-1	Givens (p)	10205	7				8			11	3		4	10	9		5	1		2	6		
42		4	CARDIFF CITY	3-0	MacDonald 3	10784	7				8			11	3			10	9		5	1		2	4		
			Apps				14	13	3	1	27	2	27	41	4	1	32	42	42	35	38	38	38	42	42	1	3
			Goals				1				8			11				4	24	1	1		3	1	5		2

One own goal

F.A. Cup

		Date	Opponent	Score	Scorers	Att	Anderson PT	Bannister J	Barber K	Branston TG	Busby VD	Collins JW	Court DJ	Givens DJ	Godeve KGA	Guild A	Hoy RE	Keen MT	MacDonald M	Moore J	Nicholl CJ	Read JA	Ryan J	Ryan JG	Slough AP	Starling AW	Tees M
R3	Jan	2	Nottm Forest	1-1	MacDonald	23230		3					8	11			4	10	9		5	1	7	2	6		
rep	Jan	11	NOTTM FOREST	3-4	MacDonald 3	23483		3					8	11			4	10	9		5	1	7	2	6		

F.L. Cup

		Date	Opponent	Score	Scorers	Att	Anderson PT	Bannister J	Barber K	Branston TG	Busby VD	Collins JW	Court DJ	Givens DJ	Godeve KGA	Guild A	Hoy RE	Keen MT	MacDonald M	Moore J	Nicholl CJ	Read JA	Ryan J	Ryan JG	Slough AP	Starling AW	Tees M
R1	Aug	19	Gillingham	1-0	MacDonald	7328							8	11			4	10	9	6	5	1	7	3	2		
R2	Sep	8	WORKINGTON	3-0	Givens 2, MacDonald	11072							8	11	4			10	7	6	5	1	12	2	3		9
R3	Oct	6	ARSENAL	0-1		27023					12		8	11			4	10	9	6	5	1	7	2	3		

		P	W	D	L	F	A	W	D	L	F	A	Pts
1	Leicester City	42	12	7	2	30	14	11	6	4	27	16	59
2	Sheffield United	42	14	6	1	49	18	7	8	6	24	21	56
3	Cardiff City	42	12	7	2	39	16	8	6	7	26	25	53
4	Carlisle United	42	16	3	2	39	13	4	10	7	26	30	53
5	Hull City	42	11	5	5	31	16	8	8	5	23	25	51
6	LUTON TOWN	42	12	7	2	40	18	6	6	9	22	25	49
7	Middlesbrough	42	13	6	2	37	16	4	8	9	23	27	48
8	Millwall	42	13	5	3	36	12	6	4	11	23	30	47
9	Birmingham City	42	12	7	2	30	12	5	6	11	28	36	46
10	Norwich City	42	11	8	2	34	20	4	6	11	20	32	44
11	Queen's Park Rgs.	42	11	5	5	39	22	6	6	10	19	31	43
12	Swindon Town	42	12	7	2	38	14	3	6	13	23	37	42
13	Sunderland	42	11	6	4	34	21	4	6	11	18	33	42
14	Oxford United	42	8	8	5	23	23	6	6	9	18	25	42
15	Sheffield Wed.	42	10	7	4	32	27	2	5	14	19	42	36
16	Portsmouth	42	9	4	8	32	28	1	10	10	14	33	34
17	Orient	42	5	11	5	16	16	4	5	12	13	36	34
18	Watford	42	6	7	8	18	22	4	6	11	20	38	33
19	Bristol City	42	9	6	6	30	28	1	5	15	16	36	31
20	Charlton Athletic	42	7	6	8	28	30	1	8	12	13	35	30
21	Blackburn Rovers	42	5	8	8	20	28	1	7	13	17	41	27
22	Bolton Wanderers	42	6	5	10	22	31	1	5	15	13	43	24

1971/72 13th in Division Two

#	Date	Opponent	Score	Scorers	Att	Anderson PT	Barber K	Busby VD	Court DJ	Garner AH	Givens DJ	Halom VL	Hindson G	Keen MT	Moore J	Nicholl CJ	Read JA	Ryan J	Ryan JG	Shanks D	Slough AP	Wainwright RK
1	Aug 14	NORWICH CITY	1-1	Givens (p)	12428	11		8	10		9			4	6	5	1	7	2		3	
2	21	Burnley	1-2	Busby	13333	11		8	10		9			4	6	5	1	7	2		3	
3	28	PRESTON NORTH END	1-1	Anderson	11772	11		7			10			4	6	5	1	12	2	3	8	9
4	Sep 1	Oxford United	1-1	Givens	10490	11		7			10			4	6	5	1		2	3	8	9
5	4	Orient	0-0		8703	11		7			10			4	6	5	1		2	3	8	9
6	11	BIRMINGHAM CITY	0-0		14678	11		7			10	9		4	6	5	1		2	3	4	
7	18	Millwall	2-2	Anderson 2	12433	11		7			10	9		8	6	5	1		2	3	4	12
8	25	MIDDLESBROUGH	3-2	Halom, Wainwright, Anderson	13001	11					10	9		8	6	5	1		2	3	4	7
9	28	FULHAM	2-0	Wainwright, Halom	14017	11	1				10	9		8	6	5		12	2	3	4	7
10	Oct 2	Hull City	0-0		13904		1		12		10	9		8	6	5		11	2	3	4	7
11	9	SWINDON TOWN	0-0		13423	11	1	12			10	9		8	6	5			2	3	4	7
12	16	Norwich City	1-3	Slough	22558	7	1				10	9	11	8	6	5			2	3	4	
13	19	Queen's Park Rangers	0-1		15858	7	1				10	9	11	8	6	5			2	3	4	
14	23	CARLISLE UNITED	0-2		11963	7	1	12			10	9	11	8	6	5			2	3	4	
15	30	Sunderland	2-2	Nicholl, Anderson	17979	7					10	9	11	8	6	5	1		2	4	3	
16	Nov 6	CHARLTON ATHLETIC	1-2	Keen	11011	7					10	9	11	8	6	5	1		2	4	3	
17	13	Watford	1-2	Halom	14000	4		7	12		10	9	11	8	6	5	1		2		3	
18	20	Blackpool	1-0	Givens	8432	7		8	4		9		11	10	6	5	1		2		3	
19	27	PORTSMOUTH	3-2	Keen, Hindson, Anderson	9910	7		8	4		9	12	11	10	6	5	1		2		3	
20	Dec 4	Bristol City	0-0		12921	7			4		10	9	11	8	6	5	1		2		3	
21	11	CARDIFF CITY	2-2	Anderson, Givens (p)	10606	7			4		10	9	11	8	6	5	1		2		3	
22	18	ORIENT	2-0	Slough, Givens	9193	7			4		10	9	11	8	6	5	1	12	2		3	
23	27	Sheffield Wednesday	2-2	Givens, Anderson	31391	7			8		10	9	11	4	6	5	1		2		3	
24	Jan 1	MILLWALL	2-1	Nicholl, Anderson	15113	7			8		10	9	11	4	6	5	1		2		3	
25	8	Preston North End	1-0	Slough	12844	7			8		10	9	11	4	6	5	1		2		3	
26	22	Fulham	1-3	Anderson	11328	7			8		10	9	11	4	6	5	1		2		3	
27	29	QUEEN'S PARK RANGERS	1-1	John Ryan	17280	7			8		10	9	11	4	6	5	1		2		3	
28	Feb 5	OXFORD UNITED	1-2	Halom	9892	7			8		10	9	11	4	6	5	1	12	2		3	
29	12	Carlisle United	0-0		8731			7	8		11	10	12	4	6	5	1		2		3	9
30	19	SUNDERLAND	1-2	Nicholl	10994	12		7	10		11	9		4	6	5	1		2		3	8
31	26	Charlton Athletic	0-2		7941	7	1	8	10		11	12		4	6	5			2	3		9
32	Mar 4	WATFORD	0-0		10816	12	1		8		10	9	11	4		5		7	2	3	6	
33	18	BURNLEY	1-0	Busby	8490	9	1	11	8	5	10			4				7	2	3	6	
34	25	Birmingham City	0-1		34395	9	1	10	8	5	11			4				7	2	3	6	
35	31	Middlesbrough	0-0		11720	9	1	10	8	5	11	7		4	12				2	3	6	
36	Apr 1	SHEFFIELD WEDNESDAY	3-1	Halom 3	9121	9	1	11	8	5	12	7		10	4				2	3	6	
37	4	HULL CITY	0-1		9763	11	1		8	5	9	10		4	12			7	2	3	6	
38	8	BLACKPOOL	1-4	Keen	7270		1	10	8	5	11	9		4	12				2	3	6	7
39	15	Portsmouth	3-0	Givens (p), John Ryan 2	8552		1			5	9	8	11	4	6			10	2	3		7
40	18	Swindon Town	1-2	Givens	8960		1			5	9	8	11	4	6			10	2	3		7
41	22	BRISTOL CITY	0-0		8329		1			5	9	8	11	4	6			10	2	3		7
42	29	Cardiff City	1-1	Wainwright	12587		1			5	9	8	11	4	6			10	2	3		7
		Apps				35	18	20	25	10	42	34	23	42	39	32	24	11	42	25	42	16
		Goals				10		2			8	7	1	3					3		3	3

F.A. Cup

#	Date	Opponent	Score	Scorers	Att	Anderson PT	Barber K	Busby VD	Court DJ	Garner AH	Givens DJ	Halom VL	Hindson G	Keen MT	Moore J	Nicholl CJ	Read JA	Ryan J	Ryan JG	Shanks D	Slough AP	Wainwright RK
R3	Jan 15	West Ham United	1-2	Givens	32099	7		8			10	9	11	4	6	5	1		2		3	

F.L. Cup

#	Date	Opponent	Score	Scorers	Att	Anderson PT	Barber K	Busby VD	Court DJ	Garner AH	Givens DJ	Halom VL	Hindson G	Keen MT	Moore J	Nicholl CJ	Read JA	Ryan J	Ryan JG	Shanks D	Slough AP	Wainwright RK
R2	Sep 7	Crystal Palace	0-2		13838	11		7			10			4	6	5	1		2	3	8	9

Watney Cup

#	Date	Opponent	Score	Scorers	Att	Anderson PT	Barber K	Busby VD	Court DJ	Garner AH	Givens DJ	Halom VL	Hindson G	Keen MT	Moore J	Nicholl CJ	Read JA	Ryan J	Ryan JG	Shanks D	Slough AP	Wainwright RK
R1	Jul 31	Colchester United	0-1		8186	7		10	8		9		11		6	5	1		2		3	14

Played at 4: R Hoy. At 12: K Goodeve

		P	W	D	L	F	A	W	D	L	F	A	Pts
1	Norwich City	42	13	8	0	40	16	8	7	6	20	20	57
2	Birmingham City	42	15	6	0	46	14	4	12	5	14	17	56
3	Millwall	42	14	7	0	38	17	5	10	6	26	29	55
4	Queen's Park Rgs.	42	16	4	1	39	9	4	10	7	18	19	54
5	Sunderland	42	11	7	3	42	24	6	9	6	25	33	50
6	Blackpool	42	12	6	3	43	16	8	1	12	27	34	47
7	Burnley	42	13	4	4	43	22	7	2	12	27	33	46
8	Bristol City	42	14	3	4	43	22	4	7	10	18	27	46
9	Middlesbrough	42	16	4	1	31	11	3	4	14	19	37	46
10	Carlisle United	42	12	6	3	38	22	5	3	13	23	35	43
11	Swindon Town	42	10	6	5	29	16	5	6	10	18	31	42
12	Hull City	42	10	6	5	33	21	4	4	13	16	32	38
13	LUTON TOWN	42	7	8	6	25	24	3	10	8	18	24	38
14	Sheffield Wed.	42	11	7	3	33	22	2	5	14	18	36	38
15	Oxford United	42	10	8	3	28	17	2	6	13	15	38	38
16	Portsmouth	42	9	7	5	31	26	3	6	12	28	42	37
17	Orient	42	12	4	5	32	19	2	5	14	18	42	37
18	Preston North End	42	11	4	6	32	21	1	8	12	20	37	36
19	Cardiff City	42	9	7	5	37	25	1	7	13	19	44	34
20	Fulham	42	10	7	4	29	20	2	3	16	16	48	34
21	Charlton Athletic	42	9	7	5	33	25	3	2	16	22	52	33
22	Watford	42	5	5	11	15	25	0	4	17	9	50	19

1972/73   12th in Division Two

#	Date	Opponent	Score	Scorers	Att	Anderson PT	Aston J	Barber K	Busby VD	Butlin BD	Carrick WF	Faulkner JG	Fern RA	French GE	Garner AH	Goodeve KGA	Hales DD	Halom VL	Harfield L	Hindson G	Horn GR	Moore J	O'Connor PK	Price PT	Ryan J	Ryan JG	Shanks D	Slough AP	Thomson RA
1	Aug 12	Cardiff City	1-2	Aston (p)	16364	4	11	1	9			5	8		6			10							7	2			3
2	19	PRESTON NORTH END	1-0	Anderson	11507	4	11	1	9			5	8		6			10							7	2		12	3
3	26	Orient	1-0	Busby	6494	4	11	1	9			5	8		6			10							7	2			3
4	30	OXFORD UNITED	0-1		10891	4	11	1	9			5	8		6			10							7	2		12	3
5	Sep 2	HUDDERSFIELD T	4-1	Halom 2, Jim Ryan, Aston (p)	8133	4	11	1	9			5	8		6			10							7	2		4	3
6	9	Nottingham Forest	1-0	Aston	9133	4	11	1	9			5	8		6			10							7		2		3
7	16	BRIGHTON & HOVE ALB	2-1	Fern, Halom	11627	4	11	1	9			5	8		6			10							7	2		12	3
8	23	Sheffield Wednesday	0-4		18913	4	11	1	9			5	8					10				12			7	2		6	3
9	26	Swindon Town	2-0	Halom 2	8469	4	11	1	9			5	8					10							7	2		6	3
10	30	BURNLEY	2-2	Aston (p), Halom	12197	4	11	1	9			5	8					10							7	2		6	3
11	Oct 7	BLACKPOOL	2-2	Slough, Aston	12073	4	11	1	9			5	8					10							7	2		6	3
12	14	Sunderland	2-0	Halom, Jim Ryan	13394	4	11	1	9			5	8					10		12					7	2		6	3
13	18	Portsmouth	2-2	Halom, Busby	9813	4	11	1	9			5	8					10							7	2		6	3
14	21	HULL CITY	1-2	Halom	11560	4	11	1					8				5	10	12	9					7	2		6	3
15	28	Bristol City	1-0	Faulkner	13562	4	11	1				5			6			10		9					7	2		8	3
16	Nov 4	SWINDON TOWN	0-1		10596	4	11	1				5	12		6			10		9					7	2		8	3
17	11	Portsmouth	2-2	Stephenson (og), Fern	7601	4	11	1				5	8		6			10		9					7	2		4	3
18	18	Aston Villa	2-0	Fern, Aston	29144	4	11	1				5	10		6					9					7	2		8	3
19	25	CARLISLE UNITED	0-1		10091	4	11	1				5	8		6	12				9					7	2		10	3
20	Dec 9	QUEEN'S PARK RANGERS	2-2	Butlin, Halom	13670	8	11	1	9			5	12		6			10							7	2		4	3
21	16	MILLWALL	2-2	Butlin, French	11550		11	1	9			8	5	12				10							7	6	2		3
22	23	Middlesbrough	1-0	Butlin	10122	7	11	1	9			8	5					10				6				4	2		3
23	26	SHEFFIELD WEDNESDAY	0-0		15799	4	11	1	9			8	5					10				6			7	2			3
24	30	Preston North End	0-2		9638	4	11	1	9				5					10				6			7	8	2	12	3
25	Jan 6	ORIENT	1-1	Aston	8344	8	11	1	9				5					10				6			7	4	2	12	3
26	20	Huddersfield Town	2-1	Butlin, Lyon (og)	3871		11	1	9				5					10				6			7	8	2	4	3
27	27	NOTTM. FOREST	1-0	Slough	10083		11	1	9				5	8								6			7	4	2	10	3
28	Feb 10	Brighton & Hove Albion	0-2		11404		11	1	9				5				12	10				6			7	8	2	4	3
29	17	CARDIFF CITY	1-1	Hales	10422		11		9				5				8	10				6			7	2		4	3
30	26	Millwall	2-3	Aston 2	10504		11		9	10			7		5	12					1	6				8	2	4	3
31	Mar 3	Blackpool	1-1	Jim Ryan	6947	8	11			10				12	5					9		6			7	2		4	3
32	10	SUNDERLAND	1-0	Shanks	12458	8			12			5			11	6	9	10		1					7	2	4		3
33	24	BRISTOL CITY	1-3	Garner	7102	8	11		9				7		6	5	12			10	1	6				4	2		3
34	27	Fulham	1-0	Fern	7442			1				5	11	8	6		9	10							7	4	2		3
35	31	Carlisle United	0-2		5517	4		1					5		11	6	9	10					12		7		2	8	3
36	Apr 7	FULHAM	1-0	Jim Ryan	8430	4	11						5	8	10	6				9	1				7	2			3
37	10	Hull City	0-4		5278	4	11	1					5	9	8	6		10							7	2			3
38	14	Queen's Park Rangers	0-2		16471	4	11	1	9				5	8				10							7	6	2		3
39	21	ASTON VILLA	0-0		10981	4	11	1	9				5	8		12		10							7	6	2		3
40	23	Burnley	0-3		6177	4		1	9				5	12	11	6		10							7	8	2		3
41	24	MIDDLESBROUGH	0-1		17689	4		1					5	9		6		10	11						7	8	2		3
42	28	Oxford United	1-2	Slough	6318	8			9				5			6						10	1	11	12	7	2	4	3
		Apps				34	36	33	21	11	4	29	30	8	27	11	7	25	1	21	5	12	2	1	39	36	22	26	42
		Goals				1	9		2	4		1	4	1	1		1	10							4		1	3	

Two own goals

F.A. Cup

#	Date	Opponent	Score	Scorers	Att	Anderson PT	Aston J	Barber K	Busby VD	Butlin BD	Carrick WF	Faulkner JG	Fern RA	French GE	Garner AH	Goodeve KGA	Hales DD	Halom VL	Harfield L	Hindson G	Horn GR	Moore J	O'Connor PK	Price PT	Ryan J	Ryan JG	Shanks D	Slough AP	Thomson RA
R3	Jan 13	CREWE ALEX.	2-0	Jim Ryan, Butlin	9411		11	1		9		5								12		6			4	7	2	10	3
R4	Feb 3	Newcastle United	2-0	Aston 2	42170		11	1		9		5						10				6			8	7	2	4	3
R5	Feb 24	Bolton Wanderers	1-0	Garner	39556		11		9	1		5						10				6			8	7	2	4	3
R6	Mar 17	Sunderland	0-2		53151	8	11	1	9			5				12		10				6			2	7	4		3

Played at 8 in R3 and substituted: SE Litt.

F.L. Cup

#	Date	Opponent	Score	Scorers	Att	Anderson PT	Aston J	Barber K	Busby VD	Butlin BD	Carrick WF	Faulkner JG	Fern RA	French GE	Garner AH	Goodeve KGA	Hales DD	Halom VL	Harfield L	Hindson G	Horn GR	Moore J	O'Connor PK	Price PT	Ryan J	Ryan JG	Shanks D	Slough AP	Thomson RA
R2	Sep 8	Birmingham City	1-1	Anderson	20962	4	11	1	9			5	8		6			10							7	2			3
rep	Sep 12	BIRMINGHAM CITY	1-1	Aston	13806	4	11	1	9			5	8		6			10							7	2			3
rep 2	Sep 19	Birmingham City	0-1		11451	4	11	1	9			5	8		6			10							7	2		12	3

R2 replay a.e.t. Replay 2 at Northampton.

Anglo-Italian Cup

#	Date	Opponent	Score	Scorers	Att	Anderson PT	Aston J	Barber K	Busby VD	Butlin BD	Carrick WF	Faulkner JG	Fern RA	French GE	Garner AH	Goodeve KGA	Hales DD	Halom VL	Harfield L	Hindson G	Horn GR	Moore J	O'Connor PK	Price PT	Ryan J	Ryan JG	Shanks D	Slough AP	Thomson RA
PR	Mar 7	BARI	4-0	Shanks 2, Moore, Thomson		8	11		9				12		5							10	1	6	7	2	4		3
PR	21	Verona	1-2	Aston			11		12		1	5	8	10		6	9								7	4	2		3
PR	Apr 4	FIORENTINA	1-0	Hindson		4	11					5	9	8		6				10	1				7	12	2		3
PR	May 2	Lazio	2-2	Anderson, John Ryan		9						5			12	6				10	1	11		2	7	8		4	3

League table on later page

1973/74 — Second in Division Two: Promoted

League matches

#	Date	Opponents	Res	Scorers	Att	Anderson PT	Aston J	Barber K	Butlin BD	Cruse PA	Faulkner JG	Fern RA	Finney T	Garner AH	Hindson G	Holmes W	Horn GR	Husband J	Litt SE	Ryan J	Ryan JG	Shanks D	Sims J	Thomson RA	West A
1	Aug 25	Nottingham Forest	0-4		10792	6	11	1	9	10	5		12	4						7	8	2		3	
2	Sep 1	CARLISLE UNITED	6-1	Finney 2, Anderson 2, Aston, Butlin	7231	4	11		9		5		10	6			1			7	8	2		3	
3	8	Bristol City	3-1	Aston, John Ryan, Finney	12208	4	11		9		5		10	6			1			7	8	2		3	
4	11	Notts County	1-1	Finney	8509	4	11		9		5		10	6			1			7	8	2		3	
5	15	PORTSMOUTH	3-3	Thomson, Garner, Finney	11552	4	11		9		5		10	6			1			7	8	2		3	
6	22	Sunderland	1-0	Butlin	27334	4	11		9		5		10	6			1			7	8	2		3	
7	29	BLACKPOOL	3-0	Butlin 2, Anderson	10365	4	11		9		5		10	6		12	1			7	8	2		3	
8	Oct 6	Crystal Palace	2-1	Anderson, Butlin	20322	4	11		9		5		10	6	7		1				8	2		3	
9	13	SWINDON TOWN	2-1	Aston (p), Anderson	10732	4	11		9	10	5			6		12	1			7	8	2		3	
10	20	Orient	0-2		11135	4	11	1	9		5			6						7	8	2		3	10
11	27	HULL CITY	2-2	Anderson, Butlin	11408	4	11	1	9		5		8	6						7		2		3	10
12	Nov 3	Middlesbrough	1-2	Butlin	22590	4	11	1	9		5		8	6						7		2		3	10
13	10	BOLTON WANDERERS	2-1	Jim Ryan (p), McAllister (og)	9528	4	11		9	12	5		8	6						7		2		3	10
14	14	Cardiff City	0-0		5999	4	11			8	5	12		6			1			7		2	9	3	10
15	17	SHEFFIELD WEDNESDAY	2-1	Aston, Sims	9543	4	11				5		8	6			1			7		2	9	3	10
16	24	Preston North End	2-2	Aston, Fern	10279	4	11				5	8		6			1			7	12	2	9	3	10
17	Dec 1	WEST BROMWICH ALB.	0-2		10192		11				5		9	6			1	8		7	4	2		3	10
18	8	Millwall	1-0	Butlin	6976	4	11		9		5			6			1	8		7		2		3	10
19	12	CARDIFF CITY	1-0	Jim Ryan	7139	4	11		9		5			6			1	8		7		2		3	10
20	15	ASTON VILLA	1-0	Anderson	10020	4	11		9		5	8		6			1			7		2		3	10
21	22	Blackpool	0-3		7796	4	11		9		5			6			1			7		2		3	10
22	26	FULHAM	1-1	Fraser (og)	15259	4	11		9		5			6			1	8		7		2		3	10
23	29	BRISTOL CITY	1-0	Anderson	11398	4	11		9		5			6			1	8		7		2		3	10
24	Jan 1	Carlisle United	0-2		9245	4	11		9		5			6			1	8		7	12	2		3	10
25	12	Portsmouth	0-0		18476	9	11				5			6			1			7		2		3	10
26	19	NOTTM. FOREST	2-2	Jim Ryan 2 (1p)	11888	9	11		12				8	6			1		5	7		2	4	3	10
27	Feb 2	Aston Villa	1-0	Jim Ryan (p)	26180	9		11					8	6			1			7		2	4	3	10
28	5	Notts County	1-1	Anderson	4908	4	11				5	9		6				8		7		2		3	10
29	23	CRYSTAL PALACE	2-1	Jim Ryan (p), Butlin	14287	4	11		9		5			6			1	8		7		2		3	10
30	26	Swindon Town	2-0	Butlin 2	2791	4	11		9		5			6			1	8		7		2		3	10
31	Mar 5	Fulham	1-2	Husband	10071	4	11		9		5			6			1	8		7		2		3	10
32	9	Hull City	3-1	West, Anderson, Aston	7027	4	11		9		5			6			1	8		7		2		3	10
33	16	ORIENT	3-1	Husband 3	17045	4	11		9		5			6			1	8		7		2		3	10
34	23	Bolton Wanderers	0-1		15903	4	11		9		5			6			1	8		7		2		3	10
35	30	MIDDLESBROUGH	0-1		19812	4	11		9		5			6			1	8		7		2		3	10
36	Apr 6	PRESTON NORTH END	4-2	Husband, Butlin 3	11806	4	11		9		5			6			1	8		7		2		3	10
37	12	Oxford United	1-1	Jim Ryan	13714	4	11		9		5			6	12		1	8		7		2		3	10
38	13	Sheffield Wednesday	2-2	Husband, Butlin	16685	4	11		9		5			6	7		1	8				2		3	10
39	16	OXFORD UNITED	0-1		16357	4	11		9		5			6			1	8		7		2		3	10
40	20	MILLWALL	3-0	Faulkner, Anderson, Hindson	15740	4	11		9		5			6	12		1	8		7		2		3	10
41	27	West Bromwich Albion	1-1	Butlin	13164	4	11		9		5			6	12		1	8		7		2		3	10
42	May 1	SUNDERLAND	3-4	Husband 2, Butlin	20285	4	11		9		5			6	11		1	8		7		2		3	10
		Apps				41	39	5	37	4	40	6	14	42	7	1	37	22	2	40	31	27	3	42	33
		Goals				11	6		17			1	1	5	1		1	8		7	1		1	1	1

Two own goals

F.A. Cup

Rd	Date	Opponents	Res	Scorers	Att	Anderson PT	Aston J	Barber K	Butlin BD	Cruse PA	Faulkner JG	Fern RA	Finney T	Garner AH	Hindson G	Holmes W	Horn GR	Husband J	Litt SE	Ryan J	Ryan JG	Shanks D	Sims J	Thomson RA	West A
R3	Jan 5	Port Vale	1-1	Jim Ryan	8127	4	11		9		5		12	6			1	8		7		2		3	10
rep	Jan 9	PORT VALE	4-2	Aston, Anderson 2, Jim Ryan	5833	9	11				5		8	6			1			7		2	4	3	10
R4	Jan 26	BRADFORD CITY	3-0	Fretwell (og), Butlin, Jim Ryan	12470	9	11				5		8	6			1			7		2	4	3	10
R5	Feb 16	LEICESTER CITY	0-4		25712	4	12		11		5	9		6			1	8		7		2		3	10

F.L. Cup

Rd	Date	Opponents	Res	Scorers	Att	Anderson PT	Aston J	Barber K	Butlin BD	Cruse PA	Faulkner JG	Fern RA	Finney T	Garner AH	Hindson G	Holmes W	Horn GR	Husband J	Litt SE	Ryan J	Ryan JG	Shanks D	Sims J	Thomson RA	West A
R2	Oct 10	GRIMSBY TOWN	1-1	Hindson	9656	4	11		9		5		10	6	7		1				8	2		3	
rep	Oct 16	Grimsby Town	0-0		13643	4	11		9	10	5			6	7		1				8	2		3	
rep2	Oct 23	Grimsby Town	2-0	Finney, Faulkner	15365	4	11	1	9		5		10	6						7		2		3	8
R3	Oct 31	Bury	0-0		8191	4	11	1	9	12	5		8	6						7		2		3	10
rep	Nov 6	BURY	3-2	Anderson, Shanks, West	7827	4	11	1	9		5		8	6						7		2		3	10
R4	Nov 21	Millwall	1-3	Jones (og)	8777	4	11				5	8		6			1			7		2	9	3	10

R2 replay a.e.t.

Division Two final table

		P	W	D	L	F	A	W	D	L	F	A	Pts
1	Middlesbrough	42	16	4	1	40	8	11	7	3	37	22	65
2	LUTON TOWN	42	12	5	4	42	25	7	7	7	22	26	50
3	Carlisle United	42	13	5	3	40	17	7	4	10	21	31	49
4	Orient	42	9	8	4	28	17	6	10	5	27	25	48
5	Blackpool	42	11	5	5	35	17	6	8	7	22	23	47
6	Sunderland	42	11	6	4	32	15	8	3	10	26	29	47
7	Nottingham Forest	42	12	6	3	40	19	3	9	9	17	24	45
8	West Bromwich Alb.	42	8	9	4	28	24	6	7	8	20	21	44
9	Hull City	42	9	9	3	25	15	4	8	9	21	32	43
10	Notts County	42	8	6	7	30	35	7	7	7	25	25	43
11	Bolton Wanderers	42	12	5	4	30	17	3	7	11	14	23	42
12	Millwall	42	10	6	5	28	16	4	8	9	23	35	42
13	Fulham	42	11	4	6	26	20	5	6	10	13	23	42
14	Aston Villa	42	8	9	4	33	21	5	6	10	15	24	41
15	Portsmouth	42	9	8	4	26	16	5	4	12	19	46	40
16	Bristol City	42	9	5	7	25	20	5	5	11	22	34	38
17	Cardiff City	42	8	7	6	27	20	2	9	10	22	42	36
18	Oxford United	42	8	8	5	27	21	2	8	11	8	25	36
19	Sheffield Wed.	42	9	6	6	33	24	3	5	13	18	39	35
20	Crystal Palace	42	8	7	6	24	24	5	5	11	19	32	34
21	Preston North End	42	7	8	6	24	23	2	6	13	16	39	31
22	Swindon Town	42	6	7	8	22	27	1	4	16	14	45	25

1974/75 20th in Division One: Relegated

#		Date	Opponent	Score	Scorers	Att	Alston A	Anderson PT	Aston J	Barber K	Buckley S	Butlin BD	Chambers BM	Faulkner JG	Fern RA	Fuccillo P	Futcher GR	Futcher P	Garner AH	Hindson G	Horn GR	Husband J	King AE	Litt SE	Ryan J	Ryan JG	Seasman J	Shanks D	Spring PJ	Thomson RA	West A
1	Aug	17	LIVERPOOL	1-2	Butlin	21216		4	11			9							6	7	1	8		5		2				3	10
2		19	West Ham United	0-2		23182		4	7			9							6	11	1	8		5		2		12		3	10
3		24	Middlesbrough	1-1	Butlin	21478		4	11			9		5						7	1	8		6		2				3	10
4		28	WEST HAM UNITED	0-0		16931	12	4	11	1		9		5						7		8		6		2				3	10
5		31	QUEEN'S PARK RANGERS	1-1	John Ryan	18535	11	4		1		9		5						7		8		6		2				3	10
6	Sep	7	Leeds United	1-1	Butlin	26516	11	4		1		9		5						7		8		6	12	2				3	10
7		14	IPSWICH TOWN	1-4	Alston	17577	11	4		1		9		5						7		8		6		2				3	10
8		21	Arsenal	2-2	Alston, Shanks	21649	11	4		1		9		5						7				6	8	2				3	10
9		24	Coventry City	1-2	Jim Ryan (p)	15643	11	4		1		9		5						7				6	8	2				3	10
10		28	CARLISLE UNITED	3-1	Anderson, Alston, Jim Ryan (p)	12987	11	4		1				5					9	7				6	8	2				3	10
11	Oct	5	Leicester City	0-0		19024	11	4		1				5					9	7		8		6		2				3	10
12		12	BIRMINGHAM CITY	1-3	Hindson	15097	11			1			4	5					9	7		8		6		2				3	10
13		16	MIDDLESBROUGH	0-1		10464	9	4	11	1				5					6	7		8				2				3	10
14		19	Manchester City	0-1		30649	9	4	11	1				5					6	7		8				2				3	10
15		26	TOTTENHAM HOTSPUR	1-1	Aston	22420	9	4	11	1				5	8				6	7						2				3	10
16	Nov	2	Newcastle United	0-1		30141	9	4	11	1				5	8				6	7						2				3	10
17		9	SHEFFIELD UNITED	0-1		12670	9	4	11	1			4	5	8	12			6	7						2				3	10
18		16	Stoke City	2-4	Anderson, Garner	20646	9	4		1				5					6			8			7	2			11	3	10
19		30	BURNLEY	2-3	Faulkner, Spring	11816	12	4	11	1				5					6			8			7	2			9	3	10
20	Dec	7	Chelsea	0-2		19009	8	4	11		3			5				6			1				7	2			9		10
21		14	Liverpool	0-2		35151		4	11		3			5				6			1	8			7	2			9		10
22		21	DERBY COUNTY	1-0	Jim Ryan (p)	12862		4	11		3			5			12	6			1	8			7	2			9		10
23		26	Ipswich Town	1-0	R Futcher	23406		4	11		3			5			9	6			1	8			7	2					10
24		28	WOLVERHAMPTON W.	3-2	R Futcher 3	19642		4	11		3			5			9	6			1	8			7	2					10
25	Jan	11	CHELSEA	1-1	Husband	23096		4	11		3			5			9	6			1	8			7	2					10
26		18	Burnley	0-1		17237		4	11		3			5			9	6			1	8			7	2					10
27	Feb	1	Sheffield United	1-1	Anderson	17270		4	11		3			5			9	6			1	8			7	2					10
28		8	NEWCASTLE UNITED	1-0	R Futcher	18019		4	11		3			5			9	6			1	8			7	2					10
29		22	STOKE CITY	0-0		19894		4	11		3			5			9	6			1	8			7	2					10
30		25	Everton	1-3	Aston	35714		4	11		3			5			9	6			1	8			7	2					10
31	Mar	1	Queen's Park Rangers	1-2	Alston	19583	8	4	11		3			5			9	6			1				7	2					10
32		8	COVENTRY CITY	1-3	Aston	14423	8	4	11		3			5			9	6			1				7	2					10
33		15	Carlisle United	2-1	Aston, R Futcher	8339	12	4	11	1	3			5			9	6				8			7	2					10
34		22	LEEDS UNITED	2-1	Aston, Anderson	23048		4	11	1	3			5			9	6				8			7	2					10
35		25	ARSENAL	2-0	Jim Ryan (p), R Futcher	22120		4	11	1	3			5			9	6				8			7	2					10
36		29	Derby County	0-5		24619		4	11	1	3			5			9	6				8			7	2	12				10
37		31	Wolverhampton Wan.	2-5	Seasman, Jim Ryan	22689		4	11	1	3			5			9	6							7	2	8		12		10
38	Apr	5	Tottenham Hotspur	1-2	West	25796		4	11	1	3			5			9	6				8			7	2			12		10
39		9	EVERTON	2-1	Anderson 2	13437	9	4	11	1	3			5								8		6	7	2					10
40		12	LEICESTER CITY	3-0	Alston, Weller (og), Husband	18298	9	4	11	1	3			5								8		6	7	2					10
41		19	Birmingham City	4-1	Jim Ryan, Alston 2, Husband	28755	9	4	11	1	3			5								8		6	7	2					10
42		26	MANCHESTER CITY	1-1	Jim Ryan	20768	9	4	11	1	3			5								8	12	6	7	2					10
			Apps				21	40	32	26	24	9	6	34	3	1	17	19	9	17	16	33	1	12	31	38	2	16	7	17	42
			Goals				7	6	5			3		1			7		1	1		3			7	1	1	1	1		1

One own goal

F.A. Cup

		Date	Opponent	Score		Att	Alston A	Anderson PT	Aston J	Barber K	Buckley S	Butlin BD	Chambers BM	Faulkner JG	Fern RA	Fuccillo P	Futcher GR	Futcher P	Garner AH	Hindson G	Horn GR	Husband J	King AE	Litt SE	Ryan J	Ryan JG	Seasman J	Shanks D	Spring PJ	Thomson RA	West A
R3	Jan	4	BIRMINGHAM CITY	0-1		17543		4	11		3			5			9	6			1	8			7	2					10

Played at 12: MA Pollock

F.L. Cup

		Date	Opponent	Score	Scorers	Att	Alston A	Anderson PT	Aston J	Barber K	Buckley S	Butlin BD	Chambers BM	Faulkner JG	Fern RA	Fuccillo P	Futcher GR	Futcher P	Garner AH	Hindson G	Horn GR	Husband J	King AE	Litt SE	Ryan J	Ryan JG	Seasman J	Shanks D	Spring PJ	Thomson RA	West A
R2	Sep	11	BRISTOL ROVERS	1-0	Alston	10073	11	4		1		9							5	7		8			6	2				3	10
R3	Oct	8	Sheffield United	0-2		14150	10	7		1	3						12	11	9			4	6	5		2					8

Texaco Cup

		Date	Opponent	Score	Scorers	Att	Alston A	Anderson PT	Aston J	Barber K	Buckley S	Butlin BD	Chambers BM	Faulkner JG	Fern RA	Fuccillo P	Futcher GR	Futcher P	Garner AH	Hindson G	Horn GR	Husband J	King AE	Litt SE	Ryan J	Ryan JG	Seasman J	Shanks D	Spring PJ	Thomson RA	West A
R1	Aug	3	SOUTHAMPTON	1-1	Butlin			4				9							6	11	1	8		5	7	2				3	10
R1		7	West Ham United	2-1	Anderson, Husband			4	14			9		12					6	11	1	8		5	7	2				3	10
R1		10	Leyton Orient	2-2	Butlin, Husband			4	12			9							6	11	1	8		5	7	2				3	10

Final Division One table

		P	W	D	L	F	A	W	D	L	F	A	Pts
1	Derby County	42	14	4	3	41	18	7	7	7	26	31	53
2	Liverpool	42	14	5	2	44	17	6	6	9	16	22	51
3	Ipswich Town	42	17	2	2	47	14	6	3	12	19	30	51
4	Everton	42	10	9	2	33	19	6	9	6	23	23	50
5	Stoke City	42	12	7	2	40	18	5	8	8	24	30	49
6	Sheffield United	42	12	7	2	35	20	6	6	9	23	31	49
7	Middlesbrough	42	11	7	3	33	14	7	5	9	21	26	48
8	Manchester City	42	16	3	2	40	15	2	7	12	14	39	46
9	Leeds United	42	10	8	3	34	20	6	5	10	23	29	45
10	Burnley	42	11	6	4	40	29	6	5	10	28	38	45
11	Queen's Park Rgs.	42	10	4	7	25	17	6	6	9	29	37	42
12	Wolverhampton Wan.	42	12	5	4	43	21	2	6	13	14	33	39
13	West Ham United	42	10	6	5	38	22	3	7	11	20	37	39
14	Coventry City	42	8	9	4	31	27	4	6	11	20	35	39
15	Newcastle United	42	12	4	5	39	23	3	5	13	20	49	39
16	Arsenal	42	10	6	5	31	16	3	5	13	16	33	37
17	Birmingham City	42	10	4	7	34	28	4	5	12	19	33	37
18	Leicester City	42	8	7	6	25	17	4	5	12	21	43	36
19	Tottenham Hotspur	42	8	4	9	29	27	5	4	12	23	36	34
20	LUTON TOWN	42	8	6	7	27	26	3	5	13	20	39	33
21	Chelsea	42	4	9	8	22	31	5	6	10	20	41	33
22	Carlisle United	42	8	2	11	22	21	4	3	14	21	38	29

1975/76 7th in Division Two

No	Date		Opponent	Score	Scorers	Att	Alston A	Anderson PT	Aston J	Barber K	Buckley S	Chambers BM	Faulkner JG	Fuccillo P	Futcher GR	Futcher P	Hill RA	Husband J	Jones G	King AE	Litt SE	Pollock MA	Price PT	Ryan J	Ryan JG	Seasman J	Spiring PJ	Thomson RA	West A
1	Aug	16	HULL CITY	2-0	R Futcher, King	10389	9	6	11	1	3		4		10					7	5				2				8
2		23	West Bromwich Albion	0-1		14062	8	4	11	1	3		5		9	6				7					2				10
3		30	CHELSEA	3-0	Anderson, Buckley (p), R Futcher	18565	8	4	11	1	3	12	5		9	6				7					2				10
4	Sep	6	Portsmouth	2-0	Alston, King	9835	8	4		1	3	10	5		9	6				7					2		11		
5		13	BOLTON WANDERERS	0-2		11217	8	4	11	1	3		5		9	6				7				10	2				
6		20	Notts County	0-1		11173	8	4	11	1	3		5		9	6			12	7				10	2				
7		24	PLYMOUTH ARGYLE	1-1	Husband	9226		4		1	3		5		9	6		8		7				10	2		11		
8		27	BLACKBURN ROVERS	1-1	Husband	8458		4		1	3		5		9	6		8						7	2		11		10
9	Oct	4	Blackpool	2-3	Anderson, Spiring	7864	8	4		1	3	12	5			6								7	2		11	9	10
10		11	Carlisle United	1-1	Seasman	6621	8	4		1			10		5	6				12				7	2	3	11	9	
11		18	FULHAM	1-0	Chambers	14086		4		1		10	5		9	6								7	2	8	11	3	12
12		21	Nottingham Forest	0-0		12290		4		1		10	5		9	6								7	2	8	11	3	
13		25	Sunderland	0-2		28338		4	11	1		8	5			6				12				7	2	9		3	10
14	Nov	1	BRISTOL CITY	0-0		11446	9		11	1		4	5			6		12		8				7	2			3	10
15		4	YORK CITY	4-0	Husband, West, King, Anderson	7982		9	11	1		4	5			6		8		7					2			3	10
16		8	Southampton	1-3	John Ryan	13885		9	11	1		4	5			6		8		7				12	2			3	10
17		15	OLDHAM ATHLETIC	2-3	Husband, Chambers	8237			11	1		4	5		9	6		8		7				12	2			3	10
18		22	Fulham	0-2		9626			11	1		4	5			6		8		7					2		9	3	10
19		29	ORIENT	1-0	Husband	7897			11	1	3	4	5			6		7		8		9			2				10
20	Dec	3	Charlton Athletic	5-1	Anderson 2, Husband 2, Chambers	8703		8	11	1	3	4	5			6		9		7					2				10
21		13	WEST BROMWICH ALB.	2-1	King, Aston	10203			11	1	3	4	5		9	6				7		12			2				10
22		20	Hull City	2-1	Husband, King	5449			11	1	3	4	5		9	6		8		7					2				10
23		26	OXFORD UNITED	3-2	R Futcher 2, King	13101			11	1	3	4	5		9	6		8		7					2				10
24		27	Bristol Rovers	1-0	King	11042			11	1	3	4	5		9	6		8		7					2				10
25	Jan	17	PORTSMOUTH	3-1	Faulkner, King, R Futcher	10464			11	1	3	4	5		9	6		8		7					2				10
26		27	Bolton Wanderers	0-3		22037			11	1	3	4	5		9	6		8						7	2				10
27		31	NOTTM. FOREST	1-1	R Futcher	8503			11	1	3	4	5		9	6		8		7					2				10
28	Feb	7	York City	3-2	Chambers, R Futcher, Fuccillo	3507				1	3	4		7	9	6		8		5			11		2				10
29		21	Oldham Athletic	1-1	Husband	8796		12		1	3	4	5	11		6		8		7		9			2				10
30		24	Plymouth Argyle	0-3		13927			11	1	3	4	5	9		6		8		7		12			2				10
31		28	SUNDERLAND	2-0	Moncur (og), R Futcher	15338				1	3	4	5	11	9	6		8		7					2				10
32	Mar	2	SOUTHAMPTON	1-0	Husband	13737				1	3	4	5	11	9	6		8		7					2				10
33		6	Bristol City	0-3		15872		12		1	3	4	5	11	9	6		8		7					2				10
34		13	CARLISLE UNITED	3-0	Husband 2, King	8856			11	1	3	5	4		9	6		8		7					2				10
35		20	Orient	0-3		5544			11	1	3	5	4		9	6		8		7		12			2				10
36		27	CHARLTON ATHLETIC	1-1	John Ryan	9947			11	1	3	4	9			6		8		7				5	2				10
37	Apr	3	Blackburn Rovers	0-3		7911			11	1	3	12			9	6						4	5		2		8		10
38		10	NOTTS COUNTY	1-1	West	8277			11	1	3	8			4	9	6						5		2				10
39		16	Chelsea	2-2	Husband, Chambers	19873			11	1	3	4			8	9	6						5		2				10
40		17	Oxford United	3-1	Buckley, Fuccillo, Husband	7881			11	1	3	8		4	9	6		7				12	5		2				10
41		19	BRISTOL ROVERS	3-1	Price, Chambers, Hill	7646				1	3	4	5	8	9	6	12	7					2		11				10
42		24	BLACKPOOL	3-0	R Futcher 2, Fuccillo	8757				1	3	4	5	8	9	6	11	7	5				2					10
			Apps				8	17	30	42	33	33	35	14	31	41	2	30	1	32	1	6	8	15	41	6	8	9	37
			Goals				1	5	1		2	6	1	3	10		1	14		9			1		2	1	1		2

One own goal

F.A. Cup

Rd	Date		Opponent	Score	Scorers	Att	Aston J	Barber K	Buckley S	Chambers BM	Faulkner JG	Futcher GR	Futcher P	King AE	Ryan JG	West A
R3	Jan	3	BLACKBURN ROVERS	2-0	R Futcher, Chambers	11195	11	1	3	4	5	9	6	7	2	10
R4	Jan	24	Norwich City	0-2		24328	11	1	3	4	5	9	6	7	2	10

F.L. Cup

Rd	Date		Opponent	Score	Scorers	Att	Anderson PT	Aston J	Barber K	Buckley S	Chambers BM	Faulkner JG	Futcher GR	Futcher P	King AE	Price PT	Ryan JG	Spiring PJ
R2	Sep	9	Darlington	1-2	R Futcher	6601	4	11	1	3	10	5	9	6	7	12	2	8

		P	W	D	L	F	A	W	D	L	F	A	Pts
1	Sunderland	42	19	2	0	48	10	5	6	10	19	26	56
2	Bristol City	42	11	7	3	34	14	8	8	5	25	21	53
3	West Bromwich Alb.	42	10	9	2	29	12	10	4	7	21	21	53
4	Bolton Wanderers	42	12	5	4	36	14	8	7	6	28	24	52
5	Notts County	42	11	6	4	33	13	8	5	8	27	28	49
6	Southampton	42	18	2	1	49	16	3	5	13	17	34	49
7	LUTON TOWN	42	13	6	2	38	15	6	4	11	23	36	48
8	Nottingham Forest	42	13	1	7	34	18	4	11	6	21	22	46
9	Charlton Athletic	42	11	5	5	40	34	4	7	10	21	38	42
10	Blackpool	42	9	9	3	26	22	5	5	11	14	27	42
11	Chelsea	42	7	9	5	25	20	5	7	9	28	34	40
12	Fulham	42	9	8	4	27	14	4	6	11	18	33	40
13	Orient	42	10	6	5	21	12	3	8	10	16	27	40
14	Hull City	42	9	5	7	29	23	5	6	10	16	26	39
15	Blackburn Rovers	42	8	6	7	27	22	4	8	9	18	28	38
16	Plymouth Argyle	42	13	4	4	36	20	0	8	13	12	34	38
17	Oldham Athletic	42	11	8	2	37	24	2	4	15	20	44	38
18	Bristol Rovers	42	7	9	5	26	15	4	7	10	18	35	38
19	Carlisle United	42	9	8	4	29	22	3	5	13	16	37	37
20	Oxford United	42	7	7	7	23	25	4	4	13	16	34	33
21	York City	42	8	3	10	28	34	2	5	14	11	37	28
22	Portsmouth	42	4	6	11	16	23	5	1	15	17	38	25

1976/77   6th in Division Two

#	Date	Opponent	Score	Scorers	Att	Aleksic MA	Aston J	Barber K	Buckley S	Carr D	Chambers BM	Deans JK	Faulkner JG	Fuccillo P	Futcher GR	Futcher P	Geddis D	Hill RA	Husband J	Jones G	Knight A	McNicholl JA	Price PT	Ryan JG	Smith TC	West A
1	Aug 21	SHEFFIELD UNITED	2-0	Deans 2	10687		11	1	3		4	9	5	10		6		8	7				2			
2	24	Hull City	1-3	Hill	5499		11	1	3		4	9	5	10		6		8	7				2		12	
3	28	Burnley	2-1	Deans, Hill	12262		11	1	3		4	9	5	10		6		8	7				2			
4	Sep 4	NOTTM. FOREST	1-1	Barrett (og)	11231		11	1	3			9	5	10	12	6		8	7				2			4
5	10	Charlton Athletic	3-4	Deans, Aston, Hill	9191		11	1	3			9	5	10	12	6		8	7				2	4		
6	18	FULHAM	0-2		19929		11	1	3			9	5	10		6		12	7				2	4		8
7	25	Wolverhampton Wan.	2-1	Husband, Deans	19826			1	3			9	5	10	11	6			7				2	4		8
8	Oct 2	Plymouth Argyle	0-1		12187			1	3			9	5	10	11	6		12	7				2	4		8
9	9	HEREFORD UNITED	2-0	Husband, P Futcher	9395			1	3		11		5	10	9	6			7				2	4		8
10	16	Carlisle United	1-1	Husband	6972		12	1	3		11		5	10	9	6			8				2	7		4
11	23	SOUTHAMPTON	1-4	Chambers	12123		11	1	3		4	9	5	10		6			7				2			8
12	30	Blackburn Rovers	0-1		8674		11	1	3		4		5	10	9	6			7				2			8
13	Nov 6	BRISTOL ROVERS	4-2	R Futcher 2, Aston, Husband	7066		11		3		4		5	10	9	6			7		1		2			8
14	13	Millwall	2-4	West, Buckley (p)	10380		11	1	3		4	12		10	9	6			7	5			2			8
15	20	CARDIFF CITY	2-1	Deans, R Futcher	8845		11	1	3		4	7		10	9	6				5			2			8
16	27	Notts County	4-0	West, Aston, Husband, Buckley	10009		11	1	3		4	7	5	10	9	6			12				2			8
17	Dec 4	BLACKPOOL	0-0		9183		11		3		4	7	5	10	9	6					1		2			8
18	21	Bolton Wanderers	1-2	Fuccillo	18463	1			3		4	7	5	10	9	6							2	11		8
19	27	Orient	0-1		8354	1			3		4		5	10	9	6			7				2	11		8
20	29	CHELSEA	4-0	Fuccillo, Chambers, Husband, Buckley (p)	14605	1			3		4		5	10	9	6			7				2	11		8
21	Jan 1	Bristol Rovers	0-1		7185	1			3		4		5	10	9	6			7				2	11		8
22	22	Sheffield United	3-0	R Futcher, Husband 2	16257	1	11		3		4		5	10	9	6			7				2			8
23	24	HULL CITY	2-1	Aston, Husband	8455	1	11		3		4		5	10	9	6			7				2			8
24	Feb 5	BURNLEY	2-0	Price, Aston	8638	1	11		3		4		5	10	9	6			7				2			8
25	12	Nottingham Forest	2-1	R Futcher, Aston	18225	1	11		3		4		5	10	9	6	12		7				2			8
26	15	BLACKBURN ROVERS	2-0	Geddis, R Futcher	9044	1	11		3		4		5	10	9	6	7						2			8
27	19	CHARLTON ATHLETIC	2-0	R Futcher 2	11625	1	11		3		4		5	10	9	6			7				2			8
28	26	Fulham	2-1	Aston, Husband	11071	1	11		3		4		5	10	9	6			7				2			8
29	Mar 5	WOLVERHAMPTON W.	2-0	Husband, Fuccillo	19200	1	11		3		4		5	10	9	6	12		7				2			8
30	8	OLDHAM ATHLETIC	1-0	Geddis	12301	1	11		3		4		5	10	9	6	12		7				2			8
31	12	PLYMOUTH ARGYLE	1-1	Aston	12793	1	11		3		4		5	10	9	6			7				2			8
32	19	Hereford United	1-0	R Futcher	6737	1	11		3		4		5	10	9	6			7	12			2			8
33	26	CARLISLE UNITED	5-0	Fuccillo, R Futcher, Husband, West, Aston	11735	1	11		3		4		5	10	9	6			7				2			8
34	Apr 2	Southampton	0-1		19923	1	11		3		4		5	10	9	6	12		7	8			2			
35	9	Chelsea	0-2		32911	1	11		3		4		5	10		6	9		7	12			2			
36	11	ORIENT	0-0		11066	1	11		3		4		5	10	12	6	9		7				2			8
37	12	MILLWALL	1-2	Fuccillo	10459	1	11		3		4		5	10	9	6			7				2			8
38	16	Cardiff City	2-4	R Futcher, Chambers	10438	1	11		3		4		5	10	9	6			7	12			2			8
39	23	NOTTS COUNTY	4-2	R Futcher, Hill 2, Geddis	9585	1	11		3		4		5	10	9	6	7	8					2			
40	30	Blackpool	0-1		9257	1	11		3		4		5	10	9	6	7	8	12				2			
41	May 7	BOLTON WANDERERS	1-1	Geddis	11164	1	11		3		4		5	10	9		8		7			6	2			
42	14	Oldham Athletic	2-1	Fuccillo, Aston	7231	1	11		3	9	4		5	10				8	7	12		6	2			

	Aleksic MA	Aston J	Barber K	Buckley S	Carr D	Chambers BM	Deans JK	Faulkner JG	Fuccillo P	Futcher GR	Futcher P	Geddis D	Hill RA	Husband J	Jones G	Knight A	McNicholl JA	Price PT	Ryan JG	Smith TC	West A
Apps	25	35	15	42	1	37	14	40	42	33	40	13	11	36	7	2	2	41	10	1	33
Goals		10		3		3	6		6	13	1	4	4	12					1		3

One own goal

F.A. Cup

	Date	Opponent	Score	Scorers	Att	Aleksic MA	Aston J	Barber K	Buckley S	Carr D	Chambers BM	Deans JK	Faulkner JG	Fuccillo P	Futcher GR	Futcher P	Geddis D	Hill RA	Husband J	Jones G	Knight A	McNicholl JA	Price PT	Ryan JG	Smith TC	West A
R3	Jan 8	Halifax Town	1-0	Aston	5519	1	11		3		4		5	10	9	6			7				2			8
R4	Jan 29	Chester	0-1		10608	1	11		3		4		5	10	9	6			7				2			8

F.L. Cup

	Date	Opponent	Score	Scorers	Att	Aleksic MA	Aston J	Barber K	Buckley S	Carr D	Chambers BM	Deans JK	Faulkner JG	Fuccillo P	Futcher GR	Futcher P	Geddis D	Hill RA	Husband J	Jones G	Knight A	McNicholl JA	Price PT	Ryan JG	Smith TC	West A
R2	Aug 31	Sunderland	1-3	Husband	22390		11	1	3		4	9	5	10		6		7	8				2	12		

	P	W	D	L	F	A	W	D	L	F	A	Pts
1 Wolverhampton Wan.	42	15	3	3	48	21	7	10	4	36	24	57
2 Chelsea	42	15	6	0	51	22	6	7	8	22	31	55
3 Nottingham Forest	42	14	3	4	53	22	7	7	7	24	21	52
4 Bolton Wanderers	42	15	2	4	46	21	5	9	7	29	33	51
5 Blackpool	42	11	7	3	29	17	6	10	5	29	25	51
6 LUTON TOWN	42	13	5	3	39	17	8	1	12	28	31	48
7 Charlton Athletic	42	14	5	2	52	27	2	11	8	19	31	48
8 Notts County	42	11	5	5	29	20	8	5	8	36	40	48
9 Southampton	42	12	6	3	40	24	5	4	12	32	43	44
10 Millwall	42	9	6	6	31	22	6	7	8	26	31	43
11 Sheffield United	42	9	8	4	32	25	5	4	12	22	38	40
12 Blackburn Rovers	42	12	4	5	31	18	3	5	13	11	36	39
13 Oldham Athletic	42	11	6	4	37	23	3	4	14	15	41	38
14 Hull City	42	9	8	4	31	17	1	9	11	14	36	37
15 Bristol Rovers	42	8	9	4	32	27	4	4	13	21	41	37
16 Burnley	42	8	9	4	27	20	3	5	13	19	44	36
17 Fulham	42	9	7	5	39	25	2	6	13	15	36	35
18 Cardiff City	42	7	6	8	30	30	5	4	12	26	37	34
19 Orient	42	4	8	9	18	23	5	8	8	19	32	34
20 Carlisle United	42	7	7	3	31	33	4	5	12	18	42	34
21 Plymouth Argyle	42	5	9	7	27	25	3	7	11	19	40	32
22 Hereford United	42	6	9	6	28	30	2	6	13	29	48	31

1977/78   13th in Division Two

Football League Division Two

#	Date	Opponent	Score	Scorers	Att	Aleksic MA	Aston J	Boersma P	Buckley S	Carr D	Faulkner JG	Fuccillo P	Futcher GR	Futcher P	Heale GJ	Hill RA	Husband J	Ingram GRA	Jones G	Knight A	McNicholl JA	Price PT	Smith TC	Sperrin MR	Stein B	West A
1	Aug 20	ORIENT	1-0	Buckley	8061	1	11	9	3	4	5	10		6		12	7					2	8			
2	27	Oldham Athletic	0-1		7553	1	11		3	4	5	10		6		8	7					2				9
3	Sep 3	CHARLTON ATHLETIC	7-1	Husband 4 (1p), Buckley, Hill, Heale	9061	1			3	4	5	10	9	6	11	8	7					2				
4	10	Bristol Rovers	2-1	Boersma, Buckley	5836	1		11	3	4	5	10	9	6		8	7					2				
5	17	BLACKBURN ROVERS	0-0		9149	1		11	3	4	5	10	9	6		8	7					2				
6	24	Tottenham Hotspur	0-2		32814	1		11	3	4	5	10	9	6		8	7					2				
7	27	Brighton & Hove Albion	2-3	R Futcher, Husband	25199	1		11	3	4	5	10	9	6		8	7					2				
8	Oct 1	NOTTS COUNTY	2-0	Fuccillo, Boersma	7593	1		11	3		5	10	9	6		8	7					2				4
9	4	MILLWALL	1-0	Price	9119	1		11	3	12	5	10	9	6		8	7					2				4
10	8	Cardiff City	4-1	Byrne (og), Fuccillo, R Futcher, Hill	8726	1		11	3		5	10	9	6		8	7					2				4
11	15	FULHAM	1-0	Faulkner	12736	1		11	3		5	10	9	6		8	7					2				4
12	22	Blackpool	1-2	Husband	12167	1		11	3		5	10	9	6		8	7					2				4
13	29	Bolton Wanderers	1-2	R Futcher	21973	1			3		5	10	9	6	11	8	7					2				4
14	Nov 5	HULL CITY	1-1	Husband	8936	1			3		5	10	9	6	11	8	7					2				4
15	12	Mansfield Town	1-3	Hill	7519	1			3		5	10	9		11	8	7		6			2			12	4
16	19	STOKE CITY	1-2	Buckley	9384	1			3		5	10	9		11	8	7		6			2			12	4
17	26	Sunderland	1-1	R Futcher	26915	1			3	11	5	10	9			8	7		6			2				4
18	Dec 3	BURNLEY	1-2	Hill	6921	1		11	3		5	10	9			8	7		6			2				4
19	10	Southampton	1-0	R Futcher	19907	1		11	3		5	10	9			8	7		6			2				4
20	17	MANSFIELD TOWN	1-1	R Futcher	6401	1		11	3		5	10	9			8	7		6			2			12	4
21	26	Crystal Palace	3-3	Price, Boersma, R Futcher	22405	1		11	3		5	10	9			8			6			2			7	4
22	27	SHEFFIELD UNITED	4-0	R Futcher, Fuccillo (p), Stein 2	10885	1		11	3	5		10	9			8			6			2			7	4
23	31	BRIGHTON & HOVE ALB	1-0	Boersma	13200	1		11	3	5		10	9			8			6			2			7	4
24	Jan 2	Orient	0-0		9270	1		11	3	5		10	9			8			6			2			7	4
25	14	OLDHAM ATHLETIC	0-1		7792	1		11		3	5	10	9			4	7		6		12	2				8
26	21	Charlton Athletic	0-0		8267	1		11		3	5	10	9	6		4	7					2				8
27	Feb 8	BRISTOL ROVERS	1-1	R Futcher	5913	1		11		3	5	10	9	6		4					12	2			7	8
28	11	Blackburn Rovers	0-2		11511	1		11		3	5	10	9	6		8	7					2			12	4
29	22	TOTTENHAM HOTSPUR	1-4	West	17024	1		11		3	5	7	9	6		4			10			2			12	8
30	25	Notts County	0-2		8558	1		11		3	5	7	9	6		4			10			2			12	8
31	Mar 4	CARDIFF CITY	3-1	Boersma 2, Faulkner	6029	1		11		3	5	10	9	6		4						2			7	8
32	10	Fulham	0-1		7796	1		11		3	5	10	9	6		12			4			2			7	8
33	18	BLACKPOOL	4-0	West, R Futcher, Boersma, Fuccillo	6041	1		11		3	5	10	9	6		4						2			7	8
34	21	BOLTON WANDERERS	2-1	West, Boersma	8306	1		11		3	5	10	9	6		4						2			7	8
35	25	Sheffield United	1-4	Calvert (og)	12587			11		3		10	9	6		4				1	5	2			7	8
36	27	CRYSTAL PALACE	1-0	Fuccillo (p)	9816			11		3		10	9	6		4				1	5	2			7	8
37	Apr 1	Hull City	1-1	West	4054			11		3		10	9	6		4				1	5	2			7	8
38	8	SUNDERLAND	1-3	Stein	7616			11		3		10	9	6		4				1	5	2		12	7	8
39	15	Stoke City	0-0		15546	1		11		3		10	9	6		4					5	2			7	8
40	22	SOUTHAMPTON	1-2	Hill	14302	1		11		3		10	9	6		4					5	2			7	8
41	25	Millwall	0-1		7593	1		11				10	9	6		4		12	3		5	2			7	8
42	29	Burnley	1-2	Ingram	11648	1		12				10		6	11	4		9	3		5	2			7	8
		Apps				38	2	35	24	27	31	42	39	31	7	40	22	3	20	4	12	40	1	1	24	36
		Goals						8	4		2	5	10		1	5	7	1				2			3	4

Two own goals

F.A. Cup

Rnd	Date	Opponent	Score	Scorers	Att	Aleksic MA	Aston J	Boersma P	Buckley S	Carr D	Faulkner JG	Fuccillo P	Futcher GR	Futcher P	Heale GJ	Hill RA	Husband J	Ingram GRA	Jones G	Knight A	McNicholl JA	Price PT	Smith TC	Sperrin MR	Stein B	West A
R3	Jan 7	OLDHAM ATHLETIC.	1-1	Fuccillo	9851	1		11		3	5	10	9			8	7		6		12	2				4
rep	Jan 10	Oldham Athletic.	2-1	Boersma 2	13802	1		11		3	5	10	9			4	7		6		8	2				
R4	Jan 31	Millwall	0-4		8763			11		3	5	10	9	6		4	7			1	8	2				

F.L. Cup

Rnd	Date	Opponent	Score	Scorers	Att	Aleksic MA	Aston J	Boersma P	Buckley S	Carr D	Faulkner JG	Fuccillo P	Futcher GR	Futcher P	Heale GJ	Hill RA	Husband J	Ingram GRA	Jones G	Knight A	McNicholl JA	Price PT	Smith TC	Sperrin MR	Stein B	West A
R2	Aug 30	Wolverhampton Wanderers	3-1	Husband, Boersma, Carr	14682	1	9		3	12	5	4		11		8	7		6			2				10
R3	Oct 25	MANCHESTER CITY	1-1	R Futcher	16443	1			3		5	10	9	6	11	8	7					2				4
rep	Nov 1	Manchester City	0-0		28254	1			3		5	10	9	6	11	8	7					2				4
rep 2	Nov 9	Manchester City	2-3	Heale 2	14043	1			3		5	10	9		11	8			6			2			12	7	4

R2 replay and replay 2 a.e.t. Replay 2 at Old Trafford.

League Table

		c	W	D	L	F	A	W	D	L	F	A	Pts
1	Bolton Wanderers	42	16	4	1	39	14	8	6	7	24	19	58
2	Southampton	42	15	4	2	44	16	7	9	5	26	23	57
3	Tottenham Hotspur	42	13	7	1	50	19	7	9	5	33	30	56
4	Brighton & Hove A.	42	15	5	1	43	21	7	7	7	20	17	56
5	Blackburn Rovers	42	12	4	5	33	16	4	9	8	23	44	45
6	Sunderland	42	11	6	4	36	17	3	10	8	31	42	44
7	Stoke City	42	13	5	3	38	16	3	5	13	15	33	42
8	Oldham Athletic	42	9	10	2	32	20	4	6	11	22	38	42
9	Crystal Palace	42	9	7	5	31	20	4	8	9	19	27	41
10	Fulham	42	9	8	4	32	19	5	5	11	17	30	41
11	Burnley	42	11	6	4	35	20	4	4	13	21	44	40
12	Sheffield United	42	13	4	4	38	22	3	4	14	24	51	40
13	LUTON TOWN	42	11	4	6	35	20	3	6	12	19	32	38
14	Orient	42	8	11	2	30	20	2	7	12	13	29	38
15	Notts County	42	10	9	2	36	22	1	7	13	18	40	38
16	Millwall	42	8	8	5	23	20	4	6	11	26	37	38
17	Charlton Athletic	42	11	6	4	38	27	2	6	13	17	41	38
18	Bristol Rovers	42	10	7	4	40	26	3	5	13	21	51	38
19	Cardiff City	42	12	6	3	32	23	1	4	14	19	48	38
20	Blackpool	42	7	8	6	35	25	5	5	11	24	35	37
21	Mansfield Town	42	6	6	9	30	34	4	5	12	19	35	31
22	Hull City	42	6	6	9	23	25	2	6	13	11	27	28

1978/79   18th in Division Two

League matches

#	Date		Opponent	Score	Scorers	Att.
1	Aug	19	OLDHAM ATHLETIC	6-1	Hatton 2, Moss 2, Stein, Fuccillo (p)	8043
2		22	Crystal Palace	1-3	Fuccillo (p)	17880
3		26	Newcastle United	0-1		24112
4	Sep	2	CHARLTON ATHLETIC	3-0	Hatton, Stein, Hill	8509
5		9	Bristol Rovers	0-2		6505
6		16	CARDIFF CITY	7-1	Moss 2, Hatton, Stein 2, Fuccillo(p), Dwyer(og)	7752
7		23	CAMBRIDGE UNITED	1-1	Stein	10801
8		30	Sheffield United	1-1	Hatton	15295
9	Oct	7	WREXHAM	2-1	Stein, Fuccillo	8683
10		14	Blackburn Rovers	0-0		7450
11		21	NOTTS COUNTY	6-0	Hatton, Stein 2, West, Moss, Fuccillo(p)	8561
12		28	Orient	2-3	Fuccillo 2	7035
13	Nov	4	LEICESTER CITY	0-1		10608
14		11	Oldham Athletic	0-2		6876
15		18	NEWCASTLE UNITED	2-0	Stein, Turner	10434
16		21	Charlton Athletic	2-1	Moss, Hatton	10191
17		25	SUNDERLAND	0-3		10249
18	Dec	9	PRESTON NORTH END	1-2	Price	7036
19		16	Brighton & Hove Albion	1-3	Moss	16216
20		26	Millwall	2-0	Moss 2	6041
21		30	Fulham	0-1		8984
22	Jan	16	BRISTOL ROVERS	3-2	Moss, Price, Hill	6002
23	Feb	3	Cambridge United	0-0		8125
24		6	STOKE CITY	0-0		6462
25		10	SHEFFIELD UNITED	1-1	Turner	7025
26		24	BLACKBURN ROVERS	2-1	West, Turner	6247
27		26	WEST HAM UNITED	1-4	Turner	14205
28	Mar	3	Notts County	1-3	Hatton	7624
29		10	ORIENT	2-1	Turner, Hill	6003
30		13	Burnley	1-2	Hatton	7691
31		24	CRYSTAL PALACE	0-1		11008
32		28	Leicester City	0-3		10464
33		31	Sunderland	0-1		23358
34	Apr	7	BURNLEY	4-1	Hatton 2, Stein., Taylor	6466
35		9	West Ham United	0-1		25398
36		14	MILLWALL	2-2	Moss 2 (1p)	8292
37		16	Stoke City	0-0		19214
38		21	BRIGHTON & HOVE ALB	1-1	Williams (og)	13132
39		25	Cardiff City	1-2	Roberts (og)	10522
40		28	Preston North End	2-2	Haslegrove (og), Moss	8946
41	May	5	FULHAM	2-0	Beck (og), West	9122
42		7	Wrexham	0-2		7842

Played at 11 in game 4: P Boersma

Player appearances (shirt numbers; 12 = substitute)

#	Aizlewood M	Aleksic MA	Birchenall AJ	Carr D	Donaghy M	Findlay JW	Fuccillo P	Hatton RJ	Hill RA	Ingram GRA	Jones G	Lawson D	McNicholl JA	Moss DJ	Philipson-Masters F	Price PT	Sherlock SE	Silkman B	Stein B	Stephens KW	Taylor SJ	Turner CJ	Turner WL	West A
1	6	1			9		8	10	4					11			3		7	2		5		
2	6	1			4		8	10	7	12				11			3		9	2		5		
3	3	1			4			10	7				12	11		6			9	2		5		8
4	3	1			7		8	10	4		2					6			9			5		12
5	3	1			7		8		4	10	2					6			9			5		12
6	3	1			7		12	10	4		2			11		6			9			5		8
7	3	1			7		12	10	4		2			11		6			9			5		8
8	3	1			6		7	10	4					11		2			9			5		8
9	3	1			6		8	10	4		12			11		2			9			5		7
10	3	1			6		8	10	4					11		2			9			5		7
11	3	1			6		8	10	4		12			11		2			9			5		7
12	3	1			2		8	10	4					11		6			9			5		7
13	3	1		12	2		8	10	4					11		6			9			5		7
14	3	1			6		8	10	4					11		2			9	12		5		7
15	3			4	6	1	8	10						11		2			9			5		7
16	3			4	6	1	8	10						11		2			9			5		7
17	3				6	1	8	10	4					11		2			9			5		7
18	3				6	1		10	4					11		2			9					7
19	3			4	6	1		10		9				11		2			12			5		7
20	3			4	6	1		10			8			11		2			9	12		5		7
21	3			4	6	1		10			8			11		2			9			5		7
22	3				6	1	8	10	4					11		5		12	9		2			7
23	3				4	1		10	8					11		6			9		2			7
24				3	4	1		10	8					11		6			9		2	5		7
25				3	4	1		10	8					11		6			9		2	12		7
26	3		8			1		10	7							6		11	9		2	12		4
27	3		8			1		10	11							6		7	9		2	12		4
28	3		8			1		10								6		11	9		2	12		7
29	3		8	4		1		10	6										9	11	2	5		7
30	3		8	4		1		10	6										9	11	2	5		7
31	8				6	1		10	7										9	11	2	5		12
32	8				4	1		10	6										9	11	2	5		7
33			6	12	4	1		10	7						5	3			9	11	2			8
34	3		6		4	1		10	7						11	5			9		2	12		8
35	3		6		4	1		10	7						11	5			9		2	12		8
36	3		11		4	1		10	6					7		5			9		2	12		8
37	3		11		4	1		10	7						5	6			9		2			8
38	3		6		4			10	7			1			11	5			9		2			8
39	3				4			10	7			1			5	6			9		2			8
40	3		11		4			10	7			1		12	5	6			9		2			8
41	3				4			10	7			1			11	5		6	9		2			8
42	3				4			10	7			1			5	6			9	12	2		11	8
Apps	39	14	8	15	40	23	18	41	38	3	10	5	1	30	10	34	2	3	34	25	20	30	1	40
Goals							7	11	3					13		2			10		1	5		3

Five own goals

F.A. Cup

Rnd	Date		Opponent	Score	Att.
R3	Jan	9	York City	0-2	6700

Players: Aizlewood 3, Carr 4, Donaghy 6, Findlay 1, Hatton 10, Hill 8, Jones 2, Price 5, Silkman 11, Stein 9, West 7.
Played at 12: GJ Heale

F.L. Cup

Rnd	Date		Opponent	Score	Scorers	Att.
R2	Aug	29	WIGAN ATHLETIC	2-0	B Stein 2	6618
R3	Oct	3	CREWE ALEXANDRA	2-1	Hill, Hatton	6602
R4	Nov	8	Aston Villa	2-0	Hatton, B Stein	32737
R5	Dec	13	Leeds United	1-4	B Stein	28177

Rnd	Aiz	Alek	Don	Find	Fuc	Hat	Hill	Moss	Price	Stein	Steph	TurCJ	West
R2	3	1	4		8	10		11	6	9	2	5	7
R3	3	1	6		8	10	4	11	2	9		5	7
R4	3	1	6		8	10	4	11	2	9		5	7
R5	3		6	1	8	10	4	11	2	9		5	7

Division Two — Final table

	Team	P	W	D	L	F	A	W	D	L	F	A	Pts
1	Crystal Palace	42	12	7	2	30	11	7	12	2	21	13	57
2	Brighton & Hove A.	42	16	3	2	44	11	7	7	7	28	28	56
3	Stoke City	42	11	7	3	35	15	9	9	3	23	16	56
4	Sunderland	42	13	3	5	39	19	9	8	4	31	25	55
5	West Ham United	42	12	7	2	46	15	6	7	8	24	24	50
6	Notts County	42	8	10	3	23	15	6	6	9	25	45	44
7	Preston North End	42	7	11	3	36	23	5	7	9	23	34	42
8	Newcastle United	42	13	3	5	35	24	4	5	12	16	31	42
9	Cardiff City	42	12	5	4	34	23	4	5	12	22	47	42
10	Fulham	42	10	7	4	35	19	3	8	10	15	28	41
11	Orient	42	11	5	5	32	18	4	5	12	19	33	40
12	Cambridge United	42	7	10	4	22	15	5	6	10	22	37	40
13	Burnley	42	11	6	4	31	22	3	6	12	20	40	40
14	Oldham Athletic	42	10	7	4	36	23	3	6	12	16	38	39
15	Wrexham	42	10	6	5	31	16	2	8	11	14	26	38
16	Bristol Rovers	42	10	6	5	34	23	4	4	13	14	37	38
17	Leicester City	42	7	8	6	28	23	3	9	9	15	29	37
18	LUTON TOWN	42	11	5	5	46	24	1	5	14	14	33	36
19	Charlton Athletic	42	6	8	7	28	28	5	5	11	32	41	35
20	Sheffield United	42	9	6	6	34	24	2	6	13	18	45	34
21	Millwall	42	7	4	10	22	29	4	6	11	20	32	32
22	Blackburn Rovers	42	5	8	8	24	29	5	2	14	17	43	30

No		Date	Opponent	Res	Scorers	Att	Aizlewood M	Birchenall AJ	Donaghy M	Findlay JW	Goodyear C	Grealish AP	Hatton RJ	Hill RA	Ingram GRA	Jones G	Judge AG	Madden N	Moss DJ	Pearson AJ	Price PT	Saxby MW	Stein B	Stephens KW	Turner WL	West A	White SJ
1	Aug	18	CAMBRIDGE UNITED	1-1	Moss	8202	5	8	1			4	10	7					11		6		9	2	3		
2		21	Bristol Rovers	2-3	Moss 2 (1p)	5621	12	8	1			4	10	7					11		6	5	9	2	3		
3		25	ORIENT	2-1	Hatton, Hill	6705			3	1		4	10	7					11		6	5	9	2		8	
4	Sep	1	Leicester City	3-1	Moss 2 (1p), Hill	16241			3	1		4	10	7					11		6	5	9	2		8	
5		8	SWANSEA CITY	5-0	Moss 2 (1p), Hatton, West, Hill	10004			3	1		4	10	7					11		6	5	9	2		8	
6		15	Notts County	0-0		9582			3	1		4	10	7					11		6	5	9	2		8	
7		22	OLDHAM ATHLETIC	0-0		8711	12		3	1		4	10	7					11		6	5	9	2		8	
8		29	Fulham	3-1	Moss (p), Hill, Hatton	9944			3	1		4	10	7					11		6	5	9	2		8	
9	Oct	6	Cardiff City	1-2	Hatton	9402			3	1		4	10	7					11		6	5	9	2		8	
10		9	BRISTOL ROVERS	3-1	Hatton 3	8507	12		3	1		4	10	7					11		6	5	9	2		8	
11		13	SUNDERLAND	2-0	Moss 2	13504			3	1		4	10	7					11		6	5	9	2		8	
12		20	West Ham United	2-1	Stein, Saxby	25049			3	1		4		7	10				11		6	5	9	2		8	
13		27	PRESTON NORTH END	1-1	Moss (p)	11648			3	1		4	10	7					11		6	5	9	2		8	
14	Nov	3	Cambridge United	2-1	Hatton, Moss (p)	8104			3	1		4	10	7					11		6	5	9	2		8	
15		10	QUEEN'S PARK RANGERS	1-1	Saxby	19619			3	1		4	10	7					11		6	5	9	2		8	
16		17	Burnley	0-0		7119			3	1		4	10	7					11		6	5	9	2		8	
17		24	BIRMINGHAM CITY	2-3	Moss (p), Stein	13720			3	1		4	10	7					11		6	5	9	2		8	
18	Dec	1	Shrewsbury Town	2-1	Stein, Hatton	8565			3	1		4	10	7					11		6	5	9	2		8	
19		8	NEWCASTLE UNITED	1-1	Moss	14845			3	1		4	10	7					11		6	5	9	2		8	
20		15	Wrexham	1-3	Hatton	9145	12		3	1		4	10	7					11		6	5	9	2		8	
21		21	CHARLTON ATHLETIC	3-0	Stein 2, Hatton	7277			3	1		4	10	7					11		6	5	9	2		8	
22		26	Watford	1-0	Stephens	20187			3	1		4	10	7					11		6	5	9	2		8	
23		29	Orient	2-2	Moss 2 (1p)	9292			3	1		4	10	7					11		6	5	9	2		8	12
24	Jan	1	CHELSEA	3-3	Donaghy, Saxby, Moss	19717	4		3	1			10	7					11		6	5	9	2		8	
25		12	LEICESTER CITY	0-0		14141			3	1		4	10	7					11		6	5	9	2		8	
26	Feb	2	NOTTS COUNTY	2-1	Saxby, Hatton	9007			3	1		4	10	7					11		6	5	9	2		8	12
27		9	Oldham Athletic	1-2	Moss	7555			3	1		4	10	7					11		6	5	9	2		8	12
28		16	FULHAM	4-0	Moss 3, Stein	9179	2		3	1		4	10	7					11		6	5	9			8	
29		23	Sunderland	0-1		25387			3	1		4	10	7					11		6	5	9	2			
30	Mar	1	WEST HAM UNITED	1-1	Hill	20040			3	1		4	10	7					11		6	5	9	2		8	12
31		4	Swansea City	0-2		12775			3	1		4	10	7					11		6	5	9	2		8	
32		8	Preston North End	1-1	Hatton	8203	7		3	1		4	12						11		6	5	9	2		8	10
33		14	CARDIFF CITY	1-2	Moss	9246			3	1		4	10	7					11		6	5	9	2		8	12
34		22	Queen's Park Rangers	2-2	Stein, Hill	15054	5		3	1		4	10	7			2			12	6		9			8	11
35		29	BURNLEY	1-1	Hatton	8507			3	1		4	10	7					11	11	6	5	9	2		8	
36	Apr	4	Charlton Athletic	4-1	Moss (p), Grealish, West, Hatton	8971			3	1		4	10	7					11		6	5	9	2		8	
37		5	WATFORD	1-0	Hatton	12783	12		3	1		4	10	7					11		6	5	9	2		8	
38		7	Chelsea	1-1	Grealish	28460	12		3	1		4	10	7					11		6	5	9	2		8	
39		12	SHREWSBURY TOWN	0-0		10793			3	1		4	10	7					11		6	5	9	2		8	12
40		19	Birmingham City	0-1		23662			3	1		4	10	7					11		6	5	9	2		8	12
41		26	WREXHAM	2-0	Moss, Stein	9049			3	1	5	4	10	7				8	11		6		9	2			
42	May	3	Newcastle United	2-2	Hatton 2	13765	7		3			4	10			1			11		6	5	9	2		8	
			Apps				10	2	42	41	1	41	41	40	1	1	1	1	40	2	42	39	42	40	2	39	9
			Goals						1			2	18	6					24			4	8	1		2	

F.A. Cup

	Date	Opponent	Res		Att	Aiz	Bir	Don	Fin	Goo	Gre	Hat	Hil	Ing	Jon	Jud	Mad	Mos	Pea	Pri	Sax	Ste	Sph	Tur	Wes	Whi
R3	Jan 5	SWINDON TOWN	0-2		12458			3	1		4	10	7					11		6	5	9	2		8	12

F.L. Cup

	Date	Opponent	Res	Scorers	Att	Aiz	Bir	Don	Fin	Goo	Gre	Hat	Hil	Ing	Jon	Jud	Mad	Mos	Pea	Pri	Sax	Ste	Sph	Tur	Wes	Whi
R1/1	Aug 11	Gillingham	0-3		6222	3	8		1		4	10	7					11		6	5	9	2			
R1/2	14	GILLINGHAM	1-1	Aizlewood	5509	3	8		1		4	10	7					11		6	5	9	2			

		c	W	D	L	F	A	W	D	L	F	A	Pts
1	Leicester City	42	12	5	4	32	19	9	8	4	26	19	55
2	Sunderland	42	16	5	0	47	13	5	7	9	22	29	54
3	Birmingham City	42	14	5	2	37	16	7	6	8	21	22	53
4	Chelsea	42	14	3	4	34	16	9	4	8	32	36	53
5	Queen's Park Rgs.	42	10	9	2	46	25	8	4	9	29	28	49
6	LUTON TOWN	42	9	10	2	36	17	7	7	7	30	28	49
7	West Ham United	42	13	2	6	37	21	7	5	9	17	22	47
8	Cambridge United	42	11	6	4	40	23	3	10	8	21	30	44
9	Newcastle United	42	13	6	2	35	19	2	8	11	18	30	44
10	Preston North End	42	8	10	3	30	23	4	9	8	26	29	43
11	Oldham Athletic	42	12	5	4	30	21	4	6	11	19	32	43
12	Swansea City	42	13	1	7	31	20	4	8	9	17	33	43
13	Shrewsbury Town	42	12	3	6	41	23	6	2	13	19	30	41
14	Orient	42	7	9	5	29	31	5	8	8	19	23	41
15	Cardiff City	42	11	4	6	21	16	5	4	12	20	32	40
16	Wrexham	42	13	2	6	26	15	3	4	14	14	34	38
17	Notts County	42	4	11	6	24	22	7	4	10	27	30	37
18	Watford	42	9	6	6	27	18	3	7	11	12	28	37
19	Bristol Rovers	42	9	8	4	33	23	2	5	14	17	41	35
20	Fulham	42	6	4	11	19	28	5	3	13	23	46	29
21	Burnley	42	5	9	7	19	23	1	6	14	20	50	27
22	Charlton Athletic	42	6	6	9	25	31	0	4	17	14	47	22

1980/81   5th in Division Two

#	Date	Opponent	Res	Scorers	Att	Aizlewood M	Antic R	Bunn FS	Donaghy M	Findlay JW	Fuccillo P	Goodyear C	Grealish AP	Harrow A	Hill RA	Ingram GRA	Judge AG	Moss DJ	Price PT	Saxby MW	Stein B	Stephens KW	Turner WL	West A	White SJ
1	Aug 16	West Ham United	2-1	Moss 2 (2p)	28033		10		3	1			4		7			11	6	5	8	2		12	9
2	19	WATFORD	1-0	White	13887		10		3	1			4		7			11	6	5	8	2		12	9
3	23	DERBY COUNTY	1-2	Stein	11025	12	10	9	3	1			4		7			11	6	5	8	2			
4	30	Newcastle United	1-2	Stein	13175	12	10	9	3	1			4		7			11	6	5	8	2			
5	Sep 6	WREXHAM	1-1	Bunn	8244		10	9	3	1			4		7			11	6	5	8	2		12	
6	13	Blackburn Rovers	0-3		9076				3	1			4		7	9		11	6	5	8	2		10	12
7	20	ORIENT	2-1	Stein, Hill	8506		10		3	1			4		7			11	6	5	8	2		9	
8	27	Grimsby Town	0-0		9044	2	10		3	1			4	12	7			11	6	5	8			9	
9	Oct 4	NOTTS COUNTY	0-1		8786	12			3	1			4	9	7			11	6	5	8			10	
10	7	Bristol City	1-2	Saxby	7571				3	1			4	9	7			11	6	5	8			10	
11	11	Preston North End	0-1		5637	12			3	1			4	9	7				6	5	8			10	11
12	18	SHREWSBURY TOWN	1-1	White	8014		10		3	1		5	4		7			11	6		8	2			9
13	21	SWANSEA CITY	2-2	Stein. Moss	8402		10		3	1		5	4		7			11	6		8	2			9
14	25	Cambridge United	3-1	Moss (p), Goodyear, Stein	7218	10	12		3	1		5	4		7			11	6		8	2			9
15	Nov 1	SHEFFIELD WEDNESDAY	3-0	Moss 2 (1p), White	12092	10			3			5	4		7		1	11	6		8	2			9
16	8	Queen's Park Rangers	2-3	Stein, Moss	10082	10			3			5	4		7		1	11	6		8	2			9
17	11	Watford	1-0	White	16993	10			3	1			4		7			11	6	5	8	2		12	9
18	15	WEST HAM UNITED	3-2	Stein 2, Moss	17031	10			3	1			4		7			11	6	5	8	2		12	9
19	22	Cardiff City	0-1		6041	10			3	1			4		7			11	6	5	8	2		12	9
20	29	BOLTON WANDERERS	2-2	Hill, Stein	8302	10			3	1			4		7			11	6	5	8	2		12	9
21	Dec 6	Oldham Athletic	0-0		4854	10			3	1			4		7			11	6	5	8	2		12	9
22	13	PRESTON NORTH END	4-2	Moss 2 (1p), Fuccillo, Ingram	7874	10	12		3	1	4				7	9		11	6	5	8	2			
23	19	Shrewsbury Town	1-0	Ingram	4521	10	12		3	1					7	9		11		5	8	2		6	
24	26	CHELSEA	2-0	Stein 2	16006	10			3	1			4		7	9		11	6		8	2		5	
25	27	Bristol Rovers	4-2	Stein 3, Hill	7010	10	12		3	1			4		7	9		11	6		8			5	
26	Jan 10	CARDIFF CITY	2-2	Moss, Price	9013	10			3	1			4		7	9		11	6	5	8	2			
27	17	NEWCASTLE UNITED	0-1		10774	10			3	1	12		4		7	9		11	6		8	2			
28	31	Derby County	2-2	Moss, Ingram	16479				3	1		10			7	9		11	6		8	2	4	5	
29	Feb 7	BLACKBURN ROVERS	3-1	Price, Hill, Moss	9350	10			3	1			4		7	9		11	6		8	2		5	
30	21	GRIMSBY TOWN	0-2		9217	10			3	1			4		7	9		11	6		8	2		5	12
31	Mar 1	Orient	0-0		7974		12		3	1		10			7			11	6	5	8	2			
32	7	Notts County	1-0	Stein	8075	10			3	1			4		7			11	6	5	8	2			9
33	14	BRISTOL CITY	3-1	White 2, Moss (p)	8745	10			3	1			4		7			11	6	5	8	2			9
34	28	CAMBRIDGE UNITED	0-0		9412	10			3	1					7			11	6	5	8	2		4	9
35	31	Wrexham	0-0		4157	10			3	1			4		7	12		11	6	5	8	2			9
36	Apr 4	Sheffield Wednesday	1-3	Ingram	17196	3	10		9	1			4		7	12		11	6		8	2			
37	11	QUEEN'S PARK RANGERS	3-0	Ingram, Stein, Antic	12112	10			3	1			4		7	9		11	6		8	2			
38	18	BRISTOL ROVERS	1-0	Moss (p)	9009	10			3	1			4		7	9		11	6		8	2			
39	20	Chelsea	2-0	Moss, Hill	12868	10			3	1			4		7	9		11	6		8	2			
40	25	OLDHAM ATHLETIC	1-2	Stein	10305	10			3	1			4		7	9		11	6		8	2		12	
41	27	Swansea City	2-2	Hill 2	21354	10			3	1					7			11	6		8	2		4	9
42	May 2	Bolton Wanderers	3-0	Stein, White, Stephens	7278	10			3	1			4		7			11	6		8	2			9
		Apps				23	24	3	42	40	5	5	37	4	42	17	2	41	41	31	42	40	1	25	21
		Goals					1	1			1	1			7	5		16	2	1	18	1			7

F.A. Cup

Rd	Date	Opponent	Res	Scorers	Att	Aizlewood M	Donaghy M	Findlay JW	Grealish AP	Hill RA	Ingram GRA	Moss DJ	Price PT	Saxby MW	Stein B	Stephens KW	West A
R3	Jan 3	Leyton Orient	3-1	Moss 2, Ingram	9891	10	3	1	4	7	9	11	6	5	8		2
R4	Jan 24	Newcastle United	1-2	Ingram	29202	10	3	1	4	7	9	11	6		8	2	5

F.L. Cup

Rd	Date	Opponent	Res	Scorers	Att	Aizlewood M	Antic R	Bunn FS	Donaghy M	Findlay JW	Grealish AP	Hill RA	Ingram GRA	Moss DJ	Price PT	Saxby MW	Stein B	Stephens KW	West A	White SJ
R2/1	Aug 27	Reading	2-0	Moss, B Stein	5778		10	9	3	1	4	7		11	6	5	8	2		12
R2/2	Sep 2	READING	1-1	Saxby	5707	6	10		3	1	4	7	12			5	8	2		9
R3	Sep 23	MANCHESTER CITY	1-2	Antic	10030		10		3	1	4	7		11	6	5	8	2	9	

Played at 11 in R2s: Heath (substituted). Played at 12 in R3: Smith.

Division Two final table

		c	W	D	L	F	A	W	D	L	F	A	Pts
1	West Ham United	42	19	1	1	53	12	9	9	3	26	17	66
2	Notts County	42	10	8	3	26	15	8	9	4	23	23	53
3	Swansea City	42	12	5	4	39	19	6	9	6	25	25	50
4	Blackburn Rovers	42	12	8	1	28	7	4	10	7	14	22	50
5	LUTON TOWN	42	10	6	5	35	23	8	6	7	26	23	48
6	Derby County	42	9	8	4	34	26	6	7	8	23	26	45
7	Grimsby Town	42	10	8	3	21	10	5	7	9	23	32	45
8	Queen's Park Rgs.	42	11	7	3	36	12	4	6	11	20	34	43
9	Watford	42	13	5	3	34	18	3	6	12	16	27	43
10	Sheffield Wed.	42	14	4	3	38	14	3	4	14	15	37	42
11	Newcastle United	42	11	7	3	22	13	3	7	11	8	32	42
12	Chelsea	42	8	6	7	27	15	6	6	9	19	26	40
13	Cambridge United	42	13	1	7	36	23	4	5	12	17	42	40
14	Shrewsbury Town	42	9	7	5	33	22	2	10	9	13	25	39
15	Oldham Athletic	42	7	9	5	19	16	5	6	10	20	32	39
16	Wrexham	42	5	8	8	22	24	7	6	8	21	21	38
17	Orient	42	9	8	4	34	20	4	4	13	18	36	38
18	Bolton Wanderers	42	10	5	6	40	27	4	5	12	21	39	38
19	Cardiff City	42	7	7	7	23	24	5	6	11	21	36	36
20	Preston North End	42	8	7	6	28	26	3	7	11	13	36	36
21	Bristol City	42	6	10	5	19	15	1	6	14	10	36	30
22	Bristol Rovers	42	4	9	8	21	24	1	4	16	13	41	23

No	Date	Opponent	Score	Scorers	Att	Aizlewood M	Aleksic MA	Antic R	Bunn FS	Donaghy M	Findlay JW	Fuccillo P	Goodyear C	Hill RA	Horton B	Ingram GRA	Jennings WJ	Judge AG	Money R	Moss DJ	Saxby MW	Small MA	Stein B	Stephens KW	Turner WL	White SJ
1	Aug 29	CHARLTON ATHLETIC	3-0	Donaghy, McAllister (og), White	8776	3		10		6	1			7	4	11					5		8	2		9
2	Sep 1	Queen's Park Rangers	2-1	Aizlewood, Hill	18703	3		10		6	1			7	4	11					5		8	2		9
3	5	Bolton Wanderers	2-1	Stein, Aizlewood	6911	3		10		6	1			7	4	11					5	12	8	2		9
4	12	SHEFFIELD WEDNESDAY	0-3		12131	3		10		6	1			7	4						5	12	8	2	11	9
5	19	Leicester City	2-1	White 2	14159	3		10		6	1			7	4					11			8	2		9
6	22	CARDIFF CITY	2-3	Saxby, Antic	9015	3		10		6	1	12		7	4					11	5		8	2		9
7	26	WATFORD	4-1	Moss 2 (2p), Stein 2	12839	3				6	1	10		7	4					11	5		8	2		9
8	Oct 3	Orient	3-0	Aizlewood, Hill, White	4944	3		12		6	1	10		7	4					11	5		8	2		9
9	10	Oldham Athletic	1-1	White	8403	3		12		6	1	10		7	4					11	5		8	2		9
10	17	GRIMSBY TOWN	6-0	Fuccillo, Moss (p), White 4	9090	3			12	6	1	10		7	4					11	5		8	2		9
11	24	Wrexham	2-0	Donaghy, White	4059					6	1	10	3	7	4					11	5		8	2		9
12	31	CRYSTAL PALACE	1-0	Moss (p)	11712			12		6	1	10	3	7	4					11	5		8	2		9
13	Nov 7	DERBY COUNTY	3-2	Moss, Goodyear, Donaghy	10784	5				6	1	10	3	7	4					11			8	2		9
14	14	Blackburn Rovers	1-0	Moss (p)	9862	5	1			6		10	3	7	4					11			8	2		9
15	21	Newcastle United	2-3	Moss (p), Donaghy	21084	3	1	12		6		10	5	7	4					11			8	2		9
16	24	BOLTON WANDERERS	2-0	Stein, Moss	8889	3	1	12		6		10	5	7	4					11			8	2		9
17	28	ROTHERHAM UNITED	3-1	White, Donaghy, Stein	11061	3	1			6		10	5	7	4					11			8	2		9
18	Dec 5	Shrewsbury Town	2-2	White, Donaghy	5259	3		12		6		10	5	7	4			1		11			8	2		9
19	28	Norwich City	3-1	Antic, White, Stein	18458	3			7	6	1	10	5		4					11			8	2		9
20	Jan 19	Charlton Athletic	0-0		7013	3			4	6	1	10	5	7						11			8	2		9
21	30	LEICESTER CITY	2-1	White, Donaghy	11810	3		12		6		10	5	7	4			1		11			8	2		9
22	Feb 6	Sheffield Wednesday	3-3	White, Moss (p), Stein	18252	3		12		6		10	5	7	4			1		11			8	2		9
23	20	Watford	1-1	Stein	22798	3				6	1	10	5	7	4					11			8	2		9
24	27	OLDHAM ATHLETIC	2-0	Moss 2 (1p)	11506	3				6	1	10	5	7	4					11			8	2		9
25	Mar 2	CAMBRIDGE UNITED	1-0	Horton	10597	3		12		6	1	10	5	7	4					11			8	2		9
26	6	Grimsby Town	0-0		7734	3		10		6	1		5	7	4					11			8	2		9
27	12	WREXHAM	0-0		10880	3		10	12	6	1		5	7	4					11			8	2		9
28	16	Barnsley	3-4	Stein 2, Law (og)	14044	3		12		6	1	10	5	7	4					11			8	2		9
29	20	Crystal Palace	3-3	Antic, Moss (p), Stein	12187			10		6	1		5	7	4				3	11			8	2		9
30	27	Derby County	0-0		15836					6	1		5	7	4				3	11			8	2	10	9
31	30	ORIENT	2-0	Moss (p), Hill	9716					6	1		5	7	4				3	11			8	2	10	9
32	Apr 3	BLACKBURN ROVERS	2-0	Stein, White	10721					6	1		5	7	4		12		3	11			8	2	10	9
33	10	Cambridge United	1-1	Turner	8815					6	1		5	7	4				3	11			8	2	10	9
34	12	NORWICH CITY	2-0	Stein, Jennings	15061					6	1		5	7	4		12		3	11			8	2	10	9
35	17	NEWCASTLE UNITED	3-2	Stein 3 (2p)	13041					6	1	10	5	7	4				3				8	2	11	9
36	20	CHELSEA	2-2	Antic, Donaghy	16185			11		6	1	10	5	7	4				3				8	2		9
37	24	Rotherham United	2-2	Fuccillo, Money	11290			12		6	1	10	5	7	4				3	11			8	2		9
38	30	SHREWSBURY TOWN	4-1	Stein, Hill, White, Moss	14563			12		6	1	10	5	7	4				3	11			8	2		9
39	May 8	Chelsea	2-1	Antic, Stein	15044			10		6	1		5	7	4				3	11			8	2		9
40	11	QUEEN'S PARK RANGERS	3-2	Hill, White, Moss (p)	16657			10		6	1		5	7	4				3	11			8	2		9
41	15	BARNSLEY	1-1	Stein	14463			12		6	1		5	7	4				3	11			8	2		9
42	17	Cardiff City	3-2	Stein 2, Donaghy	10277			10		6	1		5	7	4				3	11			8	2		9
		Apps				26	4	30	2	42	34	29	32	38	41	3	2	4	13	36	12	3	42	42	7	42
		Goals				3		5		9		2		5	2		1		1	15	1		21		1	18

Two own goals

F.A. Cup

Rd	Date	Opponent	Score	Scorers	Att	Aizlewood M	Antic R	Donaghy M	Findlay JW	Fuccillo P	Goodyear C	Hill RA	Horton B	Moss DJ	Stein B	Stephens KW	White SJ
R3	Jan 2	SWINDON TOWN	2-1	Moss, Horton	9488	3		6	1	10	5	7	4	11	8	2	9
R4	Jan 23	IPSWICH TOWN	0-3		20188	3	12	6	1	10	5	7	4	11	8	2	9

F.L. Cup (Milk Cup)

Rd	Date	Opponent	Score	Scorers	Att	Aizlewood M	Donaghy M	Findlay JW	Fuccillo P	Goodyear C	Hill RA	Horton B	Jennings WJ	Moss DJ	Saxby MW	Stein B	Stephens KW	White SJ
R2/1	Oct 6	WREXHAM	0-2		6146	3	6	1	10		7	4		11	5	8	2	9
R2/2	Oct 27	Wrexham	1-0	White	3453		6	1	10	3	7	4	12	11	5	8	2	9

Pos	Club	P	W	D	L	F	A	W	D	L	F	A	Pts
1	LUTON TOWN	42	16	3	2	48	19	9	10	2	38	27	88
2	Watford	42	13	6	2	46	16	10	5	6	30	26	80
3	Norwich City	42	14	3	4	41	19	8	2	11	23	31	71
4	Sheffield Wed.	42	10	8	3	31	23	10	2	9	24	28	70
5	Queen's Park Rgs.	42	15	4	2	40	9	6	2	13	25	34	69
6	Barnsley	42	13	4	4	33	14	6	6	9	26	27	67
7	Rotherham United	42	13	5	3	42	19	7	2	12	24	35	67
8	Leicester City	42	12	5	4	31	19	6	7	8	25	29	66
9	Newcastle United	42	14	4	3	30	14	4	4	13	22	36	62
10	Blackburn Rovers	42	11	4	6	26	15	5	7	9	21	28	59
11	Oldham Athletic	42	9	9	3	28	23	6	5	10	22	28	59
12	Chelsea	42	10	5	6	37	30	5	7	9	23	30	57
13	Charlton Athletic	42	11	5	5	33	22	2	7	12	17	43	51
14	Cambridge United	42	11	4	6	31	19	2	5	14	17	34	48
15	Crystal Palace	42	9	2	10	25	26	4	7	10	9	19	48
16	Derby County	42	9	8	4	32	23	3	4	14	21	45	48
17	Grimsby Town	42	5	8	8	29	30	6	5	10	24	35	46
18	Shrewsbury Town	42	10	6	5	26	19	1	7	13	11	38	46
19	Bolton Wanderers	42	10	4	7	28	24	3	6	12	17	37	46
20	Cardiff City	42	9	2	10	28	32	3	6	12	17	29	44
21	Wrexham	42	9	4	8	22	22	2	7	12	18	34	44
22	Orient	42	6	8	7	23	24	4	1	16	13	37	39

1982/83 18th in Division One

			Opponent	Score	Scorers	Att	Antic R	Aylott TKC	Bunn FS	Daniel RC	Donaghy M	Elliott PM	Findlay JW	Fuccillo P	Geddis D	Godden AL	Goodyear C	Hill RA	Horton B	Judge AG	Kellock W	Money R	Moss DJ	Parker GA	Small MA	Stein B	Stephens KW	Thomas MA	Turner WL	Walsh PAM	Watts MR	White SJ
1	Aug	28	Tottenham Hotspur	2-2	Lacy (og), Stein	35195	10				6		1				5	7	4			3	11			8	2			9		
2		31	WEST HAM UNITED	0-2		13403	10				6		1				5	7	4			3	11			8	2			9		
3	Sep	4	NOTTS COUNTY	5-3	Walsh 3, Hill, Moss	9071	10				6		1				5	7	4			3	11		12	8	2			9		
4		8	Aston Villa	1-4	Moss (p)	18823	10				6		1				5	7	4		12		11			8	2		3	9		
5		11	Liverpool	3-3	Stein 2, Moss	33694	12				6		1				5	7	4			3	11			8	2		10	9		
6		18	BRIGHTON & HOVE ALB	5-0	Stein 3, Turner, Moss	11342					6						5	7	4	1		3	11			8	2		10	9		
7		25	Stoke City	4-4	Walsh, Stein 2, Donaghy	18475	12				6						5	7	4	1		3	11			8	2		10	9		
8	Oct	2	MANCHESTER UNITED	1-1	Hill	17009	12				6		1				5	7	4			3	11			8	2		10	9		
9		9	Birmingham City	3-2	Stein, Walsh, Moss	13772					6		1	10			5	7	4			3	11			8	2			9		
10		16	IPSWICH TOWN	1-1	Stein (p)	13378					6		1	10			5	7	4			3	11			8	2			9		
11		23	West Bromwich Albion	0-1		16488					6			10			5	7	4	1		3	11			8	2		12	9		
12		30	NOTTM. FOREST	0-2		12648	12				6		1				5	7	4		10	3	11			8			2	9		
13	Nov	6	ARSENAL	2-2	Moss, Walsh	16597	12				6		1	10			5	7	4			3	11			8			2	9		
14		13	Sunderland	1-1	Moss	14238			12		6							7	4	1	10	3	11			8	2		5	9		
15		20	Coventry City	2-4	Horton, Stein	9670	10						1				5	7	4			3	11			8	2		6	9		
16		27	SOUTHAMPTON	3-3	Hill, Stein , Goodyear	11196	12				6		1				5	7	4			3	11			8	2		10	9		
17	Dec	4	Swansea City	0-2		9556	12				6		1				5	7	4			3	11			8	2		10	9		
18		11	MANCHESTER CITY	3-1	Walsh, Stein, Hartford (og)	11013					6		1				5	7	4			3	11			8	2		10	9		
19		18	Everton	0-5		14986					6		1	12	8		5	7	4			3	11				2		10	9		
20		27	WATFORD	1-0	Goodyear	21145					6		1	10	8		5	7	4			3	11				2			9		
21		28	Norwich City	0-1		20415	12						1	10	8		5	7	4			3	11				2		6	9		
22	Jan	1	COVENTRY CITY	1-2	Donaghy	13072	12				6		1	10	8		5	7	4			3	11				2			9		
23		4	West Ham United	3-2	Walsh 3	21435			8		6		1				5	7	4		12		11				2	3	10	9		
24		15	TOTTENHAM HOTSPUR	1-1	O'Reilly (og)	21231			8		6		1				5	7	4		12						2	3	10	9	11	
25		22	Brighton & Hove Albion	4-2	Hill 2, Stevens (og), Case (og)	11778			8		6		1				5	7	4		12		11				2	3	10	9		
26	Feb	5	LIVERPOOL	1-3	Stein	18434	12				6		1				5	7	4			3	11			8	2		10	9		
27		26	Ipswich Town	0-3		18632					6		1	10			5	7	4		12		11				2		3	9		8
28	Mar	5	WEST BROMWICH ALB.	0-0		10852					6	3	1				5	7	4				11				2		10	9		8
29		12	Nottingham Forest	1-0	Hill	14387					6	3	1				5	7	4				11				2		10	9		8
30		19	Arsenal	1-4	Moss	23987					6	3	1				5	7	4				11				2		10	9		8
31		26	SUNDERLAND	1-3	Horton (p)	11221		8		12	6	3				1	5	7	4				11				2		10	9		
32	Apr	2	NORWICH CITY	0-1		11211		8		12	10	3				1	5	7	4				11				2	6		9		
33		4	Watford	2-5	Aylott, Horton	20120	10	8			6	5				1		7	4			3	11				2			9		
34		9	ASTON VILLA	2-1	Aylott, Moss	10924	4	8			6	5				1		7				3	11				2		10	9		
35		12	BIRMINGHAM CITY	3-1	Hill 2, Horton (p)	12868	10	8			6	5				1		7	4			3	11			12	2			9		
36		16	Notts County	1-1	Donaghy	8897	10	8			6	5				1		7	4			3	11				2			9		
37		23	SWANSEA CITY	3-1	Walsh 3	11561		8			6	5				1		7	4			3	11				2		10	9		
38		30	Southampton	2-2	Elliott, Antic	18367	4	8			6	5				1	12	7				3	11				2		10	9		
39	May	2	STOKE CITY	0-0		11877	10	9			6	5				1		7	4			3	11				2		8			
40		7	EVERTON	1-5	Hill	12447	12	8			6					1	5	7	4			3	11				2		10	9		
41		9	Manchester United	0-3		34213	12	8		11	6					1	5	7	4			3		10			2			9		
42		14	Manchester City	1-0	Antic	42843	12	8			6	5				1	3	7	4							11	2		10	9		
						Apps	24	12	4	3	40	13	26	9	4	12	35	42	40	4	7	31	39	1	1	21	40	4	30	41	1	4
						Goals	2	2			3						2	9	4				9			14			1	13		

Five own goals

F.A. Cup

			Opponent	Score	Scorers	Att	Antic R	Aylott TKC	Bunn FS	Daniel RC	Donaghy M	Elliott PM	Findlay JW	Fuccillo P	Geddis D	Godden AL	Goodyear C	Hill RA	Horton B	Judge AG	Kellock W	Money R	Moss DJ	Parker GA	Small MA	Stein B	Stephens KW	Thomas MA	Turner WL	Walsh PAM	Watts MR	White SJ
R3	Jan	8	PETERBOROUGH UNITED	3-0	Horton, Hill, Walsh	11151			8		6		1				5	7	4								2	3	10	9	11	
R4	Jan	29	MANCHESTER UTD.	0-2		20516					6		1				5	7	4		12	3	11			8	2		10	9		

F.L. Cup (Milk Cup)

			Opponent	Score	Scorers	Att	Antic R	Aylott TKC	Bunn FS	Daniel RC	Donaghy M	Elliott PM	Findlay JW	Fuccillo P	Geddis D	Godden AL	Goodyear C	Hill RA	Horton B	Judge AG	Kellock W	Money R	Moss DJ	Parker GA	Small MA	Stein B	Stephens KW	Thomas MA	Turner WL	Walsh PAM	Watts MR	White SJ
R2/1	Oct	5	CHARLTON ATHLETIC	3-0	B Stein, Fuccillo 2	7030					6		1	10			5	7	4			3	11			8	2			9		
R2/2	Oct	26	Charlton Athletic	0-2		5973					6		1				5	7	4			3	11			8		2	10	9		
R3	Nov	9	BLACKPOOL	4-2	Kellock 2, Bunn, Moss	6409			12		6			10			5		4	1	7	3	11			8	2			9		
R4	Dec	1	Tottenham Hotspur	0-1		27461	12				6		1				5	7	4			3	11			8	2		10	9		

		c	W	D	L	F	A	W	D	L	F	A	Pts
1	Liverpool	42	16	4	1	55	16	8	6	7	32	21	82
2	Watford	42	16	2	3	49	20	6	3	12	25	37	71
3	Manchester United	42	14	7	0	39	10	5	6	10	17	28	70
4	Tottenham Hotspur	42	15	4	2	50	15	5	5	11	15	35	69
5	Nottingham Forest	42	12	5	4	34	18	8	4	9	28	32	69
6	Aston Villa	42	17	2	2	47	15	4	3	14	15	35	68
7	Everton	42	13	6	2	43	19	5	4	12	23	29	64
8	West Ham United	42	13	3	5	41	23	7	1	13	27	39	64
9	Ipswich Town	42	11	3	7	39	23	4	10	7	25	27	58
10	Arsenal	42	11	6	4	36	19	5	4	12	22	37	58
11	West Bromwich Alb.	42	11	5	5	35	20	4	7	10	16	29	57
12	Southampton	42	11	5	5	36	22	4	7	10	18	36	57
13	Stoke City	42	13	4	4	34	21	3	5	13	19	43	57
14	Norwich City	42	10	6	5	30	18	4	6	11	22	40	54
15	Notts County	42	12	4	5	37	25	3	3	15	18	46	52
16	Sunderland	42	7	10	4	30	22	5	4	12	18	39	50
17	Birmingham City	42	9	7	5	29	24	3	7	11	11	31	50
18	LUTON TOWN	42	7	7	7	34	33	5	6	10	31	51	49
19	Coventry City	42	10	5	6	29	17	3	4	14	19	42	48
20	Manchester City	42	9	5	7	26	23	4	3	14	21	47	47
21	Swansea City	42	10	4	7	32	29	0	7	14	19	40	41
22	Brighton & Hove A.	42	8	7	6	25	22	1	6	14	13	46	40

1983/84 16th in Division One

#	Date	Opponent	Res	Scorers	Att	Antic R	Aylott TKC	Bracker T	Bunn FS	Daniel RC	Donaghy M	Elliott PM	Goodyear C	Hill RA	Horton B	Johnson R	Moss DJ	North S	Nwajiobi E	Parker GA	Sealey L	Stein B	Stein M	Stephens KW	Thomas MA	Turner WL	Walsh PAM
1	Aug 27	Arsenal	1-2	Robson (og)	39347				10		6	5		7	4		11				1	8		2		3	9
2	31	Leicester City	3-0	Bunn, Moss, Hill	12629				10		6	5		7	4		11				1	8		2		3	9
3	Sep 3	SUNDERLAND	4-1	Hill, Walsh, Munro (og), Stein	10846				10		6	5		7	4		11				1	8		2		3	9
4	6	NORWICH CITY	2-2	Elliott, Stein	11095	12			10		6	5		7	4		11				1	8		2		3	9
5	10	Manchester United	0-2		41013	12			10		6	5		7	4		11				1	8		2		3	9
6	17	WOLVERHAMPTON W.	4-0	Walsh, Stein, Moss, Horton	10975				10		6	5		7	4		11				1	8		2		3	9
7	24	Nottingham Forest	0-1		16296	12			10		6	5		7	4		11				1	8		2		3	9
8	Oct 1	ASTON VILLA	1-0	Moss (p)	12747	12			10		6	5		7	4		11				1	8		2		3	9
9	15	Everton	1-0	Walsh	14327				10		6	5		7	4		11				1	8		2		3	9
10	22	SOUTHAMPTON	3-1	Aylott 2, Stein	12389	12	9		10		6	5		7	4		11				1	8		2		3	
11	29	Liverpool	0-6		31940	11					6	5		7	4						1	8		2	3	10	9
12	Nov 5	Queen's Park Rangers	1-0	Elliot	15053		10				6	5		7	4					11	1	8		2		3	9
13	12	BIRMINGHAM CITY	1-1	Stein	11111	12					6	5		7		4				11	1	8		2	3	10	9
14	19	TOTTENHAM HOTSPUR	2-4	Stein, Walsh	17275	11	10				6	5	4	7							1	8		2		3	9
15	26	Watford	2-1	Stein, Bunn	17791		10		11		6	5		7	4						1	8		2		3	9
16	Dec 3	COVENTRY CITY	2-4	Pearce (og), Aylott	10698	12	10		11		6	5		7	4						1	8		2		3	9
17	10	Stoke City	4-2	Walsh 3, Daniel	10329		10			11	6	5		7	4						1	8		2	3		9
18	18	WEST BROMWICH ALB.	2-0	Horton (p), Aylott	11566		10			11	6	5		7	4						1	8		2	3		9
19	26	Notts County	3-0	Aylott 2, Daniel	9789		10			11	6	5		7	4						1	8		2	3		9
20	27	WEST HAM UNITED	0-1		16343		10			11	6	5		7	4						1	8		2	3	12	9
21	31	Sunderland	0-2		19482		10		11		6	5		7	4	2					1	8				3	9
22	Jan 2	NOTTM. FOREST	2-3	Walsh, Nwajiobi	12126	12			10		6	5		7	4				11		1	8		2	3		9
23	14	ARSENAL	1-2	Kay (og)	16320		10		11		6	5			4				12	7	1	8		2	3		9
24	21	Wolverhampton Wan.	2-1	Parker, Walsh	11594		10		11		6	5	12							7	1	8		2	3		9
25	Feb 4	Aston Villa	0-0		18656		10		11		6	5								7	1	8		2	3		9
26	12	MANCHESTER UNITED	0-5		11265	12	10		11		6	5		7	4						1	8		2	3		9
27	18	LIVERPOOL	0-0		14877				11		10	5	6	7	4						1	8		2	3		9
28	25	Southampton	1-2	Donaghy	17947		10				6	5	12	7	4				11		1	8		2	3		9
29	Mar 3	QUEEN'S PARK RANGERS	0-0		11922		11				10	5	6	7	4						1	8		2	3		9
30	13	IPSWICH TOWN	2-1	Aylott 2 (1p)	8776	4	10		11		7	5	6								1	8		2	3		9
31	17	Norwich City	0-0		13112	4	10		11		7	5	6								1	8		2	3		9
32	20	Birmingham City	1-1	Stein	9592	4	10		11		7	5	6								1	8		2	3		9
33	24	LEICESTER CITY	0-0		10509						7	5	6		4		11	10			1	8		2	3		9
34	31	Ipswich Town	0-3		14586	5	10	12			7		6				11				1	8		2	3		9
35	Apr 7	EVERTON	0-3		9224		10	7	11		6	5	12		4						1	8	9	2	3		
36	14	Tottenham Hotspur	1-2	Parker	25390	12	9		10		6	5			4				11	7	1	8		2	3		
37	17	West Ham United	1-3	Walsh	15430				10		6	5	12		4				11	7	1	8		2	3		9
38	21	NOTTS COUNTY	3-2	Moss, Horton (p), Bunn	8181	12			10		6	5			4		11			7	1	8		2	3		9
39	28	WATFORD	1-2	Walsh	12594	12			10			5	6		4		11			7	1	8		2	3		9
40	May 5	Coventry City	2-2	Antic, Stein	9647	11			10		6		5		4					7	1	8		2	3		
41	7	STOKE CITY	0-1		9867	11			10		6		5		4				12	7	1	8		2	3		
42	12	West Bromwich Albion	0-3		12004	12	10		11		2	5			4				6	7	1	8				3	9
		Apps				22	20	2	30	7	40	38	17	26	37	2	16	1	4	13	42	42	1	40	26	19	39
		Goals				1	8		3	2	1	2		2	3		4		1	2		9					11

Four own goals

F.A. Cup

	Date	Opponent	Res	Scorers	Att	Antic R	Aylott TKC	Bracker T	Bunn FS	Daniel RC	Donaghy M	Elliott PM	Goodyear C	Hill RA	Horton B	Johnson R	Moss DJ	North S	Nwajiobi E	Parker GA	Sealey L	Stein B	Stein M	Stephens KW	Thomas MA	Turner WL	Walsh PAM
R3	Jan 7	WATFORD	2-2	Nwajiobi, B Stein	15007	12			10		6	5		7	4				11		1	8		2	3		9
rep	Jan 10	Watford	3-4	Donaghy, Walsh 2	20586		10		11		6	5			4				12	7	1	8		2	3		9

Replay a.e.t.

F.L. Cup (Milk Cup)

	Date	Opponent	Res	Scorers	Att	Antic R	Aylott TKC	Bracker T	Bunn FS	Daniel RC	Donaghy M	Elliott PM	Goodyear C	Hill RA	Horton B	Johnson R	Moss DJ	North S	Nwajiobi E	Parker GA	Sealey L	Stein B	Stein M	Stephens KW	Thomas MA	Turner WL	Walsh PAM
R2/1	Oct 4	Rotherham United	3-2	Walsh, Bunn, Aylott	4035		10		9			5	4		6		11				1	7		2		3	8
R2/2	Oct 25	ROTHERHAM UNITED	0-2		6755	10	9		11		6	5		7	4						1	8		2	3		

Second leg a.e.t.

		c	W	D	L	F	A	W	D	L	F	A	Pts
1	Liverpool	42	14	5	2	50	12	8	9	4	23	20	80
2	Southampton	42	15	4	2	44	17	7	7	7	22	21	77
3	Nottingham Forest	42	14	4	3	47	17	8	4	9	29	28	74
4	Manchester United	42	14	3	4	43	18	6	11	4	28	23	74
5	Queen's Park Rgs.	42	14	4	3	37	12	8	3	10	30	25	73
6	Arsenal	42	10	5	6	41	29	8	4	9	33	31	63
7	Everton	42	9	9	3	21	12	7	5	9	23	30	62
8	Tottenham Hotspur	42	11	4	6	31	24	6	6	9	33	41	61
9	West Ham United	42	10	4	7	39	24	7	5	9	21	31	60
10	Aston Villa	42	14	3	4	34	22	3	6	12	25	39	60
11	Watford	42	9	7	5	36	31	7	2	12	32	46	57
12	Ipswich Town	42	11	4	6	34	23	4	4	13	21	34	53
13	Sunderland	42	8	9	4	26	18	5	4	12	16	35	52
14	Norwich City	42	9	8	4	34	20	3	7	11	14	29	51
15	Leicester City	42	11	5	5	40	30	2	7	12	25	38	51
16	LUTON TOWN	42	7	5	9	30	33	7	4	10	23	33	51
17	West Bromwich Alb.	42	10	4	7	30	26	4	5	12	18	37	51
18	Stoke City	42	11	4	6	30	23	2	7	12	14	40	50
19	Coventry City	42	8	5	8	33	33	5	6	10	24	44	50
20	Birmingham City	42	7	7	7	19	18	5	5	11	20	32	48
21	Notts County	42	6	7	8	31	36	4	4	13	19	36	41
22	Wolverhampton Wan.	42	4	8	9	15	28	2	3	16	12	52	29

Division One

No		Date	Opponent	Score	Scorers	Att	Breacker T	Bunn FS	Daniel RC	Dibble A	Donaghy M	Droy M	Elliott PM	Elliott S	Findlay JW	Foster S	Grimes A	Harford M	Hilaire V	Hill RA	Moss DJ	Nicholas P	North S	Nwajiobi E	Parker GA	Preece D	Sealey L	Stein B	Stein M	Thomas MA	Todd C	Turner WL
1	Aug	25	STOKE CITY	2-0	P Elliott, Bunn	8626	4	10		1	6			9		3				7	11	5						8		2		
2		28	Ipswich Town	1-1	Moss	15833	4	10		1	6			9		3				7	11	5	12					8		2		
3	Sep	1	West Bromwich Albion	0-4		11653	4	10		1	6			9		3				7	11	5	12					8		2		
4		4	LIVERPOOL	1-2	Donaghy	14127	4			1	6		5	9		3				7	11				12			8		2		10
5		8	SOUTHAMPTON	1-1	Moss (p)	8657		12		1	6		5			3				7	11			9	4			8		2		10
6		16	Nottingham Forest	1-3	Moss	18605		10		1	6		5			3				7	11			9	12			8		2		4
7		22	CHELSEA	0-0		16066		10		1	6		5			3				7	11			9				8		2		4
8		29	Tottenham Hotspur	2-4	Moss, Bunn	30204		9		1	6		5			3			10	7	11				12			8		2		4
9	Oct	6	Queen's Park Rangers	3-2	S Elliott, P Elliott, Stein	12051				1	6		5	9		3				7	11				10			8		2		4
10		13	SHEFFIELD WEDNESDAY	1-2	Bunn	10285		4		1	6		5	9					10	7	11				12			8		2		3
11		20	WATFORD	3-2	Bunn 2, S Elliott	12192		10			6		5	9	1	3			11	7				4				8		2		3
12		27	Sunderland	0-3		15280	12	10			6		5	9	1	3			11	7				4				8		2		3
13	Nov	3	NEWCASTLE UNITED	2-2	Parker, Stein	10009	2		11	1	6			9					12	7		5		10				8			4	3
14		10	Norwich City	0-3		13610	2	9		1	6									7	11	5	12	10				8			4	3
15		17	Manchester United	0-2		41630	2	10		1	6	5		9					11	7				4	12			8				3
16		24	WEST HAM UNITED	2-2	Stein, Nwajiobi	10789	2	10		1	6	3		9	1					7			6	11	12			8				4
17	Dec	1	Arsenal	1-3	Stein	26336	2	10			6					5		9		7				12	11		1	8		3		4
18		8	ASTON VILLA	1-0	Preece	7696	2	9			6					5				7	11	4				10	1	8		3		
19		15	Leicester City	2-2	Stein, Harford	10476	2				6					5		9		7	11	4				10	1	8	12	3		
20		18	WEST BROMWICH ALB.	1-2	Foster	7286	2				6					5		9		11		4			12	10	1	8		3		7
21		26	COVENTRY CITY	2-0	Stein, Daniel	9237	2	12	10		6					5		9		7				11			1	8		3		4
22		29	Liverpool	0-1		35403	2	11	10		6					5		9		7				12			1	8		3		4
23	Jan	1	Everton	1-2	Harford	31641	2	12			6					5		9		7	11					10	1	8		3		4
24	Feb	2	TOTTENHAM HOTSPUR	2-2	Stein, Nwajiobi	17511	2		12		6					5		9		7		4		10			11	1	8		3		
25		23	Newcastle United	0-1		24515	2				6					5		9		7		4		10			11	1	8		3		
26	Mar	2	SUNDERLAND	2-1	Harford, Hill	8019	2				6					5		9		7		4		10			11	1	8		3		
27		16	Sheffield Wednesday	1-1	Harford	18856	2				6					5		9		7		4		10			11	1	8		3		
28		19	Watford	0-3		14185	2				6					5		9		7		4		12	10		11	1	8		3		
29		23	QUEEN'S PARK RANGERS	2-0	Harford 2	9373	2				6					5		9		7		4		10			11	1	8		3		
30		30	IPSWICH TOWN	3-1	Harford 2, Nwajiobi	12640	2		12		6					5		9		7		4		10			11	1	8		3		
31	Apr	2	Southampton	0-1		14906	2		11		6					5		9		7		4		10				1	8		3		
32		8	Stoke City	4-0	Harford 2, Nwajiobi, Moss	7108	2				6							9		7	12	4		10			11	1	8		3		5
33		16	NORWICH CITY	3-1	Nwajiobi 2, Moss, (p)	8794	2				6					5				7	9	4		10			11	1	8		3		
34		21	MANCHESTER UNITED	2-1	Harford 2 (1p)	10320	2				6					5		9		7		4		10			11	1	8		3		
35		24	NOTTM. FOREST	1-2	Moss (p)	10156	2				6					5		9		7	10	4					11	1	8		3		
36		27	West Ham United	0-0		17303	2	9			6					5				7		4		10	12		11	1	8		3		
37	May	4	ARSENAL	3-1	Harford 2 (1p), Nwajiobi	12051	2				6					5		9		7		4		10	12		11	1	8		3		
38		6	Aston Villa	1-0	Stein	14130	2				6					5		9				4		10	7		11	1	8		3		12
39		8	Chelsea	0-2		13789	2	10			6					5						4			7			1	8	12	3		11
40		11	LEICESTER CITY	4-0	Nwajiobi, Preece, Stein, Harford	11802	2				6					5		9		7		4		10			11	1	8		3		
41		23	Coventry City	0-1		14834	2		12		6					5		9		7		4		10			11	1	8		3		
42		28	EVERTON	2-0	Nwajiobi, Hill	11509	2				6					5		9		7	12	4		10			11	1	8		3		
			Apps				35	20	7	13	42	2	9	12	3	25	9	22	6	39	19	19	7	29	20	21	26	42	1	36	2	24
			Goals					5	1		1		1	3		1		15		2	7			9	1	2		9				

F.A. Cup

	Date	Opponent	Score	Scorers	Att	Breacker T	Bunn FS	Daniel RC	Dibble A	Donaghy M	Droy M	Elliott PM	Elliott S	Findlay JW	Foster S	Grimes A	Harford M	Hilaire V	Hill RA	Moss DJ	Nicholas P	North S	Nwajiobi E	Parker GA	Preece D	Sealey L	Stein B	Stein M	Thomas MA	Todd C	Turner WL
R3	Jan 5	STOKE CITY	1-1	Foster	7270	2				6					5		9		7	11			12			1	8		3		4
rep	Jan 9	Stoke City	3-2	Hill, Harford, Donaghy	9917	2				6					5		9		7				11			1	8		3		4
R4	Jan 26	HUDDERSFIELD TOWN	2-0	Donaghy, B Stein	8712	2				6					5		9		7				12	11		1	8		3		4
R5	Mar 4	WATFORD	0-0		18506	2				6					5		9		7				10			1	8		3		4
rep	Mar 6	Watford	2-2	Nwajiobi, Hill	19867	2				6					5		9		7				10	12		1	8		3		4
rep2	Mar 9	WATFORD	1-0	Turner	15586	2				6					5		9		7				10	11		1	8		3		4
R6	Mar 13	MILLWALL	1-0	Stein	17470	2				6					5		9		7				10	11		1	8		3		4
SF	Apr 13	Everton	1-2	Hill	45289	2				6					5		9		7	12			10	11		1	8		3		4

Round 5 first replay and SF a.e.t. SF at Villa Park.

F.L. Cup (Milk Cup)

	Date	Opponent	Score	Scorers	Att	Breacker T	Bunn FS	Daniel RC	Dibble A	Donaghy M	Droy M	Elliott PM	Elliott S	Findlay JW	Foster S	Grimes A	Harford M	Hilaire V	Hill RA	Moss DJ	Nicholas P	North S	Nwajiobi E	Parker GA	Preece D	Sealey L	Stein B	Stein M	Thomas MA	Todd C	Turner WL
R2/1	Sep 25	Leyton Orient	4-1	Donaghy, B Stein 2, Parker	3080		9		1	6		5			3			10	7				11	12			8		2		4
R2/2	Oct 9	LEYTON O.	3-1	Bunn, B Stein, S Elliott	3374		10		1	6		5	9		3			12	7	11							8		2		4
R3	Oct 30	LEICESTER CITY	3-1	Moss, Williams (og), Donaghy	8015	2	10		1	6		5	9						7	11				12			8			4	3
R4	Nov 20	Sheffield Wednesday	2-4	S Elliott 2	18313	2	10			6	5		9	1				11	7			4		12			8				3

1985/86   9th in Division One

No	Date	Opponent	Score	Scorers	Att	Breacker T	Daniel RC	Dibble A	Donaghy M	Elliott PM	Foster S	Grimes A	Harford M	Hill RA	Johnson R	King AE	Newell M	Nicholas P	North M	North S	Nwajiobi E	Parker GA	Preece D	Sealey L	Stein B	Stein M	Thomas MA
1	Aug 17	NOTTM. FOREST	1-1	Stein	11318	2		1	6		5		9	7				4			10	12	11		8		3
2	21	Newcastle United	2-2	Nwajiobi, Harford	21933			1	6		5	3	9					4			10	7	11		8		2
3	24	West Ham United	1-0	Harford (p)	14004			1	6		5		9		2			4			10	7	11		8		3
4	27	ARSENAL	2-2	Nwajiobi, Stein	10012	2		1	6				9	7				4			10	5	11		8		3
5	31	Aston Villa	1-3	Stein	10524	2		1	6				9	7		5		4			10	12	11		8		3
6	Sep 7	CHELSEA	1-1	Harford	10720			1	6	12	5		9	7	2			4			10		11		8		3
7	14	Everton	0-2		25487	2		1	6		5		9	7				4			10	12	11		8		3
8	21	QUEEN'S PARK RANGERS	2-0	Harford, Foster	9508	2			6		5		9	7				4			12		11	1	8	10	3
9	28	Sheffield Wednesday	2-3	Harford 2	17877	2			6	12	5		9	7				4			10		11	1	8		3
10	Oct 1	IPSWICH TOWN	1-0	Nwajiobi	8553	2			6		5		9	7				4			10		11	1	8		3
11	5	MANCHESTER UNITED	1-1	Stein	17454	2			6	12	5			7				4	9		10		11	1	8		3
12	12	Oxford United	1-1	Stein	10609	2			6		5		9	7				4			10		11	1	8		3
13	19	SOUTHAMPTON	7-0	Nwajiobi, Stein 3(1p), Hill, Preece, Daniel	8876	2	12		6		5		9	7				4			10		11	1	8		3
14	26	Liverpool	2-3	Foster, Harford	31488	2	4		6		5	12	9	7	3						10		11	1			
15	Nov 2	BIRMINGHAM CITY	2-0	Stein, Harford	8550	2			6		5		9	7				4			10		11	1	8		3
16	9	Tottenham Hotspur	3-1	Harford, Stein, Hill	19163	2			6		5		9	7				4			10		11	1	8		3
17	16	COVENTRY CITY	0-1		9607	2			6		5		9	7				4			10	12	11	1	8		3
18	23	Watford	2-1	Thomas, Terry (og)	16197	2			6		5		9	7				4			10		11	1	8		3
19	30	MANCHESTER CITY	2-1	Stein 2	10096	2	12		6		5		9	7				4			10		11	1	8		3
20	Dec 7	NEWCASTLE UNITED	2-0	Harford, M North	10319	2			6		5		9	7			10	4	12				11	1	8		3
21	14	Nottingham Forest	0-2		12078	2			6		5		9				10	4	12			7	11	1	8		3
22	21	WEST HAM UNITED	0-0		14599	2			6		5		9	7				4	10				11	1	8		3
23	26	West Bromwich Albion	2-1	M North, Harford	12508	2			6		5		9	7				4	10				11	1	8		3
24	28	Ipswich Town	1-1	M North	15607	2			6				9	7				4	10	5			11	1	8		3
25	Jan 1	LEICESTER CITY	3-1	Harford 3	10917	2			6		5		9	7				4	10				11	1	8		3
26	11	Chelsea	0-1		21102	2	12		6		5			7			9	4	10				11	1	8		3
27	18	ASTON VILLA	2-0	Newell, Stein	10217	2			6		5			7			9	4	10				11	1	8		3
28	Feb 1	Arsenal	1-2	Harford	22459	2			6		5		9	7			10	4	12				11	1	8		3
29	8	Southampton	1-2	Newell, Stein	13740	2			6		5		9	7			10	4					11	1	8		3
30	22	Queen's Park Rangers	1-1	Newell	13252				6		5		9	7	2		8	4	10				11	1			3
31	Mar 1	SHEFFIELD WEDNESDAY	1-0	Harford	10206				6		5		9	7	2		8	4	10				11	1			3
32	15	OXFORD UNITED	1-2	Preece	10633	2			6		5		9	7			10	4	12				11	1		8	3
33	19	Manchester United	0-2		33646	10	11		6					7	2		9	4		5	12			1		8	3
34	22	EVERTON	2-1	Foster, Newell	11039	10			6		5			7	2		9	4					11	1		8	3
35	29	Leicester City	0-0		9912	10			6		5		9	7	2	8		4					11	1		12	3
36	Apr 1	WEST BROMWICH ALB.	3-0	Newell, Harford (p), Hill	9226	10			6		5		9	7	2		8	4					11	1			3
37	6	Birmingham City	2-0	Harford 2	8836	10			6		5		9	7	2	8		4					11	1			3
38	12	TOTTENHAM HOTSPUR	1-3	Newell	13141				6		5		9	7	2		10	4					11	1			3
39	16	LIVERPOOL	0-1		15503	12			6		5		9	7	2		10	4					11	1		8	3
40	19	Coventry City	0-1		10161	8			6		5		9	7	2		10	4					11	1		12	3
41	26	WATFORD	3-2	Harford 3	11810	2			6		5		9	7				4			10		11	1	8		3
42	May 3	Manchester City	1-1	Nwajiobi	20361	12			6		5			7	2		9	4			10		11	1	8		3
		Apps				36	5	7	42	6	35	3	37	38	15	3	16	41	13	2	21	8	41	35	33	6	41
		Goals					1				3		22	3			6		3		5		2		14		1

One own goal

F.A. Cup

Rd	Date	Opponent	Score	Scorers	Att	Breacker T	Daniel RC	Dibble A	Donaghy M	Elliott PM	Foster S	Grimes A	Harford M	Hill RA	Johnson R	King AE	Newell M	Nicholas P	North M	North S	Nwajiobi E	Parker GA	Preece D	Sealey L	Stein B	Stein M	Thomas MA
R3	Jan 6	Crystal Palace	2-1	B Stein, Preece	9886	2			6		5		9	7				4	10				11	1	8		3
R4	Jan 25	BRISTOL ROVERS	4-0	Hill, Harford, North, Parkin (og)	12463	2			6		5		9	7				4	10				11	1	8		3
R5	Feb 15	ARSENAL	2-2	Hill, Harford	15799				6		5		9	7	2			4	10		12		11	1	8		3
rep	Mar 3	Arsenal	0-0		26547				6		5		9	7	2		8	4	10				11	1			3
rep2	Mar 5	ARSENAL	3-0	M Stein, Foster, O'Leary (og)	13251				6		5		9	7	2		10	4					11	1		8	3
R6	Mar 8	EVERTON	2-2	M Stein, Harford	15529				6		5		9	7	2		10	4	12				11	1		8	3
rep	Mar 12	Everton	0-1		44264		12		6		5	10	9	7	2			4					11	1		8	3

R5 replay a.e.t.

F.L. Cup (Milk Cup)

Rd	Date	Opponent	Score	Scorers	Att	Breacker T	Daniel RC	Dibble A	Donaghy M	Elliott PM	Foster S	Grimes A	Harford M	Hill RA	Johnson R	King AE	Newell M	Nicholas P	North M	North S	Nwajiobi E	Parker GA	Preece D	Sealey L	Stein B	Stein M	Thomas MA
R2/1	Sep 24	Sheffield United	2-1	B Stein, Nwajiobi	8943	2			6		5		9	7				4			10		11	1	8		3
R2/2	Oct 8	SHEFFIELD UNITED	3-1	Hill, North, Preece	5660	2			6		5			7				4	9		10		11	1	8		3
R3	Oct 29	NORWICH CITY	0-2		8203	2	4		6		5	12	9	7	3						10		11	1	8		

1986/87   7th in Division One

#	Date	Opponent	Res	Scorers	Att	Breacker T	Cobb G	Dibble A	Donaghy M	Foster S	Grimes A	Harford M	Harvey R	Hill RA	Johnson R	McDonough D	McEvoy R	Newell M	Nicholas P	North M	North S	Nwajiobi E	Preece D	Sealey L	Stein B	Stein M	Wilson R
1	Aug 23	Leicester City	1-1	B Stein	9801	2			6	5				7	3			9	4	12			11	1	8		10
2	26	SOUTHAMPTON	2-1	Wilson, B Stein	8777	2			6	5				7	3			9	4				11	1	8		10
3	30	NEWCASTLE UNITED	0-0		9254	2			6	5				7	3			9	4				11	1	8		10
4	Sep 3	Aston Villa	1-2	B Stein	13122	2			6	5				7	3			9	4	12			11	1	8		10
5	6	Chelsea	3-1	Newell 2, B Stein	13040				6	5	3			7	2			9	4				11	1	8		10
6	13	ARSENAL	0-0		9876				6	5	3			7	2			9	4				11	1	8	12	10
7	20	West Ham United	0-2		19133				6	5	3			7	2			9	4				11	1	8	12	10
8	27	MANCHESTER CITY	1-0	B Stein	9371				6	5	3			7	2			9	4			11		1	8	10	
9	Oct 4	Tottenham Hotspur	0-0		22738				6	5	3			7	2			9	4			11		1	8		
10	11	NORWICH CITY	0-0		10022				6	5	3			7	2	12		9	4	10		11		1	8		
11	18	Manchester United	0-1		39927	2			6	5	3			7		12		9	4			11		1	8		10
12	25	LIVERPOOL	4-1	Newell 3, Hill	13140				6	5	3			7	2			9	4			11		1	8	10	12
13	Nov 1	QUEEN'S PARK RANGERS	1-0	Neill (og)	9085				6	5	3			7	2	12		9	4			11		1	8		
14	8	Wimbledon	1-0	M Stein	6181	2			6	5				7	3		11	9	4					1	8	10	12
15	15	NOTTM. FOREST	4-2	M Stein 2, Foster, B Stein	11097	2			6	5	11				3	12		9	4					1	8	10	7
16	22	Sheffield Wednesday	0-1		21171	2			6	5	11				3	7		9	4					1	8	10	12
17	29	CHARLTON ATHLETIC	1-0	M Stein	9273	2			6	5	3				2	11		9	4					1	8	10	7
18	Dec 6	Oxford United	2-4	B Stein, M Stein	8800	7			6	5	3				2	11		9	4	12				1	8	10	
19	13	EVERTON	1-0	Newell	11151	2			6	5	11				3	7		9	4					1	8	10	
20	20	Arsenal	0-3		28213	2			6		11		3	7				9	4		5			1	8	10	
21	26	WATFORD	0-2		11140	2			6		11		3	7		12		9	4		5			1	8	10	
22	28	Nottingham Forest	2-2	B Stein, Newell	20273	2			6	5	11	10			3			9	4					1	8	12	7
23	Jan 1	Coventry City	1-0	B Stein	16667	2			6	5	11	10			3			9	4					1	8		7
24	3	CHELSEA	1-0	Newell	10556	2			6	5	11	10			3			9	4					1	8		7
25	24	LEICESTER CITY	1-0	Newell	9102	2			6	5	11	10		7	3			9	4					1	8		
26	Feb 7	Newcastle United	2-2	Grimes, Breacker	22447	2			6	5	11	10			3			9	4					1	8		7
27	14	ASTON VILLA	2-1	Foster, Harford (p)	9174	2			6	5	11	10			3			9	4					1	8		7
28	21	Manchester City	1-1	B Stein	17507				6	5	3	10		7	2			9	4					1	8		11
29	28	WEST HAM UNITED	2-1	Nicholas, Grimes	11101				6	5	3	10		7	2			9	4					1	8		11
30	Mar 7	Liverpool	0-2		32433	2			6	5	11	10		7	3			9	4					1	8		12
31	14	MANCHESTER UNITED	2-1	Harford, B Stein	12509	2			6		11	10		7	3			9	4		5			1	8		
32	21	Norwich City	0-0		16142	2			6		11	10		7	3			9	4		5			1	8		
33	24	Southampton	0-3		12117	2			6		11	10		7	3	12		9	4		5			1	8		
34	28	TOTTENHAM HOTSPUR	3-1	Harford, Newell, McDonough	13447	2			6		3	10		7		11		9	4		5			1	8		
35	Apr 4	WIMBLEDON	0-0		9729	2			6			10	3	7		11		9	4		5			1	8		
36	11	Queen's Park Rangers	2-2	M Stein, Hill	9450	2			6				3	7				9	4		5		11	1	8	10	
37	18	COVENTRY CITY	2-0	B Stein, Newell	9380	2			6		3	10		7		12		9	4		5		11	1	8		
38	21	Watford	0-2		14650	2		1	6		3	10		7				9	4		5		11		8		
39	25	SHEFFIELD WEDNESDAY	0-0		9278	2			6		3	10		7				9	4		5		11	1	8	12	
40	May 2	Charlton Athletic	1-0	Harford	5469	2	8		6			10	3	7		12		9	4		5		11	1			
41	5	OXFORD UNITED	2-3	Newell, M Stein	8917		8		6				3	7	2	12		9	4		5		11	1		10	
42	9	Everton	1-3	M Stein	44097				6					7	2	3		9	4		5		11	1	8	10	12
		Apps				29	2	1	42	28	31	18	5	30	34	18	1	42	42	5	14	6	14	41	38	21	21
		Goals				1				2	2	4		2		1		12	1						12	8	1

One own goal

F.A. Cup

Rd	Date	Opponent	Res	Scorers	Att	Breacker T	Cobb G	Dibble A	Donaghy M	Foster S	Grimes A	Harford M	Harvey R	Hill RA	Johnson R	McDonough D	McEvoy R	Newell M	Nicholas P	North M	North S	Nwajiobi E	Preece D	Sealey L	Stein B	Stein M	Wilson R
R3	Jan 11	LIVERPOOL	0-0		11085				6	5	3	10		7	2			9	4				11	1	8		
rep	Jan 26	Liverpool	0-0		34822	2			6	5	11	10		7	3			9	4					1	8		
rep2	Jan 28	LIVERPOOL	3-0	B Stein, Harford, Newell	14687	2			6	5	11	10		7	3	12		9	4					1	8		
R4	Jan 31	QUEEN'S PARK RANGERS	1-1	Harford	12707	2			6	5	11	10		7	3			9	4					1	8		
R4	Feb 4	Queen's Park Rangers	1-2	Harford	15848	2			6	5	11	10		7	3			9	4					1	8		

R3 replay a.e.t.

F.L. Cup (Littlewoods Challenge Cup)

Excluded by the Football League because of the club's ban on away supporters

1987/88 — 9th in Division One

Football League Division One

#		Date	Opponent	Score	Scorers	Att.	Allinson I	Black K	Breacker T	Cobb G	Dibble A	Donaghy M	Foster S	Grimes A	Harford M	Hill RA	James J	Johnson M	Johnson R	McDonough D	Newell M	North S	Nwajiobi E	Oldfield D	Preece D	Sealey L	Stein B	Stein M	Weir M	Wilson D	Wilson R
1	Aug	15	Derby County	0-1		17204			2			6	5	3	9	4				14	12				11	1	8			7	10
2		18	COVENTRY CITY	0-1		7506			2				5	3	9	4				6	8	12			11	1				7	10
3		22	WEST HAM UNITED	2-2	Harford 2	8073			2	8			5	3	9	4				6	10	12			11	1				7	
4		29	Chelsea	0-3		16075			2	8		4	6	3	7						9		10		11	1					6
5		31	ARSENAL	1-1	Wilson (p)	6745			2			6	5	3		4					9		10		11	1	8	12		7	
6	Sep	5	Oxford United	5-2	Breacker,Harford,Hill,Nwajiobi,B Stein	6804			2			6	5	3	9	4				14			10		11	1	8	12		7	
7		12	EVERTON	2-1	Hill, B Stein	8124			2			6	5	3	9	4				14			10		11	1	8	12		7	
8		19	Charlton Athletic	0-1		5002			2			6	5		9	4				14	3				11	1	8	10	12	7	
9		26	Queen's Park Rangers	0-2		11175		11	2			6	5	3	9	4										1	8	10		7	
10	Oct	3	MANCHESTER UNITED	1-1	Harford	9137		11	2			6	5	3	9	4				14						1	8	12	10	7	
11		10	Portsmouth	1-3	Harford (p)	12391			2			6	5	3	9	4			10	14		12				1	8		11	7	
12		17	WIMBLEDON	2-0	B Stein, Wilson	7018	12	10	2			6	5	3	9					4						1	8		11	7	
13		24	LIVERPOOL	0-1		11997	10		2			6	5	3	9					4						1	8		11	7	
14	Nov	7	NEWCASTLE UNITED	4-0	Nwajiobi, B Stein, M Stein 2	7638	11		2			6	5	3						4			9			1	8	10		7	
15		14	Sheffield Wednesday	2-0	Allinson, M Stein	16960	11		2			6	5	3						4			9			1	8	10		7	
16		21	TOTTENHAM HOTSPUR	2-0	Allison 2	10091	11		2			6	5	3							7	4	9			1	8	10			
17	Dec	5	NORWICH CITY	1-2	B Stein	7002	11		2			6	5	3			12			4			9			1	8	10		7	
18		12	Watford	1-0	Foster	12152	11		2			6	5	3	9					4						1	8	10		7	
19		18	SOUTHAMPTON	2-2	Harford, McDonough	6618	11		2			6	5	3	12	9				4						1	8	10		7	
20		26	Everton	0-2		32128	11		2			6	5	3	9	10			14	4						1	8		12	7	
21		28	CHARLTON ATHLETIC	1-0	Wilson	7243	11		2			6	5						3	4						1	8	10		7	
22	Jan	1	CHELSEA	3-0	Harford, B Stein, M Stein	8018	11		2			6	5		9				3	4						1	8	10		7	
23		2	West Ham United	1-1	M Stein	16716	11		2			6	5		9				3	4						1	8	10		7	
24		16	DERBY COUNTY	1-0	McDonough	7175	11	9	2			6	5	12					3	4						1	8	10		7	
25	Feb	6	OXFORD UNITED	7-4	Harford 2,McDonough,B Stein,M Stein 3	8063	11		2			6	5	12	9				3	4						1	8	10		7	
26		13	Arsenal	1-2	M Stein	22612	11		2			6	5	3	9					4						1	8	10		7	
27	Mar	5	Wimbledon	0-2		4854	11		2			6		3	9			5		4						1	8	10		7	
28		15	Coventry City	0-4		13711	11	12	2	14		6	5	3	9				8	4						1		10		7	
29		29	PORTSMOUTH	4-1	B Stein,M Stein,Wilson,Mariner(og)	6740	11		2			6	5	3					9	4						1	8	10		7	
30	Apr	2	Newcastle United	0-4		20752	12	11	2			6	5	3	9				8	4				14		1		10		7	
31		5	SHEFFIELD WEDNESDAY	2-2	McDonough, B Stein	7337	12		2			6	5	3	9				11	4						1	8	10		7	
32		12	Manchester United	0-3		28830	11	12	2		1	6	5		9				3	4							8	10		7	
33		19	QUEEN'S PARK RANGERS	2-1	Foster, Wilson (p)	6735			2		1		5		9			6	3	4					11		8	10		7	
34		30	Norwich City	2-2	M Stein, Wilson (p)	13171	9	11	2		1	6	5	10		4			14	3					12			8		7	
35	May	2	WATFORD	2-1	Oldfield. Wilson (p)	10409	8	11	2		1		5	3		10		6		4					9					7	
36		4	Tottenham Hotspur	1-2	Grimes	15437	9		2	12	1		5	10				6		3						7	8	11		4	
37		7	Southampton	1-1	Wilson	12722	12	11	2	8	1		5	3				14	6	4							10	9		7	
38		9	Liverpool	1-1	Oldfield	30374	8	11	2	12	1		5	4				14	6	3							9	10		7	
39		13	NOTTM. FOREST	1-1	Donaghy	9108		11	2		1	6	5	3	9				12	4							8	10		7	
40		15	Nottingham Forest	1-1	Oldfield	21055	11	12	2	4	1		5						14	6	3						9	10		7	
			Apps				27	13	40	7	9	32	39	33	25	17	3	9	25	27	5	1	12	8	13	31	28	25	8	38	3
			Goals				3		1			1	2	1	9	2				4			2	3			9	11		8	

One own goal

F.A. Cup

Rd		Date	Opponent	Score	Scorers	Att.	Allinson I	Breacker T	Donaghy M	Foster S	Grimes A	Harford M	Johnson R	McDonough D	Sealey L	Stein B	Stein M	Weir M	Wilson D	Black K	Dibble A
R3	Jan	9	Hartlepool United	2-1	Weir, McDonough	6187	11	2	6	5			3	4	1	8	10	9	7		
R4	Jan	30	SOUTHAMPTON	2-1	Allinson, B Stein	10009	11	2	6	5		(12)	3	4	1	8	10		7		
R5	Feb	20	Queen's Park Rangers	1-1	Harford	15856	11	2	6	5	3	9		4	1	8	10		7		
rep	Feb	24	QUEEN'S PARK RANGERS	1-0	Neill (og)	10854	11	2	6	5	3	9		4	1	8	10		7		
R6	Mar	12	PORTSMOUTH	3-1	Wilson, M Stein, Harford	12857	11	2	6	5	3	9	8	4	1		10		7		
SF	Apr	9	Wimbledon	1-2	Harford	25963		2	6	5	3	9	11	4		8	10		7	12	1

SF at White Hart Lane

F.L. Cup (Littlewoods Challenge Cup)

Rd		Date	Opponent	Score	Scorers	Att.	Black K	Breacker T	Donaghy M	Foster S	Grimes A	Harford M	Hill RA	Johnson R	McDonough D	North S	Nwajiobi E	Oldfield D	Preece D	Sealey L	Stein B	Stein M	Weir M	Wilson D
R2/1	Sep	22	Wigan Athletic	1-0	Weir	5018		2	6	5		9	4		3	12			11	1	8		10	7
R2/2	Oct	6	WIGAN ATHLETIC	4-2	Harford 3, McDonough	4240	10	2	6	5	3	9			4					1	8		11	7
R3	Oct	27	COVENTRY CITY	3-1	Harford 2, Weir	11448		2	6	5	3	9		10	4					1	8		11	7
R4	Nov	17	Ipswich Town	1-0	B Stein	15643	12	2	6	5				10	4		9	14		1	8	11		7
R5	Jan	19	BRADFORD CITY	2-0	Foster, Harford	11022		2	6	5		9		3	4					1	8	10		7
SF1	Feb	10	Oxford United	1-1	B Stein	12943		2	6	5	11	9		3	4					1	8	10		7
SF2	Feb	28	OXFORD UNITED	2-0	B Stein, Grimes	13010		2	6	5	3	9		11	4					1	8	10		7
F	Apr	24	Arsenal	3-2	B Stein 2, Wilson	95732		2	6	5	14	9	4	3				10		(Dibble 1)	8	12		7

Played at 3 in R4: R Harvey

Full Members Cup (Simod Cup)

Rd		Date	Opponent	Score	Scorers	Att.	Allinson I	Black K	Breacker T	Cobb G	Dibble A	Donaghy M	Foster S	Grimes A	Harford M	Johnson M	Johnson R	McDonough D	Oldfield D	Preece D	Sealey L	Stein B	Stein M	Wilson D
R3	Feb	16	Everton	2-1	Oldfield 2	5204	6	10	2	7	1		5	11			3		9					
QF	Mar	1	STOKE CITY	4-1	Harford 2, B.Stein 2	4580	11	7	2				6		9	5		4		12	1	8	10	
SF		8	SWINDON TOWN	2-1	B.Stein, M.Stein	10027	11	12	2					3	9		4	5			1	8	10	7
F		27	Reading	1-4	Harford	61740	11	14	2			6	5	3	9		12	4			1	8	10	7

SF a.e.t.
Final at Wembley Stadium

Played in R3: R McEvoy (4), Paul Gray (8, substituted), R Harvey (12)
Played in QF: R Harvey (3)

1988/89   16th in Division One

Player columns (left→right): Allinson I · Beaumont D · Black K · Breacker T · Chamberlain A · Cooke R · Donaghy M · Dowie I · Dreyer J · Foster S · Grimes A · Harford M · Harvey R · Hill RA · James J · Johnson M · Johnson R · McDonough D · Meade R · Oldfield D · Preece D · Sealey L · Wegerle R · Williams S · Wilson D

#	Date	Opponent	Score	Scorers	Att	Al	Be	Bl	Br	Ch	Co	Do	Dw	Dr	Fo	Gr	Ha	Hv	Hi	Ja	JM	JR	Mc	Me	Ol	Pr	Se	We	Wm	Wl
1	Aug 27	Sheffield Wednesday	0-1		16433	12		11	2			6		3	5		9								10		1	8	4	7
2	Sep 3	WIMBLEDON	2-2	Black, Ryan (og)	8067			11				6			5	3	9					2			10		1	8	4	7
3	10	Southampton	1-2	Foster	13214			11				6			5	3	9					2			8	10	1	12	4	7
4	17	MANCHESTER UNITED	0-2		11010			11							5	3	9		10		6	2			8		1	12	4	7
5	24	Everton	2-0	Black, Oldfield	26002	14		11	12			6		3	5		9								10		1	8	4	7
6	Oct 1	Nottingham Forest	0-0		15340	12		11				6		3	5		9								10		1	8	4	7
7	8	LIVERPOOL	1-0	Harford	12117			11				6		3	5		9								10		1	8	12	7
8	22	Middlesbrough	1-2	Wilson (p)	17792			11	12					3	5		9				6				10		1	8	14	7
9	25	ARSENAL	1-1	Black	10548			11	3						5		9				6	2		4	12		1	8		7
10	29	QUEEN'S PARK RANGERS	0-0		8453	9		11							5	3					6	2			10	12	1	8		7
11	Nov 5	Millwall	1-3	Wilson	12511			11							5	3			10	2	6			12	8		1	9	4	7
12	12	Coventry City	0-1		12625			11							5	3	9		10		6	2			12	4	1	8		7
13	19	WEST HAM UNITED	4-1	Black 2, Wegerle, Wilson	9308			11							5	3	9				6	2			10	4	1	8		7
14	26	Norwich City	2-2	Wegerle 2	13541			11							5		9	3			6	2			10	4	1	8		7
15	Dec 3	NEWCASTLE UNITED	0-0		8338	12		11							5			3	10		6	2			9	4	1	8		7
16	10	Derby County	1-0	Harford	15228			11							5		9	3	10		6	2			12	4	1	8		7
17	17	ASTON VILLA	1-1	Wegerle	8785			11							5		9	3	10		6	2				4	1	8		7
18	26	Tottenham Hotspur	0-0		27337		12								5		9	3	10		6	2			11	4	1	8		7
19	31	Wimbledon	0-4		4899		12								5		9	3	10		6	2			11	4	1	8		7
20	Jan 2	SOUTHAMPTON	6-1	Black, Harford 2, Hill, Wegerle 2	8637			11							5		9	3	10		6	2				4	1	8		7
21	14	Charlton Athletic	0-3		5212			11	12				14				9	3	10		6	2				4	1	8		7
22	21	EVERTON	1-0	Wegerle	9013			11	2				14	6	5	3	9		10				12			4	1			7
23	Feb 4	NOTTM. FOREST	2-3	Black, Harford	10465			11	2					6	5	3	9		10						12	4	1			7
24	18	MIDDLESBROUGH	1-0	Foster	8187	6		11	2						5	3	9		10							4	1			7
25	25	Arsenal	0-2		31026	6		11	2						5		9	3	10							4	1			7
26	Mar 11	MILLWALL	1-2	Wilson (p)	10722	6		11	2				12	14		3	9		10					5		4	1			7
27	14	Liverpool	0-5		31447	6		11	2				12			3	9		10		5			8		4	1			
28	18	SHEFFIELD WEDNESDAY	0-1		7776	6		11	2				12		5	3	9		10						8	4	1			7
29	21	Queen's Park Rangers	1-1	Hill	9072	6		11	2						5		9	3	10							4	1	8		7
30	25	Manchester United	0-2		36335	6		11	2	12			14		5		9	3	10							4	1	8		7
31	28	TOTTENHAM HOTSPUR	1-3	Foster	11146	6		11	2	12			8		5	3	9		10							4	1			7
32	Apr 1	Aston Villa	1-2	Hill	15640	6		11	2				14		5	3	9								7	12	1	8		4
33	15	COVENTRY CITY	2-2	Dreyer, Wilson	8610	6		11	2				12	3					10							9	1	8		7
34	22	Newcastle United	0-0		18636	6		11	2	1				3	5		9		10				14	12		4		8		7
35	29	DERBY COUNTY	3-0	Wilson (p), Harford, Black	8507	6		11	2	12				3	5		9		10							4	1	8		7
36	May 2	CHARLTON ATHLETIC	5-2	Wilson 2, Walsh (og), Harford, Wegerle	10024	6		11	2	12				3	5		9		10							4	1	8		7
37	6	West Ham United	0-1		18686	6		11	2	12				3	5		9		10							4	1	8		7
38	13	NORWICH CITY	1-0	Wilson (p)	10862	6		11	2					3	5		9		10							4	1	8		7
		Apps				5	15	37	22	6	6	6	8	18	36	12	33	12	33	1	16	21	10	4	21	26	32	30	10	37
		Goals					8							1	3		7		3						1			8		9

Two own goals

F.A. Cup

Rd	Date	Opponent	Score	Scorers	Att	Al	Be	Bl	Br	Ch	Co	Do	Dw	Dr	Fo	Gr	Ha	Hv	Hi	Ja	JM	JR	Mc	Me	Ol	Pr	Se	We	Wm	Wl
R3	Jan 7	Millwall	2-3	Black, Wilson (p)	12504			11							5		9	3	10	12	6	2			14	4	1	8		7

F.L. Cup (Littlewoods Challenge Cup)

Rd	Date	Opponent	Score	Scorers	Att	Al	Be	Bl	Br	Ch	Co	Do	Dw	Dr	Fo	Gr	Ha	Hv	Hi	Ja	JM	JR	Mc	Me	Ol	Pr	Se	We	Wm	Wl
R2/1	Sep 27	BURNLEY	1-1	R Johnson	6282			11	12			6		3	5		9					2			10		1	8		7
R2/2	Oct 11	Burnley	1-0	Hill	14036	14		11	12			6		3	5		9					2			10		1	8		7
R3	Nov 2	Leeds United	2-0	Wilson, Oldfield	19450	14		11						3	5	12			10		2				6		1	9	4	7
R4	Nov 29	MANCHESTER CITY	3-1	Oldfield, Wegerle 2	10178			11							5		9	3	12		2		6		10	4	1	8		7
R5	Jan 18	SOUTHAMPTON	1-1	Hill	11735			11	2				9		6	6	5	3							10		1	8		7
rep	Jan 25	Southampton	2-1	Harford, Hill	10250			11	2						6	5	3		9						10	12	4	1	8	7
SF1	Feb 12	West Ham United	3-0	Harford, Wegerle, Wilson (p)	24602	6		11	2						5	3	9									4	1	8		7
SF2	Mar 1	WEST HAM UNITED	2-0	Harford, Wegerle	12020	6		11	2						5	3	9									4	1	8		7
F	Apr 9	Nottingham Forest	1-3	Harford	76130	6		11	2						5	3	9							12		4	1	8		7

R5 replay a.e.t. Final at Wembley Stadium.

Full Members Cup (Simod Cup)

Rd	Date	Opponent	Score	Scorers	Att	Al	Be	Bl	Br	Ch	Co	Do	Dw	Dr	Fo	Gr	Ha	Hv	Hi	Ja	JM	JR	Mc	Me	Ol	Pr	Se	We	Wm	Wl
R3	Jan 10	Crystal Palace	1-4	Dowie	5842	6		10	2						5	11							12			3			9	

Also played: A Dibble (1), R McEvoy (4), G Cobb (7), Paul Gray (8)

1989/90 17th in Division One

#		Date	Opponent	Score	Scorers	Att	Allpress T	Beaumont D	Black K	Breacker T	Chamberlain A	Cooke R	Donaghy M	Dowie I	Dreyer J	Elstrup L	Farrell S	Gray Paul	Harford M	Harvey R	Hughes C	James J	Johnson M	Kennedy M	McDonough D	Nogan K	Poutch N	Preece D	Rees J	Rodger G	Wegerle R	Williams S	Wilson D
1	Aug	19	Tottenham Hotspur	1-2	Wegerle	17668		6	11	2	1			14	3					12			7	5				10			8	4	9
2		22	SHEFFIELD WEDNESDAY	2-0	Wilson (p), Black	9503		6	11	2	1				3	12							7	5				10			8	4	9
3		26	LIVERPOOL	0-0		11124		6	11	2	1				3	12				14			7	5				10			8	4	9
4		30	Queen's Park Rangers	0-0		10565		6	11	2	1				3	12							7	5				10			8	4	9
5	Sep	9	CHARLTON ATHLETIC	1-0	Wilson (p)	8859		6	11	2	1				3	9							7	5				10			8		4
6		16	Coventry City	0-1		11207		6	11	2	1	14			3	9				12			7	5				10			8		4
7		23	WIMBLEDON	1-1	Wegerle (p)	8449		6	11	2	1	14			3	9				12			7	5				10			8		4
8		30	Manchester City	1-3	Black	23863		6	11	2	1	14			3	9				5			7		12			10			8		4
9	Oct	14	ASTON VILLA	0-1		9433		6	11	2	1	14			3	9				12								10		5	8	7	4
10		21	NORWICH CITY	4-1	Black, Dreyer, Wilson, Williams	9038		6	11	2	1	14			3	9				12								10		5	8	7	4
11		28	Millwall	1-1	Elstrup	11140		6	11	2	1	14			3	9				12					5			10			8	7	4
12	Nov	4	DERBY COUNTY	1-0	Dowie	8919		6	11	2	1			8	3	9									5			10					12
13		11	Crystal Palace	1-1	Wilson	11346		6	11	2	1			8	3	9				12					5			10			14	7	4
14		18	MANCHESTER UNITED	1-3	Wilson	11414			11	2	1			9	6	12				3					5			10			8	7	4
15		25	Southampton	3-6	Dreyer, Black, Elstrup	14014			11	2	1			9	6	8				3		12			5			10				7	4
16	Dec	2	TOTTENHAM HOTSPUR	0-0		12620			11	2	1			9	6	14				3					5			10			12	7	4
17		9	Sheffield Wednesday	1-1	James	16339				2	1	12		9	6	10				3		8	5					11				7	4
18		16	Arsenal	2-3	Elstrup 2 (1p)	28760			11	2	1	14	5	9	6	10			12	3		8	4									7	
19		26	NOTTM. FOREST	1-1	Cooke	10754			11	2	1	14	5	9	6	10				3		8	4		12								7
20		30	CHELSEA	0-3		10068			11	2	1	7	5	9	6					12			4					10					8
21	Jan	1	Everton	1-2	Wilson (p)	21755				2	1		5	9	6				11	12	3	8	4					10	14				7
22		13	Liverpool	2-2	Black, Nogan	35312			11	2	1		5		6				9	3			4			8		10					7
23		20	QUEEN'S PARK RANGERS	1-1	Preece	9703			11	2	1			9	6					3		8	4		5	12		10					7
24	Feb	14	Wimbledon	1-1	Nogan, Dowie	3618			11	2	1			9	6	12				3			4		5	8		10					
25		19	Charlton Athletic	0-2		6201			11	2	1			9	6	12				3		8	4		5	14		10					
26		24	SOUTHAMPTON	1-1	Dowie	9417			11	2	1			9	6					3		8	4		5			10					12
27	Mar	3	Manchester United	1-4	Black	35237			11	2	1			9	6					3		8	12		5			10					4
28		7	COVENTRY CITY	3-2	Black, Gray, Dowie	8244			11	2	1			9	6			14		3		8	12		5			10					4
29		10	Aston Villa	0-2		22505	3	11		2	1			9	6			14			10	4		5		8		12					7
30		17	MANCHESTER CITY	1-1	Wilson (p)	9765			11	2	1			9	6			12		3		8	4		5			10					14
31		24	MILLWALL	2-1	McCarthy (og), Black	9027			11	2	1			9	6				8	3			4		5			10					7
32		31	Norwich City	0-2		14451			11	2	1			9	6							8	4		5			10	3				12
33	Apr	7	Chelsea	0-1		13114		12	11	2	1	8		9	6					14			4		5			10	3				
34		14	EVERTON	2-2	Dowie 2	9538		12	11	2	1	14		9	6								4		5			10	3		8		
35		16	Nottingham Forest	0-3		17001		12	11	2	1			9	6								4		5			10	3		8		
36		21	ARSENAL	2-0	Dowie, Black	11595		4	11	2	1			9	6	14							12		5			10	3		8		
37		28	CRYSTAL PALACE	1-0	Dowie	10369		4	11	2	1			9	6	14									5	12		10	3		8		
38	May	5	Derby County	3-2	Breacker, Black 2	17044		4	11	2	1			9	6	14									5		12	10	3		8		
Apps							1	19	36	38	38	11	5	29	38	23	1	7	4	26	1	20	12	32	15	10	1	32	14	2	15	14	35
Goals									11	1		1		8	2	4		1				1				2		1			2	1	7

ne own goal

F.A. Cup

		Date	Opponent	Score	Scorers	Att	Allpress T	Beaumont D	Black K	Breacker T	Chamberlain A	Cooke R	Donaghy M	Dowie I	Dreyer J	Elstrup L	Farrell S	Gray Paul	Harford M	Harvey R	Hughes C	James J	Johnson M	Kennedy M	McDonough D	Nogan K	Poutch N	Preece D	Rees J	Rodger G	Wegerle R	Williams S	Wilson D
R3	Jan	6	Brighton & Hove Albion	1-4	Wilson	10361			11	2	1			12	6				9	3		4	5	8				10					7

F.L. Cup (Littlewoods Challenge Cup)

		Date	Opponent	Score	Scorers	Att	Allpress T	Beaumont D	Black K	Breacker T	Chamberlain A	Cooke R	Donaghy M	Dowie I	Dreyer J	Elstrup L	Farrell S	Gray Paul	Harford M	Harvey R	Hughes C	James J	Johnson M	Kennedy M	McDonough D	Nogan K	Poutch N	Preece D	Rees J	Rodger G	Wegerle R	Williams S	Wilson D
R2/1	Sep	19	Mansfield Town	4-3	Wegerle 2, Elstrup 2	5361		6	12	2	1				3	9							7	5				10			8	11	4
R2/2	Oct	3	MANSFIELD TOWN	7-2	Wegerle 2, Peece, Elstrup 3, Dreye	6519		6	11	2	1				3	9							7					10		5	8		4
R3	Oct	24	Everton	0-3		18428		6	11	2	1			12	3	9				7		14		5				10			8		4

Full Members Cup (Zenith Data Systems Cup)

		Date	Opponent	Score	Scorers	Att	Allpress T	Beaumont D	Black K	Breacker T	Chamberlain A	Cooke R	Donaghy M	Dowie I	Dreyer J	Elstrup L	Farrell S	Gray Paul	Harford M	Harvey R	Hughes C	James J	Johnson M	Kennedy M	McDonough D	Nogan K	Poutch N	Preece D	Rees J	Rodger G	Wegerle R	Williams S	Wilson D
R1	Nov	8	Oxford United	3-2	Dowie 2, Gray	1754		6		2	1	7		9				12		3			5		10			11			8		4
R2		27	Crystal Palace	1-4	Dowie	3747		5		2	1	12		8	6				14	3		9	7					10					4

R1 a.e.t.

A Tighe played in R1 (at 14) and R2 (at 11)

1990/91 18th in Division One

Division One

#	Date		Opponent	Score	Scorers	Att.
1	Aug	25	CRYSTAL PALACE	1-1	Dowie	9583
2		29	Arsenal	1-2	Elstrup	32723
3	Sep	1	Southampton	2-1	Elstrup 2	13538
4		4	MANCHESTER UNITED	0-1		12576
5		8	LEEDS UNITED	1-0	Black	10185
6		15	Queen's Park Rangers	1-6	Hughes	10196
7		22	COVENTRY CITY	1-0	Dowie	8336
8		29	Norwich City	3-1	Elstrup 3	12794
9	Oct	20	Sunderland	0-2		20035
10		27	EVERTON	1-1	Elstrup	10047
11	Nov	3	Derby County	1-2	Black	15008
12		10	Liverpool	0-4		35207
13		17	MANCHESTER CITY	2-2	Dowie, Dreyer (p)	9564
14		24	ASTON VILLA	2-0	Black, Elstrup	10071
15	Dec	1	Nottingham Forest	2-2	Elstrup 2	16498
16		8	ARSENAL	1-1	Dreyer (p)	12506
17		16	Crystal Palace	0-1		15579
18		22	Tottenham Hotspur	1-2	Dowie	27007
19		26	SHEFFIELD UNITED	0-1		10004
20		29	CHELSEA	2-0	Cundy (og), Black	12005
21	Jan	1	Wimbledon	0-2		4592
22		12	SOUTHAMPTON	3-4	Elstrup, James, Dreyer (p)	9021
23		19	Leeds United	1-2	Elstrup	27010
24	Feb	2	QUEEN'S PARK RANGERS	1-2	Black	8479
25		23	LIVERPOOL	3-1	Black, Dowie 2	12032
26	Mar	2	NOTTM. FOREST	1-0	Dowie	9577
27		5	Manchester City	0-3		20404
28		9	Aston Villa	2-1	Mountfield (og), Pembridge	20587
29		13	Coventry City	1-2	Rodger	9725
30		16	NORWICH CITY	0-1		8604
31		23	Manchester United	1-4	Preece	41752
32		30	Sheffield United	1-2	Elstrup	18481
33	Apr	1	TOTTENHAM HOTSPUR	0-0		11322
34		6	Chelsea	3-3	Elstrup, Farrell, Black	9416
35		13	WIMBLEDON	0-1		8219
36		20	SUNDERLAND	1-2	Rodger	11157
37	May	4	Everton	0-1	20134
38		11	DERBY COUNTY	2-0	Harford (og), Elstrup	12889

Appearances and goals

	Beaumont D	Black K	Breacker T	Chamberlain A	Dowie I	Dreyer J	Elstrup L	Farrell S	Harvey R	Holsgrove P	Hughes C	James J	Johnson M	McDonough D	Nogan K	Pembridge M	Preece D	Rees J	Rodger G	Telfer P	Williams S
Apps	33	37	8	38	29	38	37	20	29	1	17	17	26	26	9	18	37	21	14	1	16
Goals		7			7	3	15	1			1	1				1	1	2			

Three own goals

F.A. Cup

	Date		Opponent	Score	Scorers	Att.
R3	Jan	5	Sheffield United	3-1	Elstrup 2, Farrell	13948
R4	Jan	26	WEST HAM UNITED	1-1	Black	12087
rep	Jan	30	West Ham United	0-5		25659

F.L. Cup (Rumbelows Cup)

	Date		Opponent	Score	Scorers	Att.
R2/1	Sep	25	BRADFORD CITY	1-1	Harvey	5120
R2/2	Oct	10	Bradford City	1-1	Black	6180

Lost 4-5 on penalties a.e.t.

Full Members Cup (Zenith Data Systems Cup)

	Date		Opponent	Score	Scorers	Att.
R2	Dec	19	WEST HAM UTD.	5-1	Farrell 2, Rees, Elstrup, Black	5759
R3	Feb	18	Chelsea	1-1	Dreyer	3849
SFS		26	Crystal Palace	1-3	Rees	7170

R3 won 4-1 on penalties a.e.t.   Played in SFS: M Jackson (12)

1991/92   20th in Division One: Relegated

#	Date	Opponent	Score	Scorers	Att	Beaumont D	Black K	Campbell J	Chamberlain A	Dreyer J	Farrell S	Gray Phil	Harford M	Harvey R	Hughes C	Jackson M	James J	Kamara C	Linton D	McDonough D	Nogan K	Oakes S	Peake T	Pembridge M	Preece D	Rees J	Rodger G	Salton D	Stein B	Sutton S	Telfer P	Thompson S	Varadi I	Williams M
1	Aug 17	West Ham United	0-0		25079	2	11		1	6	7	12		3						4				10	8		5		9					
2	21	Coventry City	0-5		9848	2	11		1	6	7	12		3						4				10	8		5		9					
3	24	LIVERPOOL	0-0		11132	2	11		1	6		7		3						4				10	8		5		9					
4	27	Arsenal	0-2		25898	2	11		1	3	14	7					12			4			6	10	8		5		9					
5	31	Chelsea	1-4	Gray	17457	2			1	3	11	7					12			4	14		6	10	8		5		9					
6	Sep 4	SOUTHAMPTON	2-1	Gray, Harvey	8055	12			1	5		7		3			2			4	14		6	10	8						11			
7	7	Wimbledon	0-3		3231				1	5		7		3			2			4	9		6	10	8					14	12			
8	14	OLDHAM ATHLETIC	2-1	Harford 2	9005				1	3			9				2			4	14		6	10	7				8			12	11	
9	17	QUEEN'S PARK RANGERS	0-1		9185				1	3			9				2				12		6	10	7				8			14	11	
10	21	Manchester United	0-5		46491	14			1	3			9				2				12		6	10	7				8			4	11	
11	28	NOTTS COUNTY	1-1	Gray	7629	6			1	3		8		9		12	2				14			10	7		5					4	11	
12	Oct 5	Aston Villa	0-4		18722	12			1	3			8			11	2				9		6	10	7		5		14			4		
13	19	SHEFFIELD WEDNESDAY	2-2	Harford, Nogan	9401				1	5			8	9	3	12	2						6	10	11				14		7			
14	26	Norwich City	0-1		10514				1	3					14	4	8	12			9	11	5	10	7	6							2	
15	Nov 2	EVERTON	0-1		8002				1	5			10	9	8	2		4			14	11	6	3					12				7	
16	16	Tottenham Hotspur	1-4	Harford	27543				1	5			9	3				2	4	2		11	6	10					8				7	
17	23	MANCHESTER CITY	2-2	Harford, Dreyer	10031				1	5			9	3				2	4	2		11	6	10	12				8				7	
18	30	Sheffield United	1-1	Telfer	21804			11		5			9	3				2	4				6	10	12				8	1	7			
19	Dec 7	LEEDS UNITED	0-2		11550			14		5			9	3				2	4			11		10	12				8	1	7			
20	20	COVENTRY CITY	1-0	Harford	7533					5			9	3				2	4			11	6	10	12				8	1	7			
21	26	ARSENAL	1-0	Harford	12665					5			9	3				2	4			12	6	10	11				8	1	7			
22	28	CHELSEA	2-0	Harford, Dreyer (p)	10738			12		5			9	3				2	4			14	6	10	11				8	1	7			
23	Jan 1	Nottingham Forest	1-1	Pembridge	23809			14		5			9	3				2	4			12	6	10	11				8	1	7			
24	11	Liverpool	1-2	Tanner (og)	35095					5				3				2	4		9	12	6	10	11				8	1	7			
25	18	WEST HAM UNITED	0-1		11088			14		5				3				2	4		9	12	6	10	11				8	1	7			
26	Feb 1	Sheffield Wednesday	2-3	Preece, Oakes	22291					5			9	3	12		2	4				7	6	10	11				8	1				
27	8	NORWICH CITY	2-0	Preece, Harford	8554					5			9	3	8		2	4				7	6	10	11				12	1				
28	15	Manchester City	0-4		22137					5			9	3	12		2	4				14	6	10	11				8	1	7			
29	22	SHEFFIELD UNITED	2-1	Stein, Harford	9003			12		5			9	3	14		2	4				7	6	10	11				8	1				
30	25	Crystal Palace	1-1	Pembridge (p)	12109			14		5			9	3	12		2	4				7	6	10	11				8	1				
31	29	Leeds United	0-2		28227			8		5			9	3	7		2	4					6	10	11				12	1	14			
32	Mar 7	CRYSTAL PALACE	1-1	Oakes	8591			9		5				3	12		2	4				7	6	10	11				8					
33	11	TOTTENHAM HOTSPUR	0-0		11494			9		5				3	7		2	4					6	10	11				8					
34	14	Everton	1-1	Stein	17388			14		5			9	3	12		2	4					6	10	11		7		8					
35	21	Southampton	1-2	Pembridge	14192					5			9	3	12		2	4					6	10	11		7		8					14
36	Apr 4	WIMBLEDON	2-1	Varadi, Preece	7753				1	5			9	3			2	4					6	10	11				8				7	
37	11	Oldham Athletic	1-5	Harford	13210				1	5			9	3	14		2	4					6	10	11		12		8				7	
38	14	NOTTM. FOREST	2-1	Harford, James	8014				1	5			9	3	14		2	4	14				6	10	11				8				7	
39	18	MANCHESTER UNITED	1-1	Harford	13410				1	5			9	3	12		2	4				8	6	10	11				14					
40	20	Queen's Park Rangers	1-2	Pembridge (p)	10749				1	5			9	3	12		2	4				8	6	10	11						14			
41	25	ASTON VILLA	2-0	Stein, Pembridge	11178				1	5			9	3			2	4				7	6	10	11			3	8					
42	May 2	Notts County	1-2	James	11380				1	5			12	9			2	4				7	6	10	11	14		3	8					

Played in game 6 at 9 (substituted): L Glover
Played in game 7 at 11 (substituted): P Holsgrove
Played in 4 games 32, 33, 34, 35 at 1: M Day

| | | | | | Apps | 9 | 4 | 11 | 24 | 42 | 4 | 14 | 29 | 32 | 18 | 9 | 28 | 28 | 3 | 9 | 14 | 21 | 38 | 42 | 38 | 5 | 12 | 3 | 39 | 14 | 20 | 5 | 6 | 1 |
| | | | | | Goals | | | | | 2 | | 3 | 12 | 2 | | | 2 | | | | 1 | 2 | | 5 | 3 | | | | 3 | | 1 | | 1 | 1 |

One own goal

F.A. Cup

| R3 | Jan 4 | Sheffield United | 0-4 | | 12201 | | 12 | | 1 | 5 | | | | 3 | | | 2 | 4 | | | | 9 | 6 | 10 | 11 | | | | 8 | | 7 | | | |

F.L. Cup (Rumbelows Cup)

| R2/1 | Sep 25 | BIRMINGHAM CITY | 2-2 | Gray, Nogan | 6315 | 6 | | | 1 | 3 | | 9 | | | | | 2 | | | | 12 | | | 10 | 7 | | 5 | 14 | 8 | | | 4 | 11 | |
| R2/2 | Oct 8 | Birmingham City | 2-3 | Gray 2 | 13252 | 5 | | | 1 | | | 8 | 9 | 3 | | | 2 | | | | 12 | | | 10 | 11 | | | | 14 | | 7 | 4 | | |

Full Members Cup (Zenith Data Systems Cup)

| R2 | Oct 22 | Ipswich Town | 1-1 | Telfer | 5750 | | | 1 | 14 | | | 9 | | | 4 | | | 8 | | | 10 | | | 11 | 12 | 6 | 5 | | 2 | | | | | 7 |

Lost 1-2 on penalties   Also played: T Allpress (3)

1992/93   20th in Division One of the "new" Football League

No	Date	Opponent	Res	Scorers	Att	Benjamin I	Campbell J	Chamberlain A	Claridge S	Dixon K	Dreyer J	Gray P	Greene D	Harvey R	Hughes C	James J	Johnson M	Kamara C	Linton D	Matthew D	Oakes S	Peake T	Petterson A	Preece D	Rees J	Salton D	Telfer P	Williams M
1	Aug 15	Leicester City	1-2	Campbell	17424		11	12			6	9			8	3		4	2		7	5	1	10				
2	22	BRISTOL CITY	0-3		7926		11		7		6	9			8	3	12	4	2		14	5	1	10				
3	29	Charlton Athletic	0-0		6291				7		6	9			8	3			2		12	5	1	10	11	4		
4	Sep 2	Newcastle United	0-2		27082	12			7		6	9				3			2		8	5	1	10	11	4		
5	5	TRANMERE ROVERS	3-3	Claridge, Linton, Oakes	6801	12			7		6	9				3			2		8	5	1	10	11	4		
6	13	Brentford	2-1	James, Gray	7413				7			9				3	6	8	2			5	1	10	11	4		
7	19	BIRMINGHAM CITY	1-1	Claridge (p)	8481	12			7			9				3	6	8	2		14	5	1	10	11	4		
8	26	Notts County	0-0		5992	14			7		6	9				3		8	2	5	12		1	10	11	4		
9	Oct 3	PORTSMOUTH	1-4	Dreyer	7954	14			7		6	9				3		8	2		12	5	1	10	11	4		
10	10	Barnsley	0-3		5261				7		6	9				3	5	8	2	14	12		1	10	11	4		
11	17	DERBY COUNTY	1-3	Johnson	8848	12			7			9				3	5	8	2		6		1	10	11	4		
12	24	Peterborough United	3-2	Gray 2, Telfer	7125				7			10				3	5	8	2		12	6	1	9		4	11	
13	31	SOUTHEND UNITED	2-2	James, Gray	7256				7			10				3	5	8	2		12	6	1	9		4	11	
14	Nov 3	Cambridge United	3-3	Oakes, Gray 2	5716				7			10				3	5	8	2		11	6	1	9		4		
15	7	GRIMSBY TOWN	1-4	Gray	6928	12		1	7			10				3	5	8	2		11	6		9		4	14	
16	14	Oxford United	0-4		5759			1	7			10				3	5		2		12	6		11	9	4	8	
17	21	MILLWALL	1-1	Gray	8371	8		1			2	10			5	3	14				12	6		11	9	4	7	
18	29	WATFORD	2-0	Benjamin, Oakes	8341	8		1			2	10			5	3	4				7	6		11	9			12
19	Dec 5	Bristol Rovers	0-2		6240	8		1			2	10			5	3	4		12		7	6		11	9			14
20	12	Wolverhampton Wan.	2-1	Gray 2	13932	14		1			2	10			5	3	4		12		7	6		11	9		8	
21	19	SUNDERLAND	0-0		8286	9		1			2	10			5	3	4		14		12	6		11	8		7	
22	28	West Ham United	2-2	Hughes, Dreyer	18786	14		1			2	10			5	3	4				12	6		11	9		8	7
23	Jan 9	Birmingham City	1-2	Hughes	9601			1			2	10			5	3	4				7	6		11	9		8	12
24	16	NOTTS COUNTY	0-0		6729	8		1			2	10			5	3	4				12	6		11	9		7	14
25	27	NEWCASTLE UNITED	0-0		10237	14		1			2	10			5	3	4				12	6		11	9		7	8
26	30	Bristol City	0-0		8877	14		1			2	10			5	3	4				12	6		11	9		7	8
27	Feb 6	LEICESTER CITY	2-0	Johnson, Gray	9140	14		1			2	10			5	3	4				9	6		11	12		7	8
28	9	BRENTFORD	0-0		7248			1			2	10			5	3	4				9	6		11			7	8
29	13	Tranmere Rovers	2-0	Gray, Johnson	8723			1			2	10			5	3	4				9	6		11	8		7	12
30	20	CHARLTON ATHLETIC	1-0	Gray	8443			1		8	2	10			5	3	4				9	6		11			7	
31	27	BARNSLEY	2-2	Dixon, Gray (p)	7595			1		8	2	10			5	3	4				9	6		11			7	12
32	Mar 6	Portsmouth	1-2	Gray	10457			1		8	2	10			12	3	4				9	6		11	5		7	14
33	9	OXFORD UNITED	3-1	Preece, Gray, Oakes	6687			1		8	2	10				3	4				9	6		11	12		7	5
34	13	Grimsby Town	1-3	Gray	5193			1		8	2	10		6	5	3	4				9			11	14		7	12
35	17	SWINDON TOWN	0-0		8902			1		8	2	10			12	3	4				9	6		11	5		7	14
36	20	BRISTOL ROVERS	1-1	Maddison (og)	7717			1		8	2	10			12	3	4				9	6		11	5		7	
37	24	Millwall	0-1		8287			1		12	2	10	11		8	3					9	6			5		7	14
38	27	CAMBRIDGE UNITED	2-0	Dixon, Oakes	8077			1		8	2				7		4	10			9	6			5	3		11
39	Apr 3	Watford	0-0		10656			1		8	2	10			7		4				12	6		11	5	3		
40	7	WOLVERHAMPTON W.	1-1	Gray	7948			1		8	2	10				3	4				7	6		11	5		12	14
41	10	Swindon Town	0-1		11004			1		8	2	10			7		4				12	6		11	5	3		
42	13	WEST HAM UNITED	2-0	Gray (p), Williams	10959			1		8	2	10			7		4				14	6		11	5	3		12
43	17	Sunderland	2-2	Preece, Telfer	16493			1		8	2	10			5		4				12	6		11		3	7	14
44	24	Derby County	1-1	Preece	13741			1		8	2	10			5	3	4					6		11			7	
45	May 1	PETERBOROUGH UTD.	0-0		10011			1		9	2	10				3	4	8			6	5		11			7	12
46	8	Southend United	1-2	Dixon	11913			1		9	2	10				3	4	8			6	14		11			7	12
				Apps		10	9	32	16	17	38	45	1	1	29	43	40	21	20	5	44	40	14	43	32	15	32	22
				Goals		1	1		2	3	2	19			2	2	3				5			3			2	1

One own goal

F.A. Cup

Rd	Date	Opponent	Res	Scorers	Att	Benjamin I	Campbell J	Chamberlain A	Claridge S	Dixon K	Dreyer J	Gray P	Greene D	Harvey R	Hughes C	James J	Johnson M	Kamara C	Linton D	Matthew D	Oakes S	Peake T	Petterson A	Preece D	Rees J	Salton D	Telfer P	Williams M
R3	Jan 19	BRISTOL CITY	2-0	Gray, Hughes	6092	8		1			2	10			5	3	4				14	6		11	9		7	
R4	Jan 23	DERBY COUNTY	1-5	Telfer	9170	8		1			2	10			5	3	4				14	6		11	9		7	

F.L. Cup (Coca Cola Cup)

Rd	Date	Opponent	Res	Scorers	Att	Benjamin I	Campbell J	Chamberlain A	Claridge S	Dixon K	Dreyer J	Gray P	Greene D	Harvey R	Hughes C	James J	Johnson M	Kamara C	Linton D	Matthew D	Oakes S	Peake T	Petterson A	Preece D	Rees J	Salton D	Telfer P	Williams M
R2/1	Sep 23	PLYMOUTH ARGYLE	2-2	Claridge 2	3702	14			7			9				3	6	8	2		11	5	1	10	12	4		
R2/2	Oct 6	Plymouth Argyle	2-3	Claridge, Preece	8946				7	14		9				3	6	8	2		12	5	1	10	11	4		

Anglo-Italian Cup

Rd	Date	Opponent	Res	Scorers	Att	Benjamin I	Campbell J	Chamberlain A	Claridge S	Dixon K	Dreyer J	Gray P	Greene D	Harvey R	Hughes C	James J	Johnson M	Kamara C	Linton D	Matthew D	Oakes S	Peake T	Petterson A	Preece D	Rees J	Salton D	Telfer P	Williams M
PR	Sep 15	Watford	0-0		5197	14			7			9				3	6	8	2		12	5	1	10	11	4		
PR	29	BRISTOL CITY	1-1	Claridge	2538	10			7		6	9				3		8	2	5	14		1	12	11	4		

1993/94   20th in Division One

#		Date	Opponent	Score	Scorers	Att	Aunger G	Benjamin I	Burke M	Campbell J	Davis K	Dickov P	Dixon K	Dreyer J	Greene D	Harper A	Hartson J	Houghton S	Hughes C	James J	Johnson M	Linton D	McLaren P	Oakes S	Peake T	Petterson A	Preece D	Rees J	Sommer J	Telfer P	Thomas MA	Thorpe A	Williams M
1	Aug	14	WATFORD	2-1	Telfer, Dixon	9149							9	6				12	3	2				8	5	13	11	10	1	7			4
2		21	Portsmouth	0-1		12248		14					9	6				12	10	3	2			8	5		11		1	7			4
3		28	NOTTM. FOREST	1-2	Hartson	9788							9	6		7		10	8	3	2				5		11	14	1	4			12
4	Sep	11	BOLTON WANDERERS	0-2		7199							9	6		7		10	8	3	2			12	5		11		1	4			14
5		14	Tranmere Rovers	1-4	Benjamin	5871		7						6			2		8	3				9	5		11	10	1	4			12
6		18	Middlesbrough	0-0		12487		7						6			2	12	10	14	3			8	5		11	9	1	4			
7		25	Birmingham City	1-1	Telfer	11801								6		7	11		10	3	2			8	5			9	1	4			12
8	Oct	2	BARNSLEY	5-0	Hartson, Oakes 2, James, Houghton	6201								6		11	9	12	10	3	2	14		8	5				1	7			4
9		5	BRISTOL CITY	0-2		5956								6		11	9	12	10	3	2			8	5				1	7			4
10		9	Derby County	1-2	Williams	15885				14	11			6		4	9		10	3	2			8	5				1	7			12
11		16	NOTTS COUNTY	1-0	Dickov	6366				14	11			6		4	9		10	3	2			8	5				1	7			12
12		20	Sunderland	0-2		13645				14	11			6			9		4	3	2			8	5			10	1	7			12
13		23	Oxford United	1-0	Hughes	5161				14	11	9		6		4		10	8	3	2			12	5				1	7			
14		30	LEICESTER CITY	0-2		8813					11	12		6		4	9	14	10	3	2			8	5				1	7			
15	Nov	2	Crystal Palace	2-3	Aunger, Hughes	10925	11			12		14	9	6		4			10	3	2			8	5				1	7			
16		7	CHARLTON ATHLETIC	1-0	Telfer	6327	11					14	9	6		4			10	3	2			8	5				1	7			12
17		13	Southend United	1-2	Dixon	5567	11			12		14	9	6		4		8	10		2				5				1	7		3	
18		27	STOKE CITY	6-2	Dixon 3, Hughes, Oakes, Hartson	7384							9	6		11	4	14	7		2			8	5		10		1			3	12
19	Dec	4	Charlton Athletic	0-1		7570								6		11	9	10	4	14	2			8	5			7	1		12	3	
20		11	TRANMERE ROVERS	0-1		7075								6		11	9	8	4	14	2			12	5			10	1	7		3	
21		19	Watford	2-2	Preece, Dreyer (p)	7567				12			9	6		4	14		10		2			8	5		11		1	7		3	
22		27	Peterborough United	0-0		9522				12			9	6		4		10	8	14	2				5		11		1	7		3	
23		29	GRIMSBY TOWN	2-1	Harper, Hughes	7234				12			9	6		4	11		10	14	2			8	5				1	7		3	
24	Jan	1	West Bromwich Albion	1-1	Preece	16138				12			9	6		4		10	8	14	2				5		11		1	7		3	
25		15	Notts County	2-1	Dixon 2	6589				12			9	6		4	14		10	3	2			8	5		11		1	7			
26		22	DERBY COUNTY	2-1	Telfer, Oakes	9371				11			9	6		4	12		10	3	2			8	5				1	7			
27	Feb	5	OXFORD UNITED	3-0	Oakes, Thomas, Thorpe	7366								6		4	9	14		3	2			10					1	7	11	12	
28		12	Leicester City	1-2	James	16194								6		4	9	12	10	3	2			8	5		11		1	7			
29		22	PORTSMOUTH	4-1	Telfer, Preece, Hughes, Oakes	6533							9	6		4	12		10	3	2			8	5		11		1	7		14	
30		26	SUNDERLAND	2-1	Hughes, Oakes	9367							9	6		4	14		10	3	2			8	5		11		1	7		12	
31	Mar	5	Nottingham Forest	0-2		22249			14				9	6		4			8	3	2		6				11	12	1	7		10	
32		8	MIDDLESBROUGH	1-1	Dreyer (p)	6741			11				9	6	5	4	14		8	3	2							10	1	7			12
33		19	BIRMINGHAM CITY	1-1	Telfer	7690			10					6	5	4	9			3	2			8		1	11			7		12	12
34		26	Barnsley	0-1		6289							9	6		4	12		10	3				8	5		11		1	7		14	2
35		30	Millwall	2-2	Dreyer, Hartson	9235				12				6		4	9		10	3				8	5		11		1	7		2	
36	Apr	2	PETERBOROUGH UTD.	2-0	Dixon 2	8398							9	6		4	14		10	3				8	5		11	12	1	7		2	
37		4	Grimsby Town	0-2		5542	11			12				6	5	4	14		9	8	2							10	1	7			
38		12	WOLVERHAMPTON W.	0-2		8545							9	6	5	4	12		10	3	2			8			11		1	7		14	
39		16	CRYSTAL PALACE	0-1		9880								12	5	4	9		10		2	6		8			11		1	7		3	14
40		19	Bristol City	0-1		5350	10						9	6	5	4	12		8		2	6					11		1	7		3	12
41		23	Wolverhampton Wan.	0-1		25479							9		5	4		12	8			6					11		1	7		3	10
42		26	MILLWALL	1-1	Preece	8257							9	6	5	4	12		8		2						11		1	7		3	10
43		30	SOUTHEND UNITED	1-1	Hartson	7504								6	5	4	9		10	3	2			8			11		1	7		12	14
44	May	3	WEST BROMWICH ALB.	3-2	Preece, James, Hartson	10053								6	5	4	9		10		2			8	5	13	11		1	7		3	12
45		5	Bolton Wanderers	1-2	Hughes	7102								6		4	9		10	3	2			8	5	1	12			7		11	14
46		8	Stoke City	2-2	Oakes, Telfer (p)	15893				12	1			6		4	9		10	3	2	14		8	5					7			11
				Apps			5	3	3	16	1	15	29	40	10	41	34	15	42	33	17	33	1	36	36	5	29	10	43	45	20	14	15
				Goals			1	1				1	9	3		1	6	1	7	3				8			5			7	1	1	1

F.A. Cup

Round	Date	Opponent	Score	Scorers	Att	Aunger G	Benjamin I	Burke M	Campbell J	Davis K	Dickov P	Dixon K	Dreyer J	Greene D	Harper A	Hartson J	Houghton S	Hughes C	James J	Johnson M	Linton D	McLaren P	Oakes S	Peake T	Petterson A	Preece D	Rees J	Sommer J	Telfer P	Thomas MA	Thorpe A	Williams M
R3	Jan 18	SOUTHEND UNITED	1-0	Telfer	7953			14				9	6		4	12		10	3	2			8	5		11		1	7			
R4	Jan 29	Newcastle United	1-1	Thorpe	32216			12				9	6		4			3		2			8	5		11		1	7		10	
rep	Feb 9	NEWCASTLE UNITED	2-0	Hartson, Oakes	12503			10					6		4	9	12		3	2			8	5		11		1	7		14	
R5	Feb 20	Cardiff City	2-1	Oakes, Preece	17296							12	6		4	9		10	3	2			8	5		11		1	7			
R6	Mar 14	West Ham United	0-0		27331			12				9	6	5	4	14		10	3	2			8			11		1	7			
rep	Mar 23	WEST HAM UNITED	3-2	Oakes 3	13166							9	6		4			10	3	2			8	5		11		1	7			
SF	Apr 9	Chelsea	0-2		59989							9	6		4	12		10	3	2			8	5		11		1	7			

SF at Wembley Stadium

F.L. Cup (Coca Cola Cup)

Round	Date	Opponent	Score	Scorers	Att	Aunger G	Benjamin I	Burke M	Campbell J	Davis K	Dickov P	Dixon K	Dreyer J	Greene D	Harper A	Hartson J	Houghton S	Hughes C	James J	Johnson M	Linton D	McLaren P	Oakes S	Peake T	Petterson A	Preece D	Rees J	Sommer J	Telfer P	Thomas MA	Thorpe A	Williams M
R1/1	Aug 17	Cambridge United	0-1		4065		11						6				12	10	2	3			4	5		8	7	1	9			
R1/2		24	CAMBRIDGE UNITED	0-1		3861		7		9				6					10	8	4	3		12	5		11		1				2

Anglo-Italian Cup

Round	Date	Opponent	Score	Scorers	Att	Aunger G	Benjamin I	Burke M	Campbell J	Davis K	Dickov P	Dixon K	Dreyer J	Greene D	Harper A	Hartson J	Houghton S	Hughes C	James J	Johnson M	Linton D	McLaren P	Oakes S	Peake T	Petterson A	Preece D	Rees J	Sommer J	Telfer P	Thomas MA	Thorpe A	Williams M
PR	Aug 31	Watford	1-2	Preece	2854							9	6				8	10	4	2	3			12	5		11		1	7			14
PR	Sep 7	SOUTHEND UNITED	1-1	Dixon	1823							9	6	12			8	10	4		3	2			5		11		1				7

Played in second game: M Woolgar (14)

1994/95 16th in Division One

#	Date	Opponent	Score	Scorers	Att	Adcock A	Allen P	Biggins W	Davis K	Dixon K	Greene D	Hartson J	Harvey R	Houghton S	Hughes C	James J	Johnson M	Linton D	Marshall D	Matthews R	Oakes S	Peake T	Preece D	Skelton A	Sommer J	Taylor J	Telfer P	Thomas MA	Thorpe A	Waddock G	Williams M	Woodsford J
1	Aug 13	WEST BROMWICH ALB.	1-1	Oakes	8640					9	5				11	2	3	12	14		8	6	10	4	1		7					
2	20	Derby County	0-0		13060					9	5			11		2	3	4	8			6	10		1		7					
3	27	SOUTHEND UNITED	2-2	Hartson, Hughes	5918					12	5	9			11	2	3		8		4	6	10		1		7	14				
4	30	Tranmere Rovers	2-4	Hughes, Hartson	5480						5	9			11	2	3		12		8	6	10	4	1		7					
5	Sep 3	Port Vale	1-0	Marshall	8541					9	5					2	3		8		11	6	10	4	1		7	12				14
6	10	BURNLEY	0-1		6911					14	5	9				2	3		8		11	6	10		1		7	12		4		
7	13	BOLTON WANDERERS	0-3		5764					9			11			2	3	12	14		8	6	10		1		7	5		4		
8	17	Watford	4-2	Oakes, Dixon, Telfer 2	8880					9						2	3		11		8	6	10		1		7	5		4		
9	24	Millwall	0-0		7150								12			2	3		11		8	6	10		1		7	5		4		
10	Oct 1	BRISTOL CITY	0-1		6633					9			14		12	2	3		11		8	6	10		1		7	5		4		
11	9	Stoke City	2-1	Marshall, Preece	11682								9		8	2	3		11		12	6	10		1		7	5		4		
12	15	MIDDLESBROUGH	5-1	* see below	8412								9		8	2	3		11		12	6	10		1		7	5		4		
13	22	Sheffield United	3-1	Gayle (og), James, Dixon	13317					9					8	2	3		11		12	6	10		1		7	5		4		
14	29	BARNSLEY	0-1		7212					12			9		8	2	3		11		14	6	10		1		7	5		4		
15	Nov 1	GRIMSBY TOWN	1-2	Oakes	5839								9		8	2	3		11		12	6	10		1		7	5		4		
16	5	Wolverhampton Wan.	3-2	Preece, Marshall, Dixon	26749					9			12			2	3		11		8	6	10		1		7	5		4		
17	12	Oldham Athletic	0-0		7907					9			12			2	3		11		8	6	10		1		7	5		4		
18	19	PORTSMOUTH	2-0	Dixon, Preece	8214					9						2	3		11		8	6	10		1		7	5	12	4		
19	26	Swindon Town	2-1	Dixon, Oakes	9228					9			12			2	3	11			8	6	10		1		7	5		4		
20	Dec 3	SHEFFIELD UNITED	3-6	Hartson, Gayle (og), Johnson (p)	8516					9			12			2	3	11	14		8	6	10		1		7	5		4		
21	11	Derby County	0-0		6400		11			9			14			2	3		12		8	6	10		1		7	5		4		
22	18	West Bromwich Albion	0-1		14392	4				9			12			2	3		11		8	6	10		1		7	5				
23	26	Reading	0-0		11623	8				9			14			2	3		11		12	6	10		1		7	5		4		
24	27	SUNDERLAND	3-0	Oakes 2, Hartson	8953							9				2	3		11		8	6	10	12	1		7	5		4	14	
25	31	Notts County	1-0	Telfer	6249	12						9				2	3		11		8	6	10		1		7	5		4		
26	Jan 2	CHARLTON ATHLETIC	0-1		7642	12	10					9				2	3		11		8	6			1		7	5		4		
27	14	Barnsley	1-3	Dixon	4808					9			10			2	3		11		8	6		12	1		7	5		4		
28	Feb 4	OLDHAM ATHLETIC	2-1	Marshall 2	6903		10			9						2	3		11		8	6			1		7	5	12	4		
29	11	Grimsby Town	0-5		4615		10			9						2	3		11		8	6	7		1	14	5			4		12
30	18	SWINDON TOWN	3-0	Horlock (og), Marshall 2	6595					9	12					2	3		11		8	6	10		1		7	5		4		14
31	21	Portsmouth	2-3	Telfer, James	7373					9			14			2	3		11		8	6	10		1		7	5		4		12
32	25	Bristol City	2-2	Oakes 2	7939					9						2	3		11		8	6	10		1		7	5		4	12	
33	Mar 4	MILLWALL	1-1	Marshall	6864				9		14					2	3		11	12	8	6	10		1		7	5		4		
34	7	PORT VALE	2-1	Telfer, Dixon	5947				9		14					2	3		11	12	8	6	10		1		7	5		4		
35	11	Southend United	0-3		4558				12		9					2	3		11	10	8	6			1		7	5		4		
36	18	TRANMERE ROVERS	2-0	James, Biggins	6660				9							2	3		11	12	8	6	10		1		7	5		4		
37	21	Burnley	1-2	Marshall	9551					9	12					2	3		11	8		6	10		1		7	5		4		14
38	26	WATFORD	1-1	Telfer	7984			1			5					2	3		11	8		6	10			9	7		12	4		
39	Apr 4	WOLVERHAMPTON W.	3-3	Telfer 2, Taylor	9651			1			5					2	3		11		8	6	10			9	7			4		12
40	8	NOTTS COUNTY	2-0	Telfer, Oakes (p)	6428			1			5					2	3	12	11	14	8	6	10			9	7			4		
41	11	Bolton Wanderers	0-0		13619			1			5					2	3	12	14	11	8	6	10			9	7			4		
42	15	Sunderland	1-1	Taylor	17292			1			5		12				3	2	14	11	8	6	10			9	7			4		
43	17	READING	0-1		8717			1			5					2	3	12	14	11	8	6	10			9	7			4		
44	22	Charlton Athletic	0-1		10918			1			2	14					3	12		11	8	6	10			9	7	5		4		
45	30	Middlesbrough	1-2	Taylor	23903			1			5					2	3		11		8	6	10			9	7		12	4		
46	May 7	STOKE CITY	2-3	Harvey, Waddock	8252			1			3					2			12		8	6	10			9	7	5		4		11
		Apps				2	4	7	9	29	8	20	12	1	9	42	46	10	45	11	43	46	42	5	37	9	46	36	4	40	2	7
		Goals					1			7		5	1			2	3	1	11		9		4			3	9			1		

Scorers in game 12: Wilkinson (og), Marshall 2, Preece, Hartson

Four own goals

F.A. Cup

Rd	Date	Opponent	Score	Scorers	Att	Adcock A	Allen P	Biggins W	Davis K	Dixon K	Greene D	Hartson J	Harvey R	Houghton S	Hughes C	James J	Johnson M	Linton D	Marshall D	Matthews R	Oakes S	Peake T	Preece D	Skelton A	Sommer J	Taylor J	Telfer P	Thomas MA	Thorpe A	Waddock G	Williams M	Woodsford J
R3	Jan 7	BRISTOL ROVERS	1-1	Hartson	7571	12						9				2	3		11		8	6	10		1		7	5		4		
rep	Jan 18	Bristol Rovers	1-0	Marshall	8213					9							3		11		8	6	10		1		7	5		4		
R4	Jan 28	SOUTHAMPTON	1-1	Biggins	9938		8			9							3		11		2	6	10		1		7	5		4	12	
rep	Feb 8	Southampton	0-6		15075					9	12					2	3		11		8	6	10		1		7	5	14	4		

Played at 2 in R3 replay: B Chenery

F.L. Cup (Coca Cola Cup)

Rd	Date	Opponent	Score	Scorers	Att	Adcock A	Allen P	Biggins W	Davis K	Dixon K	Greene D	Hartson J	Harvey R	Houghton S	Hughes C	James J	Johnson M	Linton D	Marshall D	Matthews R	Oakes S	Peake T	Preece D	Skelton A	Sommer J	Taylor J	Telfer P	Thomas MA	Thorpe A	Waddock G	Williams M	Woodsford J
R1/1	Aug 16	FULHAM	1-1	Oakes	3287					9	5			11	4	2	3	14	12		8	6	10		1		7					
R1/2	Aug 23	Fulham	1-1	Marshall	5134					9	5				11	2	3	4	8		14	6	10	12	1		7					

Lost 3-4 on penalties a.e.t.

Bottom of Division One: Relegated

#	Date	Opponent	Res	Scorers	Att	Alexander G	Davis K	Davis S	Douglas S	Feuer I	Grant K	Guentchev B	Harvey R	Hughes C	James J	Johnson G	Johnson M	Linton D	Marshall D	McLaren P	Oakes S	Oldfield D	Patterson D	Peake T	Riseth V	Taylor J	Thomas MA	Thorpe A	Tomlinson G	Vilstrup J	Waddock G	Wilkinson P	Woodsford J
1	Aug 13	NORWICH CITY	1-3	Guentchev (p)	7848	7	1					10	11	5			3				8			6		12	2	9			4		
2	19	Southend United	1-0	Thorpe	4630	7		4				10	11	5	2		3		8					6		9	14	13			12		
3	26	LEICESTER CITY	1-1	Hughes	7612			4				12	11	5	2	10	3	7	8					6		9	14	13					12
4	29	Grimsby Town	0-0		4289	5	1	4				9	11		2	10	3	7	8			13		6		14							12
5	Sep 2	DERBY COUNTY	1-2	Marshall	6427	5	1	4				8	11		2	10	3		7			13		6		12		9					14
6	9	Reading	1-3	Marshall	8550	6	1	4				12	11		2	10	3	7	8		9										5		
7	13	Millwall	0-1		7354			4	1			10	11		12		3	7	8			9		2							6	5	
8	16	SUNDERLAND	0-2		6955			4	1			13	11	10			3	7	8			9		2	12						6	5	
9	23	Wolverhampton Wan.	0-0		23659	7		4	1			10	11	5			3		8			13		2		9					6	12	
10	30	PORTSMOUTH	3-1	S Davis,Marshall,Guentchev(p)	7795	7		4	1			10	11	5	13		3		8					2		9					6	12	
11	Oct 7	Tranmere Rovers	0-1		6680	7		4	1			10	11				3		8	6	9	12		2							5		
12	14	WEST BROMWICH ALB.	1-2	Harvey	8042	7		4	1				11	6	12		3		8			9		2							5		10
13	22	Ipswich Town	1-0	Oldfield	9157	7		4	1			13	11	5	14		3		10		8	9		2							6	12	
14	29	CHARLTON ATHLETIC	0-1		6270	7		4	1			13	11	5			3	14	10		8	9		2		12					6		
15	Nov 4	Stoke City	0-5		9349	7		4	1				11	5		3			10		8	12		9							6		
16	11	OLDHAM ATHLETIC	1-1	Douglas	6047	7		4	10	1			11	5			3				6	8	13	12	2	9							
17	18	BIRMINGHAM CITY	0-0		7920	7			12	1			11	5	4		3		10	6	8			2	9				13				
18	21	Watford	1-1	S Davis	10042			4	14	1			11	5	7		3		10	6	8		12	2	9				13				
19	25	Barnsley	0-1		6437	14			12	1			11	5	7		3		10	6	8		4	2	9				13				
20	Dec 2	TRANMERE ROVERS	3-2	McLaren, Marshall 2	6025					1			11	5	7		3		10	6	8				9						4		
21	10	WOLVERHAMPTON W.	2-3	Oakes, Marshall	6997		1	7				12	11	5			3		10	6	8		2			13		9			4		
22	16	Portsmouth	0-4		7012	7		4	1				11				3		10	6	8		2		9	12	13			5		
23	23	HUDDERSFIELD TOWN	2-2	Marshall, Oldfield	7076			5	1			13	14				6		10	7	8	12	2		9	3	11			4		
24	Jan 13	SOUTHEND UNITED	3-1	Guentchev, Oakes 2	6566	10		5	1			7	12		2						8	13			9	3	11			4		
25	20	Norwich City	1-0	Guentchev (p)	12474	10		5	1			7	11		2			6			8	12			9	3				4		
26	31	SHEFFIELD UNITED	1-0	Guentchev	6995	10		5	1			7	13	12				6			8	12	2		9	3	11			4		
27	Feb 3	Leicester City	1-1	Thorpe	15687	10		5	1				11	8				13	12		6	2	14	9	3	7			4		
28	10	GRIMSBY TOWN	3-2	Alexander,Guentchev,Marshall	7158	10		5	1			7		8	2				13		12	6		9	3	11			4		
29	17	MILLWALL	1-0	Thorpe	7308	10		5	1			7	12	8	2				13		14	6		9	3				4		
30	21	Derby County	1-1	Marshall	14825	10		5	1			13		8	2			7			9	6	12		3	11			4		
31	24	Sunderland	0-1		16693	10			1			7	11	8	2	6			9			13	14	3	12			4		
32	27	READING	1-2	Guentchev (p)	6683				1			7			2				6	14	8	5	13	9	3	11		12	4		
33	Mar 2	CRYSTAL PALACE	0-0		8478	10		5	1			7	14		2	6			8	12		9	13	3	11			4		
34	9	Huddersfield Town	0-1		11950			5	1			7			2			12	13	8	10	6		9	3	11			4		
35	19	Crystal Palace	0-2		14703			5	1			7		12	2			13		8	10	6		9	3	11			4		
36	23	Sheffield United	0-1		14935	10		5	1			7			2				13	8	7	6		9	3	14	12		4		
37	30	IPSWICH TOWN	1-2	Grant	9151	12		5	1		10	13			2					8	7	6		3	11	14			4	9	
38	Apr 2	West Bromwich Albion	2-0	Guentchev, Grant	15130	2		5	1		10	7	11					12			13	4	6		3	8					9
39	5	Chalrton Athletic	1-1	Thorpe	14515	2		5	1		10	7	8					12			13	6		3	11	14			4	9
40	9	STOKE CITY	1-2	Grant	7689	2			1		10	7						5			11	9	6	13	3	8	12		4		
41	13	Birmingham City	0-4		15426	2			1		10	7	12					5			11	9	6	13	3	8	14		4		
42	20	WATFORD	0-0		9454	2		5	1		10	7	12					4			11	9	6		3	8	13				
43	23	Port Vale	0-1		6054	7		5	9		10						2	6			11				3	12	8		4		
44	27	BARNSLEY	1-3	Thorpe	6194	8		5	14	1	10	7	12					6			11		2		13	3	9		4		
45	30	PORT VALE	3-2	Thorpe 2, Guentchev	5443	8	1			7			10	12				6		14	11			5	13	3	9		4		
46	May 5	Oldham Athletic	0-1		6623			13	1		10	7					12	6			11			5	8	3	9		4		
		Apps				37	6	36	8	38	10	35	36	23	27	6	35	10	26	12	29	34	23	18	11	28	27	33	7	7	36	3	3
		Goals				1		2	1		3	9	1	1					9	1	3	2						7					

Played in games 2 an 3 at 1: J Sommer
Played in game 45 at 11: S Evers
Played at 2 in games 45 and 46 (substituted in 46): B Chenery

F.A. Cup

Rnd	Date	Opponent	Res	Scorers	Att	Alexander G	Douglas S	James J	Johnson M	Marshall D	Oakes S	Oldfield D	Peake T	Riseth V	Taylor J	Thomas MA	Waddock G
R3	Jan 6	Grimsby Town	1-7	Marshall	5387	13	1	5	6	11	10	8	9	2	3	12	4

F.L. Cup (Coca Cola Cup)

Rnd	Date	Opponent	Res	Scorers	Att	Alexander G	Davis S	Guentchev B	Harvey R	Hughes C	James J	Johnson M	Oakes S	Peake T	Taylor J	Thomas MA	Thorpe A	Waddock G
R1/1	Aug 15	BOURNEMOUTH	1-1	Marshall	2728	7	4	10	11	5		3	8	6	9	2	12	
R1/2	Aug 22	Bournemouth	1-2	M Johnson	4884	7	4	10	11		2	3	8	6	9	14	13	5

R1/2 a.e.t.

Played at 1 in both games: J Sommer. Played at 12 in second leg: R Matthews

Anglo-Italian Cup

Rnd	Date	Opponent	Res	Scorers	Att	Alexander G	Davis K	Davis S	Douglas S	Guentchev B	Harvey R	Hughes C	James J	Johnson M	Linton D	Marshall D	McLaren P	Oakes S	Peake T	Taylor J	Thomas MA	Thorpe A	Waddock G	Wilkinson P	Woodsford J
PR	Sep 5	PERUNGIA	1-4	Guentchev	2352		1	4		8	11	10	2		7	12			9	6				13	14
PR	Oct 11	Genoa	0-4		3759	14	1	4		10	11		2	3	7		5	8	9		12		6	13	
PR	Nov 8	Cesena	1-2	Marshall	461	7	1	4	12		11					10	5	8	2	9			6		
PR	Dec 13	ANCONA	5-0	*see below	2091		1	4		13	11			3	7	10	6	8	2	9	14	12	5		

Scored v. Ancona: Oakes, Marshall, Taylor, Thrope, Guentchev (p).
Played in first game: A Skelton (at 3), S Evers (at 5).
Played in third game: M Upson (at 3), G Simpson (13).

1996/97   3rd in Division Two

#	Date		Opponent	Score	Scorers	Att.	Alexander G	Davis S	Douglas S	Evers S	Feuer I	Fotiadis A	Grant K	Guentchev B	Harvey R	Hughes C	James J	Johnson M	Kiwomya A	Linton D	Marshall D	McGowan G	McLaren P	Oldfield D	Patterson D	Showler P	Skelton A	Thomas MA	Thorpe A	Upson M	Waddock G
1	Aug	17	BURNLEY	1-2	Thorpe	7064	8	14			1	12	10	7			2	6		13				9	5			3	11		4
2		24	Brentford	2-3	Thorpe (p), Hughes	5409	8	5			1		10	12		7	2	6						9	5			3	11		4
3		27	Bristol City	0-5		7028	13	5			1	14	10	12		8	2							9	6	7		3	11		4
4		31	ROTHERHAM UNITED	1-0	Thomas	5112	8	5			1		10	12		7	2	6						9		11		3	13	14	4
5	Sep	7	Wycombe Wanderers	1-0	Oldfield	6471	8	5			1		10			7	2	6						9				3	12		4
6		10	GILLINGHAM	2-1	Guentchev, Oldfield	5171	8	5			1		10	12	11	7	2	6						9				3			4
7		14	CHESTERFIELD	0-1		5292	8	5			1		10	12	11	7	2	6						9		13		3			4
8		21	Bury	0-0		3588	8	5	12		1		10		11	7	2	6						9				3			4
9		28	BLACKPOOL	1-0	Grant	5785	8	5	13		1	12	12	10	11		2	6						9				3	7		4
10	Oct	5	WALSALL	3-1	Thorpe, Showler, Fotiadis	5456	8	5	13		1	9		11		10	2	6						14		12		3	7		4
11		12	Shrewsbury Town	3-0	Showler, Thomas, Grant	3357	8	5	12		1		10	13		7	2	6						14		11		3	9		4
12		15	Stockport County	1-1	Davis	5352	8	5			1		10			7	2	6							12	11		3	9		4
13		19	PETERBOROUGH UTD.	3-0	Davis, Showler 2	6387	8	5			1	13		12		7	2	6						14	9	11		3	10		4
14		26	BOURNEMOUTH	2-0	Thorpe 2 (1p)	6086	8		13		1			12		10	2	5						14	9	11	6	3	7		4
15		29	Watford	1-1	Showler	14109	8	5	12		1					7	2	6							9	11		3	10		4
16	Nov	2	Plymouth Argyle	3-3	Thorpe 3	7134	8	5	9		1		13	12		7	2	6								11		3	10		4
17		9	NOTTS COUNTY	2-0	Thorpe, Hughes	6134	8	5	12		1		9	11		7	2	6								11		3	10		4
18		19	Preston North End	2-3	Davis 2	7004	8	5	9		1			10		7	2	6		14				12		11	13	3			4
19		23	BRISTOL ROVERS	2-1	Marshall, Thorpe (p)	5791	8	5			1		13	12		7	2	6			9		4			11		3	10		
20		30	Bournemouth	2-3	James, Marshall	4322	8	5			1		13	12		7	2	6			9		4			11		3	10		
21	Dec	3	YORK CITY	2-0	Marshall, Thorpe	4987	8	5			1		12			7	2	6		14	11					9	4	3	10		
22		14	CREWE ALEXANDRA	6-0	Alexander, Thorpe 3(1p), Showler, Oldfield	5977	8	5			1		13				2	6			11			7	12	9		3	10		4
23		18	Millwall	1-0	Hughes	7077	8	5			1			11		7	2	6			9				12			3	10		4
24		26	Gillingham	2-1	Thorpe 2	8491	8	5			1		9			7	2	6			11				12			3	10		4
25	Jan	18	WREXHAM	0-0		6167	8	5			1			12		7	2	6		14	11		4	13		9		3	10		4
26		27	WATFORD	0-0		7977	8	5			1					7	2	6		4	11			12		9		3	10		4
27	Feb	1	Notts County	2-1	Hughes, Alexander	4866	8	5			1		12	11		7	2	6		4	13			9				3	10		
28		8	PLYMOUTH ARGYLE	2-2	Thorpe 2	6827	8	5		4	1	12	7				2	6		13	11			9				3	10		
29		15	Bristol Rovers	2-3	Thorpe (p), Waddock	5612	8	5			1	13	7				2	6		11	14		4	9				3	10		12
30		22	PRESTON NORTH END	5-1	Oldfield 3, Waddock, Thomas	6896	8	5			1		12			7	2	6			14		13	9		11		3	10		4
31	Mar	1	York City	1-1	Davis	3788	8	5			1					7	2	6			13		12	9		11		3	10		4
32		4	Chesterfield	1-1	Thorpe (p)	3731	8	5			1		12			7	2	6			12			9	3	11			10		4
33		8	MILLWALL	0-2		9109	8	5			1		12			7	2	6			14		13	9	3	11			10		4
34		12	Wrexham	1-2	Davis	3392	8	5			1		12			7	2	6			14		13	9	3	11			10		4
35		15	Crewe Alexandra	0-0		4474	8	5			1					7	2	6			11		9	3				10		4
36		21	BRENTFORD	1-0	Thorpe	8680	8	5			1		12			7	2	6			13		9		11			3	10		4
37		29	Burnley	2-0	Thorpe 2	15490	8	5			1		12				6	11		13	2	7	9				3	10		4
38	Apr	1	BRISTOL CITY	2-2	Davis, Thorpe	7550	8	5			1	12	11			7		6		14	2	13	9				3	10		4
39		5	Rotherham United	3-0	Thorpe 3	2609	8	5			1	13				7	2	6		14	11	9	12				3	10		4
40		8	WYCOMBE WANDERERS	0-0		8117	8	5			1	12				7	2	6		13	11	9					3	10		4
41		12	Walsall	2-3	Kiwomya, Davis	5415	8	5			1	14	13				2	6	11		7	9	12				3	10		4
42		15	Blackpool	0-0		4382		5			1	8					2	6	11		7	9					3	10		4
43		19	SHREWSBURY TOWN	2-0	Thorpe (p), Marshall	7501	8	5			1	11			13		2	6			12	7	9				3	10		4
44		22	BURY	0-0		8281	8	5			1	9				7	2	6	11		13		12				3	10		4
45		26	Peterborough United	1-0	Fotiadis	9499	8	5			1	12				7	2	6	11			9					3	10		4
46	May	3	STOCKPORT COUNTY	1-1	Fotiadis	9623	8				1	10	12		11		2	6			13		7	9	5			3			4
			Apps				45	44	9	1	46	17	25	27	2	36	44	44	5	7	24	2	24	38	10	23	3	42	41	1	39
			Goals				2	8				3	2	1		4	1		1		4			6		6		3	28		2

Division Two Play-Offs

	Date		Opponent	Score	Scorers	Att.	Alex	Davis			Feuer	Fot	Grant	Guen		Hughes	James	John			Marshall		McLaren	Old	Patt	Showler		Thomas	Thorpe		Waddock
SF1	May	11	Crewe Alexandra	1-2	Oldfield	5467	8	5			1	11	13			2							12	7	9	6		3	10		4
SF2		14	CREWE ALEXANDRA	2-2	Oldfield 2	8168	8	5			1	12				6							13	7	9	2	11	3	10		4

F.A. Cup

	Date		Opponent	Score	Scorers	Att.	Alex	Davis	Doug		Feuer		Grant	Guen		Hughes	James	John			Marshall		McLaren	Old	Patt	Showler		Thomas	Thorpe		Waddock
R1	Nov	16	Torquay United	1-0	Hughes	3450	8	5	9		1			10		7	2	6			13				12	11	3				4
R2	Dec	7	BOREHAM WOOD	2-1	Marshall 2	5332	8	5			1		12	13		7	2				11			6	9	3			10		4
R3	Jan	21	BOLTON WANDERERS	1-1	Johnson	7414	8	5			1		12			7	2	6		4	11				9			3	10		
rep		25	Bolton Wanderers	2-6	Marshall, Thorpe	9713	8	5			1	13		12		7	2	6		4	11				9			3	10		

F.L. Cup (Coca Cola Cup)

	Date		Opponent	Score	Scorers	Att.	Alex	Davis			Feuer	Fot	Grant	Guen		Hughes	James	John			Marshall		McLaren	Old	Patt	Showler	Skel	Thomas	Thorpe		Waddock
R1/1	Aug	20	BRISTOL ROVERS	3-0	Grant, Thorpe (p), Oldfield	2643	8	5			1		10	12		7	2	6						9	13	14		3	11		4
R1/2	Sep	4	Bristol Rovers	1-2	Oldfield	2320	8	5			1	12		10		4	2	6		7				9		11		3			
R2/1		17	DERBY COUNTY	1-0	James	4459	8	5			1	12	10	11		7	2	6						9				3			4
R2/2		25	Derby County	2-2	Grant, Thorpe	13569	8	5			1		10	11		7	2	6						9				3	12		4
R3	Oct	22	Wimbledon	1-1	Hughes	5043	8	5			1					10	2	6						9		11		3	7		4
rep	Nov	12	WIMBLEDON	1-2	Blackwell (og)	8076	8	5	13		1		9	14		7	2	6					12			11		3	10		4

R3 replay a.e.t.

A.M. Cup (Auto Windscreens Shield)

	Date		Opponent	Score	Scorers	Att.	Alex	Davis		Evers	Feuer	Fot	Grant	Guen		Hughes	James	John			Marshall	McGowan	McLaren	Old	Patt	Showler	Skel	Thomas	Thorpe		Waddock
R1	Dec	10	LEYTON ORIENT	2-1	S Davis, Grant	1594	12	5					10	9		7	2			8	11				14	6	13	3			4
R2	Feb	4	Northampton Town	0-1		4201	8	5		4	1	12	9	11		7		6			10			13	2		3				

Played in R1: K Davis (at 1)

1972/73 Division 2

1	Burnley	42	13	6	2	44	18	11	8	2	28	17	62
2	Queen's Park Rgs.	42	16	4	1	54	13	8	9	4	27	24	61
3	Aston Villa	42	12	5	4	27	17	6	9	6	24	30	50
4	Middlesbrough	42	12	6	3	29	15	5	7	9	17	28	47
5	Bristol City	42	10	7	4	34	18	7	5	9	29	33	46
6	Sunderland	42	12	6	3	35	17	5	6	10	24	32	46
7	Blackpool	42	12	6	3	37	17	6	4	11	19	34	46
8	Oxford United	42	14	2	5	36	18	5	5	11	16	25	45
9	Fulham	42	11	6	4	32	16	5	6	10	26	33	44
10	Sheffield Wed.	42	14	4	3	40	20	3	6	12	19	35	44
11	Millwall	42	12	5	4	33	18	4	5	12	22	29	42
12	LUTON TOWN	42	6	9	6	24	23	9	2	10	20	30	41
13	Hull City	42	9	7	5	39	22	5	5	11	25	37	40
14	Nottingham Forest	42	12	5	4	32	18	2	7	12	15	34	40
15	Orient	42	11	6	4	33	18	1	6	14	16	35	36
16	Swindon Town	42	8	9	4	28	23	2	7	12	18	37	36
17	Portsmouth	42	7	6	8	21	22	5	5	11	21	37	35
18	Carlisle United	42	10	5	6	40	24	1	7	13	10	28	34
19	Preston North End	42	6	8	7	19	25	5	4	12	18	39	34
20	Cardiff City	42	11	4	6	32	21	0	7	14	11	37	33
21	Huddersfield Town	42	7	9	5	21	20	1	8	12	15	36	33
22	Brighton & Hove A.	42	7	8	6	32	31	1	5	15	14	52	29

1984/85 Division 1

1	Everton	42	16	3	2	58	17	12	3	6	30	26	90
2	Liverpool	42	12	4	5	36	19	10	7	4	32	16	77
3	Tottenham Hotspur	42	11	3	7	46	31	12	5	4	32	20	77
4	Manchester United	42	13	6	2	47	13	9	4	8	30	34	76
5	Southampton	42	13	4	4	29	18	6	7	8	27	29	68
6	Chelsea	42	13	3	5	38	20	5	9	7	25	28	66
7	Arsenal	42	14	5	2	37	14	5	4	12	24	35	66
8	Sheffield Wed.	42	12	7	2	39	21	5	7	9	19	24	65
9	Nottingham Forest	42	13	4	4	35	18	6	3	12	21	30	64
10	Aston Villa	42	10	7	4	34	20	5	4	12	26	40	56
11	Watford	42	10	5	6	48	30	4	8	9	33	41	55
12	West Bromwich Alb.	42	11	4	6	36	23	5	3	13	22	39	55
13	LUTON TOWN	42	12	5	4	40	22	3	4	14	17	39	54
14	Newcastle United	42	11	4	6	33	26	2	9	10	22	44	52
15	Leicester City	42	10	4	7	39	25	5	2	14	26	48	51
16	West Ham United	42	7	8	6	27	23	6	4	11	24	45	51
17	Ipswich Town	42	8	7	6	27	20	5	4	12	19	37	50
18	Coventry City	42	11	3	7	29	22	4	2	15	18	42	50
19	Queen's Park Rgs.	42	11	6	4	41	30	2	5	14	12	42	50
20	Norwich City	42	9	6	6	28	24	4	4	13	18	40	49
21	Sunderland	42	7	6	8	20	26	3	4	14	20	36	40
22	Stoke City	42	3	3	15	18	41	0	5	16	6	50	17

1985/86 Division 1

1	Liverpool	42	16	4	1	58	14	10	6	5	31	23	88
2	Everton	42	16	3	2	54	18	10	5	6	33	23	86
3	West Ham United	42	17	2	2	48	16	9	4	8	26	24	84
4	Manchester United	42	12	5	4	35	12	10	5	6	35	24	76
5	Sheffield Wed.	42	13	6	2	36	23	8	4	9	27	31	73
6	Chelsea	42	12	4	5	32	27	8	7	6	25	29	71
7	Arsenal	42	13	5	3	29	15	7	4	10	20	32	69
8	Nottingham Forest	42	11	5	5	38	25	8	6	7	31	28	68
9	LUTON TOWN	42	12	6	3	37	15	6	6	9	24	29	66
10	Tottenham Hotspur	42	12	2	7	47	25	7	6	8	27	27	65
11	Newcastle United	42	12	5	4	46	31	5	7	9	21	41	63
12	Watford	42	11	6	4	40	22	5	5	11	29	40	59
13	Queen's Park Rgs.	42	12	3	6	33	20	3	4	14	20	44	52
14	Southampton	42	10	6	5	32	18	2	4	15	19	44	46
15	Manchester City	42	7	7	7	25	26	4	5	12	18	31	45
16	Aston Villa	42	7	6	8	27	28	3	8	10	24	39	44
17	Coventry City	42	6	5	10	31	35	5	5	11	17	36	43
18	Oxford United	42	7	7	7	34	27	3	5	13	28	53	42
19	Leicester City	42	7	8	6	35	35	3	4	14	19	41	42
20	Ipswich Town	42	8	5	8	20	24	3	3	15	12	31	41
21	Birmingham City	42	5	2	14	13	25	3	3	15	17	48	29
22	West Bromwich Alb.	42	3	8	10	21	36	1	4	16	14	53	24

1986/87 Division 1

1	Everton	42	16	4	1	49	11	10	4	7	27	20	86
2	Liverpool	42	15	3	3	43	16	8	5	8	29	26	77
3	Tottenham Hotspur	42	14	3	4	40	14	7	5	9	28	29	71
4	Arsenal	42	12	5	4	31	12	8	5	8	27	23	70
5	Norwich City	42	9	10	2	27	20	8	7	6	26	31	68
6	Wimbledon	42	11	5	5	32	22	8	4	9	25	28	66
7	LUTON TOWN	42	14	5	2	29	13	4	7	10	18	32	66
8	Nottingham Forest	42	12	8	1	36	14	6	3	12	28	37	65
9	Watford	42	12	5	4	38	20	6	4	11	29	34	63
10	Coventry City	42	14	4	3	35	17	3	8	10	15	28	63
11	Manchester United	42	13	3	5	38	18	1	11	9	14	27	56
12	Southampton	42	11	5	5	44	24	3	5	13	25	44	52
13	Sheffield Wed.	42	9	7	5	39	24	4	6	11	19	35	52
14	Chelsea	42	8	6	7	30	30	5	7	9	23	34	52
15	West Ham United	42	10	4	7	33	28	4	6	11	19	39	52
16	Queen's Park Rgs.	42	9	7	5	31	27	4	4	13	17	37	50
17	Newcastle United	42	10	4	7	33	29	2	7	12	14	36	47
18	Oxford United	42	8	8	5	30	25	3	5	13	14	44	46
19	Charlton Athletic	42	7	7	7	26	22	4	4	13	19	33	44
20	Leicester City	42	9	7	5	39	24	2	2	17	15	52	42
21	Manchester City	42	8	6	7	28	24	0	9	12	8	33	39
22	Aston Villa	42	7	7	7	25	25	1	5	15	20	54	36

1987/88 Division 1

1	Liverpool	40	15	5	0	49	9	11	7	2	38	15	90
2	Manchester United	40	14	5	1	41	17	9	7	4	30	21	81
3	Nottingham Forest	40	11	7	2	40	17	9	6	5	27	22	73
4	Everton	40	14	4	2	34	11	5	9	6	19	16	70
5	Queen's Park Rgs.	40	12	4	4	30	14	7	6	7	18	24	67
6	Arsenal	40	11	4	5	35	16	7	8	5	23	23	66
7	Wimbledon	40	8	9	3	32	20	6	6	8	26	27	57
8	Newcastle United	40	9	6	5	32	23	5	8	7	23	30	56
9	LUTON TOWN	40	11	6	3	40	21	3	5	12	17	37	53
10	Coventry City	40	6	8	6	23	25	7	6	7	23	28	53
11	Sheffield Wed.	40	10	2	8	27	30	5	6	9	25	36	53
12	Southampton	40	6	8	6	27	26	6	6	8	22	27	50
13	Tottenham Hotspur	40	9	5	6	26	23	3	6	11	12	25	47
14	Norwich City	40	7	5	8	26	26	5	4	11	14	26	45
15	Derby County	40	6	7	7	18	17	4	6	10	17	28	43
16	West Ham United	40	6	9	5	23	21	3	6	11	17	31	42
17	Charlton Athletic	40	7	7	6	23	21	2	8	10	15	31	42
18	Chelsea	40	7	11	2	24	17	2	4	14	26	51	42
19	Portsmouth	40	4	8	8	21	27	3	6	11	15	39	35
20	Watford	40	4	5	11	15	24	3	6	11	12	27	32
21	Oxford United	40	5	7	8	24	34	1	6	13	20	46	31

1988/89 Division 1

1	Arsenal	38	10	6	3	35	19	12	4	3	38	17	76
2	Liverpool	38	11	5	3	33	11	11	5	3	32	17	76
3	Nottingham Forest	38	8	7	4	31	16	9	6	4	33	27	64
4	Norwich City	38	8	7	4	23	20	9	4	6	25	25	62
5	Derby County	38	9	3	7	23	18	8	4	7	17	20	58
6	Tottenham Hotspur	38	8	6	5	31	24	7	6	6	29	22	57
7	Coventry City	38	9	4	6	28	23	5	9	5	19	19	55
8	Everton	38	10	7	2	33	18	4	5	10	17	27	54
9	Queen's Park Rgs.	38	9	5	5	23	16	5	6	8	20	21	53
10	Millwall	38	10	3	6	27	21	4	8	7	20	31	53
11	Manchester United	38	10	5	4	27	13	3	7	9	18	22	51
12	Wimbledon	38	10	3	6	30	19	4	6	9	20	27	51
13	Southampton	38	6	7	6	25	26	4	8	7	27	40	45
14	Charlton Athletic	38	6	7	6	25	24	4	5	10	19	34	42
15	Sheffield Wed.	38	6	6	7	21	25	4	6	9	13	26	42
16	LUTON TOWN	38	8	6	5	32	21	2	5	12	10	31	41
17	Aston Villa	38	7	6	6	25	22	2	7	10	20	34	40
18	Middlesbrough	38	6	7	6	28	30	3	5	11	16	31	39
19	West Ham United	38	3	6	10	19	30	7	2	10	18	32	38
20	Newcastle United	38	3	6	10	19	28	4	4	11	13	35	31

1989/90 Division 1

1	Liverpool	38	13	5	1	38	15	10	5	4	40	22	79
2	Aston Villa	38	13	3	3	36	20	8	4	7	21	18	70
3	Tottenham Hotspur	38	12	1	6	35	24	7	5	7	24	23	63
4	Arsenal	38	14	3	2	38	11	4	5	10	16	27	62
5	Chelsea	38	8	7	4	31	24	8	5	6	27	26	60
6	Everton	38	14	3	2	40	16	3	5	11	17	30	59
7	Southampton	38	10	5	4	40	27	5	5	9	31	36	55
8	Wimbledon	38	5	8	6	22	23	8	8	3	25	17	55
9	Nottingham Forest	38	9	4	6	31	21	6	5	8	24	26	54
10	Norwich City	38	7	10	2	24	14	6	4	9	20	28	53
11	Queen's Park Rgs.	38	9	4	6	27	22	4	7	8	18	22	50
12	Coventry City	38	11	2	6	24	25	3	5	11	15	34	49
13	Manchester United	38	8	6	5	26	14	5	3	11	20	33	48
14	Manchester City	38	9	4	6	26	21	3	8	8	17	31	48
15	Crystal Palace	38	8	7	4	27	23	5	2	12	15	43	48
16	Derby County	38	9	1	9	29	21	4	6	9	14	19	46
17	LUTON TOWN	38	8	8	3	24	18	2	5	12	19	39	43
18	Sheffield Wed.	38	8	6	5	21	17	3	4	12	14	34	43
19	Charlton Athletic	38	4	6	9	18	25	3	3	13	13	32	30
20	Millwall	38	4	6	9	23	25	1	5	13	16	40	26

1990/91 Division 1

1	Arsenal	38	15	4	0	51	10	9	9	1	23	8	83
2	Liverpool	38	14	3	2	42	13	9	4	6	35	27	76
3	Crystal Palace	38	11	6	2	26	17	9	3	7	24	24	69
4	Leeds United	38	12	2	5	46	23	7	5	7	19	24	64
5	Manchester City	38	12	3	4	35	25	5	8	6	29	28	62
6	Manchester United	38	11	4	4	34	17	5	8	6	24	28	59
7	Wimbledon	38	8	6	5	28	22	6	8	5	25	24	56
8	Nottingham Forest	38	11	4	4	42	21	3	8	8	23	29	54
9	Everton	38	9	5	5	26	15	4	7	8	24	31	51
10	Tottenham Hotspur	38	8	9	2	35	22	3	7	9	16	28	49
11	Chelsea	38	10	6	3	33	25	3	4	12	25	44	49
12	Queen's Park Rgs.	38	8	5	6	27	22	4	5	10	17	31	46
13	Sheffield United	38	9	3	7	23	23	4	4	11	13	32	46
14	Southampton	38	9	6	4	33	22	3	3	13	25	47	45
15	Norwich City	38	9	3	7	27	32	4	3	12	14	32	45
16	Coventry City	38	10	6	3	30	16	1	5	13	12	33	44
17	Aston Villa	38	7	9	3	29	25	2	5	12	17	33	41
18	LUTON TOWN	38	7	5	7	22	18	3	2	14	20	43	37
19	Sunderland	38	6	6	7	15	16	2	4	13	23	44	34
20	Derby County	38	3	8	8	25	36	2	1	16	12	39	24

1991/92 Division 1

#	Team	P	W	D	L	F	A	W	D	L	F	A	Pts
1	Leeds United	42	13	8	0	38	13	9	8	4	36	24	82
2	Manchester United	42	12	7	2	34	13	9	8	4	29	20	78
3	Sheffield Wed.	42	13	5	3	39	24	8	7	6	23	25	75
4	Arsenal	42	12	7	2	51	22	7	8	6	30	24	72
5	Manchester City	42	13	4	4	32	14	7	6	8	29	34	70
6	Liverpool	42	13	5	3	34	17	3	11	7	13	23	64
7	Aston Villa	42	13	3	5	31	16	4	6	11	17	28	60
8	Nottingham Forest	42	10	7	4	36	27	6	4	11	24	31	59
9	Sheffield United	42	9	6	6	29	23	7	3	11	36	40	57
10	Crystal Palace	42	7	8	6	24	25	7	7	7	29	36	57
11	Queen's Park Rgs.	42	6	10	5	25	21	6	8	7	23	26	54
12	Everton	42	8	8	5	28	19	5	6	10	24	32	53
13	Wimbledon	42	10	5	6	32	20	3	9	9	21	33	53
14	Chelsea	42	7	8	6	31	30	6	6	9	19	30	53
15	Tottenham Hotspur	42	7	3	11	33	35	8	4	9	25	28	52
16	Southampton	42	7	5	9	17	28	7	5	9	22	27	52
17	Oldham Athletic	42	11	5	5	46	36	3	4	14	17	31	51
18	Norwich City	42	8	6	7	29	28	3	6	12	18	35	45
19	Coventry City	42	6	7	8	18	15	5	4	12	17	29	44
20	LUTON TOWN	42	10	7	4	25	17	0	5	16	13	54	42
21	Notts County	42	7	5	9	24	29	3	5	13	16	33	40
22	West Ham United	42	6	6	9	22	24	3	5	13	15	35	38

1992/93 Division 1 of the "new" Football League

#	Team	P	W	D	L	F	A	W	D	L	F	A	Pts
1	Newcastle United	46	16	6	1	58	15	13	3	7	34	23	96
2	West Ham United	46	16	5	2	50	17	10	5	8	31	24	88
3	Portsmouth	46	19	2	2	48	9	7	8	8	32	37	88
4	Tranmere Rovers	46	15	4	4	48	24	8	6	9	24	32	79
5	Swindon Town	46	15	5	3	41	23	6	8	9	33	36	76
6	Leicester City	46	14	5	4	43	24	8	5	10	28	40	76
7	Millwall	46	14	6	3	46	21	4	10	9	19	32	70
8	Derby County	46	11	2	10	40	33	8	7	8	28	24	66
9	Grimsby Town	46	12	6	5	33	25	7	1	15	25	32	64
10	Peterborough Utd.	46	7	11	5	30	26	9	3	11	25	37	62
11	Wolverhampton Wan.	46	11	6	6	37	26	5	7	11	20	30	61
12	Charlton Athletic	46	10	8	5	28	19	6	5	12	21	27	61
13	Barnsley	46	12	4	7	29	19	5	5	13	27	41	60
14	Oxford United	46	8	7	8	29	21	6	7	10	24	35	56
15	Bristol City	46	10	7	6	29	25	4	7	12	20	42	56
16	Watford	46	8	7	8	27	30	6	6	11	30	41	55
17	Notts County	46	10	7	6	33	21	2	9	12	22	49	52
18	Southend United	46	9	8	6	33	22	4	5	14	21	42	52
19	Birmingham City	46	10	4	9	30	32	3	8	12	20	40	51
20	LUTON TOWN	46	6	13	4	26	26	4	8	11	22	36	51
21	Sunderland	46	9	6	8	34	28	4	5	14	16	36	50
22	Brentford	46	7	6	10	28	30	6	4	13	24	41	49
23	Cambridge United	46	8	6	9	29	32	3	10	10	19	37	49
24	Bristol Rovers	46	6	6	11	30	42	4	5	14	25	45	41

1993/94 Division 1

#	Team	P	W	D	L	F	A	W	D	L	F	A	Pts
1	Crystal Palace	46	16	4	3	39	18	11	5	7	34	28	90
2	Nottingham Forest	46	12	9	2	38	22	11	5	7	36	27	83
3	Millwall	46	14	8	1	36	17	5	9	9	22	32	74
4	Leicester City	46	11	9	3	45	30	8	7	8	27	29	73
5	Tranmere Rovers	46	15	3	5	48	23	6	6	11	21	30	72
6	Derby County	46	15	3	5	44	25	5	8	10	29	43	71
7	Notts County	46	16	3	4	43	26	4	6	14	22	43	68
8	Wolverhampton Wan.	46	10	10	3	34	19	7	7	9	26	28	68
9	Middlesbrough	46	12	6	5	40	19	6	7	10	26	35	67
10	Stoke City	46	14	4	5	35	19	4	9	10	22	40	67
11	Charlton Athletic	46	14	3	6	39	22	5	5	13	22	36	65
12	Sunderland	46	14	2	7	35	22	5	6	12	19	35	65
13	Bristol City	46	11	7	5	27	18	5	9	9	20	32	64
14	Bolton Wanderers	46	10	8	5	40	31	5	6	12	23	33	59
15	Southend United	46	10	5	8	34	28	7	3	13	29	39	59
16	Grimsby Town	46	7	14	2	26	16	6	6	11	26	31	59
17	Portsmouth	46	10	6	7	29	22	5	7	11	23	36	58
18	Barnsley	46	9	3	11	25	26	7	4	12	30	41	55
19	Watford	46	10	5	8	39	35	5	4	14	27	45	54
20	LUTON TOWN	46	12	4	7	38	25	2	7	14	18	35	53
21	West Bromwich Alb.	46	9	7	7	38	31	4	5	14	22	38	51
22	Birmingham City	46	9	7	7	28	29	4	5	14	24	40	51
23	Oxford United	46	10	5	8	33	33	3	5	15	21	42	49
24	Peterborough Utd.	46	6	9	8	31	30	2	4	17	17	46	37

1994/95 Division 1

#	Team	P	W	D	L	F	A	W	D	L	F	A	Pts
1	Middlesbrough	46	15	4	4	41	19	8	9	6	26	21	82
2	Reading	46	12	7	4	34	21	11	3	9	24	23	79
3	Bolton Wanderers	46	16	6	1	43	13	5	8	10	24	32	77
4	Wolverhampton Wan.	46	15	5	3	39	18	6	8	9	38	43	76
5	Tranmere Rovers	46	17	4	2	51	23	5	6	12	16	35	76
6	Barnsley	46	15	6	2	42	19	5	6	12	21	33	72
7	Watford	46	14	6	3	33	17	5	7	11	19	29	70
8	Sheffield United	46	12	9	2	41	21	5	8	10	33	34	68
9	Derby County	46	12	6	5	44	23	6	6	11	22	28	66
10	Grimsby Town	46	12	7	4	36	19	5	7	11	26	37	65
11	Stoke City	46	10	7	6	31	21	6	8	9	19	32	63
12	Millwall	46	11	8	4	36	22	5	6	12	24	38	62
13	Southend United	46	13	2	8	33	25	5	6	12	21	48	62
14	Oldham Athletic	46	12	7	4	34	21	4	6	13	26	39	61
15	Charlton Athletic	46	11	6	6	33	25	5	5	13	25	41	59
16	LUTON TOWN	46	8	6	9	35	30	7	7	9	26	34	58
17	Port Vale	46	11	5	7	30	24	4	8	11	28	40	58
18	Portsmouth	46	9	8	6	31	28	6	5	12	22	35	58
19	West Bromwich Alb.	46	13	3	7	33	24	3	7	13	18	33	58
20	Sunderland	46	5	12	6	22	22	7	6	10	19	23	54
21	Swindon Town	46	9	6	8	28	27	3	6	14	26	46	48
22	Burnley	46	8	7	8	36	33	3	6	14	13	41	46
23	Bristol City	46	8	8	7	26	28	3	4	16	16	35	45
24	Notts County	46	7	8	8	26	28	2	5	16	19	38	40

1995/96 Division 1

#	Team	P	W	D	L	F	A	W	D	L	F	A	Pts
1	Sunderland	46	13	8	2	32	10	9	9	5	27	23	83
2	Derby County	46	14	8	1	48	22	7	8	8	23	29	79
3	Crystal Palace	46	9	9	5	34	22	11	6	6	33	26	75
4	Stoke City	46	13	6	4	32	15	7	7	9	28	34	73
5	Leicester City	46	9	7	7	32	29	10	7	6	34	31	71
6	Charlton Athletic	46	8	11	4	28	23	9	6	5	29	22	71
7	Ipswich Town	46	13	5	5	45	30	6	7	10	34	39	69
8	Huddersfield Town	46	14	4	5	42	23	3	8	12	19	35	63
9	Sheffield United	46	9	7	7	29	25	7	7	9	28	29	62
10	Barnsley	46	9	10	4	34	28	5	8	10	26	38	60
11	West Bromwich Alb.	46	11	5	7	34	29	6	7	11	26	39	60
12	Port Vale	46	10	5	8	30	29	5	10	8	29	37	60
13	Tranmere Rovers	46	9	9	5	42	29	5	8	10	22	31	59
14	Southend United	46	11	8	4	30	22	4	6	13	22	39	59
15	Birmingham City	46	11	7	5	37	23	4	6	13	24	41	58
16	Norwich City	46	7	9	7	26	24	7	6	10	33	31	57
17	Grimsby Town	46	8	10	5	27	25	6	4	13	28	44	56
18	Oldham Athletic	46	10	7	6	33	20	4	7	12	21	30	56
19	Reading	46	8	7	8	28	30	5	10	8	26	33	56
20	Wolverhampton Wan.	46	8	9	6	34	28	5	7	11	22	34	55
21	Portsmouth	46	8	6	9	34	32	5	7	11	27	37	52
22	Millwall	46	7	6	10	23	28	6	7	10	20	35	52
23	Watford	46	7	8	8	40	33	3	10	10	22	37	48
24	LUTON TOWN	46	7	6	10	30	34	4	6	13	10	30	45

1996/97 Division 2

#	Team	P	W	D	L	F	A	W	D	L	F	A	Pts
1	Bury	46	18	5	0	39	7	6	7	10	23	31	84
2	Stockport County	46	15	5	3	31	14	8	8	7	28	27	82
3	LUTON TOWN	46	13	7	3	38	14	8	8	7	33	31	78
4	Brentford	46	8	11	4	26	22	12	3	8	30	21	74
5	Bristol City	46	14	4	5	43	18	7	6	10	26	33	73
6	Crewe Alexandra	46	15	4	4	38	15	7	3	13	18	32	73
7	Blackpool	46	13	7	3	41	21	5	8	10	19	26	69
8	Wrexham	46	11	9	3	37	28	6	9	8	17	22	69
9	Burnley	46	14	3	6	48	27	5	8	10	23	28	68
10	Chesterfield	46	10	9	4	25	18	5	7	10	23	34	67
11	Gillingham	46	13	3	7	37	25	6	7	10	23	34	67
12	Walsall	46	12	8	3	35	21	7	2	14	19	32	67
13	Watford	46	10	8	5	24	14	6	11	6	21	24	67
14	Millwall	46	12	4	7	27	22	4	9	10	23	33	61
15	Preston North End	46	14	5	4	33	19	4	2	17	16	36	61
16	Bournemouth	46	8	9	6	24	20	7	6	10	19	25	60
17	Bristol Rovers	46	13	4	6	34	22	2	7	14	13	28	56
18	Wycombe Wanderers	46	13	4	6	31	14	2	6	15	20	42	55
19	Plymouth Argyle	46	7	11	5	19	18	5	7	11	28	40	54
20	York City	46	8	6	9	27	31	5	7	11	20	37	52
21	Peterborough Utd.	46	7	7	9	38	34	4	7	12	17	39	47
22	Shrewsbury Town	46	8	6	9	27	32	3	7	13	22	42	46
23	Rotherham United	46	4	7	12	17	29	3	7	13	22	41	35
24	Notts County	46	4	9	10	20	25	3	5	15	13	34	35

LUTON TOWN'S RECORD AGAINST OTHER LEAGUE CLUBS

Present day names used throughout

		Home:					Away:					Total:		
	P	W	D	L	F	A	W	D	L	F	A	F	A	% won
Aberdare Athletic	12	3	2	1	11	7	3	1	2	9	7	20	14	50.00
Aldershot	16	6	2	0	26	9	4	2	2	10	11	36	20	62.50
Arsenal	38	6	7	6	28	21	2	1	16	19	46	47	67	21.05
Aston Villa	32	12	3	1	24	8	5	1	10	15	29	39	37	53.12
Barnsley	44	14	5	3	61	25	3	1	18	21	55	82	80	38.64
Barrow	8	4	0	0	14	4	1	1	2	2	5	16	9	62.50
Birmingham City	50	6	8	11	29	32	4	7	14	24	53	53	85	20.00
Blackburn Rovers	36	11	7	0	43	15	2	5	11	9	27	52	42	36.11
Blackpool	28	8	3	3	26	14	3	3	8	12	24	38	38	39.29
Bolton Wanderers	30	6	5	4	13	14	3	3	9	18	31	31	45	30.00
Bournemouth	38	11	4	4	35	16	5	5	9	29	38	64	54	42.11
Bradford C	8	1	1	2	8	6	0	2	2	4	7	12	13	12.50
Bradford Park Ave.	18	5	3	1	22	12	1	3	5	10	15	32	27	33.33
Brentford	52	18	5	3	55	26	8	4	14	33	37	88	63	50.00
Brighton & Hove Alb.	50	16	7	2	52	25	3	5	17	23	49	75	74	38.00
Bristol City	42	9	7	5	33	23	5	4	12	20	45	53	68	33.33
Bristol Rovers	66	22	8	3	83	30	7	11	15	39	64	122	94	43.94
Burnley	36	8	3	7	33	26	3	4	11	19	34	52	60	30.56
Burton Swifts	6	2	1	0	9	3	0	1	2	3	6	12	9	33.33
Bury	30	11	3	1	30	13	5	2	8	22	29	52	42	53.33
Cambridge U	10	2	3	0	5	2	2	3	0	9	6	14	8	40.00
Cardiff City	48	13	8	3	66	26	4	6	14	27	40	93	66	35.42
Carlisle United	16	4	2	2	21	9	1	4	3	5	9	26	18	31.25
Charlton Athletic	62	22	3	6	61	27	7	8	16	35	51	96	78	46.77
Chelsea	38	8	6	5	29	23	4	5	10	22	37	51	60	31.58
Chester City	6	2	1	0	6	2	1	2	0	4	2	10	4	50.00
Chesterfield	24	6	3	3	19	12	3	4	5	11	16	30	28	37.50
Colchester United	6	2	1	0	7	3	1	2	0	4	3	11	6	50.00
Coventry City	60	14	6	10	51	39	2	6	22	26	70	77	109	26.67
Crewe Alexandra	12	5	1	0	21	4	0	1	5	2	10	23	14	41.67
Crystal Palace	46	12	7	4	46	27	2	8	13	29	53	75	80	30.43
Darlington	4	2	0	0	5	1	1	0	1	2	2	7	3	75.00
Darwen	4	2	0	0	11	1	1	0	1	3	4	14	5	75.00
Derby County	32	10	2	4	26	16	3	6	7	13	24	39	40	40.62
Doncaster Rovers	18	7	0	2	25	14	3	2	4	12	13	37	27	55.56
Everton	38	9	5	5	26	24	5	3	11	20	32	46	56	36.84
Exeter City	40	13	5	2	54	20	8	5	7	33	32	87	52	52.50
Fulham	44	15	1	6	43	20	4	2	16	24	48	67	68	43.18
Gainsborough Trinity	6	3	0	0	12	2	1	2	0	8	7	20	9	66.67
Gillingham	42	14	4	3	62	22	7	6	8	21	26	83	48	50.00
Glossop	2	0	0	1	0	2	0	0	1	0	5	0	7	0.00
Grimsby Town	30	7	4	4	33	21	3	5	7	15	32	48	53	33.33
Halifax Town	8	3	1	0	9	2	1	2	1	2	4	11	6	50.00
Hartlepool United	8	3	0	1	6	3	0	0	4	2	7	8	10	37.50
Hereford United	2	1	0	0	2	0	1	0	0	1	0	3	0	100.00
Huddersfield Town	14	3	1	3	14	13	3	1	3	7	9	21	22	42.86
Hull City	30	6	4	5	23	22	7	3	5	24	23	47	45	43.33
Ipswich Town	16	5	1	2	15	13	3	2	3	6	11	21	24	50.00
Leeds United	36	7	8	3	27	19	4	5	9	19	29	46	48	30.56
Leicester City	52	12	6	8	36	30	3	12	11	35	46	71	76	28.85
Leyton Orient	46	16	2	5	44	24	4	10	9	18	29	62	53	43.48
Lincoln City	22	9	1	1	33	9	3	4	4	18	28	51	37	54.55
Liverpool	28	6	3	5	17	14	0	6	8	16	38	33	52	21.43
Loughborough	6	2	1	0	13	2	0	1	2	2	7	15	9	33.33
Manchester City	34	8	6	3	33	22	3	5	9	17	31	50	53	32.35

Team	p	w	d	l	f	a	w	d	l	f	a	tf	ta	pts
Manchester Utd.	38	3	7	9	16	30	1	0	18	10	58	26	88	10.53
Mansfield Town	12	2	3	1	11	9	0	2	4	4	12	15	21	16.67
Merthyr Town	20	9	1	0	30	4	2	3	5	9	18	39	22	55.00
Middlesbrough	26	8	2	3	27	14	4	4	5	15	13	42	27	46.15
Millwall	58	11	13	5	46	28	6	9	14	28	53	74	81	29.31
New Brghton Tower	4	0	0	2	3	7	0	0	2	1	9	4	16	0.00
Newcastle United	46	14	5	4	48	28	1	5	17	24	58	72	86	32.61
Newport County	40	14	6	0	63	23	6	4	10	30	37	93	60	50.00
Northampton Town	36	15	3	0	43	15	4	3	11	19	31	62	46	52.78
Norwich City	64	15	9	8	57	36	7	9	16	37	53	94	89	34.38
Nottm Forest	54	13	8	6	51	36	6	6	15	29	47	80	83	35.19
Notts County	52	19	5	2	64	23	10	9	7	40	32	104	55	55.77
Oldham Ath.	28	7	3	4	28	16	5	4	5	12	15	40	31	42.86
Oxford United	20	5	0	5	24	16	3	3	4	16	18	40	34	40.00
Peterborough Utd.	10	2	2	1	8	4	2	2	1	4	4	12	8	40.00
Plymouth Argyle	54	10	12	5	46	37	4	6	17	29	58	75	95	25.93
Port Vale	20	6	3	1	20	9	2	2	6	5	11	25	20	40.00
Portsmouth	40	14	4	2	45	26	4	6	10	22	38	67	64	45.00
Preston North End	32	7	4	5	32	24	2	4	10	11	24	43	48	28.12
Queen's Park Rangers	78	22	11	6	70	32	6	10	23	36	73	106	105	35.90
Reading	36	11	1	6	41	18	4	4	10	15	32	56	50	41.67
Rochdale	8	4	0	0	13	3	2	1	1	6	7	19	10	75.00
Rotherham Utd.	22	8	2	1	25	13	3	4	4	17	18	42	31	50.00
Scunthorpe Utd.	8	1	2	1	3	3	0	0	4	1	13	4	16	12.50
Sheffield Utd.	34	9	2	6	29	24	3	6	8	23	27	52	51	35.29
Sheffield Wed.	48	10	8	6	37	29	2	8	14	25	53	62	82	25.00
Shrewsbury T	16	4	3	1	15	12	4	1	3	12	12	27	24	50.00
Southampton	54	10	9	8	56	44	8	6	13	44	50	100	94	33.33
Southend Utd.	50	13	8	4	51	29	7	5	13	22	42	73	71	40.00
Southport	8	2	2	0	3	0	1	1	2	7	8	10	8	37.50
Stockport County	12	4	1	1	15	9	0	2	4	4	11	19	20	33.33
Stoke City	28	4	5	5	19	13	3	6	5	20	26	39	39	25.00
Sunderland	44	10	2	10	49	37	3	7	12	16	38	65	75	29.55
Swansea	42	14	4	3	63	22	3	7	11	23	35	86	57	40.48
Swindon Town	48	16	6	2	60	24	4	8	12	25	47	85	71	41.67
Thames	4	2	0	0	10	0	1	0	1	4	3	14	3	75.00
Torquay United	26	11	1	1	41	12	3	6	4	21	24	62	36	53.85
Tottenham Hotspur	46	5	12	6	26	31	3	5	15	20	44	46	75	17.39
Tranmere Rovers	18	7	1	1	20	8	3	0	6	12	17	32	25	55.56
Walsall	30	12	1	2	39	14	4	2	9	13	36	52	50	53.33
Watford	72	21	9	6	61	38	11	8	17	41	54	102	92	44.44
West Bromwich Alb.	36	7	5	6	25	18	3	2	13	12	37	37	55	27.78
West Ham United	52	10	10	6	43	30	7	8	11	19	29	62	59	32.69
Wimbledon	12	2	3	1	7	5	2	0	4	3	12	10	17	33.33
Wolves	24	6	2	4	25	19	5	2	5	20	26	45	45	45.83
Workington	4	1	1	0	4	0	1	0	1	1	1	5	1	50.00
Wrexham	18	6	3	0	14	5	1	2	6	5	14	19	19	38.89
Wycombe Wan.	2	0	1	0	0	0	1	0	0	1	0	1	0	50.00
York City	8	4	0	0	14	2	1	2	1	6	9	20	11	62.50

OVERALL TOTALS TO THE END OF 1996/97

	p	w	d	l	f	a	w	d	l	f	a	tf	ta	pts
	3072	842	385	309	3076	1698	330	391	815	1652	2783	4728	4481	3347

Made up of:

	p	w	d	l	f	a	w	d	l	f	a	tf	ta	pts
Old Division 1	658	156	88	85	536	367	57	80	192	327	644	863	1011	725
Old Div. 2 (new Div 1	1332	334	176	156	1251	784	154	167	345	746	1161	1997	1945	1394
Old Div. 3 (new 2)	230	64	28	23	215	120	32	33	50	122	180	337	300	274
Old Div. 4	138	53	10	6	167	66	14	19	36	69	121	236	187	163
Old Div. 3 (South)	714	235	83	39	907	361	73	92	192	388	677	1295	1038	791

LUTON TOWN'S F.A. CUP RECORD IN NON-LEAGUE SEASONS

Players appearances and goals are included in the A-Z section only if they made a Football League appearance.

Season	Rd	Date	Opponent	Score	Att	P1	P2	P3	P4	P5	P6	P7	P8	P9	P10	Goalscorers
1885/86	R1	Oct 31	Great Marlow	0-3	500	Whitby F	Small	Lomax J	Deacon A	Barrett	Lawrence	Lomax E	Hunt	Martin	Long	
1886/87	R1	Oct 23	Hotspur	1-3	1000	Lomax E	Ellingham	Lomax J	Bower	Barrett	Lawrence	Taylor A	Martin	Lomax D	Boxford	Ellingham
1887/88	R1	Oct 15	Chatham	1-5	800	Lomax J	Small	Lomax E	Smart	Read	Moody	Taylor A	Martin	Sanders	Mileman	Deacon G
1888/89	Q1	Oct 6	READING	4-0	1000	Lomax J	Narburgh	Lomax E	Humphrey	Deacon G	Barrett	Moody	Thring	Sanders	Mileman	Thring, Narburgh, Lomax J 2
1888/89	Q2	Oct 27	Chesham	3-3	750	Lomax J	Narburgh	Lomax E	Humphrey	Deacon G	Barrett	Read	Thring	Sanders	Mileman	(a.e.t) Narburgh, Lomax J 2
1888/89	rep	Nov 3	CHESHAM	10-2	1500	Lomax D	Lomax J	Narburgh	Humphrey	Deacon G	Barrett	Lomax E	Thring	Sanders	Mileman	Thring 3, Deacon G 3, Narburgh 2, Lomax J 2
1888/89	Q3	Nov 17	Old Brightonians	1-3	800	Lomax D	Narburgh	Narburgh	Humphrey	Deacon G	Deacon G	Barrett	Thring	Sanders	Mileman	Deacon G
1889/90	Q2	Oct 26	Maidenhead	2-1	500	Lomax J	Narburgh	Lomax E	Whitby F	Whitby H	Miller	Moody	Humphrey	Martin	Munroe	Whitby H, Lomax J
1889/90	Q3	Nov 16	Old St. Pauls	0-4	750	Lomax J	Narburgh	Lomax E	Whitby F	Whitby H	Miller	Moody	Humphrey	Martin	Munroe	
1890/91	Q1	Oct 4	93rd Highland Regiment	0-7	1500	Lomax E	Saddington	Lomax E	Whitby F	Whitby H	Miller	Thring	Humphrey	Sanders	Read	
1891/92	Q1	Oct 3	SWINDON TOWN	4-3	1000	Deacon G	Oclee	Chesher	Whitby F	Whitby H	Wright	Paul	Hoy	Sanders	Burley	Chesher 2, Whitby H, Deacon G
1891/92	Q2	Oct 24	WINDSOR PHEONIX ATH.	3-0	1500	Deacon G	Oclee	Chesher	Whitby F	Whitby H	Wright	Paul	Hoy	Sanders	Burley	Whitby H, Chesher, Deacon G
1891/92	Q3	Nov 14	Bedminster	4-1	1500	Deacon G	Oclee	Chesher	Whitby F	Whitby H	Wright	Paul	Hoy	Sanders	Burley	Whitby F 2, Deacon G, Oclee
1891/92	Q4	Dec 5	Clifton	3-0	1000	Deacon G	Oclee	Chesher	Whitby F	Whitby H	Wright	Paul	Hoy	Sanders	Burley	Whitby H 3
1891/92	R1	Jan 16	MIDDLESBROUGH	0-3	4000	Deacon G	Oclee	Chesher	Whitby F	Whitby H	Wright	Paul	Hoy	Sanders	Burley	
1892/93	Q1	Oct 15	OLD ST. MARKS	4-0	1800	Whitby H	Whitby F	Allen	Chesher	Brown	Taylor A	Julian	Hoy	Sanders	Burley	Julian, Brown, Whitby F, Whitby H
1892/93	Q2	Oct 29	OLD ETONIANS	4-2	1500	Whitby H	Whitby F	Allen	Chesher	Brown	Taylor A	Julian	Hoy	Sanders	Burley	Sanders, Allen, Whitby F 2
1892/93	Q3	Nov 19	Polytechnic	2-4	800	Watkins	Whitby F	Allen	Chesher	Brown	Taylor A	Julian	Hoy	Sanders	Burley	Whitby F, Watkins
1893/94	Q2	Nov 4	Old Westminsters	1-0	3000	Dimmock	Allen	Galbraith	Finlayson	Brown	Taylor A	Julian	Taylor J	Wilson	Bee	Dimmock
1893/94	Q3	Nov 25	NORWICH CEYMS	5-1	2500	Dimmock	Allen	Galbraith	Finlayson	Brown	Taylor A	Julian	Vickers	Chesher	Bee	Finlayson 2, Allen 2, Julian
1893/94	Q4	Dec 16	1st Sherwood Foresters	4-2	1500	Dimmock	Allen	Galbraith	Finlayson	Brown	Taylor A	Julian	Chesher	Wilson	Bee	Brown 2, Galbraith, Dimmock
1893/94	rep	Dec 23	1ST SHERWOOD FORESTERS	2-1	2500	Allen	Brown	Finlayson	Dimmock	Galbraith	Julian	Taylor	Wilson	Chesher	Bee	Galbraith, Allen
1893/94	R1	Jan 27	Middlesbrough Ironopolis	1-2	1400	Allen	Brown	Finlayson	Dimmock	Galbraith	Julian	Taylor	Wilson	Chesher	Bee	Dimmock

Game played at Luton by arrangement (1886/87)

Game played at Luton by arrangement (1888/89)

Game played at Luton by arrangement (1890/91)

Q4 tie with Sherwood Foresters abandoned after 24 minutes of extra time (2-2 at 90 mins)

Season	Rd	Date	Opponent	Score	Att	Scorers	1	2	3	4	5	6	7	8	9	10	11
1894/95																	
	Q1	Oct 13	CITY RAMBLERS.	8-2	2000	Prentice 3, Gallacher 2, Galbraith 2, Allen	Bee	Nicholson	McEwen	Watkins	McCrindle	Howe	Gallacher	Galbraith	Allen	Prentice	Finlayson
	Q2	Nov 3	St. Albans	6-1	3000	Prentice 3, Brown, Galbraith, Dimmock	Bee	Chesher	McEwen	Watkins	McCrindle	Howe	Brown	Finlayson	Galbraith	Prentice	Dimmock
	Q3	Nov 24	Ilford	2-0	1200	Allen, Dimmock	Bee	Nicholson	McEwen	Watkins	McCrindle	Howe	Brown	Finlayson	Galbraith	Allen	Dimmock
	Q4	Dec 15	Tottenham Hotspur	2-2	3000	Finlayson, Prentice	Bee	Nicholson	McEwen	Watkins	McCrindle	Howe	Gallacher	Finlayson	Groom	Prentice	Dimmock
	rep	Dec 19	TOTTENHAM HOTSPUR	4-0	2000	Gallacher 2, Finlayson, Galbraith	Bee	Collins	McEwen	Watkins	McCrindle	Howe	Gallacher	Finlayson	Galbraith	Prentice	Dimmock
	R1	Feb 2	PRESTON NORTH END	0-2	4000		Bee	Chesher	McEwen	Collins	McCrindle	Watkins	Gallacher	Finlayson	Galbraith	Jack	Dimmock
1895/96																	
	Q1	Oct 12	TOTTENHAM HOTSPUR	1-2	3000	Galbraith	Jack	Nicholson	McEwen	Stewart	Birch	Docherty	Gallacher	Coupar	Galbraith	Parkinson	Ekins
1896/97																	
	Q3	Dec 12	1ST SCOTS GUARD	7-0	1000	McInnes 3, Docherty, Gallacher, Stewart, McCartney	Williams R	McCartney	McEwen	Davies	Stewart	Docherty	Gallacher	McInnes	Galbraith	Coupar	Ekins
	Q4	Jan 6	Marlow	5-0	1500	Galbraith,Coupar,Gallacher,Stewart,Docherty	Williams R	McCartney	McEwen	Davies	Stewart	Docherty	Gallacher	McInnes	Galbraith	Coupar	Ekins
	Q5	Jan 16	TOTTENHAM HOTSPUR	3-0	3000	McInnes 2, Galbraith	Williams R	McCartney	McEwen	Davies	Stewart	Docherty	Gallacher	McInnes	Galbraith	Coupar	Ekins
	R1	Jan 30	WEST BROMWICH ALB.	0-1	6898		Williams R	McCartney	McEwen	Davies	Stewart	Docherty	Gallacher	McInnes	Galbraith	Coupar	Birch
1900/01																	
	Q3	Nov 3	King's Lynn	4-1	1000	Blessington, Saxton 3	Ord	Lindsay	McCurdy	Clifford	Holdstock	Williams H	Blessington	Barker	Durrant	Dempsey	Saxton
	Q4	Nov 17	CIVIL SERVICE	9-1	2500	McCurdy, Lindsey 2, Holdstock, Saxton 2, Blessington 2, Johnson (og)	Ord	Lindsay	McCurdy	Clifford	Holdstock	Williams H	Blessington	Brown WR	Burbage	Dempsey	Saxton
	Q5	Dec 8	QUEEN'S PARK RANGERS	3-0	3500	Durrant 2, Dempsey	Ord	Lindsay	McCurdy	Clifford	Holdstock	Williams H	Blessington	Brown WR	Durrant	Dempsey	Saxton
	IR	Jan 5	BRISTOL ROVERS	0-2	3000		Ord	Farr	McCurdy	Clifford	Holdstock	Williams H	Blessington	Brown WR	Durrant	Tierney	Burbage
1901/02																	
	Q1	Oct 5	APSLEY	13-1	3000	Lindsay, Hawkes, White, Blessington 4, Brown 2, Tierney 3, Colvin	Ord	Lindsay	Sharp	Hawkes F	White	Williams H	Blessington	Brown WR	Durrant	Tierney	Colvin
	Q2	Oct 19	BEDFORD QUEENS WORKS	4-2	2000	Lindsay, Blessington, Durrant, Colvin	Ord	Lindsay	Hall	Hawkes F	White	Williams H	Blessington	Brown WR	Durrant	Tierney	Colvin
	Q3	Nov 2	Lowestoft Town	2-1	1500	Blessington, Brown	Ord	Lindsay	Sharp	Hawkes F	White	Williams H	Blessington	Brown WR	Durrant	Tierney	Colvin
	Q4	Nov 16	Watford	2-1	4000	Blessington, Brown	Ord	Lindsay	Sharp	Hawkes F	White	Hawkes R	Blessington	Brown WR	Durrant	Tierney	Colvin
	Q5	Nov 30	QUEEN'S PARK RANGERS	2-0	3000	Durrant, Brown	Ord	Lindsay	Williams	Hawkes F	White	Hawkes R	Blessington	Brown WR	Durrant	Tierney	Colvin
	IR	Dec 14	Woolwich Arsenal	1-1	5000	Blessington	Ord	Lindsay	Williams	Hawkes F	White	Hawkes R	Blessington	Brown WR	Durrant	Tierney	Colvin
	rep	Dec 18	WOOLWICH ARSENAL	0-2	4500		Ord	Lindsay	Williams	Hawkes F	White	Hawkes R	Blessington	Brown WR	Durrant	Tierney	Colvin
1902/03																	
	Q3	Nov 1	Queen's Park Rangers	3-0	2500	Blessington, Durrant, Allsop	Frail	Lindsay	Hall	Hawkes F	White	Hawkes R	Blessington	Hillsdon	Durrant	Moody	Allsopp
	Q4	Nov 15	LOWESTOFT TOWN	5-1	3000	Hawkes R 2, Blessington, Durrant, Moody	Frail	Lindsay	Street	Hawkes F	White	Hawkes R	Blessington	Williams	Durrant	Moody	Allsopp
	Q5	Nov 29	FULHAM	5-1	3500	Blessington, Gall 3, Moody	Frail	Lindsay	Street	Hawkes F	White	Hawkes R	Durrant	Blessington	Gall	Moody	Allsopp
	IR	Dec 13	KIDDERMINSTER	3-0	2500	Durrant, Blessington, Gall	Frail	Lindsay	Williams	Hawkes F	White	Hawkes R	Durrant	Blessington	Gall	Moody	Allsopp
	R1	Feb 7	Millwall Athletic	0-3	7000		Frail	Lindsay	Williams	Hawkes F	White	Hawkes R	Durrant	Blessington	Gall	Moody	Allsopp
1903/04																	
	Q3	Oct 31	HITCHIN	2-1	1000	Turner, Storey	Thompson	Bennett	McEwen	Hawkes F	White	Hawkes R	Eaton	Turner	Cox	Storey	Allsopp
	Q4	Nov 14	WATFORD	4-1	6000	Turner 2, McKee, Allsop	Thompson	Bennett	Holdstock	Hawkes F	White	Hawkes R	Durrant	Turner	Eaton	McKee	Allsopp
	Q5	Nov 28	Fulham	1-3	10000	Durrant	Thompson	Bennett	Holdstock	Hawkes F	McEwen	Hawkes R	Durrant	Turner	Eaton	McKee	Allsopp

Q3 game played at Luton by arrangement

Season	Rd	Date	Opponent	Score	Att	Scorers	1	2	3	4	5	6	7	8	9	10	11
1904/05																	
	Q6	Dec 10	Fulham	0-4	16000		Lindsay	Turner	White	Hawkes F	McEwen	Hawkes R	Lamberton	Spencer	Eaton	Ross	Barnes
1905/06																	
	Q4	Dec 9	Crystal Palace	0-1	8000		Platt	Blackett	McCurdy	Hawkes F	White	Hawkes R	Werner	MacDonald	Brown	Pickering	Barnes

90

1906/07

Round	Date	Opponent	Score	Scorers	Att	1	2	3	4	5	6	7	8	9	10	11
R1	Jan 12	Gainsborough	0-0		2000	Platt	Jackson	McCurdy	Hawkes F	White	Hawkes R	Warner	Fitzpatrick	Brown	Gittins	Barnes
rep	Jan 16	GAINSBOROUGH	2-1	Warner, Brown	4000	Platt	Fitzpatrick	McCurdy	Hawkes F	White	Hawkes R	Warner	Pickering	Brown	Gittins	Barnes
R2	Feb 2	SUNDERLAND	0-0		12000	Platt	Hogg	McCurdy	Hawkes F	White	Hawkes R	Murphy	Fitzpatrick	Brown	Gittins	Barnes
rep	Feb 6	Sunderland	0-1		18000	Platt	Hogg	McCurdy	Hawkes F	White	Hawkes R	Murphy	Fitzpatrick	Brown	Gittins	Barnes

1907/08

Round	Date	Opponent	Score	Scorers	Att	1	2	3	4	5	6	7	8	9	10	11
R1	Jan 11	FULHAM	3-8	Rigate, Rankin, Moody	5500	Platt	Watkins	McCurdy	Hawkes F	White	Hawkes R	Rigate	Jones	Rankin	Moody	Walders

1908/09

Round	Date	Opponent	Score	Scorers	Att	1	2	3	4	5	6	7	8	9	10	11
Q5	Dec 5	SOUTHEND UNITED	1-1	Johnson	8000	Platt	Gregory	McCurdy	Hawkes F	Jones	Hawkes R	Stansfield	Haycock	Bradley	Moody	Johnson
rep	Dec 9	Southend United	4-2	(a.e.t.) Brown, Haycock, Moody 2	5500	Platt	Gregory	McCurdy	Hawkes F	Jones	Hawkes R	Brown	Haycock	Bradley	Moody	Stansfield
R1	Jan 16	MILLWALL	1-2	Menzies	7000	Platt	Gregory	McCurdy	Hawkes F	Jones	Hawkes R	Brown	Haycock	Menzies	Moody	Stansfield

1909/10

Round	Date	Opponent	Score	Scorers	Att	1	2	3	4	5	6	7	8	9	10	11
Q4	Nov 20	Brentford	1-2	Smith	7500	Fry	Hedley	McCurdy	Hawkes F	Jones	Hawkes R	Brown	Quinn	Smith	Moody	Stansfield

1910/11

Round	Date	Opponent	Score	Scorers	Att	1	2	3	4	5	6	7	8	9	10	11
Q4	Nov 19	CAMBRIDGE UNITED	9-1	Smith 4, Moody 3, Quinn, Johnson	4000	Naisby	Chapman	Potts	Hawkes F	Bushell	Johnson	Brown	Quinn	Smith	Moody	Stansfield
Q5	Dec 3	Rochdale	1-1	Quinn	5500	Naisby	Chapman	Potts	Hawkes F	Bushell	Hawkes R	Brown	Quinn	Smith	Moody	Stansfield
rep	Dec 7	ROCHDALE	3-2	Quinn 2, Moody	3000	Naisby	Chapman	Ashton	Hawkes F	Bushell	Hawkes R	Brown	Quinn	Smith	Moody	Stansfield
R1	Jan 14	Northampton Town	1-5	Moody	8000	Naisby	Chapman	Wightman	Hawkes F	Bushell	Hawkes R	Brown	Quinn	Smith	Moody	Stansfield

1911/12

Round	Date	Opponent	Score	Scorers	Att	1	2	3	4	5	6	7	8	9	10	11
R1	Jan 13	NOTTS COUNTY	2-4	Streeton, Moody	6500	Naisby	Potts	Wightman	Hawkes F	Bushell	Hawkes R	Brown	Walker	Streeton	Moody	Stansfield

1912/13

Round	Date	Opponent	Score	Scorers	Att	1	2	3	4	5	6	7	8	9	10	11
Q4	Nov 30	TUNBRIDGE WELLS RANGERS	3-0	Hawkes R, Wileman, Streeton	4500	Bateman	Potts	Henderson	Hawkes F	Wilson	Hawkes R	Thompson	Wileman	Streeton	Worth	Stephenson
Q5	Dec 14	Croydon Common	0-2		3000	Bateman	Potts	Henderson	Hawkes F	Wilson	Hawkes R	Thompson	Wileman	Streeton	Worth	Stephenson

1913/14

Round	Date	Opponent	Score	Scorers	Att	1	2	3	4	5	6	7	8	9	10	11
Q4	Nov 29	CROYDON COMMON	3-0	Wileman, Rollinson 2	8700	Mitchell	Robinson	Jarvie	Hawkes F	Wilson	Frith	Donaghy	Wileman	Simms	Wilkie	Rollinson
Q5	Dec 13	SOUTH SHIELDS	0-0		9500	Mitchell	Elvey	Jarvie	Hawkes F	Hawkes R	Frith	Durrant	Wileman	Simms	Wilkie	Rollinson
rep	Dec 17	South Shields	0-2		9000	Mitchell	Elvey	Jarvie	Hawkes F	Hawkes R	Frith	Durrant	Wileman	Simms	Wilkie	Rollinson

1914/15

Round	Date	Opponent	Score	Scorers	Att	1	2	3	4	5	6	7	8	9	10	11
Q4	Nov 21	GT. YARMOUTH	15-0	Simms 4, Rollinson 4, Wileman 2, Hawkes F, Frith, Roberts, Hoar, Housego (og)	4000	Mitchell	Elvey	Dunn	Hawkes F	Frith	Hawkes R	Roberts	Wileman	Simms	Rollinson	Hoar
Q5	Dec 5	Oxford City	1-0	Simms	2500	Mitchell	Elvey	Dunn	Hawkes F	Frith	Hawkes R	Roberts	Wileman	Simms	Rollinson	Hoar
Q6	Dec 19	BROMLEY	5-1	Simms 3, Hawkes F, Wileman	2500	Mitchell	Elvey	Dunn	Hawkes F	Frith	Hawkes R	Roberts	Wileman	Simms	Rollinson	Hoar
R1	Jan 9	Southampton	0-3		11000	Mitchell	Elvey	Dunn	Hawkes F	Frith	Hawkes R	Roberts	Wileman	Simms	Chipperfield	Hoar

1919/20

Round	Date	Opponent	Score	Scorers	Att	1	2	3	4	5	6	7	8	9	10	11
Q6	Dec 20	Brighton & Hove Albion	1-0	Williams	7000	Whitehead	Elvey	Dunn	Urwin	Rutherford	Parker	Dodd	Bookman	Simms	Williams	Hoar
R1	Jan 10	COVENTRY CITY	2-2	Parker, Dodd	10000	Summers	Elvey	Dunn	Urwin	Rutherford	Parker	Hoar	Roe	Simms	Dodd	Bookman
rep	Jan 16	Coventry City	1-0	Hoar	20000	Whitehead	Elvey	Dunn	Urwin	Rutherford	Parker	Hoar	Roe	Simms	Dodd	Bookman
R2	Jan 31	LIVERPOOL	0-2		12640	Summers	Elvey	Dunn	Urwin	Rutherford	Parker	Hoar	Roe	Simms	Dodd	Bookman

1945/46

Round	Date	Opponent	Score	Scorers	Att	1	2	3	4	5	6	7	8	9	10	11
R3	Jan 5	DERBY COUNTY	0-6		16792	Duke	Beach	Dunsmore	Goodyear	Vinall	Campbell	Daniel	Brice	Vinall	Gardiner	Needham
R3s	Jan 9	Derby County	0-3		18000	Duke	Lake	Dunsmore	Goodyear	Gager	Campbell	Isaacs	Daniel	Vinall	Vinall	Needham

Player			D.O.B	Place of Birth	Died	First Season	Last Season	Previous Club	Next Club	Appearances				Goals			
										League	FAC	FLC	Other	Leagu	FAC	FLC	Oth.
Abbott	H	Harry	15/03/1895	Preston		1927	1928	Nelson	Exeter City	55	8	0	0	0	0	0	0
Adam	J	Jimmy	13/05/31	Glasgow		1953	1958	Spennymoor U	Aston Villa	137	1	0	2	22	0	0	2
Adamson	T	Terry	15/10/48	Houghton-le-Spring		1966		Sunderland	Hartlepool Utd	2	0	0	0	0	0	0	0
Adcock	AC	Tony	27/02/63	Bethnal Green		1994		Peterborough Utd	Colchester Utd	2	1	0	0	0	0	0	0
Agnew	W	Billy	09/01/1898	Pollokshaws		1925	1926	Arthurlie		35	1	0	0	8	0	0	0
Aherne	T	Tom	26/01/19	Limerick		1948	1956	Belfast Celtic	(coaching staff)	267	21	0	0	0	0	0	0
Aizlewood	M	Mark	01/10/59	Newport		1978	1981	Newport County	Charlton Ath.	98	5	7	0	3	0	1	0
Alderson	T	Tom	01/04/09	West Auckland		1932		Leeds United	Darlington	14	4	0	0	5	1	0	0
Aleksic	M	Milija	14/04/51	Newcastle-u-Lyme		1976	1978	Plymouth Argyle	Tottenham H	81	4	7	0	0	0	0	0
						1981			Tottenham H (loan)								
Alexander	G	Graham	10/10/71	Coventry		1995	1996	Scunthorpe Utd		82	5	8	8	3	0	0	0
Allen	DS	Derrick 'Sos'	18/04/30	Luton	1978	1954		Alton Town	Watford	1	0	0	0	0	0	0	0
Allen	K	Keith	09/11/43	Newport, IoW		1966	1969	Stockport Co.	Plymouth Argyle	137	7	10	0	36	4	3	0
Allen	PK	Paul	28/08/62	Aveley		1994		Southampton (loan)		4	0	0	0	0	0	0	0
Allinson	IJR	Ian	01/10/57	Hitchin		1987	1988	Stoke City	Colchester Utd	32	5	2	5	3	1	0	0
Allpress	TJ	Tim	27/01/71	Hitchin		1989	1991	YTS	Bayer Uerdigen	1	0	0	2	0	0	0	0
Alston	A	Adrian	06/02/49	Preston		1974	1975	Safeways (AUS)	Cardiff City	29	0	2	0	8	0	1	0
Anderson	PT	Peter	31/05/49	Hendon		1970	1975	Hendon Town	Royal Antwerp	181	7	13	7	34	2	2	2
Anderson	R	Bobby	1902	Ardrossan		1923	1925	Ardrossan W. Rov.	Newport County	74	3	0	0	0	0	0	0
Anderson	SMJ	Sam				1933		Stockton	West Stanley	10	0	0	0	5	0	0	0
Andrews	H	Harold	13/08/03	Lincoln	1988	1935		Barnsley	Accrington Stanley	1	0	0	0	0	0	0	0
Antic	R	Raddy	22/11/49	Zitiste (Yug)		1980	1983	Real Zaragoza	retired	100	2	6	0	9	0	1	0
Armstrong	JW	Jimmy	06/09/01	Swalwell-upon-Tyne	1977	1930		Tottenham H	Bristol Rovers	10	1	0	0	1	0	0	0
Arnison	JW	Joe	27/06/24	Johannesburg (SA)	1996	1948	1950	Glasgow Rangers	Berea Park (SA)	44	2	0	0	19	2	0	0
Ashworth	A	Alec	01/10/39	Southport	1995	1960	1961	Everton	Northampton Town	63	6	2	0	20	4	0	0
Aston	J	John	28/06/47	Manchester		1972	1977	Manchester Utd	Mansfield Town	174	12	11	4	31	4	1	1
Aunger	GE	Geoff	04/02/68	Red Deer, Canada		1993		Ipswich Town	Sudbury	5	0	0	0	1	0	0	0
Aylott	TKC	Trevor	26/11/57	Bermondsey		1982	1983	Millwall	Crystal Palace	32	1	2	0	10	0	1	0
Bailey	H	Harry	1897	Macclesfield		1920	1922	Millwall	Exeter City	82	7	0	0	0	0	0	0
Baker	A	Albert	1912			1929		Redhill		1	0	0	0	0	0	0	0
Ball	JT	Jack	13/09/07	Southport	1976	1934	1935	Huddersfield T	Excelsior Roubaix	65	6	0	3	47	3	0	0
						1936		Excelsior Roubaix	Vauxhall Motors								
Banes	CS	Claude	01/07/04	Beeston Green	1977	1928	1930	Biggleswade T	Biggleswade T	57	3	0	0	0	0	0	0
Banks	JA	Jimmy	28/04/1893	Wigan	1942	1927		Norwich City	London Omnibus (p/c)	13	0	0	0	2	0	0	0
Bannister	J	Jack	26/01/42	Chesterfield		1968	1970	Crystal Palace	Cambridge Utd	83	8	5	0	0	0	0	0
Barber	K	Keith	21/09/47	Luton		1970	1976	Dunstable T	Swansea City	142	5	10	1	0	0	0	0
Barnes	WT					1899				6	0	0	0	0	0	0	0
Barton	KR	Ken	20/09/37	Caernarfon	1982	1964		Millwall	Dunstable T	11	1	0	0	0	0	0	0
Bassett	EJ	Ted	01/01/1889	Deptford	1970	1921		Watford	Dartford	21	3	0	0	3	1	0	0
Bates	WH	William	13/01/22	Eaton Bray		1946		Waterlows	Watford	1	0	0	0	0	0	0	0
Bayliss	R	Dick	28/04/1899	Alfreton	1947	1920		Alfreton Rose Villa	Mansfield	1	0	0	0	0	0	0	0
Baynham	RL	Ron	10/06/29	Birmingham		1952	1964	Worcester City	Ampthill (coach)	388	31	5	8	0	0	0	0
Beach	DF	Doug	02/02/20	Watford		1946		Sheffield Wednesday	Southend Utd	23	3	0	0	0	0	0	0
Beaumont	DA	Dave	10/12/63	Edinburgh		1988	1991	Dundee Utd	Hibernian	76	1	10	4	0	0	0	0
Beaven	KH	Ken	26/12/49	Bovingdon		1967		App.	Chesham Utd.	1	0	0	0	0	0	0	0
Beck	W	William	1905	Silvertown		1934		South West Ham	Carlisle Utd	2	0	0	1	0	0	0	0
Bedford	L	Lewis	26/03/04	Erdington	1975	1928	1929	Walsall	Walsall	49	5	0	0	15	2	0	0
Bedford	SG	Syd	1897	Northampton	1958	1925		Brighton & Hove A.	Rushden	1	0	0	0	0	0	0	0
Bell	S	Sam	06/02/09	Burnhope	1982	1933	1934	Norwich City	Tottenham Hotspur	30	3	0	2	20	1	0	2
Bell	T	Tommy	09/11/06	Seaham Colliery	1983	1933	1934	Southport	Northampton Town	34	1	0	3	15	0	0	2
Benjamin	IT	Ian	11/12/61	Nottingham		1992	1993	Southend Utd	Brentford	13	2	2	0	2	0	0	0
Bennett	EW	Edgar	29/03/29	Stoke-on-Trent		1953		Vauxhall Motors	Chelmsford	1	0	0	0	0	0	0	0
Beresford	FE	Frank	08/10/10	Chesterfield	1974	1935	1936	Preston NE	Crystal Palace	12	0	0	3	1	0	0	2
Biggins	W	Wayne	20/11/61	Sheffield		1994		Stoke C (loan)		7	2	0	0	1	1	0	0
Billington	HJR	Hugh	24/02/16	Ampthill	1988	1938	1947	Waterlows	Chelsea	86	8	0	0	63	7	0	0
Bingham	WL	Billy	05/08/31	Belfast		1958	1960	Sunderland	Everton	87	12	0	3	27	6	0	0
Birch	E	Edwin	07/10/1869	Newhall		1897	1898	Burton Swifts		29	1	0	0	10	0	0	0
Birch	W	Wallace	06/03/10	Wortley		1929		Grenoside Sports	Sheffield Wed.	15	1	0	0	3	0	0	0
Birchenall	AJ	Alan	22/08/45	East Ham		1978	1979	Blackburn Rovers	Hereford Utd	10	0	0	0	0	0	0	0
Bird	SA	Sid	1904	Luton		1922		Luton Ams.	Kettering	1	0	0	0	0	0	0	0
Black	AJ	Alf	15/03/01	Milton	1972	1931		Millwall	Folkestone	1	0	0	0	0	0	0	0
Black	JR	John	26/05/00	Denny		1926	1929	Chesterfield	Bristol Rovers	91	10	0	0	3	0	0	0
Black	K	Kingsley	22/06/68	Luton		1987	1991	Juniors	Nottm. Forest	127	6	18	6	26	2	1	1
Boersma	P	Phil	24/09/49	Kirkby		1977	1978	Middlesbrough	Swansea City	36	3	1	0	8	2	1	0
Bonsall	C	Cyril	1903	East Kirkby		1922	1923	New Hucknall Colliery	Sutton Town	8	0	0	0	2	0	0	0
Bookman	LO	Louis	6/11/1890	Dolphin Bar (Eire)	1943	1920	1921	West Bromwich A.	Port Vale	72	9	0	0	4	1	0	0
Booton	H	Harold	02/03/06	Annesley	1976	1935	1936	Birmingham	Atherstone Town	7	0	0	2	0	0	0	0
Boutwood						1898				1	0	0	0	0	0	0	0
Boyd	WG	Willie	27/11/05	Cambuslang	1967	1935		Workington	Southampton	13	0	0	0	11	0	0	0
Boylen	RH	Robert	05/01/07	Newcastle	1992	1928	1929	St. Peters Albion	Gillingham	11	0	0	0	1	0	0	0
Bradley	JL	James	1896	Lismaghow		1920		Dundee Hibernian	Clapton Orient	5	0	0	0	1	0	0	0
Bramwell	J	John	01/03/37	Ashton-in-Makerfield		1960	1964	Everton	Rugby Town	187	11	8	0	0	1	0	0
Branston	TG	Terry	25/07/38	Rugby		1967	1970	Northampton Town	Lincoln City	101	6	11	0	9	0	1	0
Breacker	TS	Tim	02/07/65	Bicester		1983	1990	App.	West Ham Utd	210	21	24	7	3	0	0	0
Brennan	M	Matt	03/01/43	Glasgow		1962		St. Rochs	Chelmsford C	4	0	0	0	1	0	0	0
Brennan	RA	Bobby	14/03/25	Belfast		1947	1948	Distillery	Birmingham City	69	7	0	0	22	8	0	0
Brice	GHJ	Gordon	04/05/24	Bedford		1946		Bedford St Cuthberts	Wolves	13	1	0	0	0	0	0	0
Briggs	H	Harold	1904	Middlesbrough		1927		Darlington	Newark Town	2	0	0	0	0	0	0	0
Brock	JS	John	12/01/1878	Glasgow		1898	1899	Vale of Clyde		52	6	0	0	14	1	0	0

Player			D.O.B	Place of Birth	Died	First Season	Last Season	Previous Club	Next Club	Appearances				Goals			
										League	FAC	FLC	Other	League	FAC	FLC	Oth.
Brogan	D	Dave	11/01/39	Glasgow		1960		St. Anthonys		4	0	2	0	0	0	2	0
Brookes	GH	Gilbert	02/04/1895	Kidderminster	1952	1924		Swansea Town	Merthyr Town	42	1	0	0	0	0	0	0
Brown	AC	Albert	1895	Bedford		1922		Kettering	Kettering	1	0	0	0	0	0	0	0
Brown	AD	Allan	12/10/26	Kennoway		1956	1960	Blackpool	Portsmouth	151	15	2	4	51	6	0	2
Brown	J	James	1880	Luton		1899			Middlesbrough	13	0	0	0	1	0	0	0
Brown	MJ	Mick	11/04/44	Farnham Common		1967	1968	Millwall	Colchester Utd	14	1	2	0	2	0	0	0
Brown	TH	Tommy	1896	Glasgow		1924		South Shields		15	0	0	0	0	0	0	0
Brown	WI	William 'Buster'	06/09/09	West Silvertown	1993	1930	1934	Fairbairn House	Huddersfield T	49	5	0	3	4	0	0	0
Brown	WR	Roland	1875	Luton	1940	1899		Woodville	Watford	26	14	0	0	3	6	0	0
Bryce	RS	Robert	17/11/04	Grangemouth	1970	1930	1931	Bournemouth	Kings Park	34	3	0	0	8	1	0	0
Buckley	S	Steve	16/10/53	Brinsley		1974	1977	Burton Albion	Derby County	123	5	7	0	9	0	0	0
Bunn	FS	Frankie	06/11/62	Birmingham		1980	1984	App.	Hull City	59	4	7	0	9	0	3	0
Burbage	RW	Robert				1899		Hertford	Bedford Queens Engnrs	3	2	0	0	1	0	0	0
Burgess	W	William	1919	Wellingborough		1938		Rushden Town		5	0	0	0	0	0	0	0
Burke	MS	Mark	12/02/69	Solihull		1993		Wolves (loan)		3	1	0	0	0	0	0	0
Burtenshaw	CE	Charlie	16/10/22	Portslade		1948	1949	Southwick	Gillingham	11	0	0	0	1	0	0	0
Burtenshaw	WF	Bill	13/12/29	Portslade		1948		Southwick	Gillingham	1	0	0	0	0	0	0	0
Busby	VD	Viv	19/06/49	Wycombe		1969	1972	Wycombe W	Fulham	77	1	5	3	16	0	0	0
Butcher	G	George	25/10/1890	St Albans	1970	1920	1924	West Ham Utd		121	8	0	0	24	2	0	0
Butlin	BD	Barry	09/11/49	Rosliston		1972	1974	Derby County	Nottm. Forest	57	6	6	3	24	2	0	2
Buxton	IR	Ian	17/04/38	Cromford		1967	1968	Derby County	Notts County	47	3	1	0	14	1	0	0
Bywater	NL	Les	08/02/20	Lichfield		1946		Huddersfield T	Rochdale	19	4	0	0	0	0	0	0
Caleb	GS	Graham	25/05/45	Oxford		1963	1964	Oxford City	Kettering Town	20	3	1	0	0	0	0	0
Campbell	J	Jamie	21/10/72	Birmingham		1991	1993	Bramingham Spitfires	Barnet	36	4	2	3	1	0	0	0
Carr	D	David	31/01/57	Aylesham		1976	1978	Thanet	Lincoln City	43	4	1	0	0	0	1	0
Carrick	WF	Willie	26/09/52	Dublin		1972		Manchester Utd	Chelmsford C	4	1	0	1	0	0	0	0
Carroll	JT	Tony		Glasgow		1938		Leicester City	retired	13	0	0	0	0	0	0	0
Carte	R	Robert	11/10/13	Denaby	1986	1937	1938	Gainsborough Trin.	Bristol Rovers	6	0	0	0	0	0	0	0
Catlin	W	Walter				1897			Watford	1	0	0	0	1	0	0	0
Chamberlain	AFR	Alec	20/06/64	March		1988	1992	Everton	Sunderland	138	7	7	6	0	0	0	0
Chambers	BM	Brian	31/10/49	Newcastle-upon-Tyne		1974	1976	Arsenal	Millwall	76	4	2	0	9	1	0	0
Chandler	RAS	Robin	19/12/42	Luton		1960	1964	Juniors	Kettering	13	3	0	0	0	1	0	0
Chapman	JR	Joe	1908	Whittington Moor		1931		Fulham	Scunthorpe	1	0	0	0	0	0	0	0
Chenery	B	Ben	28/01/77	Ipswich		1994	1995	YTS	Cambridge United	2	1	0	0	0	0	0	0
Clapton	DR	Danny	22/07/34	Stepney	1986	1962		Arsenal	Corinthians (AUS)	10	1	0	0	0	0	0	0
Claridge	SE	Steve	10/04/66	Portsmouth		1992		Cambridge Utd	Cambridge Utd	16	0	2	2	2	0	3	1
Clark	AW	Archie	04/04/02	Shoreham, Kent	1967	1928	1930	Arsenal	Everton	87	5	0	0	11	0	0	0
Clark	C	Charlie		Fleet	1944	1938		QPR		14	1	0	0	6	0	0	0
Clark	J	John	1900	Bo'ness		1926		Arsenal	Bo'ness	29	1	0	0	2	1	0	0
Clarke	A	Alan	10/04/42	Houghton Regis		1961	1964	Juniors	Dunstable T	9	0	1	0	0	0	0	0
Clarke	J					1897				1	0	0	0	0	0	0	0
Clarke	PR	Percy				1923			Peterborough	1	0	0	0	0	0	0	0
Clarke	WE	Walter	1874	Rushden		1898		Rushden Town		4	0	0	0	0	0	0	0
Clarkson	W	Billy	1891	Wombwell	1954	1922		Rotherham County	Pontpridd	32	1	0	0	3	0	0	0
Cobb	GE	Gary	06/08/68	Luton		1986	1988	Limbury BC	Fulham	9	0	0	2	0	0	0	0
Cockerill	HL	Harry	14/01/1894	Ryhope	1960	1920		Arsenal	Mid Rhondda	8	0	0	0	0	0	0	0
Cockle	ES	Ernie	12/09/1896	East Ham	1966	1924		Arsenal	Northampton Town	7	0	0	0	1	0	0	0
Coen	JL	Joe	04/12/11	Glasgow	1941	1934	1938	Bournemouth		142	11	0	5	0	0	0	0
Collier	AS	Alan	24/03/38	Markyate		1958	1960	Juniors	Chelmsford C	10	0	0	3	0	0	0	0
Collins	JW	John	10/08/42	Chiswick		1969	1970	Reading	Cambridge Utd	42	3	3	0	10	2	0	0
Collins	MJA	Mike	01/02/38	Bermondsey		1959	1961	Juniors	Bedford T	8	0	2	0	0	0	0	0
Collins	WH	Bill	15/02/20	Belfast		1947	1948	Belfast Celtic	Gillingham	7	0	0	0	0	0	0	0
Colquhoun	DW	David	23/01/06	Motherwell	1983	1934	1935	Tottenham H	Rochdale	16	0	0	1	0	0	0	0
Conboy	FJA	Frank	05/09/47	Marylebone		1966		Chelsea	Cheltenham T	19	2	0	0	1	0	0	0
Connelly	E	Eddie	09/12/16	Dumbarton	1990	1937	1938	Newcastle United	West Bromwich A.	88	2	0	0	24	0	0	0
						1946	1947	West Bromwich A.	Leyton Orient								
Cook	C	Colin	08/01/09	North Shields		1934	1935	Chesterfield	Northampton Town	8	0	0	1	5	0	0	0
Cooke	RE	Richard	04/09/65	Islington		1988	1989	Bournemouth	Bournemouth	17	0	0	2	1	0	0	0
Cooke	WH	Harry	07/03/19	Whittington	1992	1946	1952	Bournemouth	Shrewsbury Town	210	18	0	0	4	0	0	0
Coote	SA	Stanley	1909	Harpenden		1932		Arden Wednesday	Reading	1	0	0	0	0	0	0	0
Cope	R	Ron	05/10/34	Crewe		1961	1962	Manchester Utd	Northwich Vic.	28	2	1	0	0	0	0	0
Corkindale	WJ	Billy	19/05/01	Birmingham	1972	1932		Millwall	Shrewsbury	1	1	0	0	0	0	0	0
Cottingham	T	Tom		Lanark		1922		Hamilton Acad.	Dundee Utd	1	0	0	0	0	0	0	0
Coupar	J	James	1873	Dundee		1897		Rotherham Town	Swindon T	26	8	0	0	9	1	0	0
Court	DJ	David	01/03/44	Mitcham		1970	1971	Arsenal	Brentford	52	3	3	1	0	0	0	0
Crompton	W	Wilf	01/04/08	Blackburn	1971	1934	1936	Gillingham	retired injury	48	6	0	0	15	1	0	0
Crook	MS	Mark	29/06/03	Morley	1977	1935		Wolves		5	0	0	1	1	0	0	0
Crump	WH	William	10/02/1874	Smethwick	1943	1898		Tottenham Hotspur	Tottenham Hotspur	25	5	0	0	0	1	0	0
Cruse	PL	Peter	10/01/51	Camden		1973		Arsenal	Enfield	4	0	2	0	0	0	0	0
Cullen	MJ	Mick	03/07/31	Glasgow		1951	1957	Douglasdale Jnrs.	Grimsby Town	112	9	0	4	17	3	0	0
Cummins	GP	George	12/03/31	Dublin		1953	1960	Everton	Cambridge C	184	17	0	11	21	4	0	5
Cupit	WW	Billy	1912	Huthwaite		1931		Sutton Junction	Mansfield Town	8	0	0	0	1	0	0	0
Curwen	W	Billy	1905	High Spen		1928		Willington	Thames Assoc.	1	0	0	0	0	0	0	0
Daly	J	Joe	28/12/1897	Lancaster		1928	1929	Northampton Town	Gillingham	70	6	0	0	5	0	0	0
Daniel	AW	Alan	05/04/40	Ashford, Kent		1958	1963	Bexleyheath & W.		50	2	2	2	3	0	0	0
Daniel	MJ	Mel	26/01/16	Llanelli	1997	1946	1948	Ashford T	Aldershot	53	5	0	0	20	2	0	0
Daniel	RC	Ray	10/12/64	Luton		1982	1985	App.	Hull City	22	6	2	0	4	0	0	0
Danskin	C	Charlie		Stockport		1923		Aberdare Ath.	Dragon (Pontypridd)	11	0	0	0	0	0	0	0
Davie	AG	Sandy	10/06/45	Dundee		1968	1969	Dundee	Southampton	58	6	2	0	0	0	0	0

Player			D.O.B	Place of Birth	Died	First Season	Last Season	Previous Club	Next Club	Appearances				Goals			
										League	FAC	FLC	Other	Leagu	FAC	FLC	Oth.
Davie	WC	Willie	07/01/25	Paisley		1950	1951	St Mirren	Huddersfield T	42	2	0	0	11	1	0	0
Davies	AS	Bert	01/03/1894	Swindon	1976	1927		Swindon Town	Garrard Athletic	4	0	0	0	0	0	0	0
Davies	RA	Roy	23/08/24	Capetown (SA)	1973	1951	1957	Clyde	Bedford T	150	16	0	5	24	2	0	1
Davies	RT	Ron	25/05/42	Holywell		1962	1963	Chester	Norwich City	32	1	0	0	21	0	0	0
Davies	S	Samuel		Nantwich		1897		Bury	Gravesend	25	7	0	0	1	1	0	0
Davis	KG	Kelvin	29/09/76	Bedford		1993	1996	YTS		16	0	0	5	0	0	0	0
Davis	SM	Steve	30/10/68	Hexham		1995	1996	Burnley		80	4	8	10	10	0	0	1
Daw	EC	Edwin 'Teddy'	23/01/1875	Doncaster	1944	1899		Rushden	Leicester City	34	4	0	0	2	0	0	0
Dawson						1899				2	0	0	0	0	0	0	0
Dawes	AG	Bert	23/04/07	Frimley Green	1973	1936	1937	Crystal Palace	Crystal Palace	44	3	0	0	18	1	0	0
Day	MR	Mervyn	26/06/55	Chelmsford		1991		Leeds Utd (loan)		4	0	0	0	0	0	0	0
Deans	J	John 'Dixie'	30/07/46	Johnstone Linwood		1976		Celtic	Partick Thistle	14	0	1	0	6	0	0	0
Dennis	GT	George	12/09/1897	Moira	1969	1924	1928	Nottm. Forest	Norwich City	139	11	0	0	42	3	0	0
Dent	F	Fred	24/01/1896	Sheffield	1983	1930		Swindon Town	Sheff. Emplymnt Exchnge	13	3	0	0	5	0	0	0
Denton	PR	Peter	01/03/46	Gorleston		1967	1968	Coventry City	Canterbury	5	0	0	0	0	0	0	0
Diaper	AWF	Albert	11/02/09	Woolston		1932		Arsenal	Fulham	3	0	0	0	0	0	0	0
Dibble	AG	Andy	08/05/65	Cwmbran		1984	1988	Cardiff City	Manchester City	30	2	4	2	0	0	0	0
Dickov	P	Paul	01/11/72	Glasgow		1993		Arsenal (loan)		15	0	0	0	1	0	0	0
Dimmock	R					1899				12	0	0	0	2	0	0	0
Dixon	KM	Kerry	24/07/61	Luton		1992	1994	Southampton	Millwall	75	9	2	2	19	0	0	1
Dixon	M	Mike	14/03/37	Willesden		1958	1960	Hitchin T	Coventry City	3	0	0	1	1	0	0	0
Docherty	J	James		Pollokshaws		1897		Derby County	Cowes	30	8	0	0	0	2	0	0
Dolman	HW	Bill	30/08/03	Bloxwich	1964	1935	1938	Bristol City		62	4	0	1	0	0	0	0
Donaghy	MM	Mal	13/09/57	Belfast		1978	1988	Larne T	Manchester Utd	415	36	34	3	16	3	2	0
						1989			Manchester Utd (loan)								
Donaldson	R	Robert				1897		Manchester Utd	Glossop	17	1	0	0	10	0	0	0
Dougan	MS	Max	23/05/38	Stoneyburn		1966	1969	Leicester City	Bedford T	118	6	8	0	0	0	0	0
Douglas	SA	Stuart	09/04/78	Enfield		1995	1996	YTS		17	1	1	1	1	0	0	0
Dow	JM	John	1873	Dundee		1898	1899	Glossop	Middlesbrough	56	9	0	0	1	1	0	0
Dowie	I	Iain	09/01/65	Hatfield		1988	1990	Hendon	West Ham U	66	3	4	4	15	0	0	4
Downie	JD	Johnny	19/07/25	Lanark		1953		Manchester Utd	Hull City	26	0	0	0	12	0	0	0
Draper	F	"Bob"	1876	Luton	1901	1898	1899			9	1	0	0	3	0	0	0
Dreyer	G	Gordon	1914	Sunderland		1937	1938	Hartlepool Utd	Bedford T	23	1	0	0	0	0	0	0
Dreyer	JB	John	11/06/63	Alnwick		1988	1993	Oxford United	Stoke City	214	14	14	7	13	0	1	1
Drinnan	JMcK	Jimmy	28/05/06	Harthill	1936	1929		Brentford	Burnley	31	1	0	0	12	0	0	0
Driver	A	Allenby	29/09/18	Blackwell, Derbyshire		1946	1947	Sheffield Wed.	Norwich City	41	4	0	0	13	0	0	0
Droy	MR	Micky	07/05/51	Highbury		1984		Chelsea (loan)		2	0	1	0	0	0	0	0
Duggan	EJ	Ted	27/07/22	Plaistow	1982	1946	1948	Juniors	QPR	48	1	0	0	20	0	0	0
Duke	GE	George	06/09/20	West Hampnett		1946	1948	Southwick	Bournemouth	16	1	0	0	0	0	0	0
Duncan	D	Douglas 'Dally'	14/10/09	Aberdeen	1990	1946	1947	Derby County	manager	32	4	0	0	4	0	0	0
Dunne	S	Shay	13/04/30	Wicklow		1951		Shelbourne	Yiewsley	301	14	0	8	0	0	0	0
Dunsmore	TH	Tom		Motherwell		1938	1938	Hibernian		40	3	0	0	0	0	0	0
Durrant	AF	Arthur 'Jimmy'	1878	Luton	1927	1897	1899	Luton Stanley	Leicester City	32	22	0	0	8	10	0	0
Eckford	J	John	13/02/1878	Buckhaven		1899		Raith Rovers	Middlesbrough	34	4	0	0	4	1	0	0
Edwards	GG	Gerald		Hong Kong		1930		Cambridge University		2	0	0	0	0	0	0	0
Edwards	RL	Dick	05/11/43	Kingsbury		1964	1965	Admult	Kettering T	17	3	2	0	1	0	0	0
Ekins	FG	Frederick	27/09/1871	New Brompton		1897	1898	Burton Swifts		33	10	0	0	5	1	0	0
Elliott	PM	Paul	18/03/64	Lewisham		1982	1985	Charlton Ath.	Aston Villa	66	2	5	0	3	0	0	0
Elliott	SB	Steve	15/09/58	Haltwhistle		1984		Preston NE	Walsall	12	0	3	0	3	0	3	0
Elstrup	L	Lars	24/03/63	Rarby, Denmark		1989	1990	OB Odense	OB Odense	60	3	4	3	19	2	5	1
Evers	S	Sean	10/10/77	Hitchin		1995	1996	YTS		2	0	0	2	0	0	0	0
Fairchild	MP	Mick	24/11/42	Brixworth		1960	1963	Lowestoft Town	Reading	21	2	4	0	1	1	1	0
Fairgrieve	RW	Walter	30/08/1874	Edinburgh		1899		Southampton	Partick Thistle	15	4	0	0	5	2	0	0
Farr	H					1898			Southend	1	0	0	0	0	0	0	0
Farrell	SP	Sean	28/02/69	Watford		1989	1991	App.	Fulham	25	3	0	3	1	1	0	2
Faulkner	JG	John	10/03/48	Orpington		1972	1977	Leeds United	Memphis Rogues	209	12	15	3	6	0	1	0
Fellowes	WJ	Bill	15/03/10	Bradford		1935	1937	Clapton Orient	Exeter City	110	11	0	3	3	0	0	0
Ferguson	C	Charlie	22/11/10	Dunfermline	1995	1937	1938	Notts County	Aberdeen	29	4	0	0	10	3	0	0
Fern	RA	Rodney	13/12/48	Measham		1972	1974	Leicester City	Chesterfield	39	1	4	3	5	0	0	0
Feuer	AI	Ian	20/05/71	Las Vegas		1995	1996	West Ham Utd		84	5	6	3	0	0	0	0
Fincham	GR	Gordon	08/01/35	Peterborough		1963	1964	Plymouth Argyle	Port Elizabeth (SA)	64	3	2	0	0	0	1	0
Findlay	JW	Jake	13/07/54	Blairgowrie		1978	1984	Aston Villa	Swindon Town	167	8	12	0	0	0	0	0
Finlayson	J	John		Thornliebank		1935	1938	Clapton Orient		154	12	0	2	9	0	0	0
Finney	T	Tom	06/11/52	Belfast		1973		Crusaders	Sunderland	14	3	4	0	5	0	1	0
Fleming	JP	Jim	07/01/42	Alloa		1960	1962	Partick Thistle	Partick Thistle	66	3	5	0	9	1	1	0
Forbes	AS	Alex		Bo'ness		1928		Musselburgh Bruntonians	Bournemouth	1	0	0	0	0	0	0	0
Ford	C	Charles	04/03/1878	Arbroath		1898		Arbroath	Reading	24	6	0	0	0	0	0	0
Ford	WG	Bill	07/05/1876	Albion	1948	1898		New Brompton	Gravesend	23	3	0	0	7	0	0	0
Foster	JH	John	1889	Wombwell		1921	1923	Notts County	Hartlepool Utd	47	3	0	0	3	0	0	0
Foster	SB	Steve	24/09/57	Portsmouth		1984	1988	Aston Villa	Oxford United	163	27	20	3	11	2	1	0
Fotiadis	A	Andrew	06/09/77	Hitchin		1996		(youth)		17	1	2	3	3	0	0	0
Fraser	CR	Charles	1907	Plaistow		1926	1934	Fairbairn House Lads		246	24	0	2	4	0	0	0
French	GE	Graham	06/04/45	Wolverhampton		1965	1972	Wellington T	Southport	182	8	10	2	21	1	0	0
Fry	BF	Barry	07/04/45	Bedford		1965		Bolton Wanderers	Gravesend & Northfleet	6	1	0	0	0	0	0	0
Fuccillo	P	Pasquale 'Lil'	02/05/56	Bedford		1974	1982	App.	Tulsa Roughnecks	160	7	13	0	24	1	2	0
Fulton	JJ	John	22/12/03	Kilmarnock	1963	1927	1929	Kilbirnie Ladeside	Norwich City	81	5	0	0	0	0	0	0
Futcher	P	Paul	25/09/56	Chester		1974	1977	Chester	Manchester City	131	6	4	1	1	0	0	0
Futcher	GR	Ron	25/09/56	Chester		1974	1977	Chester	Manchester City	120	8	5	0	40	1	2	0
Gager	HE	Horace	25/01/17	West Ham	1984	1946	1947	Vauxhall Motors	Nottm. Forest	59	5	0	0	2	0	0	0

Player			D.O.B	Place of Birth	Died	First Season	Last Season	Previous Club	Next Club	Appearances				Goals			
										League	FAC	FLC	Other	League	FAC	FLC	Oth.
Galbraith	H	Hugh	02/12/1868	Govan		1930	1898	Burnley	Glossop	3	18	0	0	0	10	0	0
Gale	EWA	Ernie	14/08/11		1972	1930	1931	Southall		11	0	0	0	0	0	0	0
Gallacher	W					1897		Bootle	Glossop	30	12	0	0	7	6	0	0
Galloway	SR	Randolph	22/12/1896	Sunderland	1964	1927		Nottm. Forest	Coventry City	2	0	0	0	1	0	0	0
Gardiner	D	Doug	29/03/17	Douglas		1946	1950	Auchinleck Talbot	Bedford Town	121	13	0	0	1	0	0	0
Garner	AH	Alan	02/02/51	Lambeth		1971	1974	Millwall	Watford	88	8	11	5	3	1	0	0
Garratt	A					1899				1	0	0	0	0	0	0	0
Geddis	D	David	12/03/58	Carlisle		1976		Ipswich Town (loan)		17	0	0	0	4	0	0	0
						1982		Aston Villa (loan)									
Gentle						1898		Luton Amateurs		5	0	0	0	0	0	0	0
Gibbon	T	Tommy	24/03/1891	West Hartlepool	1975	1922	1923	Dundee	QPR	69	1	0	0	0	0	0	0
Gibson	J	Jim	04/09/40	Belfast		1964	1965	Cambridge U	South Africa	32	4	2	0	0	0	1	0
Gibson	JR	Jock	23/03/1898	Philadelphia, USA	1974	1933		Sheffield Utd	Vauxhall Motors	3	0	0	0	0	0	0	0
Givens	DJ	Don	09/08/49	Limerick		1970	1971	Manchester Utd	QPR	83	3	4	1	19	1	2	0
Glover	A	Alec	28/02/22	Glasgow		1949	1950	Bradford PA	Blackburn Rovers	56	3	0	0	6	0	0	0
Glover	EL	Lee	24/04/70	Kettering		1991		Nottm. Forest (loan)		1	0	0	0	0	0	0	0
Godden	AL	Tony	02/08/55	Gillingham		1982		West Brom (loan)		12	0	0	0	0	0	0	0
Godfrey	WP	Will	29/04/10	Stenhousemuir	1978	1935	1936	Plymouth Argyle	Vauxhall Motors	6	0	0	0	0	0	0	0
Goldie	J	Jim	29/06/40	Denny		1962		Kilsyth Rangers	York City	7	0	1	0	2	0	0	0
Goodeve	KGA	Ken	03/09/50	Manchester		1970	1972	Manchester Utd	Brighton & Hove A.	15	0	0	4	0	0	0	0
Goodyear	C	Clive	15/01/61	Lincoln		1979	1983	Lincoln United	Plymouth Argyle	90	4	5	0	3	0	0	0
Goodyear	GW	George	05/07/16	Luton		1946		Hitchin Town	Southend Utd	10	2	0	0	0	0	0	0
Gooney	WH	Bill	08/10/10	Sheffield	1978	1935		Plymouth Argyle		4	0	0	0	0	0	0	0
Gordon	J	John		Kirkcudbright		1926	1927	Greenock Morton	Dunfermline Ath.	14	0	0	0	0	0	0	0
Graham	RC	Bob	25/08/00	Muirkirk		1921	1928	Kilwinning Rangers	Norwich City	164	11	0	0	5	0	0	0
Grant	K	Kim	25/09/72	Sekondi-Takaradi, Ghana		1995	1996	Charlton Ath	Millwall	35	2	4	3	5	0	2	1
Gray	RP	Paul	28/01/70	Portsmouth		1987	1989	YTS	Wigan Ath.	7	0	0	4	1	0	0	1
Gray	P	Phil	02/10/68	Belfast		1991	1992	Tottenham H	Sunderland	59	2	4	2	22	1	3	0
Grealish	AP	Tony	21/09/56	Paddington		1979	1980	Orient	Brighton & Hove A.	78	3	5	0	2	0	0	0
Green	HR	Rodney	24/06/39	Halifax		1967		Charlton Ath.	Watford	11	0	2	0	3	0	0	0
Green	J	John		Blackburn	1927	1923		Nottm. Forest	Southend U (trial)	26	1	0	0	5	1	0	0
Greene	DM	David	26/10/73	Luton		1992	1994	St Joseph's	Colchester Utd	19	1	2	1	0	0	0	0
Gregory	AC	Tony	16/05/37	Luton		1955	1959	Vauxhall Motors	Watford	59	11	0	8	17	7	0	1
Griffiths	EO	Edward	1916	Tipton		1937		Stourbridge		6	0	0	0	1	0	0	0
Grimes	AA	Ashley	02/08/57	Dublin		1984	1988	Coventry City	Osasuna	88	11	14	4	3	0	1	0
Gripton	EW	Billy	02/07/20	Tipton	1981	1948		West Bromwich A.	Bournemouth	3	0	0	0	0	0	0	0
Groves	J	John	16/09/33	Derby		1953	1962	Juniors	Bournemouth	218	16	6	11	15	0	0	2
Guentchev	BL	Bontcho	07/07/64	Tchosevo, Bulgaria		1995	1996	Ipswich T	(Bulgaria)	62	4	7	7	10	0	0	2
Guild	AN	Alan	27/03/47	Forfar		1970		East Fife	Cambridge Utd	1	0	1	0	0	0	0	0
Hacking	RE	Bob	30/03/18	Blackburn		1946		Blackburn Rovers	Brighton & Hove A.	1	0	0	0	0	0	0	0
Hails	W	Billy	19/02/35	Nettlesworth		1964		Northampton Town	(assistant manager)	3	0	0	0	0	0	0	0
Hale	A	Alf 'Pally'	24/01/06	Kiveton Park	1972	1930	1931	Lincoln City	Llanelly	22	1	0	0	0	0	0	0
Hales	DD	Derek	15/12/51	Lower Halstow		1972		Dartford	Charlton Ath.	7	1	0	1	1	0	0	0
Hall	LF	Les	01/10/21	St Albans		1947	1954	St Albans City	Hemel Hempstead	79	12	0	0	0	0	0	0
Halom	VL	Vic	03/10/48	Coton Park		1971	1972	Fulham	Sunderland	59	1	3	0	17	0	0	0
Hancock	E	Ted	29/03/07	Denaby Main		1936	1937	Burnley	Lincoln City	26	1	0	0	3	0	0	0
Harber	WH	Billy	03/12/44	Hitchin		1964	1965	Swindon Town	Corby Town	28	4	1	0	3	0	0	0
Hare	T	Tommy	01/04/44	Motherwell		1967		Southampton	Workington	12	2	2	0	0	0	0	0
Harfield	LP	Les	22/11/52	Southampton		1972		Southampton	Folkestone	1	0	0	0	0	0	0	0
Harford	GB	George	1910	Abbey Wood		1929	1933	Millwall	Carlisle Utd	99	7	0	1	0	0	0	0
Harford	MG	Mick	12/02/59	Sunderland		1984	1989	Birmingham City	Derby County	168	27	17	4	69	10	10	3
						1991		Derby County	Chelsea								
Harkins	J	James		Paisley		1927		Third Lanark	Port Vale	4	0	0	0	3	0	0	0
Harper	A	Alan	01/11/60	Liverpool		1993		Everton	Burnley	41	7	0	0	1	0	0	0
Harper	WG	Bill	22/03/02	Bothwell		1926		Crystal Palace	Weymouth	31	3	0	0	0	0	0	0
Harris	B	Bernard	14/03/1899	Sheffield		1928		Sheffield Utd	QPR	19	5	0	0	0	0	0	0
Harrison	MJ	Mike	18/04/40	Ilford		1968	1969	Plymouth Argyle	Dover	31	3	3	0	6	2	2	0
Harrow	A	Andy	06/11/56	Kirkcaldy		1980		Raith Rovers	Aberdeen	4	0	0	0	0	0	0	0
Hartson	J	John	05/04/75	Swansea		1993	1994	YTS	Arsenal	54	6	0	2	11	2	0	0
Harvey	RG	Richard	17/04/69	Letchworth		1986	1996	App.	Stevenage Borough	155	8	8	13	4	0	1	0
Hatton	RJ	Bob	10/04/47	Hull		1978	1979	Blackpool	Sheffield Utd	82	2	6	0	29	0	2	0
Havenga	WS	Willie	06/11/24	Bloemfontein		1950	1951	Birmingham City	Ipswich Town	18	1	0	0	6	1	0	0
Hawkes	B	Barry	21/03/38	Easington, Co Durham		1958	1959	Shotton Colliery Welfare	Darlington	8	1	0	0	0	0	0	0
Hawkes	JF	Fred	17/4/1881	Luton		1899		Luton Stanley		2	0	0	0	1	0	0	0
Hawkes	KK	Ken	06/05/33	Easington, Co Durham		1957	1960	Shotton Colliery Welfare	Peterborough Utd	90	10	0	2	1	0	0	0
Hawkes	T	Thomas				1898				2	0	0	0	0	0	0	0
Hayhurst	A	Bert	17/09/05	Birdwell	1991	1932		Frickley Colliery	Reading	1	1	0	0	0	0	0	0
Heale	GJ	Gary	15/07/58	Canvey Island		1977	1978	Canvey Island	Reading	7	1	3	0	1	0	2	0
Henderson	WJ	Bill	11/01/1899	Carlisle	1934	1922	1923	Arsenal	Southampton	2	0	0	0	0	0	0	0
Heslop	AS	Archie		Annfield Plain		1930	1931	West Stanley	Spennymoor Utd	27	0	0	0	8	0	0	0
Hewitt	G	George	1878	Burslem		1898		Burslem Port Vale		12	5	0	0	6	2	0	0
Higginbotham	H	Harry		Sydney		1920	1922	South Shields	Clapton Orient	80	8	0	0	26	4	0	0
Hilaire	VM	Vince	10/10/59	Forest Hill		1984		Crystal Palace	Portsmouth	6	0	3	0	0	0	0	0
Hill	FWP	Percy	25/03/1895	Luton	1970	1920		Luton Clarence	Exeter City	6	0	0	0	4	0	0	0
Hill	RA	Ricky	05/03/59	Paddington		1975	1988	App.	Le Havre	436	33	38	0	54	6	5	0
Hindson	G	Gordon	08/01/50	Flint Hill		1971	1974	Newcastle United	Hartford Bicentennials	68	5	4	6	3	0	1	1
Hoar	S	Syd	28/11/1895	Leagrave	1969	1920	1924	Luton Clarence	Arsenal	160	16	0	0	26	3	0	0
Hodge	J	Jack		Plymouth		1935	1936	Bristol City	Colchester United	20	2	0	3	1	0	0	0
Hodgson	T	Tommy	19/01/03	Hetton-le-Hole	1989	1930	1932	West Ham Utd	Luton Postal	67	7	0	0	0	0	0	0

Player			D.O.B	Place of Birth	Died	First Season	Last Season	Previous Club	Next Club	Appearances				Goals			
										League	FAC	FLC	Other	Leagu	FAC	FLC	Oth.
Hogg	F	Fred	24/04/18	Bishop Auckland		1937		West Auckland	Mansfield Town	4	0	0	0	0	0	0	0
Holbeach	F	Fred	17/03/10	Mansfield		1933		Grantham	Yeovil & Petters	2	0	0	0	0	0	0	0
Holdstock	H	Herbert	29/10/1879	St Albans		1899		Luton Star	Nottm. Forest	13	4	0	0	1	1	0	0
Holmes	WG	Billy	04/02/51	Balham	1987	1973		Millwall	Barnet	1	0	0	0	0	0	0	0
Holsgrove	P	Paul	26/08/69	Wellington, Salop		1990	1991	Wokingham Town	Heracles	2	0	0	0	0	0	0	0
Horn	GR	Graham	23/08/54	Westminster		1972	1974	Arsenal	Los Angeles Aztecs	58	5	3	6	0	0	0	0
Horton	B	Brian	04/02/49	Hednesford		1981	1983	Brighton & Hove A.	Hull City	118	6	8	0	9	2	0	0
Hoten	RV	Ralph	27/12/1896	Pinxton	1978	1922	1924	Portsmouth	Northampton Town	59	1	0	0	13	0	0	0
Houghton	SA	Scott	22/10/71	Hitchin		1993	1994	Tottenham Hotspur	Walsall	16	0	3	2	1	0	0	0
Hoy	RE	Roger	06/12/46	Poplar		1970	1971	Crystal Palace	Cardiff City	32	2	2	1	0	0	0	0
Hubbard	AA	Arthur	1911	Erdington		1935	1936	Birmingham	Dunstable Town	4	0	0	2	0	0	0	0
Hughes	CM	Ceri	26/02/71	Llwynpia		1989	1996	Llwynpia Boys Club	Wimbledon	175	11	13	7	17	2	1	0
Hughes	I	Iorrie	26/05/25	Llandulas	1993	1949	1950	Llandudno	Cardiff City	36	0	0	0	0	0	0	0
Hughes	WM	Billy	06/03/18	Carmarthen	1981	1947		Birmingham City	Chelsea	31	3	0	0	0	0	0	0
Hull	F	Frank	1896	Dunstable		1920		Luton Amateurs	Torquay Utd	3	0	0	0	0	0	0	0
Husband	J	Jimmy	15/10/47	Newcastle-upon-Tyne		1973	1977	Everton	Memphis Rogues	143	10	6	3	44	0	2	2
Hutchinson	A	Albert		Sheffield		1929		Atlas & Norfolk	Torquay United	5	0	0	0	1	0	0	0
Hutchison	D	Davie	29/10/08	Shotts		1932	1934	Carlisle Utd	Airdrie	55	2	0	1	22	0	0	0
Imlach	JJS	Stuart	06/01/32	Lossiemouth		1960		Nottm. Forest	Coventry City	8	0	1	0	0	0	0	0
Imrie	JJ	James		Markinch		1931	1932	Crystal Palace	Doncaster Rovers	63	7	0	0	0	0	0	0
Inglis	JA	James	1872	Kirkland		1899		Small Heath		4	0	0	0	3	0	0	0
Ingram	GPA	Godfrey	26/10/59	Luton		1977	1981	App.	San Jose Earthquakes	27	4	2	0	6	2	0	0
Irvine	TB	Tommy	06/07/1898	Springside		1922		Dreghorn	Bedford Town	8	0	0	0	0	0	0	0
Jackson	MA	Matthew	19/10/71	Leeds		1990	1991	Juniors	Everton	9	0	2	1	0	0	0	0
James	JC	Julian	22/03/70	Tring		1987	1996	Tring Tornados		258	22	16	13	13	0	1	0
James	PGB	Percy	09/03/17	Rhondda		1949		Oxford City	Worcester City	2	0	0	0	1	0	0	0
Jardine	F	Fred	27/09/41	Edinburgh		1961	1969	Dundee	Torquay United	220	12	11	0	9	0	1	0
Jennings	W	Bill	25/02/1891	Cinderhill		1922	1925	Merthyr Town	Northampton Town	114	3	0	0	2	0	0	0
Jennings	WJ	Billy	20/02/52	Hackney		1981	1981	Orient	Dagenham	2	0	0	0	1	0	0	0
Jinks	JT	Jimmy	19/08/16	Camberwell	1981	1949	1950	Fulham	Aldershot	9	0	0	0	2	0	0	0
Johnson	B	Brian	12/11/48	Newcastle-upon-Tyne		1966	1967	Sunderland	Darlington	10	2	0	0	0	0	0	0
Johnson	G	Gavin	10/10/70	Eye		1995	1995	Ipswich T	Wigan Ath	6	0	0	0	0	0	0	0
Johnson	J	Joe		Stamford		1924	1924	Watford		11	0	0	0	0	0	0	0
Johnson	MA	Marvin	29/10/68	Wembley		1987	1996	App.		245	13	16	15	4	1	1	0
Johnson	RS	Rob	22/02/62	Bedford		1983	1988	Bedford T	Leicester City	97	15	11	3	0	0	1	0
Jones	G	Graham	02/06/59	Worsley		1975	1979	App.	Torquay United	39	4	0	0	0	0	0	0
Jones	LC	Les	01/01/30	Mountain Ash		1950	1957	Craig Athletic	Aston Villa	98	7	0	5	1	0	0	0
Jones	VW	Vince	01/07/00	Carmarthen	1950	1931		Millwall	Norwich City	3	0	0	0	0	0	0	0
Judge	AG	Alan	14/05/60	Kingsbury		1979	1982	Juniors	Reading	11	0	1	0	0	0	0	0
Kamara	C	Chris	25/12/57	Middlesbrough		1991	1992	Leeds United	Sheffield Utd	49	1	2	2	0	0	0	0
Kean	FW	Fred	10/12/1898	Sheffield	1973	1931	1934	Bolton Wanderers	Sutton Town	117	13	0	1	5	1	0	0
Keen	MT	Mike	19/03/40	High Wycombe		1968	1971	QPR	Watford	144	6	9	1	11	0	0	0
Keen	WJ	Billy		Hazelmere		1924		Millwall		3	0	0	0	0	0	0	0
Kellock	W	Billy	07/02/54	Glasgow		1982		Peterborough Utd	Wolves	7	1	1	0	0	0	2	0
Kelly	TWJ	Terry	16/01/32	Luton		1954	1962	Vauxhall Motors	Cambridge City	136	9	0	5	1	0	0	0
Kemplay	J	James	17/01/1876	Middlesbrough		1898		Middlesbrough St John		29	5	0	0	11	1	0	0
Kennedy	MF	Mick	09/04/61	Salford		1989		Leicester City	Stoke City	32	1	2	1	0	0	0	0
Kerr	A	Andy		Falkirk		1923	1924	Androssen Winton Rov.	Reading	68	1	0	0	25	0	0	0
Kettley	SC	Spencer	22/05/21	Rhondda		1946		Newbury Town		1	0	0	0	0	0	0	0
Kevan	DT	Derek	06/03/35	Ripon		1966		Peterborough Utd	Stockport Co.	11	1	0	0	4	2	0	0
Kidd	GI	George	20/05/09	Dundee	1988	1934	1935	Gillingham	Gillingham	9	0	0	1	0	0	0	0
Kiernan	T	Tommy	20/10/18	Coatbridge		1948	1950	Stoke City	St, Mirren	55	5	0	0	10	5	0	0
Kilgannon	J	John	26/06/36	Stenhousemuir	1967	1958	1959	Stenhousemuir	Stirling Albion	13	0	0	3	1	0	0	0
King	AE	Andy	14/08/56	Luton		1974	1975	App.	Everton	36	5	1	0	9	0	0	0
						1985		Wolves	Aldershot								
King	GH	Gerry	09/04/47	Radnor		1966		Torquay United	Newport County	22	1	2	0	4	0	1	0
King	TP	Tom	29/06/09	Woolsthorpe, Belvoir	1993	1936	1938	Bournemouth		55	2	0	0	0	0	0	0
Kingham	HR	Henry	19/11/04	Harpenden		1926	1936	St. Albans City	Yeovil & Petters	250	22	0	3	0	0	0	0
Kirkwood	D	Dan	24/12/00	Dalserf		1933		Brighton & Hove A.	Swindon Town	2	0	0	0	1	0	0	0
Kitchen	H	Harry	1914	Bolsover		1933		Bolsover Colliery		1	0	0	0	1	0	0	0
Kiwomya	A	Andy	01/10/76	Huddersfield		1996		Bradford City (loan)		5	0	0	0	1	0	0	0
Knight	A	Tony	06/03/59	Romford		1976	1977	App.	Dover	6	1	0	0	0	0	0	0
Knights	AF	Anthony	13/02/40	Grimsby		1964		Grimsby Town	Aldershot	2	0	2	0	0	0	0	0
Lake	LE	Leslie	29/01/23	Luton	1976	1946	1950	Holly Rangers		59	4	0	0	0	0	0	0
Lamb	JW	John	1892	Claycross		1920		Sheffield Wed.	Matlock Town	24	4	0	0	0	0	0	0
Lawson	D	David	22/12/47	Wellsend		1978		Everton	Stockport Co.	5	0	0	0	0	0	0	0
Lawson	H	Bert	12/04/05	Luton		1933		Brentford	Bedford T	1	0	0	0	0	0	0	0
Legate	RA	Roly	04/05/39	Arlesey		1956	1961	Arlesey Town	Yiewsley	15	3	0	0	8	0	0	0
Lennon	GF	George	24/05/1889	Kilwinning	1984	1920	1922	St Mirren	Stoke City	107	8	0	0	0	0	0	0
Lewis	B	Brian	26/01/43	Woking		1968	1969	Coventry City	Oxford United	50	3	6	0	22	0	3	0
Lewis	J	Jack		Gwersyllt		1937		Wrexham		2	0	0	0	0	0	0	0
Lindsay	D	David	23/09/19	Dumbarton		1948		St. Mirren	Barnsley	7	0	0	0	0	0	0	0
Linton	DM	Des	05/09/71	Birmingham		1991	1996	Leicester City	Peterborough Utd	83	9	5	7	1	0	0	0
Litt	SE	Steve	21/05/54	Carlisle		1972	1975	Blackpool	Minnesota Kicks	15	1	1	3	0	0	0	0
Little	T	Tommy	00/04/72	Dumfries		1897		Wellingborough	Swindon	22	3	0	0	9	1	0	0
Littlewood	SC	Stewart	1906	Treeton		1925		Sheffield Wed.	Alfreton	6	1	0	0	2	1	0	0
Loosby	H	Harry	1910	Kettering		1931		Gillingham	Kettering Town	15	0	0	0	14	0	0	0
Long	C	Chris	07/02/48	Hatfield		1965		Hatfield T	Stevenage T	1	0	0	0	0	0	0	0
Lornie	J	Jack	02/03/39	Aberdeen		1961	1962	Leicester City	Carlisle Utd	19	0	2	0	6	0	0	0

Player			D.O.B	Place of Birth	Died	First Season	Last Season	Previous Club	Next Club	Appearances				Goals			
										League	FAC	FLC	Other	League	FAC	FLC	Oth.
Loughran	JL	Joe	12/08/15	Consett	1994	1937	1938	Birmingham	Burnley	25	0	0	0	0	0	0	0
Love	T	Thomas				1925		Dumbarton	Alloa	2	0	0	0	0	0	0	0
Lownds	MU	Mark	28/11/40	Sunderland		1961	1964	Ryhope Colliery	(South Africa)	59	1	1	0	3	0	0	0
Lumsden	R	Robert	10/07/02	West Calder	1974	1927		West Calder Swifts		1	0	0	0	0	0	0	0
Lunniss	RE	Roy	04/11/39	Islington		1966		Addington	Oakland Clippers	1	0	0	0	0	0	0	0
Lutterloch	BR	Bert	12/08/10	Poplar	1996	1936	1937	Aldershot	Vauxhall Motors	10	0	0	2	0	0	0	0
Macdonald	MI	Malcolm	07/01/50	Fulham		1969	1970	Fulham	Newcastle United	88	5	8	0	49	5	4	0
MacEwan	MP	Peter	23/05/33	Roodeport, SA		1953	1955	Germiston (SA)		26	0	0	0	11	0	0	0
Mackey	JA	Jim	1898	Ryton-on-Tyne		1924		Lincoln City	Crewe Alexandra	10	1	0	0	1	0	0	0
Mackey	TS	Tom	22/10/08	Cassop	1969	1932	1937	Sheffield Wed.	(coaching staff)	183	20	0	5	2	0	0	0
Madden	N	Neil	06/02/62	Luton		1979		Vauxhall Motors	Hitchin Town	1	0	0	0	0	0	0	0
Marsh	WE	Eddie	14/12/27	Croydon		1957	1958	Charlton Ath.	Torquay United	2	0	0	0	0	0	0	0
Marshall	DW	Dwight	03/10/65	St. Lucea, Jamaica		1994	1996	Plymouth Argyle		95	9	4	9	24	5	2	2
Marshall	FR					1899		Wishaw Ath		3	0	0	0	1	0	0	0
Martin	GS	George	14/07/1899	Bothwell	1972	1933	1936	Middlesbrough	(coaching staff)	98	5	0	2	27	1	0	1
Mathieson	A	Allan	1897	Belfast		1920	1921	Glentoran	Exeter City	54	2	0	0	16	0	0	0
Matthew	D	Damian	23/09/70	Islington		1992		Chelsea (loan)		5	0	0	1	0	0	0	0
Matthews	RD	Rob	14/10/70	Slough		1994	1995	Notts County	York City	11	0	1	0	0	0	0	0
Mayberry	S	Sam	1918	Bellshill		1938		Gainsborough Trinity		1	0	0	0	0	0	0	0
McAuley	PJ	Pat	31/07/21	Barrhead		1950		Celtic	Kettering Town	8	0	0	0	1	0	0	0
McBain	A	Alan	10/02/40	Aberdeen		1963	1964	Carlisle Utd	Corby Town	60	4	2	0	0	0	0	0
McBride	J	Joe	10/06/38	Kilmarnock		1959	1960	Wolves	Partick Thistle	25	0	2	0	9	0	0	0
McCann	A	Albert	01/11/41	Maidenhead		1959	1960	Juniors	Coventry City	6	0	0	0	0	0	0	0
McCartney	WJ	John	1866	Glasgow	1933	1897		Manchester Utd	Barnsley	27	7	0	0	0	1	0	0
McCreadie	WH	Harvey	01/10/42	Glenluce		1959		Accrington Stanley	Wrexham	1	0	0	0	0	0	0	0
McCurdy	W	Bill	06/09/1876	Bridgton		1899		Vale of Clyde	Nottm. Forest	31	8	0	0	0	0	0	0
McDerment	WS	Billy	05/01/43	Paisley		1967	1968	Leicester City	Notts County	40	4	6	0	1	0	0	0
McDonough	DK	Darron	07/11/62	Antwerp, Belgium		1986	1991	Oldham Athletic	Newcastle United	105	10	11	3	5	1	1	0
McEvoy	RP	Ricky	06/08/67	Gibraltar		1986	1988	App.	Shamrock Rovers	1	0	0	2	0	0	0	0
McEwen	J	Jimmy 'Punch'	1873	Bootle	1942	1897		Liverpool South End	Glossop	30	14	0	0	1	0	0	0
McGinnigle	H	Hugh		Bargeddie		1930	1936	Falkirk	Aldershot	159	17	0	1	2	1	0	0
McGowan	GG	Gavin	16/01/76	Blackheath		1996		Arsenal (loan)		2	0	0	0	0	0	0	0
McGuffie	AS	Alwyn	13/04/37	Stranraer		1955	1963	Queen of the South	St Albans	79	3	5	0	10	0	0	0
McInnes	T	Tom	22/03/1870	Glasgow		1897	1899	Everton	Bedford Queens Engnrs	93	16	0	0	18	9	0	0
McInnes	WA	Willy		Beith		1929		Arthurlie		22	0	0	0	1	0	0	0
McJarrow	H	Hugh	29/01/28	Motherwell		1951	1953	Sheffield Wed.	Plymouth Argyle	15	0	0	0	10	0	0	0
McKechnie	J	James		Helensburgh		1920			Mid Rhondda	1	0	0	0	0	0	0	0
McKechnie	TS	Tommy	09/02/40	Milngavie		1961	1965	Kirkintilloch Rob Roy	Bournemouth	131	8	7	0	31	2	1	0
McLaren	PA	Paul	17/11/76	High Wycombe		1993	1996	YTS		37	1	1	5	1	0	0	0
McLeish	H	Hugh	10/06/48	Shotts		1967		Sunderland	Stevenage T	2	0	0	0	0	0	0	0
McLeod	GJ	George	30/11/32	Inverness		1955	1958	Inverness Clachnaccudin	Brentford	51	3	0	3	6	0	0	2
McNally	JB	Brendan	22/01/35	Dublin		1956	1962	Shelbourne	Cambridge C	134	17	7	6	3	0	0	0
McNestry	G	George	07/01/08	Chopwell		1930	1931	Sunderland	Bristol Rovers	69	7	0	0	26	3	0	0
McNichol	JA	Jim	09/06/58	Glasgow		1976	1978	Ipswich Town	Brentford	15	0	2	0	0	0	0	0
Meade	RJ	Raphael	22/11/62	Islington		1988		Dundee Utd	OB Odense	4	0	0	0	0	0	0	0
Millar	RM	Rob		Dalry		1920	1929	Dalry Thistle	Belfast Celtic	205	8	0	0	4	0	0	0
Miller	J	James	16/02/1899	Tynemouth		1925		Swansea Town		10	1	0	0	3	0	0	0
Miller	W	Bill	31/03/08	Stockport	1974	1931	1931	Bolton Wanderers	Runcorn	3	0	0	0	0	0	0	0
Mills	AS	Arthur	1906	Karachi, India		1932		Gainsboro' Trinity	Gillingham	37	4	0	0	14	0	0	0
Mills	HM	Hugh	09/02/12	Dumbarton		1936		Celtic	Carlisle Utd	2	0	0	0	0	0	0	0
Mills	J	Joe	10/04/1895	Cresswell	1938	1924		Nottm. Forest	Bentley Colliery	31	1	0	0	2	0	0	0
Mingay	HJ	Henry	19/10/1895	Luton	1969	1925	1926	Clapton Orient	Watford	29	0	0	0	0	0	0	0
Mitchell	AJ	Bert	22/01/22	Corbridge		1951	1954	Northampton Town	Middlesbrough	106	13	0	0	41	2	0	0
Mittell	JL	James 'Jackie'	28/02/06	Merthyr Tydfil	1976	1933		Birmingham	Derry City	8	0	0	0	0	0	0	0
Moffat	H	Hugh	1900	Camerton		1925		Guildford Utd.	Everton	33	1	0	0	4	0	0	0
Moir	RM	Robert		Maryhill		1926		Morton		1	0	0	0	0	0	0	0
Molyneux	W	William		St Helens		1920	1923	Liverpool	Kettering T	80	5	0	0	1	0	0	0
Money	R	Richard	13/10/55	Lowestoft		1981	1982	Liverpool	Portsmouth	44	1	4	0	1	0	0	0
Moore	BJ	Bernard	18/12/23	Brighton		1950	1953	Hastings Utd	Brighton & Hove A.	74	11	0	0	31	3	0	0
Moore	J	John	21/12/43	Harthill		1965	1972	Motherwell	Brighton & Hove A.	274	15	14	3	13	0	0	1
Moore	JAO	James	20/06/1877	Middlesbrough		1898		Middlesbrough		19	2	0	0	0	0	0	0
Morgan	FG	Gerry	25/07/1899	Belfast	1959	1929		Nottm. Forest	Grantham	4	0	0	0	0	0	0	0
Morrison	FR	Frank	1874	Greenbank		1899		Millwall	Barnsley	13	4	0	0	0	0	0	0
Morrison	M	Murdoch	09/10/24	Glasgow	1975	1946		Bell Haven Stars	Leyton Orient	1	0	0	0	0	0	0	0
Morton	RH	Bob	25/09/27	Aston Clinton		1948	1963	Waterlows	Bletchley	495	58	7	12	48	4	0	3
Mosley	HT	Herbert	1900	Shuttlewood	1962	1922		Chesterfield	Sutton Town	3	0	0	0	0	0	0	0
Moss	DJ	David	18/03/52	Witney		1978	1984	Swindon Town	Swindon Town	221	8	16	0	88	3	3	0
Muir	J	James		Longcroft		1927		Bo'ness		10	0	0	0	0	0	0	0
Muir	JB	John	18/11/03	Hamilton		1930		Falkirk	Bristol Rovers	4	0	0	0	0	0	0	0
Mulvaney	J	Jimmy	27/04/21	Airdrie		1948	1949	Dumbarton	Brighton & Hove A.	8	1	0	0	2	0	0	0
Neal	S	Sid	1899	Mosbrough		1924	1925	Mosbrough	Frickley Colliery	27	1	0	0	0	0	0	0
Nelson	A	Arthur	15/05/09	Sheffield	1977	1932		Stockport Co.	Nuneaton Town	21	5	0	0	5	1	0	0
Nelson	JH	Jack	15/03/05	Chorley	1984	1935	1938	Wolves		134	11	0	3	0	0	0	0
Nelson	SE	Sammy	26/05/24	Belfast		1947	1948	Blackpool	Kettering Town	4	0	0	0	1	0	0	0
Newell	MC	Mike	27/01/65	Liverpool		1985	1987	Wigan Ath.	Leicester City	63	5	0	0	18	1	0	0
Nicholas	P	Peter	10/11/59	Newport		1984	1986	Crystal Palace	Aberdeen	102	12	2	0	1	0	0	0
Nicholl	CJ	Chris	12/10/46	Wilmslow		1969	1971	Halifax Town	Aston Villa	97	4	4	1	6	0	0	0
Noake	DJ	David	09/06/40	Dorchester		1959	1960	Dorchester T	Bristol City	17	3	1	0	0	0	0	0
Nogan	K	Kurt	09/09/70	Cardiff		1989	1991	YTS	Brighton & HA	33	0	4	2	3	0	1	0

Player			D.O.B	Place of Birth	Died	First Season	Last Season	Previous Club	Next Club	Appearances				Goals			
										League	FAC	FLC	Other	Leagu	FAC	FLC	Oth.
North	MV	Marc	29/05/66	Ware		1985	1986	App.	Grimsby T	18	5	1	0	3	1	1	0
North	SS	Stacey	25/11/64	Luton		1983	1987	App.	West Bromwich Albion	25	0	1	0	0	0	0	0
Northover	SO	Stan	03/07/26	Weymouth		1949		Weymouth	Yeovil T	1	0	0	0	0	0	0	0
Nunn	AS	Alf	15/11/1899	Holborn		1927		Folkestone	Hugonians	14	0	0	0	3	0	0	0
Nwajiobi	C	Chukwuemeka	25/05/59	Nibo Awka, Nigeria		1983	1987	Dulwich Hamlet	(retired)	72	9	6	0	17	2	1	0
O'Brien	J	Joe	09/05/24	Dundalk		1947	1948	Dundalk	Ipswich Town	11	3	0	0	3	0	0	0
O'Connor	PK	Phil	10/10/53	Romford	1985	1972		Bexley Utd.	emigrated Australia	2	0	0	0	0	0	0	0
O'Hara	MJ	Mike	30/08/44	Belfast		1960		App.	Swindon Town	2	0	2	0	0	0	0	0
O'Rourke	J	John	11/02/45	Northampton		1963	1965	Chelsea	Middlesbrough	84	5	1	0	64	2	0	0
Oakes	SJ	Scott	05/08/72	Leicester		1991	1995	Leicester City	Sheffield Wednesday	173	15	6	6	27	5	1	1
Oldfield	DC	David	30/05/68	Perth, Australia		1987	1988	App.	Manchester City	101	2	13	11	12	0	4	5
						1995	1996	Leicester C									
Orr	J	John		Kilbirnie		1923		Kilwinning Rangers	Dunfermline Ath.	9	1	0	0	0	0	0	0
Ottewell	S	Syd	23/10/19	Horsley		1947		Birmingham City	Nottm. Forest	15	3	0	0	4	1	0	0
Owen	SW	Syd	29/09/22	Small Heath		1947	1958	Birmingham City	Club manager	388	27	0	8	3	0	0	0
Pacey	D	David	02/10/36	Luton		1957	1964	Hitchin Town	Kettering T	246	22	6	3	16	3	0	0
Pacey	HJ	Harry	02/12/12	Clophill	1984	1932		St. Albans City	Bedford Town	4	0	0	0	0	0	0	0
Page	JE	John	23/09/01	Grays	1979	1930		Millwall	Chatham Town	4	0	0	0	1	0	0	0
Palmer	JF	John				1898		London Junior Club		1	0	0	0	0	0	0	0
Panther	FG	Fred	04/04/03	Manchester	1971	1926	1927	Peterboro' & Fletton	Brighton & Hove A.	8	0	0	0	3	0	0	0
Parker	GA	Garry	07/09/65	Oxford		1982	1985	App.	Hull City	42	8	4	0	3	0	1	0
Parker	TB	Tom		Carr Vale		1920	1921	Bolsover Colliery	Portsmouth	36	8	0	0	0	1	0	0
Parris	JE	Eddie	31/01/11	Pwllmeyric	1971	1936	1937	Bournemouth	Northampton Town	7	0	0	0	2	0	0	0
Patterson	DJ	Darren	15/10/69	Belfast		1995	1996	Crystal Palace		33	3	1	6	0	0	0	0
Payne	J	Joe	17/01/14	Brinnington Common	1975	1934	1937	Biggleswade T	Chelsea	72	5	0	0	83	4	0	0
Peake	T	Trevor	10/02/57	Nuneaton		1991	1995	Coventry City	reserve coach	178	13	7	3	0	0	0	0
Pearce	RS	Reg	12/01/30	Liverpool		1954	1957	Winsford Utd	Sunderland	75	4	0	5	5	0	0	0
Pearson	AJ	Andy	19/11/60	Newmarket		1979		App.	Hitchin Town	2	0	0	0	0	0	0	0
Pearson	GWM	George	21/09/07	West Stanley		1933		Chelsea	Walsall	14	0	0	0	1	0	0	0
Pearson	J	John	22/01/1892	Arbroath		1923		Tottenham H		1	0	0	0	0	0	0	0
Pease	WH	Billy	30/09/1898	Leeds	1955	1933	1934	Middlesbrough		33	1	0	1	8	0	0	1
Pemberton	JT	Jim	14/11/25	Birmingham		1950	1957	Stourbridge	King's Lynn	92	4	0	4	8	0	0	2
Pembridge	MA	Mark	29/11/70	Merthyr Tydfil		1990	1991	YTS	Derby County	60	4	2	4	6	0	0	0
Perkins	WH	Bill	26/01/1876	Wellingborough		1898		Kettering	Liverpool	26	6	0	0	0	0	0	0
Perrins	G	George	24/02/1873	Birmingham		1897		Manchester Utd	Chatham	6	0	0	0	0	0	0	0
Pett	EF	Ernie	1892	Edmonton		1920		Barnet		1	0	0	0	0	0	0	0
Petterson	AK	Andy	26/09/69	Fremantle, Australia		1992	1993	East Fremantle	Charlton Ath	19	0	2	2	0	0	0	0
Phillips	EJ	Ted	21/08/33	Leiston		1964		Leyton Orient	Colchester Utd	12	0	0	0	8	0	0	0
Phillips	PS	Peter	29/06/46	Wellingborough		1969	1969	Bishops Stortford	Cambridge U	5	0	0	0	0	0	0	0
Phillipson-Masters	FE	Forbes	14/11/55	Bournemouth		1978		Southampton (loan)		10	0	0	0	0	0	0	0
Pleat	DJ	David	15/01/45	Nottingham		1964	1966	Nottm. Forest	Shrewsbury Town	70	6	3	0	9	1	0	0
Pointon	J	Joe	02/1905	Leek	1940	1926	1927	Port Vale	Brighton & Hove A.	65	6	0	0	12	1	0	0
Pollock	MAI	Maitland	31/10/52	Dumfries		1974	1975	Burton Albion	Portsmouth	6	1	0	0	0	0	0	0
Potter	GR	George	07/10/46	Arbroath		1967	1968	Forfar Athletic	Torquay United	8	1	0	0	0	1	0	0
Pounder	JA	John	16/03/35	Sheffield		1955	1956	Atlas Sports	Coventry City	3	0	0	0	0	0	0	0
Poutch	NA	Neil	27/11/69	Dublin		1989		YTS	Shamrock Rovers	1	0	0	0	0	0	0	0
Preece	DW	David	28/05/63	Bridgnorth		1984	1994	Walsall	Derby County	336	27	23	8	21	2	3	1
Preedy	CJF	Charlie	11/01/00	Neemuch, India	1978	1934		Bristol Rovers	Margate	5	0	0	0	0	0	0	0
Prentice	H	Horace		Weedon		1923		Brickstock St.Peters		1	0	0	0	0	0	0	0
Price	PT	Paul	23/03/54	St Albans		1972	1980	Welwyn Garden Utd	Tottenham H	207	9	13	1	8	0	0	0
Purdy	A	Arthur	23/07/04	Evenwood	1970	1925		Tottenham H	Southend Utd	24	2	0	0	0	0	0	0
Pye	J	Jesse	22/12/19	Treeton	1984	1952	1954	Wolves	Derby County	61	4	0	0	32	4	0	0
Ralley	W	William				1898		Luton Stanley	Bedford Queens Engnrs	21	4	0	0	0	0	0	0
Ramage	GM	George	29/01/37	Dalkeith		1965		Leyton Orient	Dartford	7	0	0	0	0	0	0	0
Ramage	J	Jock		Bonnyrigg		1927		Coventry City	Hearts	9	0	0	0	0	0	0	0
Read	JA	Tony	05/03/42	Haydock		1965	1971	Peterborough Utd	(retired)	199	11	18	1	12	0	0	0
Reader	AR	Dickie	03/06/1894	Derby		1922		Bristol City	(United States)	7	0	0	0	0	0	0	0
Redfern	WJ	Billy	15/10/10	Connahs Quay	1988	1937	1938	Newry Town	Derby County	41	1	0	0	19	0	0	0
Reece	HJ	Harry	1911	Darlaston		1933	1934	Blackpool	Barrow	29	1	0	1	0	0	0	0
Reed	BRF	Barry	24/11/37	Peterborough		1961		Leicester City	Worcester City	1	0	1	0	0	0	0	0
Rees	JM	Jason	22/12/69	Aberdare		1989	1993	Penywauyn	Portsmouth	82	3	5	6	0	0	0	2
Reid	J	John	20/08/32	Newmains		1963		Northampton Town	Torquay United	111	7	3	0	7	0	0	0
Reid	S	Syd		Troedyrhiw		1921	1927	Troedyrhiw Star	Luton Amateur	134	9	0	0	70	11	0	0
Rennie	A	Andy	1901	Baillieston	1938	1925	1934	Kilwinning Rangers	Newport County	307	26	0	2	148	15	0	0
Rennie	J	Joe				1933		Maryhill Hibernian		4	0	0	0	0	0	0	0
Reynolds	JW	Joe	25/12/06	Leicester	1993	1927		Mount Sorrell	Watford	2	0	0	0	0	0	0	0
Rich	LT	Len	03/11/12	Camelford		1935	1936	Plymouth Argyle	Exeter City	19	1	0	1	5	0	0	0
Richards	AC	Albert	18/07/03	Chatham	1973	1924		Charlton Ath.	Chatham T	2	0	0	0	0	0	0	0
Richards	D	David	01/10/1896	Wolverhampton	1971	1925	1930	Dundee United	Watford	147	5	0	0	0	0	0	0
Richmond	J	Jimmy	12/12/03	Auchinleck		1930		Partick Thistle		2	0	0	0	0	0	0	0
Rickett	WJ	Billy		Plaistow		1930		Colchester Utd	Gateshead	1	0	0	0	0	0	0	0
Riddick	GG	Gordon	06/11/43	Langleybury		1962	1966	Juniors	Gillingham	102	7	5	0	16	1	0	0
Rioch	BD	Bruce	06/09/47	Aldershot		1964	1968	App.	Aston Villa	149	9	9	0	47	2	3	0
Riseth	V	Vidar	21/04/72	Levanger,Norway		1995		Kongsvinger	Linz	11	0	0	1	0	0	0	0
Rivers	AD	Alan	27/01/46	Portsmouth		1965	1966	App.	Watford	30	0	4	0	1	0	0	0
Roberts	F	Frederick	09/10/08	Greets Green	1979	1934	1938	Birmingham	Kettering T	180	15	0	3	38	6	0	1
Roberts	J	Joe	02/09/00	Birkenhead	1984	1932		Clapton Orient	Millwall	17	5	0	0	2	0	0	0
Robinson	F	Foster	1901	South Shields		1925		Bournemouth		1	0	0	0	1	0	0	0
Rodger	G	Graham	01/04/67	Glasgow		1989	1991	Coventry City	Grimsby Town	28	0	2	3	2	0	0	0

Player			D.O.B	Place of Birth	Died	First Season	Last Season	Previous Club	Next Club	Appearances				Goals			
										League	FAC	FLC	Other	Leagu	FAC	FLC	Oth.
Roe	A	Arthur	1892	South Normanton		1920	1924	South Normanton	Arsenal	93	7	0	0	1	0	0	0
Roe	TW	Tommy	08/12/00	Evenwood	1972	1928		Nottm. Forest	Walsall	17	2	0	0	7	0	0	0
Rowe	DH	Doug	09/07/09	Nottingham	1978	1931	1932	Sneinton	Lincoln City	23	2	0	0	8	0	0	0
Rowland	DC	David	12/09/40	Arlesey		1957			West Ham Utd	1	0	0	0	0	0	0	0
Ruffett	RD	Ray	20/07/24	Luton		1948			Christ Church	1	0	0	0	0	0	0	0
Russell	CJ	Jack	19/06/04	Northfield		1934			Bournemouth	8	0	0	1	1	0	0	0
Ryan	J	Jimmy	12/05/45	Stirling		1970	1975	Manchester Utd	Dallas Tornado	174	11	12	7	19	4	0	0
Ryan	JG	John	20/07/47	Lewisham		1969	1976	Fulham	Norwich City	276	17	15	6	12	0	0	1
Ryan	JO	John	28/10/44	Liverpool		1967	1968	Wigan Athletic	Notts County	18	1	3	0	1	0	0	0
Salisbury	G	Gareth	11/03/41	Caernarfon		1963		Norwich City	Colchester Utd	12	0	1	0	2	0	2	0
Salton	DB	Darren	16/03/72	Edinburgh		1991	1992	Salveson Boys	(retired)	18	0	3	3	0	0	0	0
Sanderson	JR	John	05/02/18	Carlisle	1993	1946		Wolves	(club groundsman)	6	0	0	0	0	0	0	0
Saxby	MW	Mike	12/08/57	Mansfield		1979	1981	Mansfield Town	Newport County	82	2	7	0	6	0	1	0
Scott	JC	Joe	09/01/30	Fatfield		1952	1953	Spennymoor	Middlesbrough	13	0	0	0	2	0	0	0
Sealey	LJ	Les	29/09/57	Bethnal Green		1983	1988	Coventry City	Manchester Utd.	207	28	21	3	0	0	0	0
Seasman	J	John	21/02/55	Liverpool		1974	1975	Tranmere Rovers	Millwall	8	0	0	0	2	0	0	0
Semple	J	John		Kirkintilloch		1920		Ayr United		7	0	0	0	0	0	0	0
Sexton	DJ	Dave	06/04/30	Islington		1951	1952	Chelmsford City	West Ham Utd	9	0	0	0	1	0	0	0
Shankland	J	John		Kirkconnel		1920		Nithsdale Wanderers	Galston	3	0	0	0	0	0	0	0
Shankly	J	John		Glenbuck	1960	1924	1925	Portsmouth	Alloa Ath	46	2	0	0	20	1	0	0
Shanks	D	Don	02/10/52	Hammersmith		1971	1974	Fulham	QPR	90	6	9	5	2	0	1	2
Shanks	WG	Wally	01/05/23	Valetta, Malta		1946	1956	Chelsea		264	11	0	0	6	0	0	0
Sharpe	DA	David		Glasgow		1898		Ashfield		21	4	0	0	0	0	0	0
Sheffield	LJ	Laurie	27/04/39	Swansea		1968	1969	Oldham Athletic	Doncaster Rovers	35	1	9	0	12	0	5	0
Sheldon	W	Wilf		Bulwell		1929		Grantham		2	0	0	0	0	0	0	0
Shepherd	JWV	Billy		Sunderland		1923		Ashington	West Stanley	3	0	0	0	0	0	0	0
Sherlock	SE	Steve	10/05/59	Birmingham		1978		Manchester City	Stockport Co.	2	1	0	0	0	0	0	0
Showler	P	Paul	10/10/66	Doncaster		1996		Bradford City		23	4	4	2	6	0	0	0
Sidney	H	Hilton	14/4/1895	Horden	1957	1920		Horden Ath	Mansfield Town	2	0	0	0	0	0	0	0
Silkman	B	Barry	29/06/52	Stepney		1978		Plymouth Arg. (loan)		3	0	0	0	0	0	0	0
Simms	E	Ernie	23/07/1891	South Shields	1971	1920	1921	Barnsley	South Shields	65	18	0	0	46	13	0	0
Sims	J	John	14/08/52	Belper		1973		Derby County (loan)		3	0	1	0	1	0	0	0
Skelton	AM	Aaron	22/11/74	Welwyn Garden City		1994	1996	YTS	Colchester Utd	8	2	1	2	0	0	0	0
Slatter	LAH	Les	22/11/31	Reading		1949		Mount Pleasant	Crusaders	1	0	0	0	0	0	0	0
Slicer	J	Jackie	24/11/02	Bramley	1979	1930	1931	Norwich City	Ashton National	45	3	0	0	13	1	0	0
Sloan	FJ	Frank	26/12/04	Chapelhall	1974	1935	1936	Plymouth Argyle		4	3	0	0	0	1	0	0
Slough	AP	Alan	24/09/47	Luton		1965	1972	App.	Fulham	275	16	19	2	28	2	2	0
Small	MA	Mike	02/03/62	Birmingham		1981	1982	Bromsgrove	Go Ahead Eagles	4	0	0	0	0	0	0	0
Small	PV	Peter	23/10/24	Horsham		1947	1949	Horsham	Leicester City	28	3	0	0	5	1	0	0
Smeaton	AR	Alec	29/09/00	South Shields	1956	1929		Torquay United	Gillingham	6	0	0	0	0	0	0	0
Smith	E	Ted	22/02/02	Sunderland		1929	1930	Reading	Preston NE	32	1	0	0	0	0	0	0
Smith	GH	George				1898				1	0	0	0	0	0	0	0
Smith	HR	Ray	13/09/34	Hull		1963	1963	Northampton Town	(retired)	10	3	0	0	1	1	0	0
Smith	RS	Ray	14/04/29	Evenwood		1951	1957	Evenwood Town	Southend Utd	12	0	0	4	0	0	0	1
Smith	TC	Tim	19/04/59	Gloucester		1976	1977	App.	Trowbridge	2	0	0	0	0	0	0	0
Smith	TS	Tom		Higham		1934	1938	Rochdale	Burnley	157	14	0	1	1	0	0	0
Sommer	JP	Juergen	27/02/64	New York, USA		1993	1995	Indiana University (USA)	QPR	82	11	6	4	0	0	0	0
Soo	FC	Hong 'Frank'	08/03/14	Buxton	1991	1946	1947	Leicester C	Chelmsford City	71	7	0	0	4	1	0	0
Spencer	L	Les	16/09/36	Manchester		1960		Rochdale	(retired)	7	0	0	0	1	0	0	0
Sperrin	MR	Martyn	06/12/56	Edmonton		1977		Edgware T	Barnet	1	0	1	0	0	0	0	0
Spiring	PJ	Peter	13/12/50	Glastonbury		1974	1975	Liverpool	Hereford Utd	15	0	1	0	2	0	0	0
Standen	JA	Jim	30/05/35	Edmonton		1960	1962	Arsenal	West Ham Utd	36	3	3	0	0	0	0	0
Stark	WR	Billy	27/05/37	Glasgow		1965	1965	Doncaster	Chesterfield	10	0	0	0	4	0	0	0
Starling	AW	Alan	02/04/51	Barking		1969	1970	App.	Northampton T	7	0	0	0	0	0	0	0
Steen	AW	Alan	26/06/22	Crewe		1946		Wolves	Northwich Victoria	10	0	0	0	0	0	0	0
Stein	B	Brian	19/10/57	Cape Town, SA		1977	1987	Edgware T	Caen	427	31	35	3	130	6	15	3
						1991		Caen	Barnet								
Stein	EMS	Mark	28/01/66	Cape Town, SA		1983	1987	Juniors	QPR	54	9	5	3	19	3	0	1
Stephens	KW	Kirk	27/02/55	Coventry		1978	1983	Nuneaton Borough	Coventry City	227	8	13	0	2	0	0	0
Stephenson	GH	George	29/08/08	Stillington		1934	1938	Aston Villa	Leeds United	192	15	0	5	59	5	0	5
Stephenson	J	John	01/06/1899	Crawcrook	1969	1921	1922		Kettering T	10	0	0	0	0	0	0	0
Stevens	R	Ron	26/11/14	Luton		1936	1938	Hitchin T		7	0	0	1	1	0	0	1
Stevenson	MJ	Morris	16/04/43	Tranent		1968		Morton	Met Police	1	0	0	0	0	0	0	0
Stewart	WS	William	11/02/1872	Coupar Angus	1945	1897		Newton Heath	Millwall	45	12	0	0	10	4	0	0
						1899		Millwall	Thames Ironworks								
Stobbart	GC	George	09/01/21	Pegswood		1949	1951	Newcastle United	Millwall	107	9	0	0	30	0	0	0
Stone	PJ	Peter	08/10/22	Oxford		1951		Oxford City	Worcester City	1	0	0	0	0	0	0	0
Strathie	WJ	James	12/02/13	Beancross	1976	1937	1938	St. Bernards	Northampton Town	2	0	0	0	0	0	0	0
Streten	BR	Bernard	14/01/21	Gillingham	1994	1946	1957	Shrewsbury T	King's Lynn	276	22	0	3	0	0	0	0
Sutton	SJ	Steve	16/04/61	Hartington		1991		Nottm. Forest (loan)	Nottm. Forest	14	0	0	0	0	0	0	0
Swan	RM	Ron	08/01/41	Plean		1966		Oldham Athletic	Buxton	14	0	0	0	0	0	0	0
Tait	T	Tommy	20/11/08	Hetton-le-Hole	1976	1931	1933	Bolton Wanderers	Bournemouth	84	12	0	0	50	7	0	0
Taylor	AA	Arthur	05/04/31	Lambeg		1952	1955	Glentoran		8	1	0	0	0	2	0	0
Taylor	JE	Jack	11/09/24	Newcastle		1948	1951	Stockton-on-Tees	Wolves	85	6	0	0	29	4	0	0
Taylor	JP	John	24/10/64	Norwich		1994	1995	Bradford City	Cambridge Utd	37	0	2	3	3	0	0	1
Taylor	JT	Joe	11/03/13	West Bromwich	1977	1934	1934	Shrewsbury T	Carlisle Utd	1	0	0	0	0	0	0	0
Taylor	SJ	Steve	18/10/55	Royton		1978		Oldham Athletic	Mansfield Town	20	0	0	0	1	0	0	0
Taylor	WD	Billy	03/06/38	Keldholm		1967	1968	Partick Thistle	Epping Town	6	1	0	0	0	0	0	0
Tees	M	Matt	13/10/39	Johnstone		1969	1970	Charlton Ath.	Grimsby Town	35	3	2	0	13	2	0	0

Player			D.O.B	Place of Birth	Died	First Season	Last Season	Previous Club	Next Club	League	FAC	FLC	Other	Leagu	FAC	FLC	Oth.
Telfer	PN	Paul	21/10/71	Edinburgh		1990	1994	Salveson BC	Coventry City	144	14	5	2	19	2	0	1
Thayne	W	Billy	13/12/09	West Hartlepool	1986	1934	1935	Hartlepool Utd	Northampton Town	30	2	0	2	0	0	0	0
Thear	AC	Tony	04/02/48	Edmonton		1966	1966	Arsenal	Gillingham	13	0	2	0	5	0	0	0
Thirlaway	WJ	Billy	01/10/1896	New Washington	1983	1924		Southend Utd	South Shields	13	0	0	0	0	0	0	0
Thomas	MA	Mitchell	02/10/64	Luton		1982	1985	Limbury Boys Club	Tottenham H	232	25	13	6	5	0	0	0
						1993	1996	West Ham Utd									
Thompson	A	Alan	02/09/31	Goole		1956		West Park Juniors	Bedford Town	1	0	0	0	0	0	0	0
Thompson	JWJ	Jimmy	19/04/1898	West Ham	1984	1925		Clapton Orient	Chelsea	72	1	0	0	41	0	0	0
Thompson	R	Robert		Eldon		1922		Ashington	Pontypridd	17	0	0	0	7	0	0	0
Thompson	SJ	Steve	02/11/64	Oldham		1991		Bolton Wanderers	Leicester City	5	0	2	0	0	0	0	0
Thomson	NS	Norman	20/02/01	Glasgow	1984	1925	1926	Hibernian	Clapton Orient	43	2	0	0	10	0	0	0
Thomson	R	Bobby	21/11/39	Menstrie		1965	1966	Liverpool	(Australia)	74	7	3	0	0	0	0	0
Thomson	RA	Bobby	05/12/43	Smethwick		1972	1975	Birmingham City	Hartford Bi-Centennials	110	8	10	7	1	0	0	1
Thorpe	A	Tony	10/04/74	Leicester		1993	1996	Leicester City		92	7	6	7	36	2	2	1
Till	J	Joe		Stoke-on-Trent		1923	1927	St. Mirren	Crewe Alex	138	6	0	0	1	0	0	0
Tinsley	C	Colin	24/10/35	Redcar		1963	1967	Exeter City	Kettering T	55	4	3	0	0	0	0	0
Tirrell	A	Alf	7/2/1894	Desborough		1920	1923	West Ham Utd	(retired)	122	8	0	0	5	1	0	0
Todd	C	Colin	12/12/48	Chester-le-Street		1984		Vancouver Whitecaps	Whitley Bay	2	0	1	0	0	0	0	0
Tomlinson	G	Graeme	10/12/75	Watford		1995		Manchester Utd (loan)		7	0	0	0	0	0	0	0
Tracey	MG	Mike	14/02/35	Durham		1959	1960	Crook Town	Lincoln City	23	0	2	0	3	0	0	0
Tricker	RW	Reg	05/10/05	Karachi, India		1924		(Teacher training col.)	Beccles	4	1	0	0	0	0	0	0
Turner	CJ	Chris	03/04/51	St Neots		1978		Peterborough Utd	New England Teamen	30	0	4	0	5	0	0	0
Turner	G	George	05/05/10	Mansfield		1931		Notts County	Everton	20	1	0	1	5	0	0	0
						1935		Bradford City	Northampton Town								
Turner	GR	Gordon	07/06/30	Hull	1976	1950	1963	(Navy)	Wisbech Town	406	25	7	12	243	18	4	11
Turner	WL	Wayne	09/03/61	Luton		1978	1984	Lewsey Youth	Coventry City	84	10	8	0	2	1	0	0
Upson	M	Matthew	18/04/79	Eye		1995	1996	youth	Arsenal	1	0	0	1	0	0	0	0
Varadi	I	Imre	08/07/59	Paddington		1991		Leeds Utd (loan)		6	0	0	0	1	0	0	0
Vaughan	W	Billy	18/12/1898	Willenhall	1976	1928		Merthyr Town	Scunthorpe Utd	3	0	0	0	2	0	0	0
Vilstrup	J		27/2/69	Copenhagen		1995		Lyngby		7	0	0	2	0	0	0	0
Vinall	EJ	Jack	16/12/10	Witton		1937	1945	Norwich City	Walsall	44	6	0	0	18	2	0	0
Waddock	GP	Gary	17/03/62	Kingsbury		1994	1996	Bristol Rovers		115	7	6	5	3	0	0	0
Wainwright	RK	Robin	09/03/51	Luton		1971		App.	Millwall	16	0	1	1	3	0	0	0
Walden	HB	Harry	22/12/40	Walgrave		1960	1963	Kettering T	Northampton Town	96	5	5	0	11	0	1	0
Wales	A	Abraham	1907	Kilwinning		1931		Montrose	Kilwinnig Eglinton	3	0	0	0	0	0	0	0
Walker	DG	Dennis	05/07/48	Spennymoor		1967		West Ham Utd	Stevenage T	1	0	0	0	0	0	0	0
Walker	JR	Jimmy		Port Glasgow		1920	1925	Port Glasgow Ath.	Exeter C	133	5	0	0	4	0	0	0
Walker	R	Bob		Beith		1929		Arthurlie		5	0	0	0	0	0	0	0
Wallbanks	WH	Horace	04/09/18	Chopwell		1946	1947	Grimsby Town	Weymouth	4	0	0	0	1	0	0	0
Walsh	P	Peter	18/10/22	Dublin		1949	1983	Dundalk	Brighton & Hove A.	8	0	0	0	2	0	0	0
Walsh	PAM	Paul	01/10/62	Plumstead		1982	1983	Charlton Ath.	Liverpool	80	4	5		24	3	1	
Walsh	W	Billy		Horden		1920	1921	Horden Athletic	Horden Athletic	17	0	0	0	2	0	0	0
Walters	AV	Albert	05/1902	Wolverhampton		1928		Aldershot	Walsall	1	0	0	0	0	0	0	0
Warner	J	John	06/05/40	Ashington		1959			Yiewsley	1	0	0	2	0	0	0	1
Watkins	C	Charlie	14/01/21	Glasgow		1948	1954	Glasgow Rangers		218	21	0	0	16	4	0	0
Watson	J	Jim		Motherwell		1920		Dundee	Exeter City	4	0	0	0	0	0	0	0
Watts	MR	Mark	24/09/65	Welham Green		1982		App.		1	1	0	0	0	0	0	0
Waugh	WL	Bill	27/11/21	Edinburgh		1946	1949	Bathgate Thistle	QPR	135	12	0	0	9	3	0	0
Weaver	RS	Bob		Ponkey		1932		Burnley	Bristol City	3	0	0	0	1	0	0	0
Wegerle	RC	Roy	19/03/64	Johannesburg, SA		1988	1989	Chelsea	QPR	45	1	10	2	10	0	8	0
Weir	J	Jimmy 'Jock'	12/04/39	Glasgow		1963		Mansfield Town	Tranmere Rovers	12	1	1	0	1	0	0	0
Weir	MG	Mickey	16/01/66	Edinburgh		1987		Hibernian	Hibernian	8	1	3	0	0	1	2	0
West	A	Alan	18/12/51	Hyde		1973	1980	Burnley	Millwall	285	14	15	3	16	0	1	0
Whalley	R	Robert	1905	Flimby		1932		Peterboro' & Fletton		4	1	0	0	1	0	0	0
Whent	JR	Jackie	03/05/20	Darlington		1950		Brighton & Hove A.	Kettering T	11	0	0	0	3	0	0	0
Whitby	BK	Brian	21/02/39	Luton		1957	1958	Vauxhall Motors	Bedford T	7	0	0	1	1	0	0	0
White	SJ	Steve	02/01/59	Chipping Sodbury		1979	1981	Bristol Rovers	Charlton Ath.	76	3	4	0	25	0	1	0
						1982		Charlton Ath. (loan)									
Whittaker	RH	Ray	15/01/45	Bow		1963	1968	Arsenal	Colchester Utd	170	11	7	0	40	3	2	0
Wilkinson	P	Paul	30/10/64	Louth		1995		Middlesbrough (loan)		3	0	0	0	0	0	0	0
Williams	H	Harry				1898	1899	Sr Albans	Reading	54	13	0	0	2	0	0	0
Williams	MK	Martin	12/07/73	Luton		1991	1994	Leicester City	Reading	40	1	1	3	2	0	0	0
Williams	R	Richard				1897		Everton	Glossop	30	7	0	0	0	0	0	0
Williams	SC	Steve	12/07/58	Hammersmith		1988	1990	Arsenal	Exeter City	40	2	5	1	0	0	0	0
Wilson	DJ	Danny	01/01/60	Wigan		1987	1989	Brighton & Hove A.	Sheffield Wed.	110	8	20	4	24	2	2	0
Wilson	GG	Gordon	1904	West Auckland	1947	1931		Hull City	Norwich City	7	0	0	0	0	0	0	0
Wilson	JA	Jim	28/06/22	Musselburgh		1947	1950	Peterborough U	Northampton Town	39	3	0	0	1	0	0	0
Wilson	RJ	Robert	05/06/61	Kensington		1986	1987	Millwall	Fulham	24	0	0	0	1	1	1	0
Woods	H	Harry	12/03/1890	St Helens		1926	1929	Arsenal	North Shields	97	8	0	0	21	5	0	0
Woods	M	Matt	01/11/31	Skelmersdale		1965		Hakoah (Australia)	Stockport Co.	34	4	0	0	0	0	0	0
Woodsford	JM	Jamie	09/11/76	Ipswich		1994	1995	YTS	Boreham Wood	10	0	0	2	0	0	0	0
Wyldes	RJ	Bobby	06/10/28	Southport		1949	1951	Desborough	Southend United	26	1	0	0	8	0	0	0
Yardley	G	George	08/10/42	Kirkcaldy		1966		Australia Soccer	Tranmere Rovers	1	0	0	0	0	0	0	0
Yardley	J	Jimmy	16/4/07	Wishaw		1926	1931	Clapton Orient	Charlton Ath.	173	15	0	0	77	16	0	0
Young	JW	Joe		Flimby		1929		Spennymoor United	Northampton Town	3	0	0	0	0	0	0	0

Played in 1939/40 only

Stockill	RR	Reg		23/11/13	York	1995	1939		Derby County	

Played in FA Cup Only

Campbell	R	Robson		Pegswood		1945				0	2	0	0		0	0	0	0
Isaacs	FC					1945				0	1	0	0		0	0	0	0
Needham	D					1945				0	2	0	0		0	0	0	0

Played in FL Cup only

Heath	SJMP	Seamus	06/12/61	Belfast	1980	Cromac Albion	Wrexham	0	0	1	0		0	0	0	0
Riley	R	Robert			1964	Leicester City		0	0	1	0		0	0	0	0
Smith	H	Herbie	06/12/59	London	1980	Tooting & Mitcham		0	0	1	0		0	0	0	0

Played in Miscellaneous Games Only

Simpson	G	Gary	14/12/76	Ashford	1995		Aylesbury	0	0	0	1		0	0	0	0
Tighe	A	Aaron	11/07/69	Banbury	1989		Hitchin Town	0	0	0	2		0	0	0	0
Walker	J	Jackie	1941	Co. Durham	1958			0	0	0	1		0	0	0	0
Woolgar	M	Matthew	05/01/76	Bedford	1993		Baldock Town	0	0	0	1		0	0	0	0

MANAGERS

		From:	To:	
Green	Charlie	1901	1928	*Secretary*
Thompson	George Alexander	16/02/25	26/10/25	
McCartney	John	14/09/27	21/12/29	
Kay	George	23/12/29	13/05/31	
Wightman	Harold	01/06/31	09/10/35	
Liddell	Edward (Ned)	13/08/36	26/02/38	
McBain	Neil	01/06/38	5/6/39	
Martin	George Scott	04/12/44	24/05/47	*Appointed coach 1/8/39*
Duncan	Douglas (Dally)	13/06/47	16/10/58	
Owen	Sydney William	27/04/59	16/04/60	
Bartram	Samuel	18/07/60	14/06/62	
Crompton	John	29/06/62	06/07/62	
Harvey	William	24/07/62	21/11/64	
Watkins	Charlie			*Caretaker Manager*
Martin	George Scott	16/02/65	03/11/66	
Brown	Allan Duncan	04/11/66	17/12/68	
Stock	Alexander William Alfred	20/12/68	27/04/72	
Haslam	Harold	04/05/72	23/01/78	
Pleat	David John	24/01/78	16/05/86	
Moore	John	03/06/86	16/06/87	
Harford	Raymond	16/06/87	03/01/90	
Ryan	James	11/01/90	13/05/91	*Caretaker 3/1/90 to 11/1/90*
Pleat	David John	07/06/91	11/06/95	
Westley	Terence	03/07/95	18/12/95	
Lawrence	Robin Michael (Lennie)	21/12/95	to date	

Messrs Martin, Duncan, Owen, Watkins, Brown, Pleat, Moore and Ryan were former Luton players.
John Crompton was never manager for a competitive match!

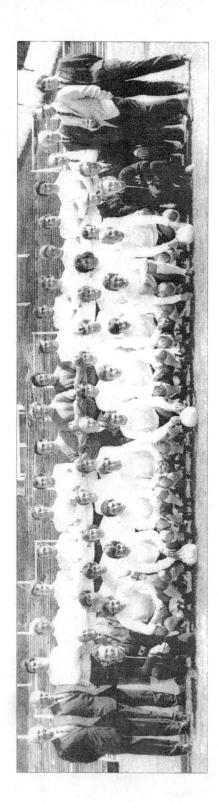

1936/37: Back: Pakes (trainer), Finlayson, King, Dolman, Nelson, Coen, Mackey, Smith, Fellows. Front: Hancock, Dawes, Payne, Roberts, Stephenson.

Nearly 40 years ago.
A Cup Final ticket for 17½p and 5p for the programme!

A wide angle camera was needed for the 1970 team group!
© The Luton Museum Service/Luton News